Expert Systems

Edited by

Petrică Vizureanu

Expert Systems
Edited by Petrică Vizureanu

Republished by InTech
Janeza Trdine 9, 51000 Rijeka, Croatia

Additional hard copies can be obtained from orders@intechopen.com

Expert Systems, Edited by Petrică Vizureanu
p. cm.
ISBN 978-953-307-032-2

For EU product safety concerns:
IN TECH d.o.o., Prolaz Marije Krucifikse Kozulić 3, 51000 Rijeka, Croatia, info@intechopen.com or visit our website at intechopen.com.

Meet the editor

Dr. Petrică Vizureanu was born on the 17th of October 1967, in Barlad, Romania. He received the following degrees: M.Sc. in Heating Equipment, from „Gh. Asachi" Technical University of Iasi (1992), and Ph.D. at „Gh. Asachi" Technical University of Iasi (1999). Vizureanu's past and present positions include Assistant (1993-1999), Lecturer (1999-2002), Ass. Professor (2002-2009), Professor (2009-today) in „Gh. Asachi" Technical University of Iasi – Romania. Dr. Petrică Vizureanu is a professor with a teaching experience over 25 years, with a very rich experience in project management of national and international research projects (Director-5, member-34), concerning different areas including: unconventional energy, heating equipment, refractory materials, materials science, computer assisted design, biomaterials (characterization; testing and material expertise; medical devices; surface properties; tissue-implant interaction phenomena), geopolymers, safety and health at work, management and commercial engineering.

Preface

The artificial intelligence concept defined in 1956 at Berkeley (USA). In those days, it was the endowment of a computer with certain capabilities normally attributed to human intelligence such as:

- knowledge acquisition;
- perception (visual, auditory sensation;
- reasoning;
- decisions.

Since the early `80, the artificial intelligence entered in economic life too. It has been developed to allow a settlement of outstanding issues by algorithmic method. It aims the approach of the human reasoning.

Studying the share of artificial intelligence, it shows that expert systems prevail in artificial intelligence domains. As a result, this part of artificial intelligence was that which led to the greatest number of industrial applications (see figure below).

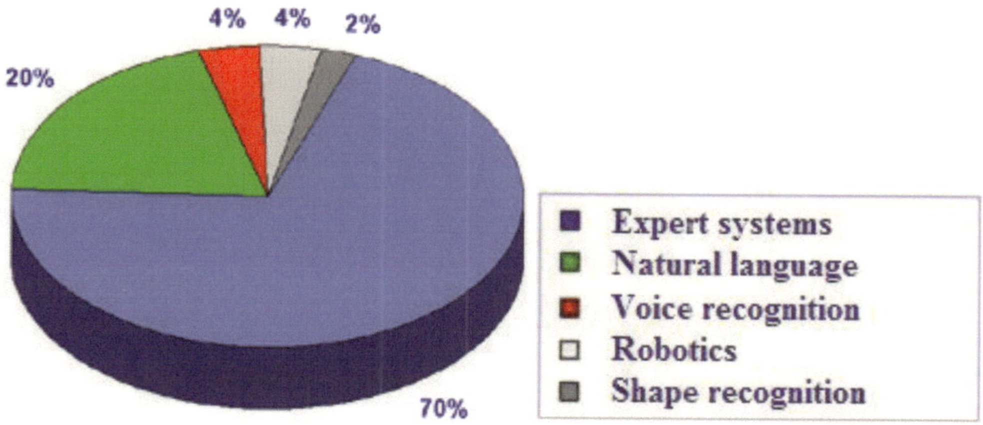

Figure.

Expert systems represent a branch of artificial intelligence, aiming to take the experience of human specialists and to transfer to a computer system. Specialty knowledge is stored in the computer, which by an execution system (inference engine) is reasoning and it derives specific conclusions for the problem.

The purpose of the expert systems is to help and support user's reasoning and not by replacing human judgment! In fact, expert systems offer to the inexperienced user a solution when human experts are not available.

Expert systems are digit structures of adjustment and automatic control using a range of knowledge, an operating system, a programming environment, a database, and a series of execution bodies that implement promptly the expert system controls.

The connection between the expert system and a technical system is a logical and physical interface embedded by an algorithm, a hardware component. The relationship between the two systems is that the expert system determines the thermal system, because the first one based on knowledge, professional experience (of the human element that made it!) as well as on logic reasoning. While the second is the necessary and sufficient infrastructure for the relationship between these two systems could exist (technology, equipment, control elements, measuring devices etc.).

Expert systems are products of the artificial intelligence, branch of computer science that seeks to develop intelligent programs. What is remarkable for expert systems is the applicability area and solving of different issues in many fields of architecture, archeology, commerce, trade, education, medicine to engineering systems, production of goods and control/diagnosis problems in many industrial branches.

Editor

Petrică Vizureanu

The "Gheorghe Asachi" Technical University from Iasi
Romania

Contents

1

Darwin, Culture and Expert Systems

Dr. Yoram Romem,
The Cohn Institute for the History and Philosophy of Science and Ideas Tel-Aviv University, P.O. Box 39040, Tel-Aviv 69978, Israel

1. Introduction

Darwin's theory of evolution by natural selection targeted the living parts of nature. This paradigm, which is one of the foundations of the living world, attracted scholars as a mechanism which might apply to other areas that change over time.

This paper creates an analogy between Darwinian evolution processes and Expert Systems (ES), where human expertise is utilized by computerized technology. Firstly, Darwinian theory is applied to social and cultural areas in general; then, as a special case of culture, it is applied to science and technology; lastly, as a special case of technology, Darwinian processes are applied to ES.

The revelation of the strong resemblance that ES bears to Darwinian processes may trigger new approaches for future generations of ES.

2. Initial step: Cultural evolution

A natural extension of Darwin's evolution theory is to the social and cultural behavior of humans. As physical characteristics are governed by genes, there is no reason to restrict the theory to this layer. Since behavior is a phenotypic (i.e. observable) phenomenon, and behavior includes social and cultural aspects, there is an obvious interest in studying how evolutionary ideas apply to these layers too.

One of the earliest and most influential scholars to apply Darwinian theory to human cultural evolution was Donald Campbell. In his view (Campbell, 1960; Campbell, 1965), cultural inheritance is a process of imitation, in which successful people are imitated. This, of course, differs from natural inheritance which is "blind": the descendant cannot choose to inherit from his ancestor only the desired genes.... Cultural evolution includes all that humans learn from each other. There is a kind of "injustice" in this process, for what some individuals learn by themselves through hard effort others often imitate, typically at much less cost to themselves[1]. However, this "cheaper" way is not perfect and involves variations, intended or unintended.

---

[1] Latour (1987) referred to another type of cultural inheritance (without using this term), by analyzing knowledge and expertise. While those who have the "real" knowledge (whom he called "insiders") know the actual facts and understand them, the others (whom he called "outsiders") have only the perception of the real knowledge, or "beliefs" in Latour's

As such, cultural evolution applies to technical knowledge, to the language, the habits, sentiments and ideas that guide participation in social and political life, systems based on belief, like religion, and artistic traditions.

Cultural inheritance involves variation as humans pick and choose their adopted elements. Moreover, the inherited culture is modified by experience. On the other hand, each individual has only marginal influence on the group culture, which is shaped by the cumulative choices of the whole group. These cultural changes are the evolutionary forces.

In some cases, natural selection operates directly on cultural variation. For example, the mortality rate for drunken drivers directly affects this type of cultural behavior.

On a personal level there is a clear distinction between genetic and cultural inheritance: a childless person can still transmit his or her culture. Even if a person's genetic fitness is in doubt, he or she may nevertheless be favored by cultural natural selection if he or she succeeds and is influential. However, both approaches intervene in the theories of group selection: when the unit of selection is a group, e.g. a species, the forces that act must include both the social and cultural aspects [2].

Socio-cultural forces affect Darwinian natural selection processes: natural selection will, for example, cause a species to develop appropriate measures better adapted to cool weather or other climatic conditions; similarly, societies and corporations find new niches in which to prosper in changing economic and competitive environments (surviving or disappearing, as the case may be, by natural selection processes)[3].

Just as evolution in living nature is based on many forces in the struggle for survival of any particular variation of species, cultural evolution is affected by various forces as well: in the economic market, for example, the success (or even survival) of a company or business depends on or is influenced by market conditions, workers' morale, government regulations, random catastrophes and so on. Also, in the case of cultural evolution, the variation is "guided" and the inherited transmission is biased, as people, societies and companies make changes in order to improve or even survive. Even the term "innovation" is used both in classic Darwinian evolution for variation, and obviously in social changes, especially in science and technology.

An even greater connection between evolution in living nature and cultural evolution is found when considering cooperation and altruism vs. selfishness in both domains. In the classical Darwinian theory these phenomena were deeply researched, with the resulting

---

definition. Thus, the imitators (in the present context), acquire only the "surface" of the knowledge, gaining only perceived knowledge but not the real thing. This observation will be very important later as we focus on Expert Systems.

2 Richerson & Boyd (2000, 4): "Suppose, for example, a tendency to be more cooperative arose through natural selection on cultural variation. A cultural environment might thus arise in which excessively belligerent or selfish individuals suffered discrimination or ostracism, reducing their chances of acquiring mates. A population composed of more compliant personalities would follow, perhaps quite rapidly on the paleontological time scale." Other theories suggest that selfish individuals might prosper when residing among altruistic societies, e.g. Dawkins (1976).

3 In order to adapt to the dynamic economic and technological environment, companies need to change their strategies (e.g. find new niches) and their structure (e.g. becoming more responsive).

conclusion that cooperative species are usually better fitted in many cases of struggles for survival: "A tribe including many members who...were always ready to give aid to each other and sacrifice themselves for the common good, would be victorious over most other tribes; and this would be natural selection" Darwin (1871, 166)[4].

Once the theory of evolution has been found to relate to the phenomena associated with cooperation as a driving force affecting natural selection, the next logical step is the determination of the unit of selection. While genetic inheritance affects individuals, thereby pointing to their fitness as the selection criterion, the cooperation aspect may change this. Less fitted individuals can survive when the group forces "protect" them. The cooperation tactics employed by the whole group may change natural selection effects.

The next step is a short one: if group tactics practically affect natural selection, then we must treat the "unit of selection" as group-centric and not only as gene-centric. According to this approach, in the struggle for survival, what matters (in addition to the fitness of the individual) is the group's fitness or ability to adapt to the environment and the threats[5].

This discussion reciprocally affects the altruism vs. selfishness dilemma: since altruism is, by definition, acting against one's immediate selfish benefit (e.g. sharing food with others, alerting the group while risking oneself, self-sacrifice), when considering the wider group aspects, one can benefit from the group's wellbeing. So may we refer to an altruistic behavior caused by selfish considerations....

The recognition of the importance of the group's characteristics, beyond the individual's, leads to focus on the forces that affect groups' behavior. Obviously, one of the main forces in human societies is culture, which like physical phenomena, is continuously changing, thus laying the basis for research of its variation, adaptation, survival and inheritance.

In a sense, cultural selection operates sometimes to prevent natural selection forces from having their way: when societies and corporations make changes (like reorganization, replacing management, mergers etc.), they fight against the forces of natural selection that would otherwise extinguish them. Sometimes the fight is against problems created by the same self society, such as the contamination of the ozone layer, where both the fighters and the perpetrators belong to the same species. So, evolution provided us with the intellectual capabilities to create problems and then to solve them.

Human societies created institutions (like universities) to enable better adaptation of the society to the dynamic environment by inventing new ways and technologies. This is their tactical way of guiding the way for the variations needed for adaptation and survival. Cooperation is another method of coping with threats in the struggle for survival, although natural selection sometimes favors uncooperative, selfish individuals[6]. Cooperation is,

---

[4] In animals, self-sacrifice and other altruistic behavior is very common (e.g. vampires sharing blood, bees caring for the queen, vervet monkeys alerting the group while risking themselves).

[5] One of the scholars promoting the group selection approach is Wynne-Edwards (1962), as well as Campbell (1965) and Richerson & Boyd (2005). On the other hand, critiques like Williams (1966) and Dawkins (1976) emphasized the dominance of gene-selection over the group's aspects.

[6] Various scholars (e.g. Dawkins [1976]) contended that selfishness is the regular "winning" strategy for individuals, especially within cooperative societies. This may be traced to Adam Smith's "invisible hand" principle as a major theory of directing a society comprising selfish

therefore, part of the broader argument about the unit of selection (group or individual). This argument is even broader when applied to nations and states: the socialist system which included government controlled economies (maybe the ultimate example of cooperation is the multinational one), collapsed while capitalist paradigms prevailed[7]. However, when applied to former communist states, not all absorbed it at the same success rate. It seems that the cooperative forces are less dominant compared to open-mindedness for changes as a winning strategy.

The ultimate outcome of cooperation, trust and collective decision making (which by definition apply only when groups are involved) is group selection on cultural variation: the survival of the fittest, in this context, relates to the culture of the group as a whole. Personal survival is not relevant, as even unfitted individuals (in the biological sense) may still transmit their culture. However, cultural group selections (e.g. political systems) affect only short-term phenomena (less than half a millennium), and not phenomena which take longer to develop. Capitalism vs. communism is an example of a short term phenomenon, while an example of a long term phenomenon is the transition from an agricultural society to an industrial one.

The reason why humans were able to develop complex societies compared to other species seems to be what Darwin called their "social instincts". Other close species, like chimpanzees, could not adapt and cooperate by inventing tools and machines that need large-scale planning and cooperation in their cultural evolution.

When we judge these social instincts using Darwinian methods, we should be cautious and not conclude as to which is better (or more fitted). Just as Darwinian evolution cannot predict future developments, we cannot state which of the various social approaches will prevail in the long run.

The attractiveness in applying Darwinian theory when analyzing cultural processes is in the use of its methods of dealing with change. The forces which pertain in the global evolutionary equilibrium include religious fundamentalism (of various religions), liberalism, global weather, free market economics and the like. The immediate evolutionary effect can be measured by birth rates, which may be regarded as a measure of natural selection[8], or standard of living. Another force which affects cultural evolution is human "happiness" (i.e. what makes individuals more comfortable or "happy"), as a driver of preference among societies when variation exists. However, this force is difficult to monitor as it varies from society to society. Open economies as a driving force, on the other hand, seem to be directly correlated to dynamic change, especially technological change, which affects social change.

The general tendency for people to cooperate and be trustworthy (at least within their own in-groups), to follow group norms, to be altruistic as expected when the group's well-being

---

individuals, however even he added another social aspect: "How selfish soever man may be supposed, there are evidently some principles in his nature, which interest him in the fortune of others, and render their happiness necessary to him, though he derives nothing from it, except the pleasure of seeing it" (Smith [1790, II.1])

[7] After the recent global economic crisis of 2008-2009 we may see the signs of yet another needed adaptation cycle, mainly in capitalist societies.

[8] However, it is not clear what is meant by high birth rate: either a winning successful species or one doomed because of its inability to provide itself with food and therefore lagging behind.

is at stake – is basic to a social natural selection. In the struggle for survival, groups which developed high cooperative cultures were able to prevail when only a whole group effort could provide technological or economic solutions.

The above ideas about cultural evolution lacked a major element which resides in natural evolution: the mechanism for transmitting the genetic information. Since genes provide the physical data platform which is transmitted by inheritance, there must be an equivalent mechanism in cultural evolution to make it a real "colleague". This missing link was bridged by Dawkins (1976), who coined the term "memes" to describe units of human cultural evolution analogous to the genes. In his book "The Selfish Gene', Dawkins contended that the meme[9] is a unit of information residing in the brain and is the mutating replicator in human cultural evolution.

Memes contain the information about habits, skills, songs, stories, or any other kind of information that is copied from person to person. Memes, like genes, are replicators. That is, they are information that is copied with variation and selection. Because only some of the variants survive, memes (and hence human cultures) evolve. Memes are copied by imitation, teaching and other methods, and they compete for space in our memories and for the chance to be copied again[10]. Large groups of memes that are copied and passed on together are called co-adapted meme complexes, or memeplexes.

Blackmore (1999) took Dawkins' ideas to the extreme: as the memes are the replicators, they also have a selfish nature (like Dawkins' selfish genes). This selfishness drives human thoughts, talking, sex, and even communication instruments and Internet, for one major purpose: distribution of memes and their survival…The human large brain serves, of course, the same purpose; we are just Meme Machines (which is the name of her book). So, according to Dawkins and Blackmore, humans serve a dual purpose: the continuation of genes at the physical level, and the continuation of memes at the cultural level.

Several scholars criticized Dawkins' ideas (and those of other cultural evolutionists as well), especially his neglect of human special characteristics which differentiate us from other species. The main weak point, in the view of the critiques, was the randomness of variation in Darwinian evolution theory, which is not applicable in the human case. One of the most extreme objections was Midgley's (1999) attack on Dawkins' theories[11]. She claimed that since humans are actively making choices, affecting their environment and not only being affected, their progress cannot be determined by the same scientific methods that are

[9] The word "meme" has recently been included in the Oxford English Dictionary where it is defined as follows: "meme (mi:m), n. Biol. (shortened from mimeme ... that which is imitated, after GENE n.) "An element of a culture that may be considered to be passed on by non-genetic means, esp. imitation".

[10] It seems that Dawkins missed the dual meaning of inheritance in his memes analogy: on the one hand there are ideas and habits that are just memorized as existing; on the other hand, there are ideas and habits which influence the behavior of the "descendants". The difference between simply storing the information without causing any behavioral change (or continuity) vs. transmitting behavioral direction is significant, I believe, in cultural evolution. Interestingly, this distinction is equally important in genetic evolution: in fact, most genes of most organisms play no direct role in changing - either their behaviors or their morphologies.

[11] Midgley also attacked Dawkins' attribution of selfish motivations to genes; this backfired on her when she was accused of misunderstanding Dawkins' metaphor.

applicable to other species. Another argument (Frank, 1988) was that in the case of humans emotions like love, sympathy, hate, preferences for fairness, anger or fear are strong incentives to people to react in certain ways; these emotions may even induce them to behave in ways not in accordance with conscious selfish rational calculus in a narrow sense. However even Frank concluded that emotions are a stable phenomenon in a selfish rational competitive environment[12].

Another criticism against Dawkins was of his elimination of God's role once evolutionary theories are adopted (McGrath, 2005). However, as religion is part of culture, it seems that it may nevertheless serve as an example of cultural inheritance, variation and evolution by natural selection.

Whether fully or only partially, it is clear that cultural evolution resembles almost all the ingredients of "classical" Darwinian evolution in nature[13]. Next, we will take a special case of culture – science and technology – and examine whether Darwinian methods can apply and be helpful in creating deeper understanding.

3. Second step: science and technology as an evolutionary process

Campbell (1974) took another step towards the application of Darwinian theory to science (although we can consider science as a subset of culture, hence every aspect is relevant by definition), by comparing new ideas to mutations in genes: as a prerequisite for a mutant gene to be able to survive, it must first meet the structural selective requirements of "being a

---

12 I think that both Midgley and Frank attacked one of the weak points of the whole Darwinian evolution theory, and not only cultural evolution per se: the random variation component. While their criticism points to the intentional characteristics of human culture and motivation, it seems that there is a lack of any intentional direction or any kind of connection between challenges and the resulting "responsive" variations in the adaptation process, in current evolution theories. An initial step towards bridging the gap may be attributed to Jablonka & Lamb (2005), showing the existence of non-random semi-directed mutations and "induced and acquired changes" that play a role in evolution. They also strongly back the analogy between cultural and biological evolution.

13 Darwin himself was rather surprised that his ideas were applied to social and cultural phenomena, but he nevertheless favored this approach: "You will readily believe how much interested I am in observing that you apply to moral and social questions analogous views to those which I have used in regard to the modification of species. It did not occur to me formerly that my views could be extended to such widely different and most important subjects." (Charles Darwin's letter to Hugo Thiel, 1869, in: Weikart (1995)). Darwin similarly corresponded with K. Marx as well. Later, Darwin adopted some of the cultural implications of his theory: "Selfish and contentious people will not cohere, and without coherence nothing can be affected. A tribe rich in the above qualities would spread and be victorious over other tribes: but in the course of time it would, judging from all past history, be in its turn overcome by some other tribe still more highly endowed. Thus the social and moral qualities would tend slowly to advance and be diffused throughout the world." Darwin (1871, Ch. 5). He also discussed the psychological forces driving human behavior in society while affecting evolutionary processes, e.g. the need to be praised by colleagues and to conform to the majority.

gene". Likewise, new scientific ideas must meet the implicit requirements of being accepted by the scientific community. Just as genes must adhere to the DNA "rules" which preserve the ever developing inheritance, the scientific community has its "tribal" continuity which must be maintained. There is a difference, however, between "illegally mutated" ideas and genes: ideas can still cause a paradigm shift which will make them "legal" in the new paradigm, whereas illegal genes (as defined above) will not survive.

So, in Campbell's view, the survival of scientific ideas depends not only on their actual compliance with some objective truth, but also on their conformity to the tribal basic instinct for survival[14]. Similar ideas were expressed by Collins (1985) who coined the term "core set" (which basically means the leaders who keep the scientific tribe together).

This criterion should be regarded as the environment which affects the natural selection of scientific ideas. Moreover, a strategy of maintaining tribal continuity is probably inherited in the scientific community and resides in the genes (or memes) of the members. In a way it resembles the "selfishness" of the genes, as discussed in Dawkins (1976), where the main driving force for survival in the natural selection is described as the need to preserve the genes' continuity.

After establishing the survival strategy, the next step must be to determine the variation mechanism: in natural Darwinism, it consists of random mutation and natural selection preferring the fittest; what is the equivalent in the scientific case? In fact, at first glance one might wonder if there is any resemblance, as science advances by logic, deduction, engineering and mathematical reasoning; how can these fundamental advantages of scientific thought be compared to a random, "blind" process?

Campbell's (1960) second major contribution was indeed the insight of the pseudo-random nature of scientific progress. In his paper he describes scientific progress as something which cannot be deduced from prior knowledge. Each step which expanded knowledge beyond anything that could be deduced, was "blind" and taken in a trial-and-error process. Thus we may have found the missing element in the analogy between scientific progress and Darwinian theory: "A blind-variation-and-selective-retention process is fundamental to all inductive achievements, to all genuine increases in knowledge, to all increases in fit of system to environment." Campbell (1960, 2.1.1).

Campbell was probably aware of the "hole" in his theory, which neglected the intentional nature of scientific progress, but he nevertheless contended that even planned steps (to which he referred as "shortcuts") are more blind than deductive.[15]

A more comprehensive theory of how scientific progress is achieved was presented by Pickering (1995). He referred to the two sides, scientists ("human agency") and science/technology ("material agency"), as participating in the same "actor-network", mutually affecting each other. The technological progress is an unstable process until it

---

14 "An idea is not followed up because it would offend the laboratory head, or because it would give comfort to a rival research group, or because of lack of funding... an idea is rejected because of reasons why it will not work, or because of rumors that a trusted researcher is known to have tried it and failed." Campbell (1997, 8.12).

15 "The many processes which shortcut a more full blind-variation-and-selective-retention process are in themselves inductive achievements, containing wisdom about the environment achieved originally by blind variation and selective retention." Campbell (1960, 2.1.3).

becomes "tuned". As human agencies strive to advance by modifying the material agencies, they encounter "resistance" (i.e. things are not working exactly as planned), which in turn needs to be accommodated by further modification.

This resistance-accommodation relationship was described as a kind of dance which has a direction. This direction is not straightforward and is continuously modified by redefining of the gaps and the new goals. This type of progress was called by Pickering "the mangle of practice", with an evolutionary type of unpredictable behavior.[16]

Thus, Pickering was able to show that although technological progress appears to have an intentional nature coupled with engineering logic, it is much closer to the trial-and-error process judged by the force of natural selection, as are other evolutionary blind-variation-and-selective-retention phenomena[17].

Lastly, as a special case of technological change, we will examine Expert Systems' fundamental paradigms, and endeavor to identify additional analogies with Darwinian evolution processes, beyond those that are common to every technology.

4. Third step: expert systems in evolutionary perspective

4.1 Knowledge renewal – expertise as an evolutionary process

Expert Systems (ES)[18] are based on a simple and attractive paradigm: since experts are able to perform better than others, if their unique knowledge is extracted, stored in a computerized system, and then made available to the "users" to be applied by them - we can achieve an expert-level performance by any user.

However, there is a fundamental concern when we look at the future: may we assume that something that worked in the past will work in a similar way in the future? The underlying paradigm of ES is that if we apply the unique expert knowledge, based on past experience, in future events, we will be able to succeed. This assumption seems obvious, when applying the same rules repeatedly with the same results. However, various scholars warned in the past that this inductive assumption is dangerous. David Hume (1748), as early as the eighteenth century, doubted that any prediction of future events based on past experience, is justified. Karl Popper (1972) added the insight that we believe in causal relationship only because we observe the repetition of past results coupled with our expectation that there is an underlying rule which is the reason for them. Actually, claimed Popper, this is a deductive process rather than an inductive one[19].

---

16 Others (Tenner (1997); Brown & Duguid (2000)) referred to the same phenomenon as "technologies bite back" and "fight back".

17 "Scientists do not simply fix their goals once and for all and stick to them, come what may. In the struggles with material agency that I call tuning, plans and goals too are at stake and liable to revision. And thus the intentional character of human agency has a further aspect of temporal emergence, being reconfigured itself in the real time of practice, as well as a further aspect of intertwining with material agency, being reciprocally redefined in the contours of material agency in tuning." Pickering (1995, 20).

18 The discussion on ES and the analogy suggested in this paper is limited to "Rule-Based Expert Systems", which are the most popular type of ES. Also, much debate exists on ES's successes and failures, limitations, social resistance and others; this paper deals only with the basic paradigms. A more comprehensive discussion on ES may be found in Romem (2007) and Romem (2008).

19 Popper (1972) even named his book as providing "an evolutionary approach"…

So, if we want to be cautious, we should not just take for granted that what has worked in the past will do so in the future. Still, the rules are written in ES for future use, so perhaps this paradigm is too dangerous?

A partial answer to this concern is that experts, at least the better ones, are aware of the fact that what has worked in the past might not work in the future. Those who are fixated by former experience, always performing as they did in the past, are probably not 'good experts". Only those who are capable of adapting past experience to new circumstances may be considered good experts. The rules, which refer to past experience, are only adequate as one input for the right decision in a new scenario. This "adaptation" capability is most important for making a good expert[20].

The issue of adaptation is strongly related to the dynamic nature of the relevant environment. If everything is stable, including the goals, then we may expect that all the concerns about updates of the rules are less significant. Once there is a "steady state" where the rules function as a "close enough" recipe for decision making, there will be no need to change them. All that is required is to learn how to use them properly. However, we must assume that organizations experience continuous changes, where the business and cultural environments are dynamic. As ES are static in nature, the adaptation issue becomes crucial.

There are various researches dealing with "adaptive expertise", trying to trace what makes experts employ adaptive capabilities[21]. However, the fact that experts can adapt better than others to new circumstances, is beyond our current knowledge extraction capability. This tacit, non-algorithmic and possibly intuitive capability, remains out of the reach of current ES, as further analyzed in Romem (2008). Since the need for adaptation originates from changes, and we assume that experts have good adaptation skills, the key to understanding this phenomenon is by trying to understand how successful knowledge changes occur.

Various scholars described the process of knowledge renewal as "a trial-and-error process, which leads unconsciously to improvement without specifically knowing how we do it" Polanyi, (1957, 101). The dynamics of this process presents an obvious challenge to ES: "...beliefs held by individuals are modified through negotiation with other individuals...But the information encoded in a knowledge base is not modified in this way" Forsythe (1993, 466). What is especially challenging is the innovation aspect. How experts find new ways to cope with new circumstances remains mystifying. Collins (1990) described innovation not as a structured methodological strategy, but rather more like a "gang of cutthroats" fighting for the wheel to direct a truck, with almost random result. Similarly, as mentioned in the previous chapter, Pickering (1995) described it as a kind of "dance of agencies" where human and material agencies participate in a "resistance - accommodation" relationship, resulting in unpredictable progress.

---

20 Polanyi (1958) found a clear distinction between assimilation of experience into an existing fixed environment, and the adaptation of a current framework according to the lessons of a new experience. The degree of novelty and an even heuristic approach is much stronger in the second case. In our case, the users of ES are required to perform the more challenging task of adaptation of the rules provided to them, which correspond to what Polanyi defined as "current framework". Shanteau (1992, 257) referred to "The competence seen in experts [which] depends on having stable strategies developed in response to their environments."

21 E.g. Fisher & Peterson (2001).

Combining all the above observations on expertise renewal, a dynamic, trial-and-error process, with random steps, which eventually lead to improvements (or "adaptation") - it is tempting to compare it to a Darwinian evolutionary phenomenon. Darwinian Theory is based on similar processes and even uses similar terminology[22]. As revealed here, ES and Darwinian evolution have similar characteristics, apart from a crucial one: natural selection's retention criterion. How can we compare these two processes if there is no mechanism which determines the "winning direction"?

A careful consideration may lead to an answer to the missing component: experts gain their positions as the ones who are able to adapt; the natural selection criterion is the survival of experts in their position. Those who do not adapt successfully do not survive as experts. Fisher & Peterson (2001) and Wineburg (1998) distinguished between "sure-footed" experts whose expertise is based almost solely on "prior knowledge" and experts who continuously seek new insights with a broader perspective, thus employing an "adaptive expertise". In the present context, the latter are the "winning species".

Thus, we may have found the missing link: experts react to dynamic environments; they (sometimes unconsciously[23]) engage in trial-and-error processes while creating intuitive "mutations" of previous behavior; as long as they are successful, thereby maintaining their expert status, they have successfully adapted; those who fail to adapt, are passed over as future expertise reference.

Although the analogy contains all the required ingredients, it seems that one step is weaker than the others: the variation step. While biological variation originates from random mutations, the usual strategy of experts when striving to solve an unprecedented problem is not to try "all" possible mutations, at random, until one prevails; they rather apply more thoughtful considerations, favoring those directions which seem to offer better solutions[24].

---

22 In the classical Darwinian Theory literature, the terms of "random variation", "mutations", "adaptation" and "survival of the fittest" are fundamental. The last is discussed in this section; another basic Darwinian term - "inheritance" - is discussed in the next section.

23 Penrose's (1989) analysis reveals a somewhat surprising conclusion about the way humans make decisions: their consciousness enables them to make "non-algorithmic" decisions; only when they are unconscious do they make pre-defined procedural decisions. Therefore, we can conclude that rule-based Expert Systems are closer to simulated unconscious decisions. Unlike ES, when experts make conscious decisions, these decisions may be different from their corresponding rules…

24 Brandon (1994) contended that humans, unlike other species, act thoughtfully. Combining this idea with Penrose's (1989) (mentioned above) about humans' conscious non-algorithmic behavior, it may strengthen the concern that Expert Systems' rules can only cover unconscious decisions by experts. However, one explanation is that the reason that experts' conscious decisions seem to be intuitive/tacit/non-algorithmic is because the experts do not know their algorithm; yet when experts make conscious decisions (or thoughtful, as Brandom would say), the fact that they cannot tell us how they did it, may suggest that at *the moment of decision* they made it unconsciously. So, there might be some underlying rules which caused the decision (although experts are not aware of them). This means that even conscious decisions may be governed by rules; we simply asked the wrong person…

This difference between the human approach to solving unprecedented problems and nature's approach may indeed be regarded as, on the one hand, a gap in the analogy revealed in this paper and, on the other hand, a trigger for further research. For such research two potential directions are recommended: one, in the area of "genetic algorithms" - which currently imitate nature's approach by applying random variations when trying to find the best way to solve a problem; and the other in the post-Darwinian evolution theory itself - by seeking some hidden mechanism in the genes that reacts to problems which the species experience. I believe that such a mechanism which "shortcuts" the blind-variation-and-selective-retention process (by making it less blind) will make the evolution theory more comprehensive.

The two suggested areas of further research may strengthen the analogy suggested in this paper; nevertheless, there are much more important reasons for adopting them. In any case, the similarities between knowledge renewal (in life and in ES) and evolutionary process were shown; we are ready now to turn to another area of resemblance: the inheritance process.

4.2 Knowledge transference as an inheritance process

ES' common process of knowledge transference from experts to the users seems to be very straightforward: the expert tells a "Knowledge Engineer" (KE) all the details of his or her knowledge, than the KE codifies the knowledge as rules in the Knowledge-Base (KB) of the ES. These rules are in the form of: IF {A} THEN {B}: when situation {A} occurs, the users should do {B}. This process of knowledge extraction from the expert and the use of it by the user are described in figure 1.

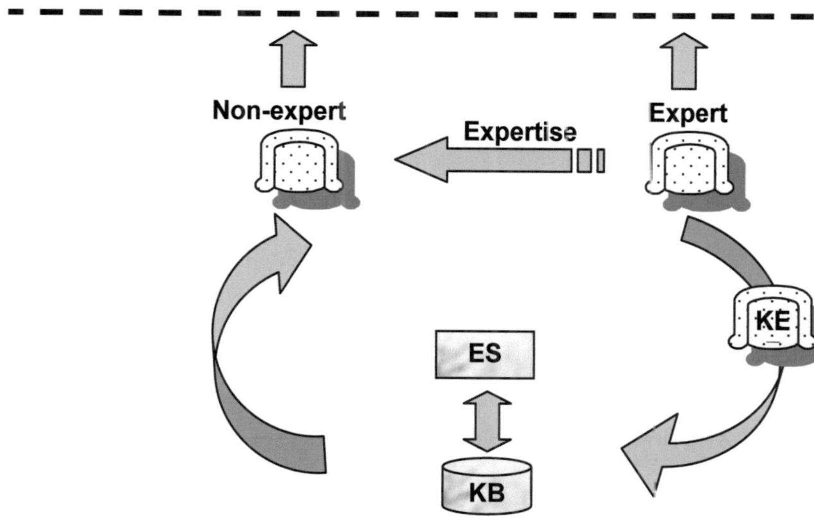

Fig. 1. Knowledge Transfer in Expert Systems

The goal of knowledge transfer is to enable the non-expert to act as an expert, or to be regarded by the outside world (above the dashed line in figure 1) as an expert. Adopting the Darwinian connotation, we may define the behavior of the expert as the phenotypic characteristics which should be transmitted to the non-expert, like an inheritance process (the upper arrow in figure 1). This can be regarded as "memetic" inheritance (using memes as the unit of selection). It differs from the original Darwinian inheritance only in that it is not between generations but rather between colleagues, but this is similar to any cultural evolution.

This difference should not detract from the analogy: Mameli (2005) contended that even the use of the term 'inheritance' for genetic transmission was always a metaphorical one. In his view, the reference by evolutionists (including Darwin himself) to the practice of parents giving property to their offspring to describe the "like-begets-like" phenomenon, should not mislead us in our research. In fact, knowledge transference and genetic inheritance seem to be closer than the original metaphor of gift of property: unlike the latter which involves the transition from one owner to another, in the knowledge case as well as the biological case, the donor remains in possession of the original "property".

Now, the next step is to examine how this inheritance mechanism is implemented in ES: the knowledge is articulated as rules in the Knowledge-Base (KB). Thus the rules in the KB are in essence the "code" representing an expert's behavior, just as genes are the code for the characteristics of any species. In other words: rules represent expertise, just as genotype represents phenotype. This relationship is shown in figure 2.

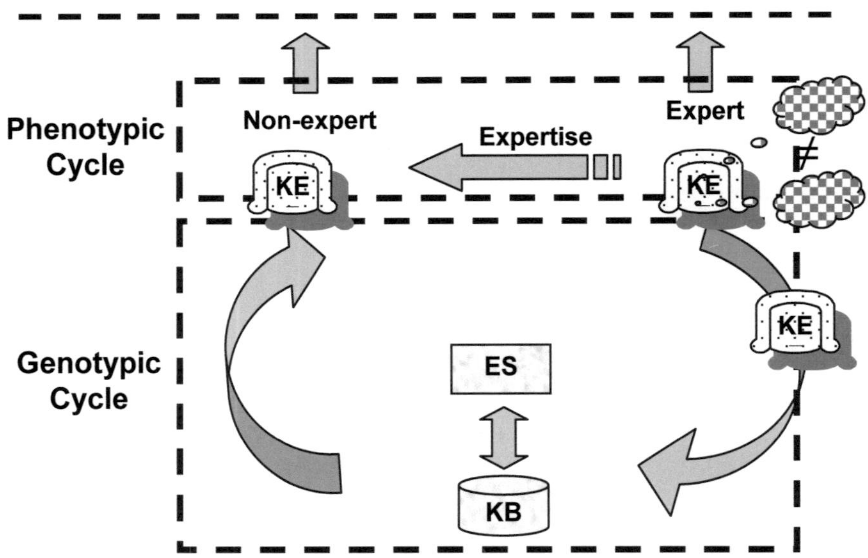

Fig. 2. Knowledge Transfer in Expert Systems

In the expertise inheritance process, the expert is asked to articulate his or her expertise. There is a hidden assumption in equating what we are doing with what we think or say we are doing namely, that when we do things we can always tell how we did them. This assumption is found to be wrong. This is marked in figure 2 in the gap between the expert's mind and the expert's words.

This gap was recognized by various philosophers such as Polanyi who argued that there is a distinction between practicing expertise and being able to explain it explicitly: "the aim of a skilful performance is achieved by the observance of a set of rules which are not known as such to the person following them" Polanyi (1958, 49). His conclusion: "even in the modern industries the indefinable knowledge is still an essential part of technology". For this kind of indefinable knowledge Polanyi coined the term "tacit knowledge".

This is a rather surprising observation, as people naturally tend to assume that experts know the rules by which they practice their expertise. Examples include: the skill of swimming, a cyclist's balance, the 'touch' of the pianist, flying, skiing, cooking and many others. It is very difficult for experts to shift their attention from doing what they are doing to being aware of *how* they are doing it. In many cases, they cannot do both at the same time Polanyi (1957; 1958). The point is that describing explicitly what one does requires different skills from just doing it[25]. Proclaimed experts will have "earned" their title not on account of any skills of articulation they may have but because of their practicing skills. Yet, the whole process of knowledge transfer relies heavily on the ability of experts to describe what they do, something in which they are not experts at all.

But after our conclusion that knowledge transfer resembles inheritance in evolution, this difficulty is not so surprising: determining the underlying rules from the behavior of the expert is similar to determining the genetic structure from the phenotypic appearance… Just as the latter is not likely to succeed, we should not be surprised about the tremendous challenges that are encountered in expertise transference.

Another challenge was pointed out by Mameli (2005); in his view, simple DNA-copying is not sufficient for transmitting the full phenotypic behavior which is influenced by the environment and culture in a non-genetic way. ES knowledge transference resembles the same phenomenon: the rules must be interpreted in the context of the original environment when they were coded. As this environment is not part of the rules themselves, following them may produce wrong results.

There is a limit, however, to the suggested analogy: in the ES case, there is an ultimate measure of success: users performing in an expert-like way or being able to do "the right thing" as needed; in the genetic inheritance case the measure of success, if any, is more vague. Is the offspring "as good" as the ancestors? It seems that this direction is more philosophical than practical, although one may conclude, in the Dawkins' way of thinking, that the success of genetic inheritance is in the survival and continuity of the genes.

5. Conclusion

In summary, there is a close analogical relationship between Expert Systems fundamental processes and Darwinian evolution processes: Just as evolution reaches a stabilization phase only after a successful mutation survives the natural selection, so does the new knowledge of the expert become a habit and noticeable only after it has been successfully transmitted as rules in the Expert System[26].

---

[25] Polanyi (1958, 88) summarized this phenomenon: "I know that I know perfectly well how to do such things, though I know the particulars of what I know only in an instrumental manner and am focally quite ignorant of them; so that I may say that I know these matters even though I cannot tell clearly, or hardly at all, what it is that I know." Polanyi (1957) also quoted Gauss: 'I have had my solutions for a long time but I do not yet know how I am to arrive at them.'

[26] This is not enough to make the new knowledge inheritance successful: Romem (2008) showed that even if the rules are correct, the user might wrongly interpret them, the future scenario might be different, the goals or motivation for acting in a certain way may have changed and various other conditions may cause unexpected results.

The challenge of transforming phenotypic new knowledge to genotypic new explicit rules is the articulation challenge. In this analogy, rules in the Knowledge-Base act as does DNA in humans. The rules are implicit in their phenotypic phase and become explicit in their genotypic phase, thus enabling "inheritance" by the users. This inheritance is, in a sense, the goal of Expert Systems.

6. Acknowledgement

Dr. Oren Harman's important comments helped me sharpen the ideas; Professor Menachem Fisch and Professor Niv Ahituv's guidance in my original Dissertation; Dr. Noah Efron's continuous encouragement - they all turned my research and writing into an enjoyable and fulfilling experience.

7. References:

Avital, Eytan and Jablonka, Eva. 2000. *Animal Traditions: Behavioral Inheritance in Evolution.* Cambridge, MA: Cambridge University Press.

Blackmore,S.J. 1999. *The Meme Machine.* Oxford, UK: Oxford University Press.

Brandom, Robert B. 1994. Making it Explicit: Reasoning, Representing, and Discursive Commitment. Harvard University Press.

Brown, John S.and Duguid, Paul. 2000. *The Social Life of Information.* Cambridge, MA: Harvard Business School Press

Campbell, Donald. T. 1960. Blind variation and selective retention in creative thought as in other knowledge processes. *Psychological Review*, 67: 380-400.

Campbell, Donald T. 1965.Variation and Selective Retention in Sociocultural Systems. In: *Social Change in Developing Areas* . Edited: Barringer et al.

Campbell, Donald T. 1997. From evolutionary epistemology via selection theory to a sociology of scientific validity. *Evolution and Cognition* 3: 5-38.

Collins, H.M. 1985 Changing Order: Replication and Induction in Scientific Practice Thousand Oaks, CA: Sage

Darwin, Charles. 1871. *The Descent of Man*. Penguin Classics (republished 2004).

Dawkins, Richard. 1976. *The Selfish Genes*. Oxford, UK: Oxford University Press

Fisher, Frank T.and Peterson, Penelope L. 2001. A tool to Measure Adaptive Expertise in Biomedical Engineering Students. Proceedings of the 2001 American Society for Engineering Education Annual Conference & Exposition: 2793.

Forsythe, Diana E. 1993. Engineering Knowledge: The Construction of Knowledge in Artificial Intelligence. *Social Studies of Science* 23(3): 445-77

Frank, Robert. 1988. *The Strategic Role of Emotions.* New York & London: W.W. Norton & Company.

Greisemer, James. 2000., *Philosophy of Science* Vol. 67, Supplement. Proceedings of the 1998 Biennial Meetings of the Philosophy of Science Association. Part II: Symposia Papers: 348-68

Hume, David. 1748. *Enquiries Concerning Human Understanding and Concerning the Principles of Morals.* Oxford: Oxford University Press, 1975. Original: 1748; (ed. L.A. Selby-Bigge, rev. P.H. Nidditch).

Jablonka, Eva and Lamb, Marion. 2005. Evolution in Four Dimensions: Genetic, Epigenetic, Behavioral and Symbolic Variation in the History of Life. Cambridge, MA: MIT Press.

Latour, Bruno. 1987. *Science in Action*. Cambridge, MA: Harvard University Press

Mameli, Matteo. 2005. The inheritance of Features. *Biology and Philosophy* 30: 365-99

McGrath, Alister. 2005. Has Science Eliminated God? – Richard Dawkins and the Meaning of Life. *Science & Christian Belief* 17(2): 115-35

Midgley, Mary. 1999. *Science and Poetry.* New York: Routledge.

Penrose, Roger. 1989. *The Emperor's New Mind.* Oxford, UK: Oxford Univ. Press.

Pickering, Andrew. 1995. The Mangle of Practice: Time, Agency and Science. Chicago, IL:The University of Chicago Press.

Polanyi, Michael. 1957. Problem Solving. *British Journal for the Philosophy of Science.* 8 (30): 89-103

Polanyi, Michael. 1958. *Personal Knowledge: Towards a Post-Critical Philosophy.* Chicago, IL: The University of Chicago Press 1958,1962.

Popper, Karl R. 1972. *Objective Knowledge: An Evolutionary Approach.* Oxford, UK: Oxford University Press.

Richerson, Peter J.and Boyd, Robert. 2000. Evolution: the Darwinian Theory of Social Change, an Homage to Donald T. Campbell. In: *Paradigms of Social Change: Modernization, Development, Transformation, Evolution.* Edited: Schelkle, W. et als. Frankfurt: Campus Verlag.

Richerson, Peter J.and Boyd, Robert. 2005. *Not by Genes Alone: How Culture Transformed Human Evolution.* Chicago, IL: University of Chicago Press.

Ridley, Matt. 1998. The Origins of Virtue: Human Instincts and the Evolution of Cooperation. USA: Penguin.

Romem, Yoram. 2007. The Social Construction of Expert Systems. *Human Systems Management.* 26: 291-309.

Romem, Yoram. 2008. *Expert Systems: the Promise, the Disappointment, the Comeback.* Bar-Ilan Univ. Israel, (Ph.D. dissertation)

Shanteau J. 1992. Competence in Experts: The Role of Task Characteristics. *Organizational Behavior and Human Decision Processes* 53: 252-66.

Smith, Adam. 1790. *The theory of Moral Sentiments.* London, UK: A. Millar 6th edition (1st published 1759)

Tenner, Edward. 1997. Why Things Bite Back: Technology and the Revenge of Unintended Consequences. New York: Vintage Books.

Weikart, Richard. 1995. A recently discovered Darwin Letter on Social Darwinism. *ISIS* 86: 609-11

Williams, G.C. 1966. *Adaptation and Natural Selection*. Princeton, N.J: Princeton University Press

Wineburg, S. 1998. Reading Abraham Lincoln: An Expert/Expert Study in the Interpretation of Historical Texts. *Cognitive Science* 22(3): 319-46

Wynne-Edwards, V.C. 1962. *Animal Dispersion in Relation to Social Behaviour*. Edinburgh: Oliver & Boyd

2

NALUPES – Natural Language Understanding and Processing Expert System

Andrzej Pułka
Institute of electronics, Silesian University of Technology, Gliwice
Poland

1. Introduction

Today, modern electronic devices are supplied with many new sophisticated functions, and expectations of their users are constantly growing. Abilities of natural language handling, i.e. understanding and processing commands given in natural language undoubtedly increase the attraction of such equipment. Moreover, this property makes them useful for those persons who have problems with standard communication, with limited manual dexterity, handicapped or even blind persons. This problem can be extended to other fields of human's activity. Also electronic design automation (EDA vendors work on facilitation of the design process for engineers and simplification of their tools. (Pułka & Kłosowski, 2009) described the idea of such expert system supplied with the speech recognition module, dialog module with speech synthesis elements and inference engine responsible for data processing and language interpreting. That approach is dedicated to system-level electronic design problems. The authors focused on automatic generation of modules based on speech and language processing and on data manipulating.

This chapter focuses on highest level language processing phase - the heart of the system – the intelligent expert system responsible for appropriate interpretation of commands given in natural language and formulation of responses to the user. We concentrate on inference engine that works on the text strings that are far from the lowest, signal level.

Automated processing and understanding of natural language have been recognized for years and we can find these problems in many practical applications (Manning & Schultze, 1999, Jurafsky & Martin, 2000). They belong to hot topics investigated in many academic centers (Gu et al. 2006, Ammicht et al. 2007, Infantino et al. 2007, Neumeier & Thompson 2007, Wang 2007). The main objective of the presented contribution is to develop an expert system that aids the design process and enriches its abilities with speech recognition and speech synthesis properties. The proposed solution is intended to be an optional tool incorporated into the more complex environment working in the background. The goal is to create a system that assists the working.

These objectives can be met with the AI-based expert system consisting of the following components: speech recognition module, speech synthesis module, language processing module with knowledge base (dictionary and semantic rules), knowledge base of the design components and design rules and the intelligent inference engine which ties together entire system, controls the data traffic and checks if the user demands are correctly interpreted.

Next section addresses the entire EDA system architecture and localizes the Natural Language Understanding and Processing Expert System (NALUPES).

2. Entire system architecture

The architecture of entire EDA system presented in (Pułka & Kłosowski, 2009) is depicted in Fig. 1. Main elements belonging to the NALUPES expert system are denoted by shaded area. Certainly, the presented scheme covers all levels of the language processing and synthesis ranging from the signal level through all necessary transformations to phonemes and allophones to the text level (Pułka & Kłosowski, 2009). Because this chapter is devoted to the expert system responsible for data analysis, and not detection of signals and their transformations, we concentrate on text level. The heart of the NALUPES system is the inference engine based on Fuzzy Default Logic (Pułka, 2009). The inference engine works on semantic rules implemented within the system and it cooperates with two additional modules: the speech recognition module and the speech synthesis module. The brief description of levels handled by these modules is given in the next section.

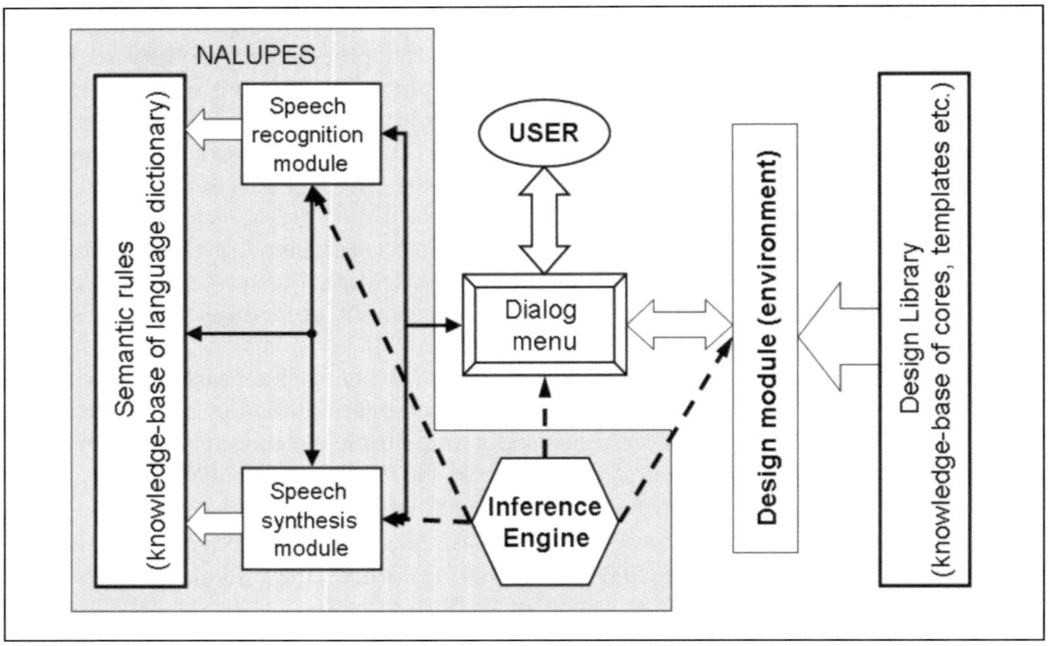

Fig. 1. A Dialog System Architecture

3. System layers – a brief overview

3.1 Speech recognition module

The speech recognition module is responsible for finding the message information hidden inside the acoustic waveform [4]. The nature of this procedure heavily depends on speaker, speaking conditions and message context. Usually, it is performed in two steps (Fig. 2). In the first step speech signal is transformed into a sequence of phonemes or allophones. Phonemes are sound units that determine meaning of words. In phonetics, an allophone is

one of several similar phones that belong to the same phoneme. A phone is a sound that has a defined wave, while a phoneme is a basic group of sounds that can distinguish words (i.e. change of one phoneme in a word can produce another word). In the second step the sequence of phonemes is converted into the text by phonemes-to-text conversion unit.
The conversion process is of course more complicated and consists of many calculations and involves many modules, among others we have to determine the number of distinctive parameters for each phoneme (Pułka & Kłosowski, 2009), but the obtained text not necessarily is correct, i.e. reflects real meaning and the speaker intentions. In this moment the NALUPES system starts and tries to verify the correctness.

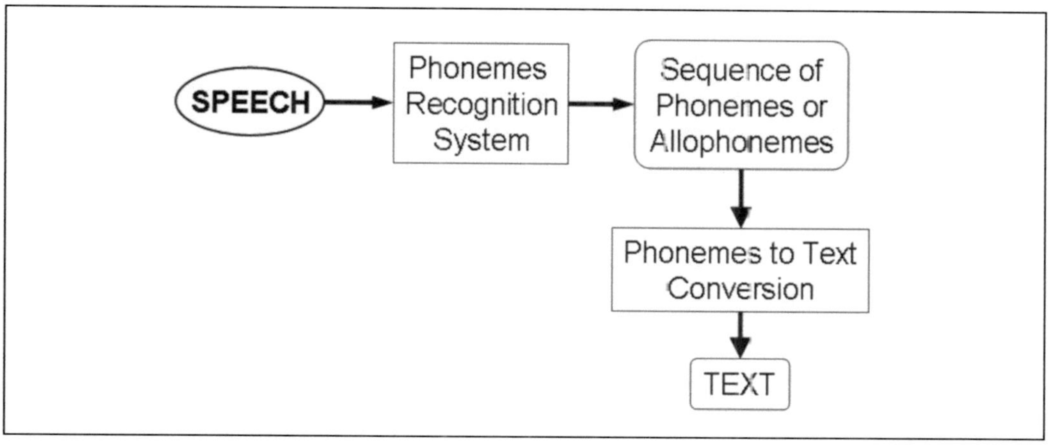

Fig. 2. The speech recognition process seen as a transformation speech-to-text (STT).

3.2 Speech synthesis module

The speech synthesis process is widely used in many practical applications, especially in telecommunication devices. Usually the full text-to-speech (TTS) system converts an arbitrary ASCII text to speech. In the first step the phonetic components of the message are extracted and we obtain a string of symbols representing sound-units (phonemes or allophones), boundaries between words, phrases and sentences along with a set of prosody markers (indicating the speed, the intonation etc.). The second step of the process consists of finding the match between the sequence of symbols and appropriate items stored in the phonetic inventory and binding them together to form the acoustic signal for the voice output device (Fig. 3). So, the NALUPES system is responsible for appropriate composition of text strings, and the rest is performed on the phonetic and signal levels, respectively.

4. FDL based inference engine – a heart of the system

As it was mentioned above, the most important part of the NALUPES is its inference engine enriched with sophisticated heuristic tools based on Fuzzy Default Logic (FDL) (Pułka, 2009). The classical logic based approaches usually fail in cases where flexibility is strongly required and the system has to search for a solution which is based on vague and incomplete prerequisite. In our case of phrases recognition, the system is expected to guess the meaning of voice commands even though the original (initial) information is in a useless (incomplete, distorted, mispronounced, misspelled, etc.) form.

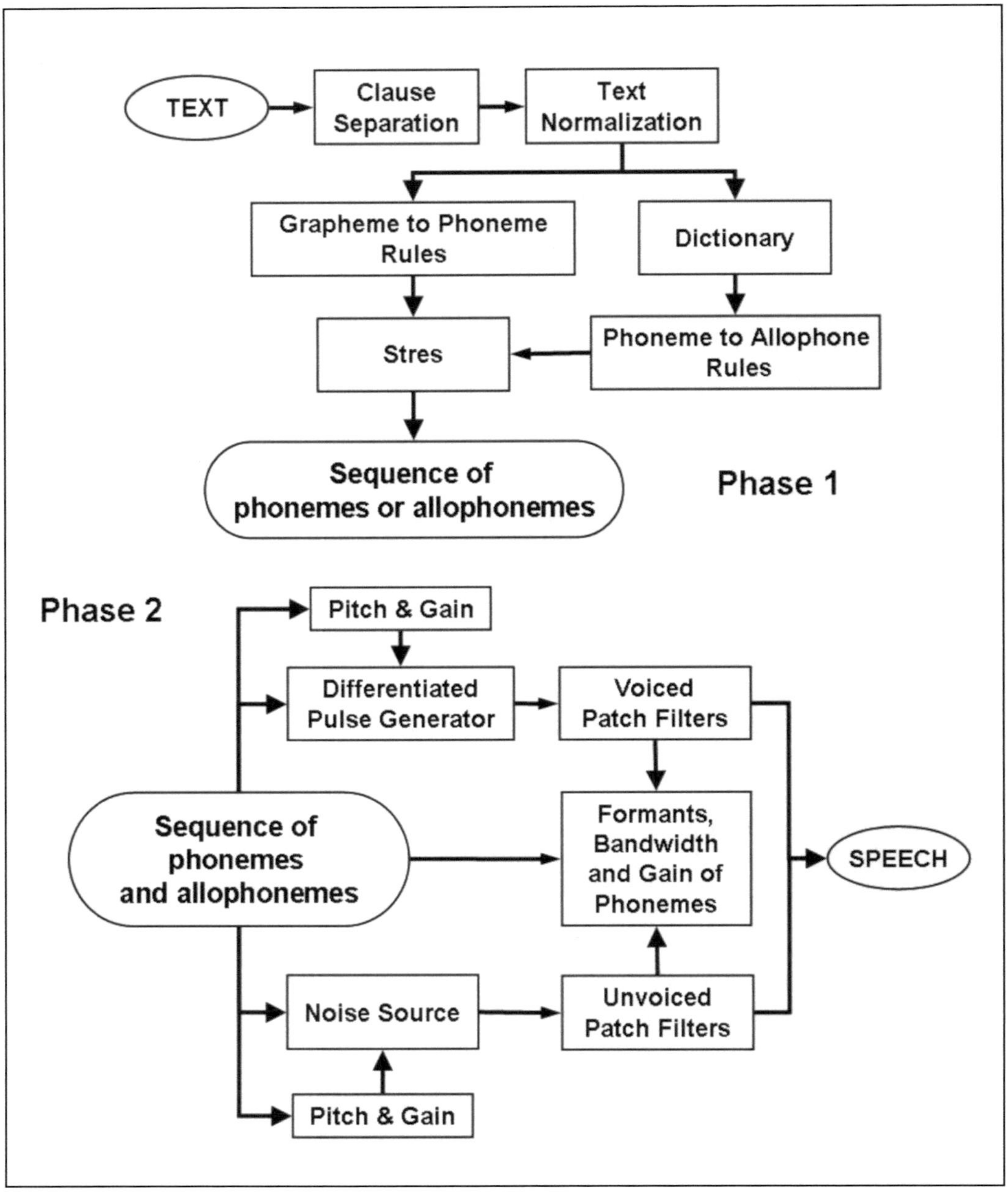

Fig. 3. The speech synthesis process seen as a two steps transformation text-to-speech (TTS).

4.1 Fuzzy Default Logic (FDL)

Considerations on the one hand on nonmonotonic reasoning and answer set programming, and on the other hand, on fuzzy logic and generalized theory of uncertainty lead to the formulation of Fuzzy Default Logic (Pułka, 2009). This new methodology combines techniques of modeling and handling cases with incomplete information with various types of imprecise information and vagueness. Main definitions of FDL are presented below.

Definition 1

The ***Fuzzy Hypothesis*** (***FH***) is defined as a vector:

$$\Phi^{\lambda}=\left\{\left[h_1^{\lambda},\mathrm{Tw}\left(h_1^{\lambda}\right)\right],\left[h_2^{\lambda},\mathrm{Tw}\left(h_2^{\lambda}\right)\right],\ldots,\left[h_m^{\lambda},\mathrm{Tw}\left(h_m^{\lambda}\right)\right],\right\} \tag{1}$$

where: h_i^{λ} (i = 1...m) are wffs in propositional language L, and $Tw(h_i^{\lambda})$ denotes ***Trustworthiness***; i.e. one of the modality of generalized constraints in the Zadeh's sense (Zadeh 2006) (bivalent, probabilistic, fuzzy, veristic etc.). For the simplest case the trustworthiness can be treated as a membership function or probability (Zadeh 2008).

Definition 2

The ***Fuzzy Default Rule*** (***FDR***) is the following inference rule:

$$\frac{\alpha:\beta_1,\beta_2\ldots\beta_N}{\Phi^{\lambda}} \tag{2}$$

α, $\beta_1 \ldots \beta_N$ are *wffs* (well formed formulas) in a given propositional language L and Φ^{λ} is a Fuzzy Hypothesis. Moreover, we assume that prerequisite (like in Reiter 2001) is represented by strong information (facts in the sense of (Reiter 1980)), while the possible uncertainty or missing of information is represented by justifications $\beta_1 \ldots \beta_N$. Two assumptions reflect the nonmonotonicity of the inference system: *NaF* (Negation as a Failure) and *CWA* (Closed World Assumption). This scheme reduces the problem of inference path propagation and tracing for trustworthiness. If we would like to have a FDR based fully on ignorance and/or vagueness, the prerequisite is an empty set ($\alpha \equiv \varnothing$).

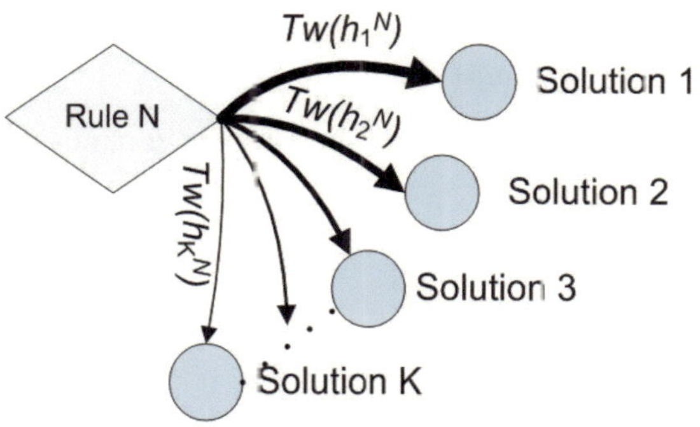

Fig. 4. Hypotheses generation based on FDR scheme – the granular view.

The fuzzy default rules are interpreted similarly to their *classical* predecessors (default rules Reiter 1980). The main difference is in the form of the hypothesis (FH), which consists of different aspects (views, extensions) of the same problem and each of these sub-hypothesis has its own *Tw* coefficient. Trustworthiness reflects the *significance* of a given solution, which usually is subjective and can be modified. Elementary hypotheses (components) of a given FH Φ^{λ}, i.e. are h_1^{λ}, h_2^{λ},..., h_m^{λ} are mutually exclusive. At first glance it looks like inconsistency, because we would like to derive different hypotheses about the same world, but we should remember that each of them has its own trustworthiness level, and moreover, it is the preprocessing phase before the final assessment of hypotheses. In this sense we can call the inference process as a ***multistage procedure***. To eliminate some very weak hypotheses we can add an additional cut-off mechanism (see the implementation) which preserves inferring a hypothesis with a small level of the trustworthiness. Such a solution of the inference engine simplifies the hypothesis derivation and the problem of priorities and existence of various extensions of default theories (Reiter 1980, Brewka 1991) does not limit the application. It is possible, during the inference process, to watch various options (debug the inference engine) and their number can be controlled by the cut-off level. Granular representation of the FDR reasoning procedure presents Fig.4, (the width of arrows corresponds to the values of the trustworthiness).

Definition 3

The ***Credible Set*** (***CS***) $\boldsymbol{H^\lambda}$ of a given Fuzzy Hypothesis $\boldsymbol{\Phi^\lambda}$ is a subset of $\boldsymbol{\Phi^\lambda}$ consisting of those elements $\boldsymbol{h_i^\lambda}$ that have appropriate Trustworthiness i.e.:

$$H^\lambda \subseteq \Phi^\lambda \quad \text{and} \quad \underset{h_i^\lambda \in H^\lambda}{\forall} \; Tw\left(h_i^\lambda\right) \geq \text{cut\_off} \tag{3}$$

Naturally, the CS corresponds to those hypotheses that are considered during the further inferring process. The presented mechanisms of hypotheses selection may be more complicated or adjusted dynamically, according to other constraints. The trustworthiness of hypotheses and its ordering corresponds to ordering of literals $\boldsymbol{l_0}$ to $\boldsymbol{l_k}$ in the head of the answer set programming disjunction rules and preference rules (Balduccini & Mellarkod 2004, Balduccini et al. 2006, Gelfond & Lifschitz 1988, Łukasiewicz & Straccia 2008, Van Nieuwenborgh & Vermeir 2006).:

$$\begin{gathered} l_0 \; or \; l_1 \; or \ldots l_k \leftarrow l_{k+1}, \ldots l_m, \; \textbf{not} \; l_{m+1}, \ldots \textbf{not} \; l_n \\ \text{pref}(l_1, l_2); \text{pref}(l_2, l_3); \ldots \end{gathered} \tag{4}$$

We will call a given CS ***coherent*** if no its hypothesis is contained in any prerequisite or justification of a FDR, i.e.:

$$\underset{h_i^\lambda \in H^\lambda}{\forall} \Rightarrow \neg \left[\underset{\frac{\alpha^\varphi : \beta_1^\varphi, \beta_2^\varphi \ldots \beta_N^\varphi}{\Phi^\varphi}}{\exists} \middle| \begin{array}{c} h_i^\lambda \cap \alpha^\varphi \neq \varnothing \\ h_i^\lambda \cap \beta_1^\varphi, \beta_2^\varphi \ldots \beta_N^\varphi \neq \varnothing \end{array} \right] \tag{5}$$

Definition 4

The ***hypotheses reduction*** (***HR***) at a given level, we will call the transformation (simplification) of all Credible Sets inferred at this level. This reduction (logical sum of Credible Sets) generates all good (possible for further considerations) hypotheses and reduces the number of trustworthiness per a single hypothesis. After the reduction we obtain all concluded hypotheses that could be considered for the final assessment, and each hypothesis <u>**contains**</u> only one trustworthiness.

$$HR\left\{\bigcup_i H_i^\lambda\right\} = \left\{\left[h_i, Tw(h_i)\right] \middle| \exists H_k^{\lambda_k} \; h_i \in H_k^{\lambda_k} \text{ and } Tw(h_i) = opt\left(Tw\left(h_i^{\sum \lambda_k}\right)\right)\right\} \tag{6}$$

where: $opt\left(Tw\left(h_i^{\sum \lambda_k}\right)\right)$ denotes ***optimal*** value of the trustworthiness for a given element (hypothesis) selected from all Credible Sets.

Selection of optimal function (opt) is another, very interesting problem and it can be a field for user interaction to the inferring process. The optimal function can be flexible, i.e. it can have different meaning for various kinds of trustworthiness (bivalent, probabilistic, veristic, and fuzzy - Zadeh 2008). The optimal function can be also strict (the same for every trustworthiness), which means that it corresponds to one of the following cases: maximum (optimistic approach), mean (no priorities), minimum (worst case analysis), max-min(fuzzy approach) etc.

Definition 5

The ***Fuzzy Default Logic*** (**FDL**) is the theory Δ_{fuzzy} for modeling the commonsense reasoning, which splits the inferring process into stages (steps) Δ^{s}_{fuzzy} and at every stage a given hypothesis is generated. The stage Δ^{s}_{fuzzy} is represented by a quadruple: axioms, simple relations between the knowledgebase elements (classical logic relations), fuzzy default rules and constraints (Apt & Monfroy 2001). The stage Δ^{s}_{fuzzy} is responsible for generation a hypothesis h_s. Formally:

$$\Delta_{fuzzy} = \{ \Delta^{s1}_{fuzzy}, \Delta^{s2}_{fuzzy}, \ldots \Delta^{sN}_{fuzzy} \}; \quad \Delta^{sk}_{fuzzy}\{ A, Facts, FDRs, C \} \mapsto h_{sk} \qquad (7)$$

The FDL reminds its ancestors of Default Logic (DL) (Reiter 1980) and Cumulative Default Logic (CDL) (Brewka 1991), however this mechanisms is supplied with vagueness and uncertainty (Zadeh 2004 and Zadeh 2008), and thanks to complex form of hypotheses with their trustworthiness and possibility of generation and consideration of various conclusions it is very close to answer set programming. Instead of preference operator in answer set disjunction logic (Gelfond & Lifschitz 1988), final conclusion is selected on the hypotheses assessment stage. Fig. 5 brings in the scheme of this multi stage inference process. Those pieces of information which are known (stated in a form of axioms, facts or constraints) are not derived. We assume that there is no connections (loop-backs) between FDRs (represented by hexagons) of the same stage, which is very important for the model stability (Pułka 2009). The fuzzy default rules (FDRs) that take part in the inference process (generation of credible sets) are represented by shaded hexagons.

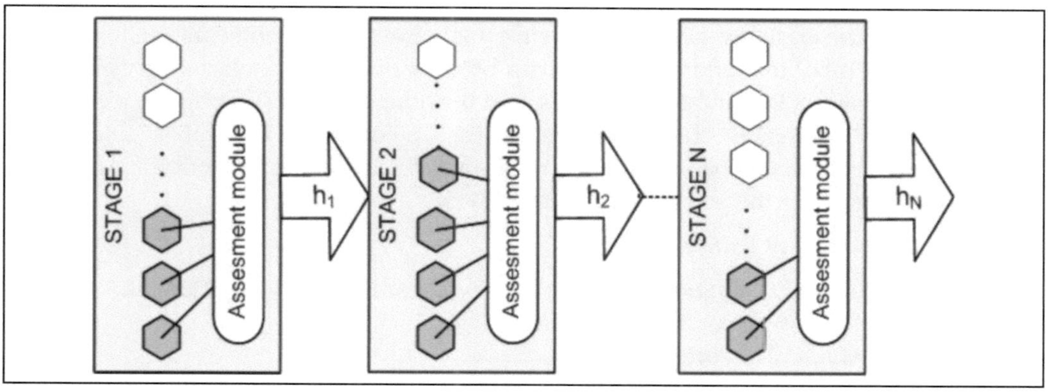

Fig. 5. Generation of Basis Extension (BE) – a multiple stage view.

4.2 Hypotheses generation

As it was mentioned above, very important is the problem of the model stability (Gelfond & Lifschitz 1988), which may lead to unexpected results. The proposed solution (Pułka 2009) is to avoid feedbacks (briefly: concluded hypotheses are not the prerequisites for the other rules) in the inference chain and construction of coherent credible sets. So, the main drawback of the presented methodology is its application specific property, i.e. the implementation of the knowledge base and structure of rules is strongly dependent on the application, and the technique is not a general purpose commonsense modeling. Only the main backbone (shell) of the deduction structure is generalized. On the other hand, however it gives some flexibility to the implementation. In the form presented here, the FDL based inference engine implements the idea of cumulativity (Brewka 1991) and generates so-called Basis Extension (BE) (Pułka & Pawlak 1997). The cumulativity is achieved by calling all nonmonotonic rules and asserting all possible hypotheses as well as justifications (exactly their negations). These *extra* FDL rules control the process of information generation and supplies the system with missing pieces of information. There is no need to keep control on generation rules (priorities of extensions), because every possible hypothesis is considered (the inferring procedure resembles multithread process) and the final selection of the conclusion is performed in the end (assessment phase of Algorithm 1). The implementation requires the appropriate construction of the knowledge-base (addressed in the following section).

Algorithm 1 (Generation of Basis Extension – BE)

forall fuzzy_default_rule(α, β, FH^λ)
  if α true ***then***
    if β cannot be proved ***then***
      assert every hypothesis $h_i^\lambda \in FH^\lambda$ ***for each***
        $Tw(h_i^\lambda)$ > cut off level;
update the knowledge-base;
assess inferred hypotheses.

4.3 Revision of beliefs

Every formal model of commonsense reasoning has to consider the problem of revision of beliefs, i.e. consistency checking with new pieces of information or occurrence of inconsistency. The meaning of the inconsistency in the fuzzy system should be explained at first. Of course, the existence of two or more mutually exclusive hypotheses is allowed, but we have to remember that after the assessment process, only one conclusion is valid. So, if we find somewhere in the subsequent stages, that the other solution is assumed, we have to reconstruct the deduction chain and verify the hypotheses. The other solution is investigation of more than one paths and parallel analysis of various possibilities. Algorithm 2 given below describes the process of revision of beliefs.

Algorithm 2 (Revision of Beliefs)

forall hypothesis ([h_i^λ, $T\omega$], $Source_i$, $Level_i$) | fuzzy_default_rule(α, β, FH^λ) ***and*** $h_i^\lambda \in FH^\lambda$
when one of the following conditions is true:
  1° negation of h_i^λ can be proved ***or***
  2° β can be proved ***or***
  3° α cannot be proved

remove hypothesis h_ι^λ and every hypothesis hypothesis ([h_κ^λ, $T\omega$], $Source_k$, $Level_k$) such that $Level_k > Level_i$;
update the knowledge-base;
complete (generate) basis extension (BE);
assess inferred hypotheses.

Cases 1°, 2° and 3° represent various situations when consistency of the information has to be verified. This somehow complicated mechanism is forced by the deduction structure within the system that creates a deduction chain. Hypotheses can be generated directly from fuzzy default rules (as their hypotheses) and then we call them as hypotheses of zero level or we can deduce given information basing on the hypothesis which is a result of non-monotonic inference process. The latter has also to be classified as a non-monotonic hypothesis, because is based not on strong fact but on other non-monotonic hypothesis and can be invalidated later. So each hypothesis *has to remember* its predecessor. Because of this deduction structure we can call the inference engine as ***multilevel***. After the revision of beliefs the system is ready to check the completeness of the basis extension and make any necessary supplements, to have a full set of the design information.

4.4 Hypotheses assessment

The generated hypotheses form a deduction chain, and every hypothesis remembers its ancestor. If we denote a hypothesis in a form of a clause hypothesis ([h_ι^λ, $T\omega$], $Source_i$, $Level_i$) it means that the assumed hypothesis has been derived from $Source_i$, which is also a hypothesis of the level $Level_i$. The final assessment and selection of the *best* hypothesis as a final conclusion at a given level can be based on different schemes, which depend on chosen demands: we can take a simple criterion of trustworthiness value (like *verity* in veristic modality of generalized constraints), analyze the entire path (paths) from the $Source_0$ to $Source_i$ and find the global trustworthiness (regarding it like probabilities or possibilities) or use fuzzy criteria max(min) (Łukasiewicz & Straccia 2008, Zadeh 2006). Many examples show that the assessment mechanism gives additional ability to control the model (selected extension). Let's assume that a given FDL model consists of A = ∅: Facts = {C, D, E} and the FDR set contains 3 rules:

(1) (C :B/ {[A_1,0.8], [A_2,0.7], [A_3,0.6]}).
(2) (D :B/ {[A_1,0.4], [A_2,0.6], [A_3,0.4]}).
(3) (E :B/ {[A_1,0.2], [A_2,0.3], [A_3,0.4]}).

So, we have the following trustworthiness for hypotheses A_1, A_2 and A_3, respectively:

$Th(A_1) = \{0.8, 0.4, 0.2\}$.
$Th(A_2) = \{0.7, 0.6, 0.3\}$.
$Th(A_3) = \{0.6, 0.4, 0.4\}$.

The hypotheses reduction process could be controlled by different functions, which are based on altered criteria. This may allow obtaining different solutions as a finally accepted hypothesis: worst case scheme generates A_3 as a positively selected hypothesis with trustworthiness 0.4; the mean criterion based on average value of trustworthiness chooses hypothesis A_2 (average 0.53); and if we employ the classifier based on the best (highest) trustworthiness, we obtain hypothesis A_1 with 0.8 value.

In this sense the assessment of hypothesis gives a lot of flexibility to the user and is application dependant. Moreover, we can split the hypotheses reduction process into two steps: first, selection of the optimal value of the trustworthiness for each hypothesis and then, final assessment and selection of the best one solution. We can use different criteria for each step.

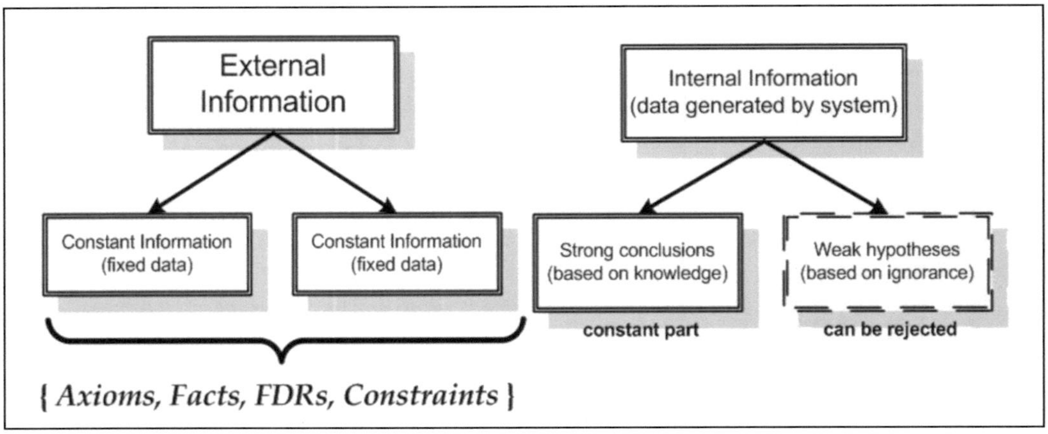

Fig. 6. The knowledge-base structure.

5. Knowledge-base construction

The knowledge-base and data-base structure on one hand corresponds to the requirements of the inference engine, and on the other hand reflects the properties of the implementation environment (here PROLOG). Details concerning the implementation are addressed in the next section, so let's focus only on main elements constituting the system database.
The entire information stored in the knowledge-base can be divided into two parts: external data acquired by the system from the user and internal data generated by the system. Fig. 6 presents the diagram of the data structure within the entire system. This formal scheme simplifies the information handling and controlling of its consistency (Pułka 2000).

5.1 NLU and NLP rules

The entire dialog system described in Fig.1 consists of many elements handling the voice commands on various levels. The NALUPES system deals only with highest levels of abstraction uses results of modules working on signal level that extract appropriate parameters necessary to recognize and classify phonemes and corrects errors that may occur on lower layers (Fig.7).
The main objectives of the expert system are:

1. correction of unrecognized or wrongly recognized commands;
2. interpretation of entire language phrases constituting commands;
3. understanding and execution of the orders included within commands;
4. preparation of answers or comments to the user (system feedback).

The above goals are achieved during the different phases of the decision process and they relate to the natural language processing (NLP) and the natural language understanding (NLU) processes (Jurafsky & Martin 2008, Bird et al. 2009).

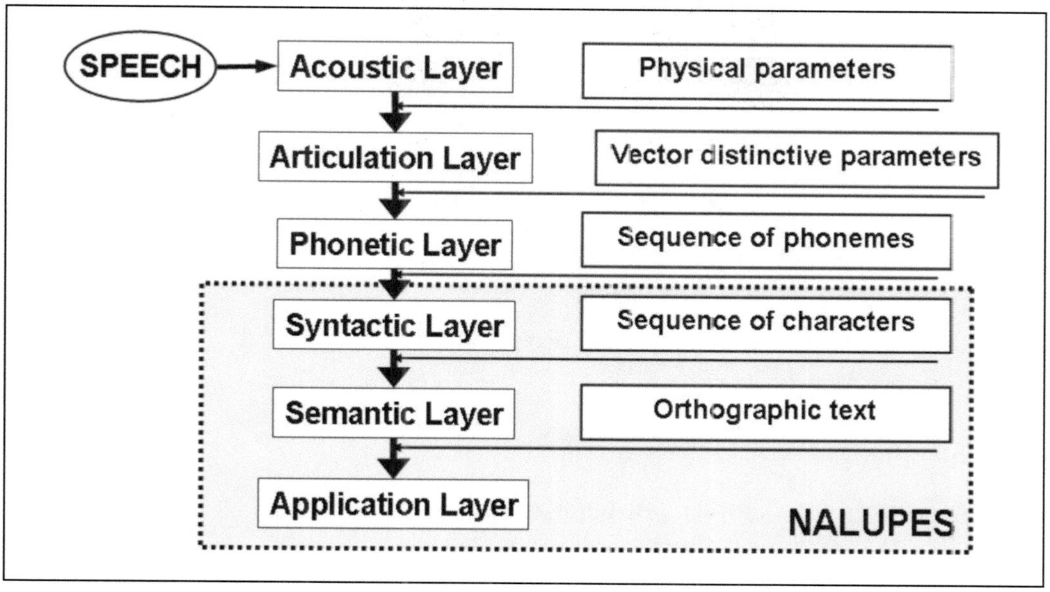

Fig. 7. Multilayer speech recognition process.

First group of tasks concerns recognition of single words. The system should answer the following questions: if a given word exists (belongs to our dictionary)? If a given word has an exact meaning (if a given command makes sense)?

The second phase concerns analyses and verification of sequences of words (entire commands with all necessary and optional parameters). System controls if a given combination of words exists? If this conjunction has a sense?, If it is possible to execute this command within a given phase (context)?

The third group of tasks is responsible for understanding the semantic and meaning of the entire phrase and execution of the appropriate operation. The fourth element of the system generates answers and/or comments to a user or optionally questions in problematic situations.

The system decisions depend on a given context, the menu (here: the design system) and possible actions. Moreover, the deduction structure may look differently for various kinds of situations - there is no unique scheme of the system behavior. However, on the other hand the process of commands correction or understanding is based on templates of phrases and patterns of semantic constructions. The same situation is with the system answers, every response is based on selection of appropriate model from the knowledgebase.

The above scheme justifies the usage of a sophisticated inference mechanism. We can find here: nonmonotonicity (Reiter 1980, Brewka 1991) and incomplete granular information (Kudo & Murai 2004) as well as vagueness and various forms of uncertainty (Zadeh 2006).

Feedback loops present in the verification procedures reflects the nonmonotonic nature of hypotheses (conclusions), which are only temporal and weak. Statistical nature of linguistic information, frequency of appearance of characters, similarity of sounds (allophones and phonemes), the probability of the situation that two or more letters (sounds) are adjacent to each other and many more observations allow incorporating fuzzy models to the processing rules. The scheme depicted in Fig.8 contains small feedback loops (let's say local) and loops covering bigger regions of the deductive process.

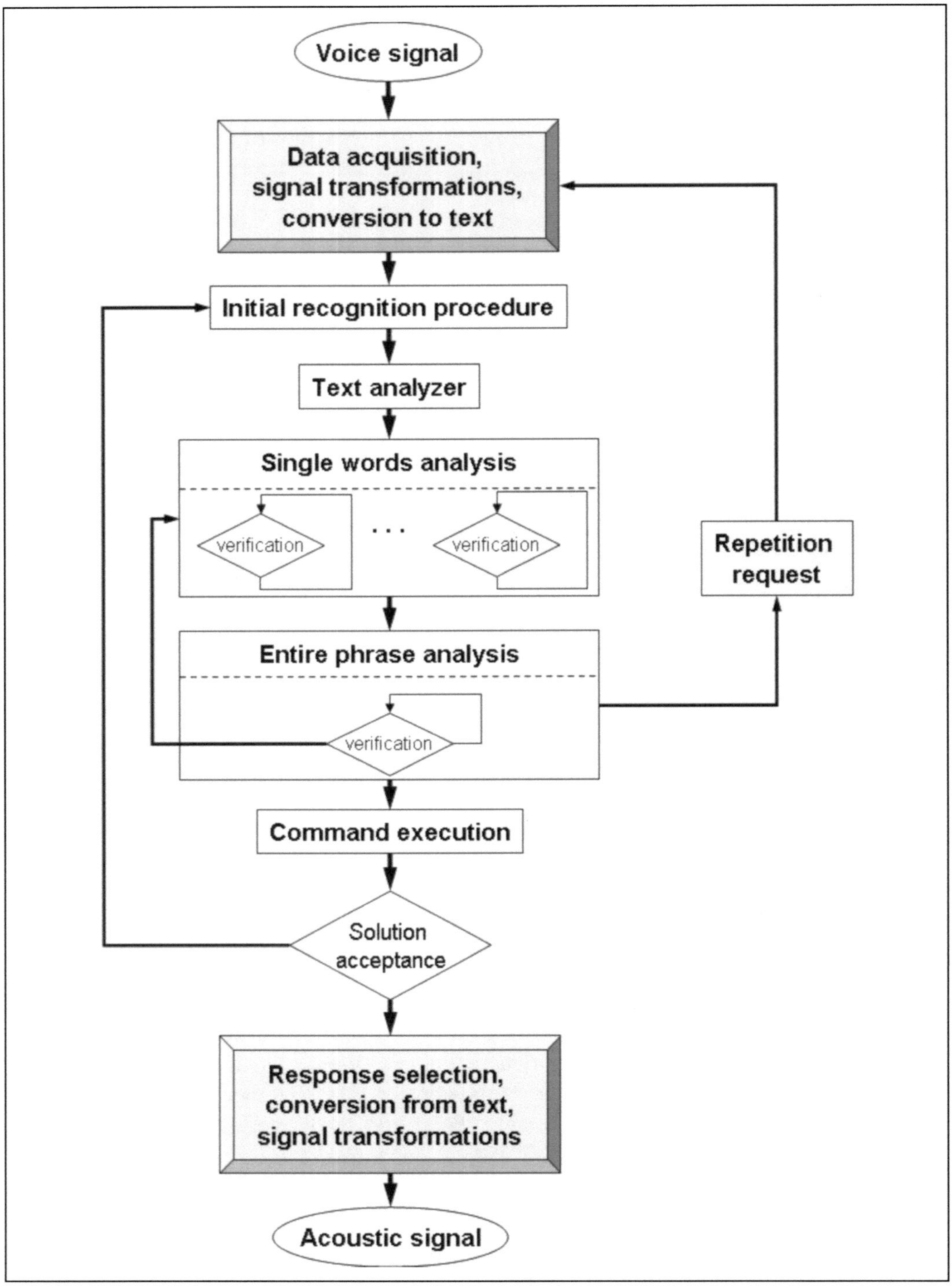

Fig. 8. Natural language processing and understanding sequence.

A single word verification process, which could (but not necessarily must) be executed concurrently, requires examination only short parts of the entire string. In case of any errors, basing on statistical information and current context, the system tries to find in the knowledgebase candidates that best match to a given sequence, i.e. we have an initial chain of characters: $\{C_0, C_1, C_2, \ldots C_N\}$ that

- can have a correct meaning,
- can have meaning but with no sense in a given situation,
- can have no meaning (represents no word)

Each of the above cases should be handled and system is expected to select from the templates present in the knowledgebase candidates: $\{\{T^1_0, T^1_1, T^1_2, \ldots T^1_N\}, \{T^2_0, T^2_1, T^2_2, \ldots T^2_N\}, \ldots\{T^k_0, T^k_1, T^k_2, \ldots T^k_N\}\}$. These candidates together with their trustworthiness create the fuzzy hypothesis from definition 1. The values of trustworthiness may depend on other factors represented in prerequisite and/or justification, so the FDR rule looks as follows:

$$\frac{\text{Prerequisite} : \text{Justification}}{\Phi^{\lambda}} \tag{8}$$

where: **Prerequisite** represent ***context*** (the menu item, edition phase, evaluation phase or another step of the design process) together with the initial chain $\{C_0, C_1, C_2, \ldots C_N\}$; **Justification** could be connected with context (not present elements) or other optional parameters concerning the design process. Φ^{λ} is a fuzzy hypothesis of the form: $\{[\{T^1_0, T^1_1, T^1_2, \ldots T^1_N\},Tw_1], [\{T^2_0, T^2_1, T^2_2, \ldots T^2_N\},Tw_2], \ldots[\{T^k_0, T^k_1, T^k_2, \ldots T^k_N\},Tw_k]\}$ where each trustworthiness coefficient Tw_i is selected individually depending on a given case (rule). Also the prerequisites could be modeled as a stack with nesting priorities, i.e. ***context***$^{\gamma}$, ***context***$^{\gamma-1}$, ***context***$^{\gamma-2}$, etc. This mechanism allows obtaining another property – controlled deep of backtracking mechanisms.

Process of entire phrase analysis deals with bigger elements: words. Because of the specific nature of the commands to the design system, usually the most important part of a command is the head, i.e. the first element of the chain. The complex semantic tree analysis (Chou & Juang 2002, Gu et al. 2002, Lee & Leong 1992, Bird et al. 2009) is not necessary. We can distinguish three main kinds of commands: actions, descriptions and questions. Furthermore, a command could be simple (trivial case) or complex. In general, the first keyword decides about the command classifying. The analysis is limited to some class of commands, however it is possible to use synonyms (a kind of thesaurus has been implemented). The action commands begin with verbs denoting appropriate activity that should be performed. The description commands denote some execution, but they start with a noun describing a real element in the database of the project. The property of this component has an impact of the analysis of the rest of the chain. The question commands may begin with some limited set of words, like *is, what, why, how* etc. Another commands partitioning presents listing in Fig. 11, we can distinguish global, editing and reviewing commands depending on the current state of the design process.

If the analysis of a given phrase (a chain of words) fails, i.e. gives no real results and corresponds to no order, the verification procedure has to start the revision of beliefs and the system has to invalidate the hypothesis and consider another possibility. This situation may involve deep backtracking and correction of the previous assumptions. The same problem may occur if the solution generated after the execution of the selected command is not satisfying for the user or it contradicts some earlier actions. In such a case, the deduction process could be turned back to previous stages or the user is asked to repeat a command. The latter case usually appears, when several attempt of correction failed.

6. Implementation

The NALUPES system has been implemented in PROLOG language (LPA Prolog) on MS Windows platform. PROLOG language is used for automatic theorem proving, it enables very compact, coherent and consistent implementation of knowledge-base rules. PROLOG is based on linear resolution and uses the backtracking search mechanism. Unfortunately, this mechanism is not very efficient and is not complete - for incompletely defined worlds it can be non-soluble. We can point out some approaches that propose optimization of the search process and reduce the searching space (Prestwich 2001), but the problem of the resolvability is still open in the pure PROLOG. However, in the application domain presented here, where we can assume closed description of the world, this limitation is not very annoying.

6.1 FDL expressed in PROLOG

In order to incorporate the proposed inference mechanisms into the first-order based linear resolution, we have to make few assumptions: the hypothesis of CWA (Closed-world Assumption), existence of more then two logical states for some of the variables representing mutually exclusive solutions and as a consequence the modified logical negation. In other words, the presented fuzzy (cumulative) default logic extends the soundness and strength of the linear resolution and gives new abilities to PROLOG language. The proposed syntax reminds the Cumulative Default Logic engine presented in (Pułka & Pawlak 1997), but introduces the vagueness with Trustworthiness (Fig.9).

```
conclude([Hypothes,Trustworth],Source,Lev):-
        \+(no(Hypothesis)),
        cut_off_level(Cut_Level),Trustworth > Cut_Level,
        \+(hypothesis([[Hypothes,Trustworth],Source,Lev])),
        assertz(hypothesis([[Hypothes,Trustworth],Source,Lev])),
        \+(Hypothesis),
        assertz(Hypothesis).

conclude(_,_,_).

negation(Fact) :- no(Fact),!.          /* modified negation*/
negation(Fact) :-  \+ Fact.
```

Fig. 9. PROLOG implementation of the predicate conclude handling FDR rules.

Fig.9 presents one of the crucial predicates conclude that is responsible for generation of basis extension. It handles fuzzy default rules and a uses the *artificial negation* (predicate no) that complements the gap in PROLOG (PROLOG negation is interpreted as a *negation as a failure*). This philosophy can be used only for limited application and domains that covers *the entire world description*. The more general solution of the negation is still NP-hard problem, however if we assume (and allow) that some parts of knowledge are imprecise and represented not only by two value-logic (true and false), but taking values from more states, we can take advantage of this PROLOG drawback, so the prerequisites as well as conclusions can be of the fuzzy type.

```
phrase_recognize(Phrase):-
        find_list_of_words(Phrase,[Head|Tail),
        menu_select([Head|Tail]).

menu_select([Command|ListOfParameters]):-
        check_command(Command,Menu,MenuType),
        check_sense(Menu,ListOfParameters,Menu1),
        execute(Menu1,ListOfParameters).
/* If the command is not recognized system */
/* generates voice information to the user */
menu_select(_):-
        speech_generate('Command not recognized'),
        speech_generate('Try once more').

check_command(X,X,Type):-               command(X,Type), !.
check_command(Command,X,_):-  conclude(X, Command).
```

Fig. 10. Examples of PROLOG rules of a semantic checker.

6.2 Knowledge-base rules

The inference engine is responsible for solving *difficult* situations where the system meets problems with recognition and understanding of the user intensions. The significance of a given conclusion depends on the strength of hypotheses that belong to the root of the deduction structure. However the entire process is controlled by linear resolution and all rules are implemented in a form of clauses (Fig. 10). In case of any problems with recognition, the FDL engine is invoked (predicate conclude).

6.3 Database templates

To simplify some recognition operations, the database contains patterns of commands and thesaurus dictionary. The system can find appropriate template and reduce number of fuzzy default engine invocations. The templates has a form of lists (compare to framelists described in (Pułka & Pawlak 1997, Pułka & Kłosowski 2009)). The main problem occurred with names (of modules, ports, signals etc.) that could be often wrongly interpreted, so the system generates subsequent numbers and prescribes fixed names followed by numbers.

```
template(['start', 'edition', 'of', 'data']).
template(['start', 'data', 'edition']).
template(['cancel', 'previous', 'operation']).
template(['insert', 'new', 'port']).
template(['insert', 'new', 'signal']).
template(['add', 'signal', 'name']).
template(['show', 'recently', 'inserted', 'module']).
template(['what', 'is', '10', 'port', 'direction']).
synonym(['start', 'begin', 'initiate', 'set up', 'establish']) .
```

Fig. 11. Examples of the database templates (PROLOG clauses).

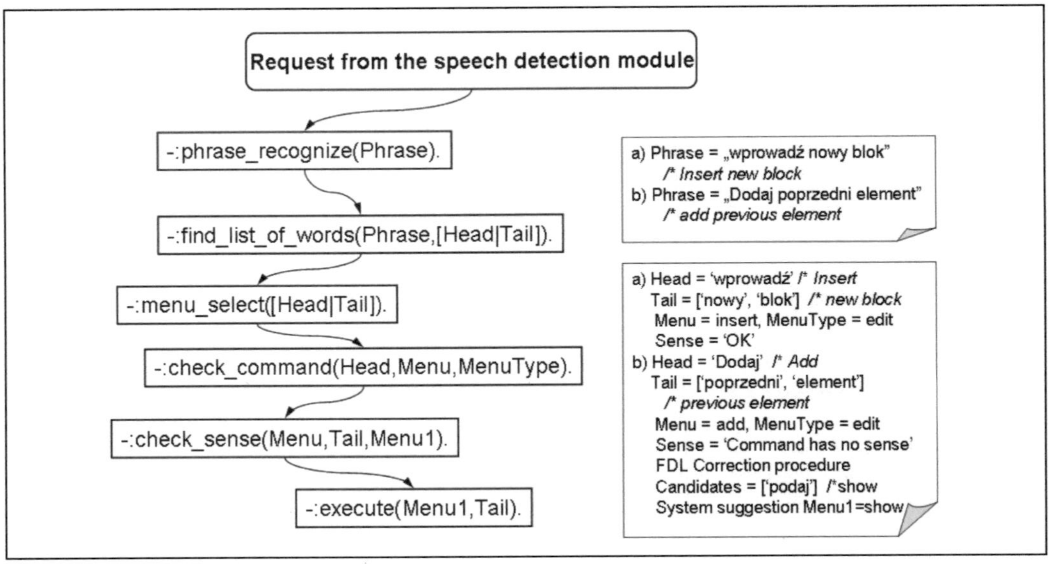

Fig. 12. Examples of the system run.

7. Experiments

Previously, the system has been designed and dedicated to Polish dictionary, it has used characteristic properties of Polish language (Kłosowski 2002). Main advantage of the first version of the system was the very good conversion mechanism at the allophonic level. However the test with modified NALUPES shell (the expert system) supported by FDL inference engine show a radical improvement of the correctly recognized commands. Moreover, the effectiveness could be increased thanks to the user interactions (feedbacks). Currently, the system has been extended to English language and first experiments seem to be very promising.

8. Final remarks

In this chapter the NALUPES - the expert system for understanding and processing of commands in natural language has been presented. The system is based on statistical and numerical semantic language analysis methodologies developed for year and described in literature. However, the main novelty of the system is its sophisticated inference engine which allows improving the efficiency of the recognition process at the textual level.
The area for further investigations is research on system universality, i.e. introduction general rules that allow handling different languages with different databases.

9. References

Ammicht E., Fosler-Lussier E., Potamianos A. (2007). *Information Seeking Spoken Dialogue Systems: Part I and Part II*, IEEE Transactions on Multimedia, Vol.9(3), 2007, pp.532–566.

Apt K. R. and Monfroy E. (2001). Constraint programming viewed as rule-based programming, *Theory and Practice of Logic Programming*, 1(6): pp.713–750, 2001.

Balduccini M. and Mellarkod V. (2004). Cr-prolog2: Cr-prolog with ordered disjunction, In ASP04 Answer Set Programming: *Advances in Theory and Implementation, volume 78 of CEUR Workshop proceedings*, 2004, pp.98–112.

Balduccini M., Gelfond M., and Nogueira M. (2006). Answer Set Based Design of Knowledge Systems, *Annals of Mathematics and Artificial Intelligence*, 2006.

Bird S., Klein E., Loper E. (2009). Natural Language Processing with Python, O'Reilly Media, June 2009.

Brewka G. (1991). Cumulative Default Logic: in defense of nonmonotonic inference rules, *Artificial Intelligence* 50 (1991), pp.183 - 205.

Chou W. and Juang B. H. (2002). *Pattern Recognition in Speech and Language* Processing, Eds. 2002, CRC Press, Inc.

Gelfond, M. and Lifschitz V. (1988). The stable model semantics for logic programming. In Logic Programming, *Proceedings of the Fifth International Conference and Symposium*, R. A. Kowalski and K. A. Bowen, Eds. The MIT Press, Seattle,Washington 1988, pp.1070–1080.

Gu L., Gao Y., Liu F-H. and Picheny M. (2006). *Concept-Based Speech-to-Speech Translation Using Maximum Entropy Models for Statistical Natural Concept Generation*, IEEE Transactions on Audio, Speech and Language Processing, Vol.14, No.2, March 2006.

Infantino I., Rizzo R., Gaglio S. (2007). *A Framework for Sign Language Sentence Recognition by Commonsense Context*, IEEE Transactions on Systems, Man and Cybernetics: Part C: Appl. & Rev., Vol.37, No.5, 2007, pp. 1034–1039.

Jurafsky D. and Martin J. H. (2008). *Speech and Language Processing*, Speech Recognition and Computational Linguistics, Prentice-Hall, 2008.

Kłosowski P. (2002). *Improving of speech recognition process for Polish language*, Transactions on Automatic Control and Computer Science Vol.47 (61), 2002, pp. 111–115.

Kudo Y., Murai T. (2004). Non-monotonic reasoning in prioritized knowledge bases based on granular reasoning, Proc. *of IEEE Intern. Conf. on Fuzzy Systems*, 2004, vol. 1, pp.275–280.

Lee M. C. and Leong H. V. (1992). *NLUS – a Prolog Based Natural Language Understanding System*, Proceedings of 4th IEEE International Conference on Computing and Information, ICCI'92, pp. 204-207.

LPA Prolog. *http://www.lpa.co.uk*.

Łukasiewicz T. and Straccia U. (2008). Tightly Coupled Fuzzy Description Logic Programs under the Answer Set Semantics for the Semantic Web, *International Journal on Semantic Web and Information Systems*, 4(3), 2008, pp. 68–89.

Manning C. D. and Schütze H. (1999). *Foundations of Statistical Natural Language Processing, Cambridge*, MA: MIT Press 1999.

Neumeier K., Thompson C. (2007). *Parameterizing Menu Based Natural Language Interfaces with Location Models*, Proc. of IEEE KIMAS 2007, pp. 236–240.

Prestwich S. (2001). Local Search and Backtracking vs. Non-Systematic Backtracking, *Proceedings of AAAI 2001 Fall Symposium on Using Uncertainty Within Computation*, 2-4 November, AAAI Press 2001, pp. 109-115.

Pułka A., Pawlak A. (1997). Experiences with VITAL Code Generator Controlled by a Nonmonotonic Inference Engine, *Proc. of WORKSHOP on Libraries Component*

Modelling and Quality Assurance with CHDL'97, Toledo, Spain, April 20-25, 1997, pp.309-320.

Pułka A. (2000). *Modeling Assistant - a Flexible VCM Generator in VHDL*, In R. Seepold, N. Martinez (Ed.): Virtual Components Design and Reuse, Kluwer Acad. Pub., 2000.

Pułka A. (2009). Decision Supporting System Based on Fuzzy Default Reasoning, *Proceedings of the HSI'08 Human Systems Interaction Conference*, Catania, Italy, May 21-23, 2009, pp. 32–39.

Pułka A. and Kłosowski P (2009). Polish Speech Processing Expert System Incorporated into the EDA Tool, in: *Human-Computer Systems Interaction Backgrounds and Applications*, Series: *Advances in Intelligent and Soft Computing* , Vol. 60, Hippe, Z. S.; Kulikowski, J. L. (Eds.), *Springer Verlag* 2009, ISBN: 978-3-642-03201-1, pp. 281–293.

Reiter R. (1980). A logic for default reasoning, *Artificial Intelligence* 13, 1980, pp.81–132.

Reiter R. (2001). Knowledge in Action: Logical Foundations for Specifying and Implementing Dynamical Systems, Cambridge, Massachusetts: *The MIT Press*, 2001.

Van Nieuwenborgh D. and Vermeir D. (2006). Preferred Answer Sets for Ordered Logic Programs, *Theory and Practice of Logic Programming, Volume 6 Issue* 1-2, January 2006, pp. 107–167.

Wang Y. (2007). *A Systematical Natural Language Model by Abstract Algebra*, 2007 IEEE International Conference on Control and Automation, Guangzhou, China, 2007, pp. 1273–1277.

Zadeh L. A. (2004). *Precisiated natural language* (*PNL*), AI Magazine, Vol. 25(3), 74-91, 2004.

Zadeh L. A. (2006). Generalized theory of uncertainty (GTU)--principal concepts and ideas, *Computational Statistics & Data Analysis* 51, 15-46, 2006.

Zadeh, L. A. (2008). Is there a need for fuzzy logic? *Information Sciences: an International Journal*, 178, 13 (Jul. 2008), 2751-2779.

3

ET: an Enrolment Tool to Generate Expert Systems for University Courses

Neil Dunstan
University of New England
Australia

1. Introduction

Expert Systems are in use today in many fields where there exists a well-defined problem domain (Giarratano & Riley, 2005). In this chapter, XML is used to help define a knowledge domain for academic course rules and used as the starting point for web-base expert systems.

Requirements for the satisfactory completion of university and college courses can be quite complex. Courses such as undergraduate bachelor degrees and postgraduate masters degrees are typically composed of units (sometimes called subjects) that must be completed according to the course rules. Such rules may impose constraints on the units that may be taken from specific groups of units, as well as constraints like prerequisite units and corequisite units. Many universities designate a human expert – the Course Coordinator, to guide students through their enrolment process to ensure that students' programs conform to course rules. In addition, many universities provide web-based descriptions of courses and units. However, such web sites are usually purely descriptive and lack a level of interaction with students that would enable answers to complex enrolment questions. It is therefore tempting to consider the automation of the course coordinator's role and its delivery. This chapter will provide a detailed description of the generation of a variety of expert system products intended to provide online advice to students about university bachelor and masters level courses. These products include course rules, unit descriptions, enrolment advice and course planners. They are designed following knowledge acquisition from experienced academic course coordinators about typical student queries in relation to their enrolment choices.

An XML Document Type Definition (DTD) will be described for university and college courses. It will be compatible with the European Credit Transfer System (EU, 2004), thus allowing a course to be composed of units with set credit points, term or semester of offering, and other unit constraints. Course rules may be expressed in terms of credit point requirements from groups of units. The XML data definition is sufficient to express the typical course requirement rules of higher education institutions such as universities and colleges.

The automatic generation of course-specific expert system products is accomplished via ET, an XML parser that translates XML course documents into Prolog predicates. This is the knowledge base. A Prolog interpreter then acts as the inference engine to solve course enrolment queries based on the course knowledge base.

The expert system products are intended for use by the students. A user-friendly web-based interface is described. The XML parser can also generate course-specific HTML and CGI files that interact with the Prolog interpreter to report the results of enrolment queries through a web browser in a use-friendly fashion.
There is an interesting synergy of XML and Web technologies, following the adoption of XHTML (W3C, 2000) and growing browser support for XML (Ciancarnini et al., 1998; Ghislain et al., 2009). Consideration is given to the place of the course XML DTD in the higher education knowledge domain.

2. Discussion.

A prototype ET was used to describe the method in (Dunstan, 2008) for generating domain-specific web-based expert systems. That method used Open Source products Linux (Moody, 2001), Perl (Wall & Schwartz, 1992) and SWI-Prolog (Wielemaker, 2003) and a domain-specific XML parser to generate a web-based expert system. The prototype produced a single web page with limited functionality and used low-level parsing techniques.
A recommender system that matches student interests with elective units was proposed in (O'Mahony & Smyth, 2007) and decision support for enrolment at the institutional level is described in (Maltz et al., 2007). Current generation university and college web sites provide only minimal online support for the complex task of guiding student enrolment. Web services typically only provide tables of rules and unit descriptions. ET produces expert systems with a web-based user interface.
An overview of requirements for expert systems on the internet is described in (Grzenda & Noemczak, 2004) and (Caldwell et al., 2003) compares two possible architectures. There have been many approaches to building web-based expert systems (Li et al., 2002; Li, 2005; Huntington, 2000; Riva et al., 1998). They propose solutions in isolation. The approach of the ET project features an XML DTD and takes advantage of the growing synergy of XML and Web technologies. Many browsers include XML parsers and are able to display raw XML files in a tree fashion at least, or use style guides to present XML data. Web-based applications can request XML data files from remote servers for processing and presentation. The XML DTD provides a vocabulary, namespace and data file structure for Web and XML applications that use academic course rule data.

3. Rules, groups and units in XML

University and college courses such as Bachelors and Masters degrees are composed of units (or subjects taught over teaching periods called semesters or terms) that are selected from groups according to course rules. Grouping of units might be by year level, subject theme, or even just to distinguish between compulsory and non-compulsory. There may be further constraints on unit selection such as prerequisites requirements. Units may carry different credit point values towards a total required for course completion. A course document type definition is needed to standardize course information for applications, including data transfer across the internet. Here is the XML DTD for academic course rules.

```
<?xml version="1.0"?>
<!ELEMENT course (aname, acode, adescr, rules, group+, unit+, prog*)>
<!ELEMENT rules (maximum*, minimum*)>
```

```
<!ELEMENT group (gname, gunits)>
<!ELEMENT unit (uname, udescr, usem, uprer, ucore,urest, ucps)>
<!ELEMENT prog (pname, punits) >
<!ELEMENT maximum (#PCDATA)>
<!ELEMENT minimum (#PCDATA)>
<!ELEMENT aname  (#PCDATA)>
<!ELEMENT acode  (#PCDATA)>
<!ELEMENT adescr  (#PCDATA)>
<!ELEMENT gname  (#PCDATA)>
<!ELEMENT gunits  (#PCDATA)>
<!ELEMENT uname  (#PCDATA)>
<!ELEMENT udescr  (#PCDATA)>
<!ELEMENT usem  (#PCDATA)>
<!ELEMENT uprer  (#PCDATA)>
<!ELEMENT ucore  (#PCDATA)>
<!ELEMENT urest  (#PCDATA)>
<!ELEMENT ucps  (#PCDATA)>
<!ELEMENT pname  (#PCDATA)>
<!ELEMENT punits (#PCDATA)>
```

A *course* document is composed of these elements:

aname : a name,
acode : a code,
adescr : a short description,
rules : rules governing course requirements
group : one or more groupings of units
unit : one or more units
prog : zero or more recommended programs

In the *rules* section, there can be any number of *maximum* or *minimum* elements. The text for each one consists of *group_name : credit_points*. For example:

```
<maximum>
firstYear : 36
</maximum>
```

meaning that at most 36 credit points can be counted for units from the group *FirstYear*. For *minimum*, the meaning is that at least that number of credit points must come from that group.

A *group* has a name and a list of unit names that belong to the group. For use in *maximum* and *minimum*, the group name *all* indicates a maximum or minimum number of credit points required from all groups. A unit has

uname : a name or code,
udescr : a short description that should include keywords for searching,
usem : a list of semester names or numbers when the unit is offered,
uprer : a list of unit names that are required before enrolment in this unit,
ucore : a list of unit names that must accompany enrolment in this unit,
urest : a list of unit names that may not be in a program with this unit,
ucps : the number of credit points towards course completion.

For convenience when converting the XML to Prolog, the lists are in Prolog list form, that is:

[name1, name2, ... ,namen]

For example: here is the XML data for the unit *stat354*

```
<unit>
  <uname> stat354 </uname>
  <udescr> 'Distribution Theory and Inference' </udescr>
  <usem> [1] </usem>
  <uprer> [stat260, pmth212] </uprer>
  <ucore> [] </ucore>
  <urest> [] </urest>
  <ucps> 6 </ucps>
</unit>
```

A *prog* is a recommended program meant to represent a valid program for the course that focuses on a particular interest area or theme. It has a name and a list of unit names that belong to the program.

4. The parser

ET version 2 is an XML parser based on the Perl XML::Parser module. It processes the XML data for a course and:

- translates the XML data into Prolog rules and facts,
- generates web modules for use as enrolment guides,
- generates a SWI-Prolog script file to execute Prolog queries.

Fig 1. shows the operation of ET.

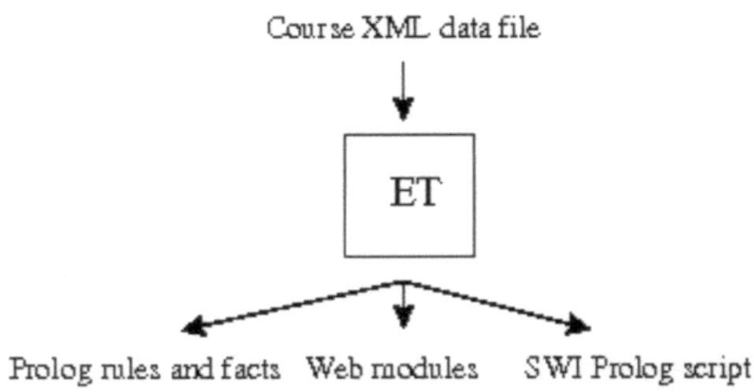

Fig. 1. ET operation.

The ET usage message is:

```
Usage: ET course.xlm -ieprl
            i rules and units
            e enrolment guide
            p course planner
            r recommended programs
            l output in indented xml layout
or Usage: ET course.xlm
            for the lot.
```

The options permit selective re-generation of web modules. The web modules consist of HTML and CGI files to generate user-interface pages and CGI programs to execute queries. Some HTML files are used to establish a home page for this course. These files are described in Table 1.

File name	Description
{coursecode}.html	Establish a frameset with title, navigation and display frames
links.html	Navigation panel with links to modules
title.html	Display the course title and description
blank.html	Initial blank page in display frame.

Table 1. Course HTML files

ET produces files for each web module required. These files are described in Table 2.

Web Module	File name	Description
Rules and units	*rulesunits.cgi*	General rule and unit information page
	allrules.cgi	Get course rules
	allunits.cgi	Get all unit information
	findkeyword.cgi	Find a keyword in a unit description
	unitinfo.cgi	Get unit information
	prerchain.cgi	Get the chain of prerequisite units
Enrolment guide	*enrolguide.cgi*	Enrolment guide page
	required.cgi	Get requirements to complete course
Planner	*planner.cgi*	Course planner page
	check_plan.cgi	Check a program against course rules
Recommended programs	*recomprog.cgi*	Recommended programs page
	findprog.cgi	Find a recommended program that includes chosen units
	showprog.cgi	Show a program

Table 2. Course Web modules.

Other files are listed in Table 3.

File name	Description
{acode}.pl	Prolog rules and facts for the course
auxiliary.pl	Auxiliary Prolog functions
{acode}_script	SWI-Prolog script file
{acode}.css	Cascading Style Sheet for the web site.

Table 3: Other Course files

The Cascading Style Sheet file describes the presentation of ET Web modules. This provides some web site customization.

5. The prolog

ET converts the XML course rules and units into Prolog predicates. A group of units from the XML data file such as:

```
<group>
  <gname> firstYear </gname>
  <gunits>
    [comp131, comp132, comp100, comp170,
     amth140, comp160, maths101, maths102]
  </gunits>
</group>
```

becomes:

```
get_group( M, firstYear ):-
  M = [comp131, comp132, comp100, comp170,
       amth140, comp160, maths101, maths102].
```

A rule such as:

```
<minimum> firstYear : 36 </minimum>
```

is included in a predicate to check a program against all the rules of the course, such as:

```
check_rules( N ):-
  get_group( G1, firstYear ),
  check_min( N, G1, firstYear, 36 ),
  ....
```

where *N* is a list of unit names and the intention is to check that the program represented by *N* contains units from group *firstYear* with a minimum of 36 credit points. If a rule is not satisfied the checking predicate outputs the reason. For example, the query

```
check_rules( [comp131, comp160] ).
```

has the response:

```
At least 24 more credit points required from Group firstYear:
comp131 comp132 comp100 comp170 amth140 comp160 math101 math102
```

along with the output from other rule predicates, such as:

```
At least 132 more credit points required altogether.
```

An XML unit representation such as that of *stat534*, shown in section 3, becomes in Prolog:

```
unit( stat354, 'Distribution Theory and Inference',
      [1], [stat260, pmth212], [], [], 6 ).
```

Auxiliary predicates include those that check prerequisites and other constraints, as well as providing answers to targeted queries. Here is an example:

```
prer_chain( [], A, A ).
prer_chain( [ H | T ], A, D ):-
  not( member( H, A ) ),
```

```
  unit( H, _, _, P, _, _, _ ),
  append( A, [H], B ),
  write( H ), write( ' :has prerequistes: ' ),
  show( P ),
  prer_chain( P, B, C ),
  prer_chain( T, C, D ).

prer_chain( [ H | T ], A, D ):-
  member( H, A ),
  unit( H, _, _, P, _, _, _ ),
  prer_chain( P, A, B ),
  prer_chain( T, B, D ).
```

This predicate will report on the prerequisites required by the units in the list of the first parameter, and the prerequisites required of those units. That is, it recursively finds all units required directly or indirectly by the units in the list.
Queries are put to the Prolog course file via an SWI-Prolog script:

```
#!/usr/bin/pl -q -t main -f
% bcompsci_script : for bcompsci enrolment guide
% Generated by ET version 2
% This script file uses auxiliary.pl
% This script file loads bcompsci into pl and executes
% a query given by the first command line arg
% Example: bcompsci_script 'check_rules( [ ] )'
main :-
    [award-aux],
    [bcompsci],
    current_prolog_flag(argv, Argv),
    append(_, [--|Args], Argv),
    concat_atom(Args, ' ', SingleArg),
    term_to_atom(Term, SingleArg),
    config_term_to_object(_,Term,Object),
    Object,
    halt.
main :-
    halt(1).
```

The script supresses all output except the application output from *write* statements in the predicates. An example of running a query using the script is:

```
$ award_script 'prer_chain( [stat354], [], [] )'
stat354 :has prerequisites: stat260 pmth212
stat260 :has prerequisites: math102
math101 :has prerequisites:
math102 :has prerequisites: math101
pmth212 :has prerequisites: math102
```

That is, *stat534* has prerequisites *stat260* and *pmth212*. In turn, *stat260* has prerequisite *math102*. And *pmth212* also had as prerequisite *math102*, which in turn has prerequisite *math101*, which has no prerequisites. Note that the output lists the prerequisites of each required unit only once. This invites the comparison between presenting a flat table of unit details and the capabilities of an expert system. The expert system is able to infer indirect requirements.

6. Web interface

The Web modules are a graphical user interface to the expert system. Instead of having to enter queries in Prolog syntax, users enter information into forms whose actions initiate appropriate queries and display results. That is, the web modules read form data, convert it into Prolog queries that are put to the expert system using the SWI-Prolog script. Responses are displayed to the user. This process is illustrated in Fig 2.

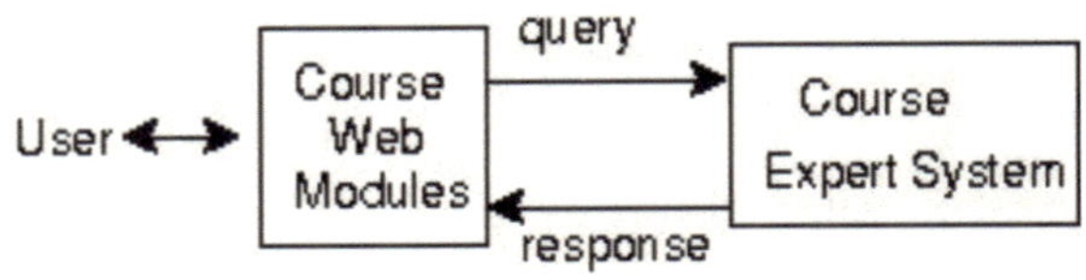

Fig. 2.Web interface

The Rules and Units module displays a web page like Fig 3.

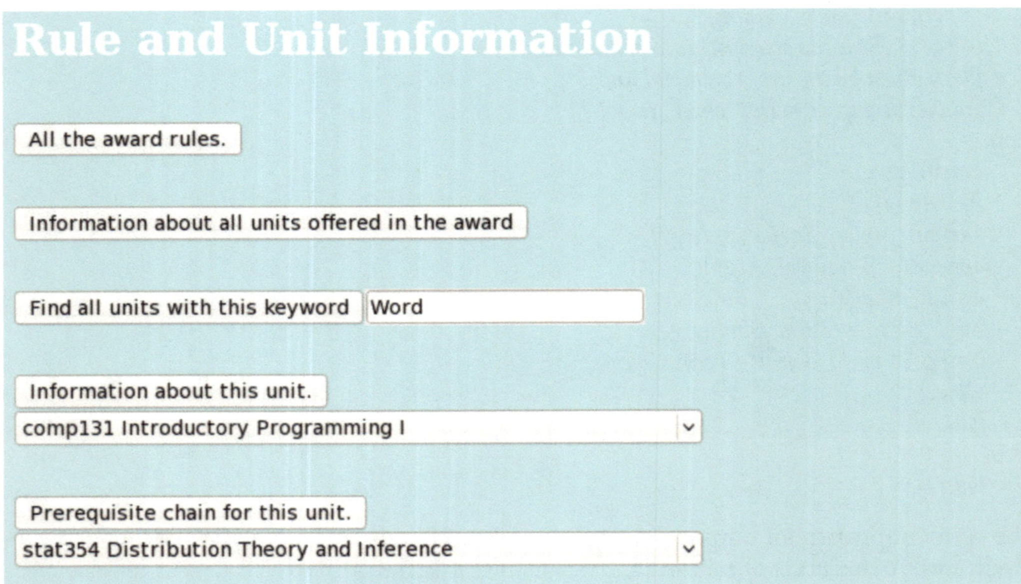

Fig. 3. Rule and Unit Information Web interface

The user selects or enters required information and clicks on the buttons. Should the user select unit *stat354* and click *Prerequisite chain for this unit*, the form action executes *prerchain.cgi*, which executes the query:

prer_chain([stat354], [], []).

via the script, and displays the application output response on screen.
The Enrolment guide web interface is shown in Fig 4. It enables three questions that are based on the list of units already completed and the course rules. The Course Planner

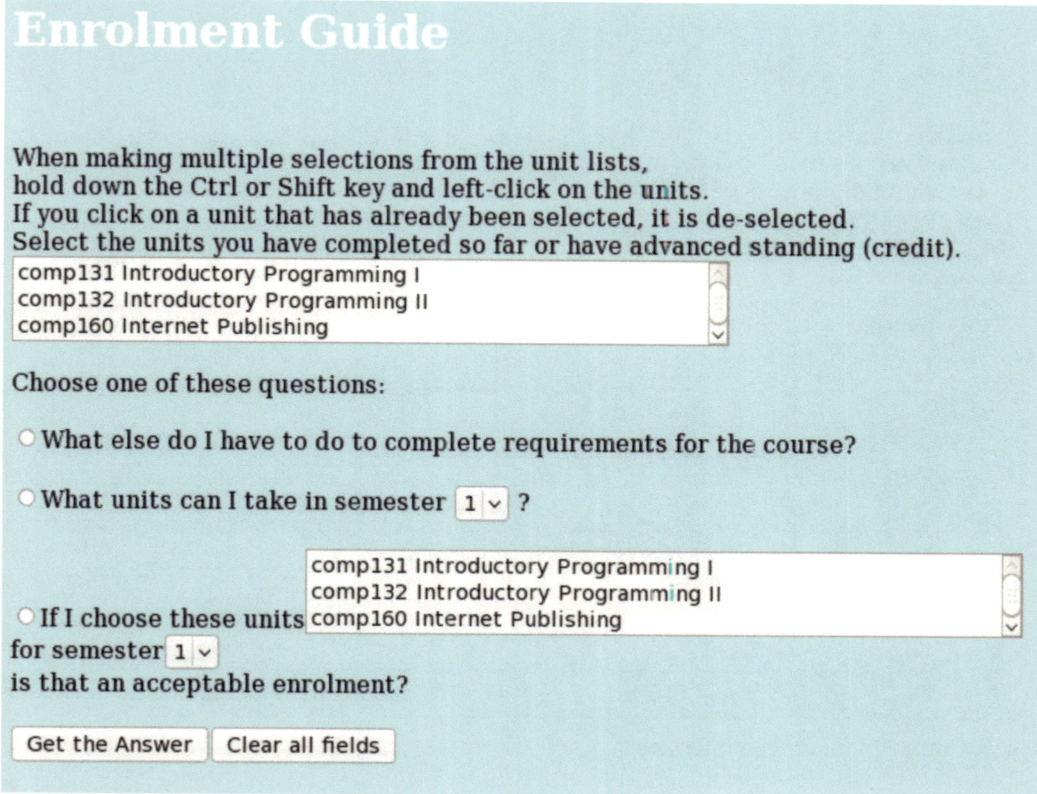

Fig. 4. Enrolment guide module web interface

module web interface is shown in Fig 5. It permits free-hand construction of a valid program of study scheduled over a period of years. The Recommended Programs web interface is shown in Fig 6. It permits the searching of valid recommended programs to find those with units of interest to students.

The web sites generated by ET have few HTML elements and conform to the XHTML 1.0 transitional DTD. In order to provide a customizable and consistent presentation a site style sheet is provided:

```
/* style sheet for ET html documents */
body         {background-color: lightblue; color: black}
input        {background-color: white}
input:focus  {background-color: yellow}
label        {color: red}
h1           {color: white}
```

It is also desirable to provide a style sheet for the raw XML data files.

7. Conclusion and future work

The potential of web-based expert systems as knowledge servers was recognised in (Erikson, 1996). An XML DTD was developed to represent academic course rules and formalize this knowledge domain. The DTD can be used to validate course rule documents

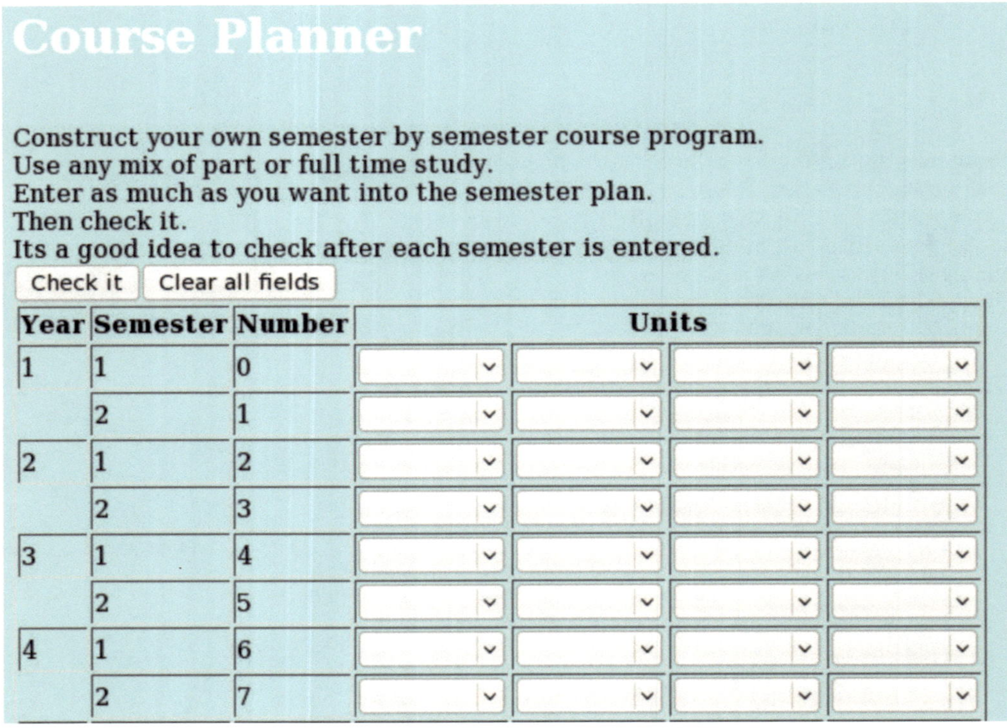

Fig. 5. Course planner web interface

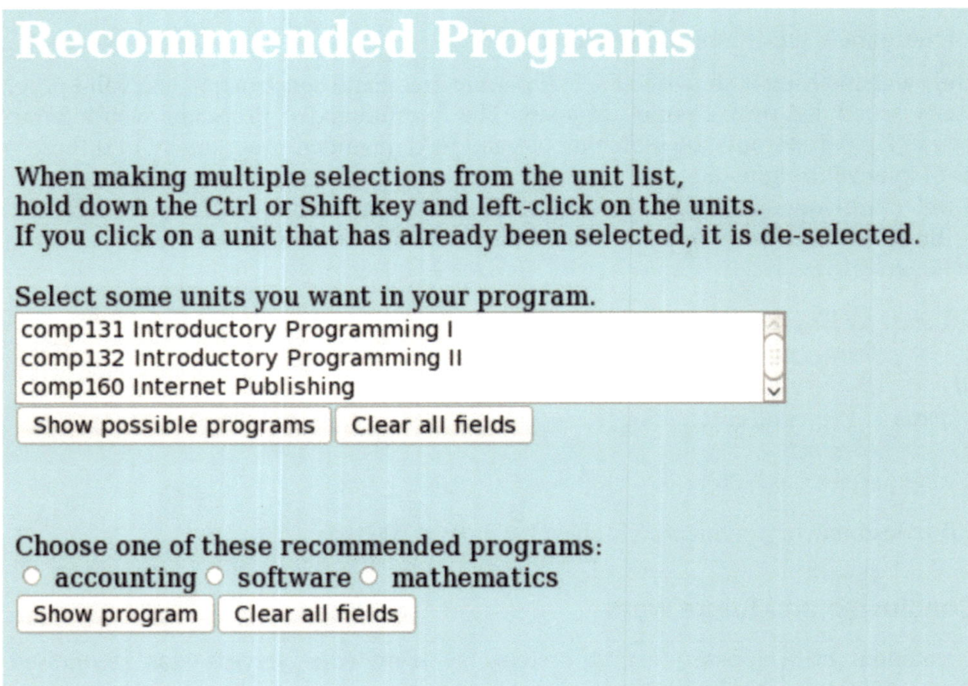

Fig. 6. Recommended programs web interface

and provide a standard format for representing course rules. The DTD thus supports application programs that process academic course rules. Applications may be web-based since there is script language support for fetching XML data files from remote servers, such as the *JavaScript XMLHttpRequest.* The DTD provides a *namespace* and vocabulary for such web-based applications. The adoption of the DTD by a network of university and college servers hosting XML course data files would enable comparative studies of courses and programs. Simply publishing XML course data files on the Web with a suitable style sheet to assist browser presentation would be an effective way to distribute course information.

An XML parser was described that converts a course rule data file to a Prolog knowledge base. It also generates web modules that serve as a graphical user interface to expert system. The web modules permit users to pose complex queries about their proposed enrolment choices. The range of types of queries is limited but future research will investigate:

- the addition of new types of enrolment queries
- new web-based interface methods for posing queries.

The open source products used to implement ET proved to be convenient and powerful. Perl continues to be an effective language for writing CGI scripts and SWI-Prolog is a mature implementation of the popular Prolog language for building expert systems.

Web-based applications of course data files are now planned with a view to supporting comparative studies of courses both within universities and across the higher education sector.

8. References

Caldwell, N. H. M., Breton, B. C. and Holburn, D. M. (2003). Information clients versus knowledge servers, In: *Studies in Fuzziness and Soft Computing: Intelligent exploration of the Web,* 402-417, Physica-Verlag, ISBN: 3-7908-1529-2, Heidelberg.

Ciancarnini, P., Rizzi, A. And Vitali, F. (1998). An extensible rendering engine for XML and HTML, *Computer Networks and ISDN Systems,* Vol. 30, Issues 1-7, (April, 1998), 225-237, ISSN: 0169-7552.

Dunstan, N. (2008). Generating Domain-specific Web-based Expert Systems, *Expert Systems with Applications,* Vol. 35, No. 3, (October, 2008), 686-690, ISSN: 0957-4174.

Eriksson, H. (1996). Expert systems as knowledge servers, *IEEE Expert: Intelligent Systems and their Applications,* Vol. 11, No. 3, (June, 1996), 14-19, ISSN: 0885-9000.

European Union (EU) (2004), ECTS User's Guide - European Credit Transfer System for Lifelong Learning, European Commision, 2004.

Ghislain, F., Pilman, M., Floresu, D., Kossmann, D., Kraska, T. And MacBeath, D. (2009), Xquery in the browser, *Proceedings of the 18th International Conference on WWW,* pp. 1011-1020, Madrid, April, 2009.

Huntington, D. (2000), Web-based expert systems are on the way: Java-based Web delivery, *PC AI Intelligent Solutions for Desktop Computers,* Vol. 14, No. 6, (June, 2008), 34-36.

Grzenda, M. And Niemczak, M. (2004). Requirements and solutions for web-based expert systems, In: *Lecture Notes in Artificial Intelligence 3070,* Rutkowski, L. et al. (Ed.), 866-871, Springer-Verlag, Berlin.

Maltz, E., Murphy, K. E. And Hand, M. L. (2007)). Decision support for university enrolment management: implementation and experience, *Decision Support Systems,* Vol. 44, No. 1, (November, 2007), 106-123.

Moody, G. (2001). *Rebel code: Linux and the open source revolution,* Perseus Publishing, ISBN: 0738206709.

O'Mahony, M. P. And Smyth, B. (2007). *A recommender system for online course enrolment: an initial study, Proceedings of the 2007 ACM Conference on Recommender Systems,* pp. 133-136, ISBN: 978-1-39593-730-8, ACM, Minneapolis.

Riva, A., Bellazzi, R., and Montani, S. (1998). A knowledge-based Web server as a development environment for Web-based knowledge servers. In *EIEE colloquium on web-based knowledge servers (Digest No 1998/307).*

W3C (2000). XHTML 1.0 The Extensible Hypertext Markup Language (second edition) : A Reformulation of HTML 4 in XML 1.0. Retrieved from www.w3.org/TR/xhtml1/ in Ocober, 2009.

Wall L., Christainsen, T. and Schwartz, R. L. (1996). Programming in Perl, O'Reilly and Associates, ISBN: 1-56592-149-6, USA, Second Edition, 1996.

Wielemaker, J. (2003). *An overview of the SWI-Prolog programming environment (Vol. CW371, pp. 1-16).* WLPE Report. Katholeike Univiersiteit Leuven, Department of Computer Science, Celestijnenlaan 200A, B3001 Heverlee (Belgium).

4

Expert System used on Heating Processes

Vizureanu Petrică
The "Gheorghe Asachi" Technical University from Iasi
Romania

1. Introduction

The expert systems are numerical structures of regulating and automat control using an operation system, a programming environment and a series of execution organs that fulfill promptly the commands of the expert systems.

The thermal system represents the totality of the equipment and parameters of the thermal process concerning at the achieving of a heating region according to the technological conditions and these of the material to be processed.

The link between the expert system and the thermal system can be done through a logic and physic interface materialised in an algorythm and a hardware component. The relation between the two systems is that the expert system *determines* the thermal system, because the first is based on knowledge, professional experience (of human factor who build it!), as well as a logic reasoning, while the second is the necessary and sufficient infrastructure enabling the relation between the two systems (equipment, command elements, measurement apparatus etc.).

2. Industrial systems assisted by expert systems

An expert system undertakes a human problem of which solutions can be logically determined by a natural deductive system (natural system based on a series of solid knowledge) and codes it with the help of a computer. It results in this manner a software component that interprets the logical solution and transforms it into a codes solution. If all this process takes place in its expected order, then one can foresee the expected results.

The relevance of these systems results from the fact that the economy of energy is a priority for the human society, especially form Romania. The proposal estimates economies of resources up to 25 % on the assembly of the processing industry of metallic and non-metallic materials.

There is a *present tendency* in the development of industrial processes of thermal processing of materials, consisting in the computer assisting of processes and heating equipment, expressed here by the shape of thermal systems.

An another *national preoccupation* refers to the integration of the thermal processes among other fabrication processes by computer assisting.

The proposed expert system is a software instrument for the automate command of a heating system, with modern means, by processing the specific knowledge and expertise in the field. The automate planning of the technological process supposes the integration of the

entire production process, integration between the constructive designing, computer aided-CAD, and the computer aided fabrication designing CAM, through a designing system of the technological process - CAPP. The system is an interactive medium, modern and efficient in view of technologies designing.
The system of planning of the technological process enable the rapid processing of knowledge, achieving a simple and efficient dialog with the user, the control and management of a great quantity of dots and necessary knowledge, the adequate representation of information of geometric and technical type.
The main goal is the implementation, in Romania, of this modern solution on international level for command, control and programming of the thermal equipment used in materials processing, in view to enabling economical revamping of the Romanian economic agents, by increasing the products quality and enabling a true competitivity during UE integration, to ensure the stability on internal market and real succes in European competition.
The ***expert systems*** (figure 1) are numerical structures of regulating and automat control using an operation system, a programming environment and a series of execution organs that fulfill promptly the commands of the expert systems.

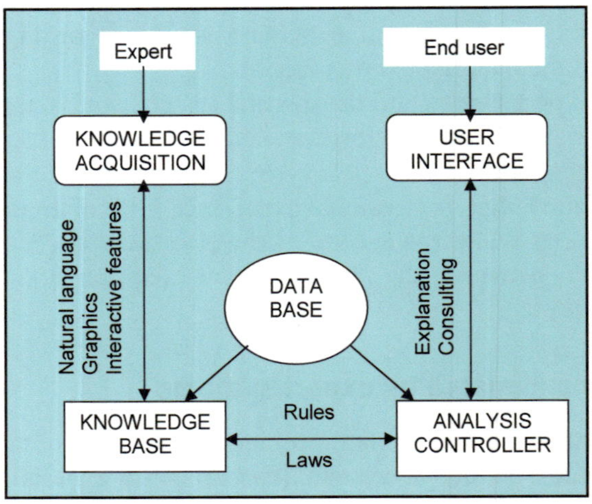

Fig. 1. The expert system.

Knowledge accumulation - specific for the field (in the shape of rules and laws), gathered by an expert and associated with the problem.
Database - relevant information, hystory, statistics, components, coefficients etc.
Analysis, command - analysis the rules, laws together with the actions of the user for the determination of the new conditions of identification of the possible solutions. The system will react in the field of the problem being based on the data base and using the input data from the **final user.**
The user interface - ensures the link between the expert system and user and designed in such a manner than to offer explanations of the system actions.
The ***heating system*** (figure 2) represents the totality of the equipment and parameters of the thermal process concerning at the achieving of a heating region according to the technological conditions and these of the material to be processed.
The **power source SP** can be constituted in a steady state convertor type M3, ensuring a three phase supplying of the thermal system with a continuum voltage.

Heating elements R ensures the temperature of the thermal process according to the technological needs.
Measurement amplifiers A1, A2 used to increase the signals power from the temperature transducers.

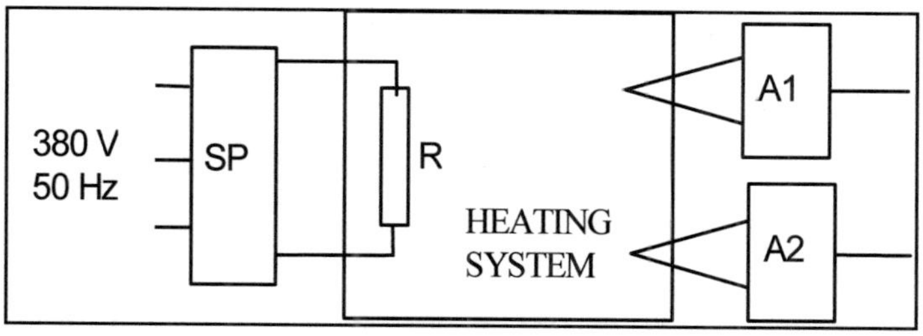

Fig. 2. The heating system.

The link between the expert system and the thermal system can be done through a logic and physic interface materialised in an algorythm and a hardware component. The relation between the two systems is that the **expert system** *determines* the **thermal system**, because the first is based on knowledge, professional experience (of human factor who build it!), as well as a logic reasoning, while the second is the necessary and sufficient infrastructure enabling the relation between the two systems (equipment, command elements, measurement apparatus etc.).
The variant A (figure 3) represents an expert system OFF-LINE type, the computer is not connected directly to the process and the exchange of data between the computer and the process is established by means of an operator. The computer receives information about the process by means of the operator that introduces the dates and following the processing the operator gets the results of the calculus and applies them in a manual manner in the process. In this case the computer is "off-line" (outside the line). The input dates referring to the process can be taken completely manual or in an automatic way. Such an expert system can be used in places when the delays do not matter and where the dates handling is not expressive.

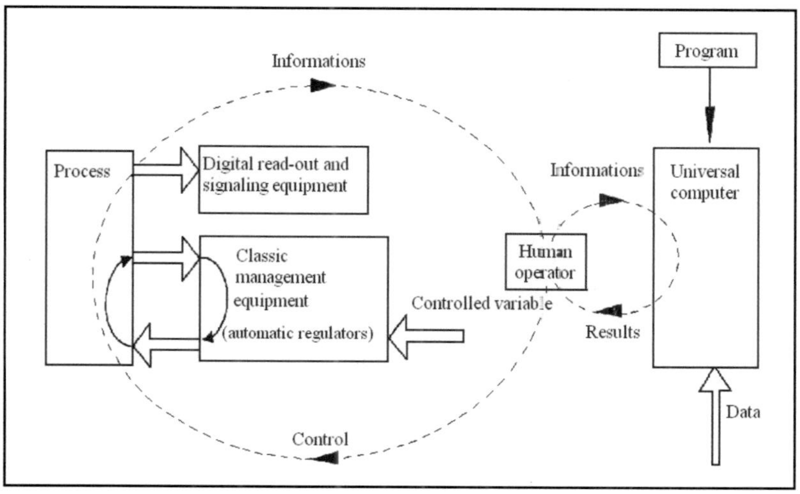

Fig. 3. The expert system OFF-LINE type.

The variant B (figure 4) represents an expert system of IN-LINE type: in the case of this kind of connecting the operator introduces dates concerning the process, directly in the computer, rapidly with the process, introduces in the computer can be processed immediately and the results are manually applied by the operator. In this type of expert system, as in the "off-line" one the information from the computer exists as shown as a typed message or on a display.

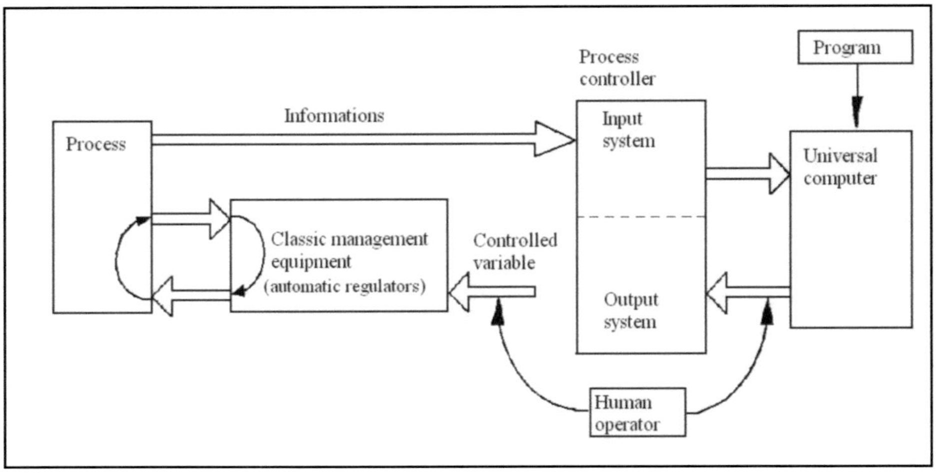

Fig. 4. The expert system IN-LINE type.

The variant C (figure 5) is an expert system of "ON-LINE" type: an expert system connected physically with the process so it gets information physically with the process so it gets information without human intervention and without delay.

The computer can get information directly from the process through its peripheries. In this case the computer works "on-line". The "on-line" system sends information from the process to the computer memory without immediately processing information, in a compulsory manner. When the processing of "on-line" sent information takes place immediately, during the process, the system is named "on line" in real time.

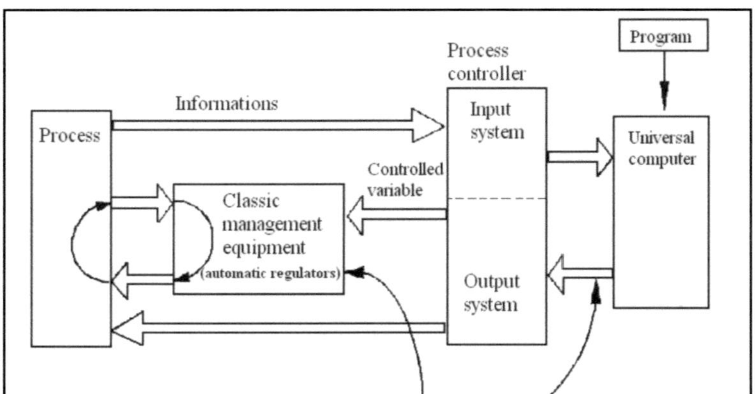

Fig. 5. The expert system ON-LINE type.

The output dates given by the computer after processing the inputs can be applied manually or directly to the process regulating devices In the case of output dates transmission as messages and the decisions of commanding the regulation devices of the process, the system is named "on line" in open circuit, the computer operates in a regime "guide-operator", in the quality of process conduction consultant.
The variant taken into consideration is D (figure 6) because it shows the most advantages way of conducting because it can be implements on an existing conventional automation structure and in the case at failure of the computer the conduction of the process can be done with conventional equipments.

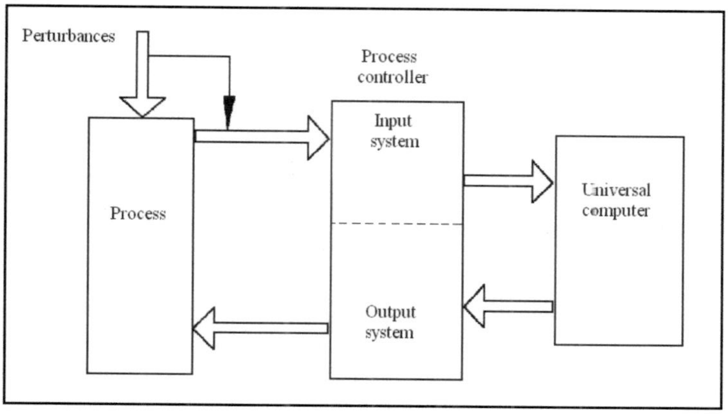

Fig. 6. The expert system ON-LINE type in closed circuit.

In the case there is no need of human intervention, the conduction actions are estimated by the computer and applied directly in the process, the system is called "ON LINE" in closed circuit.

3. Expert system designed for heating processes

The novel degree and the originality of such equipment consists in the regulation method that will be used as a combination between the variation of the quantity of energy in the heating elements and the variation of the connecting time of them as well as the replacing of the command of the thermal system, type "all or nothing" with a command with continuous regulation, ensuring in this way the growing of reliability and life duration of the thermal system.
In the figure 7 is shown the block scheme of on expert system of command of a thermal system is given; it is supplied at the industrial power network 380V, 50Hz and it has as a measurement parameter the temperature.
The power source SP can be constituted in a steady state convertor type M3, ensuring a three phase supplying of the thermal system with a continuum voltage.
IBM - PC represents a personal computer, compatible IBM, that has the role of numeric regulator and achieves it by the software component.
The **parallel programmable interface IPP** has as a purpose the expanding of the number of outputs available on the parallel standard interface LPT of a computer compatible IBM-PC. Given the necessity of existence of two parallel parts of 8 bytes, for data exchange with the block D/A and A/D, as well as a part for commands, for configurating the system, one can use a specialized circuit in the INTEL family.

The **block of digital-analogic conversion D/A** has as a purpose the supplied at its output of an electric signal (voltage or current), proportional with the numeric expression received at the output. In this case, through the foreseen channel in the block scheme, the block D/A receive from the IBM-PC system a numeric value and supplies at the output a continuum voltage ranging between 0-10V, necessary for the command of the power source SP.

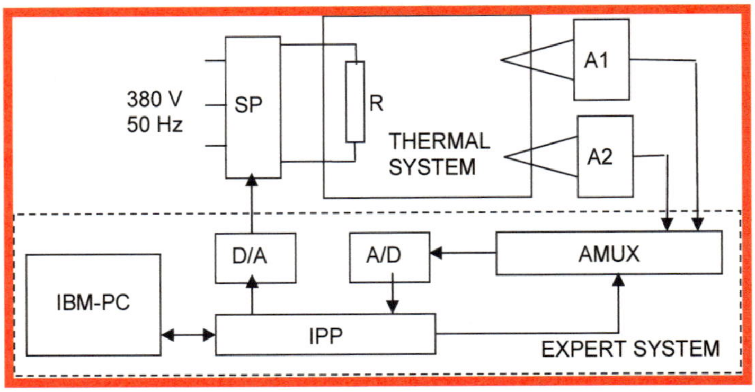

Fig. 7. The expert system for heating system programming.

The **block of analogic-digital conversion A/D** supplies at the output a number in binary representation, proportional with the analogical measure from the output. The convention A/D supposed the superposition of the imput signal at two operations: sampling and quanting. The first operating defines the temporal aspect of the conversion and the way of taking the sample and the second defines even the way of obtaining of the numeric equivalent of the analogue measure.

The **block of analogic multiplexing AMUX** has the role to enable the reception of ware electric signals on a single channel, it actually achieves a time partitioning of the input channel of the block A/D. The analogic multiplying operating needs commutation devices to direct the useful signal on a desire channel. In a simple variant the analogic swich can be assimilating with a rotative switch with a position or with an ensemble of n swiches one being closed during the other stay opened.

Measurement amplifiers A1, A2 – the majority of the expert system working with analogic dates work with high level tension signals (0..5V, 0..10V), but not always the transducers used (in the case of measuring some non-electrical measures) can supply such signals. It appears the necessity of amplifying the signals supplied towards the expert system up to values compatible to these it is able to read as input data. For solving this problem the measure amplifiers are being used. The practical implementing of the measurement amplifies has at the basis the operational amplifiers that is capable to ensure a big gain in a wide range of frequencies and as characterized by symmetric output, amplification and input impedance very big.

Performance parameters of the system:

- Ensuring a precision of achievement of the heating diagram in the range 3 and 5 °C;
- Achieving of an energy recovery, comparing eith the classic varriant of the thermal system about 25 %, economic efficiency estimated as an average of the solutions that will be applied in industry;
- The expert system achieved will enable the obtaining of low heating speeds of 8 - 10 °C/h.

Quality parameters of the system:

- The functioning of the proposed solution at the series production level;
- The industrial implementation with minimum costs of the new proposed technology;
- The success rate of the application (degree of repetability of the results);
- The clarity of definition and framing of the technologic parameters accoring to the estimated success rate in industrial conditions.

Estimated technical performance:

- The thermal system functional revamping;
- Simplifying the thermal system elements;
- The significant growing of thermal systems durability;
- The enhance of the fiability in exploitation of the industrial thermal systems with 8 - 10 %;
- The productivity growing by reduction of technological operation and a fabrication cycle with 10 %.

Prognosed economic efficiency:

- The development of the production capacity by upgrading the fabrication technology;
- The productivity growing goes to the significant growing of profitability for potential economical partners, when they will produce such expert systems;
- The oportunity of valorization of product, inside and outside market, because of big demanding that exists and because the advantages that the system have;
- Growing of skill level of people by expert systems implementation.

Impact on technological development at regional level:

- Promotion at the regional level of a higher performance and quality level of the technologies/products through the collaboration among partners of the same unfavorable region;
- The increase of the competence level through re-technology based on the modernizing and research, through the initiation of the partner among the economic agents and the research-development units.

The impact on the scientific and technical medium:

- The increase of the agents' economic capacity to assimilate in an efficient way the latest technologies and the results of the research activity;
- The development within the D-R units of the activity of promoting new materials and technologies, as well as of the advanced analysis and control techniques.

Social and medium impact:

- Social stability through the improvement of the economic medium;
- Creation of new working places and the perfecting of the working force which will assure the success of the technological transfer and the efficient implementation of the proposed solution;
- The increase of the biosecurity and bioethical levels through stimulation within the project of the responsible factors of ec. agents to enforce working discipline and the environment protection through the personnel conscience in the perspective of Romania's adherence in the EU.

Economical impact:

- The increase of economic efficiency at the level of the beneficiary through the reducing of the manufacturing expenses and maintenance of the heating systems;
- The possibility to obtain new contracts in order to assure financial stability and investments;

- The extension of the application field through the diversity of the heating systems, obtained through the technical solution;
- The increase of the affair figure through the promotion of quality and new products.

4. Expert system designed for heat treatment furnaces

Measurement and control digital systems had mainly enforced in the last decades cause to the technological revolution within electronic components domain. It is hereby obtained a bigger accuracy in digital information processing by facilitating the direct connecting with computer, a bigger speed work and an increased automation degree of the process.
The expert system is made on the basis of an original mathematical model theoretically and experimentally obtained. The mathematical model respects and combines static and dynamic behavior of an industrial furnace and the model of a temperature regulator with PID behavior.
Measurement and numeric control (digital) systems have mainly imposed in the last decades because the technological revolution within electronic components domain. It is thus obtained a bigger accuracy in numeric information processing by facilitating the direct connection with computer, a higher work speed and an increased automation degree of the process.
It was accomplished an original "on-line" management system in closed circuit with gradual command of heating electric power and self-adaptive control with PID behavior of temperature. The hard structure is made of a command unit with thyristor connected to an electronic device specialized on its interface with an electronic computer.
The calculus program is based on an original mathematical model theoretically and experimentally obtained. The mathematical model respects and combines static and dynamic behavior of an electric furnace and the model of a temperature regulator with PID behavior. That is why the model can be used for any other furnace than the one used during experiments. As any theoretical model, it has a lot of coefficients whose identification can be made only experimentally in order to respect the constructive functional particularities of the installation.
The expert system assures the self-adjusting parameters of the temperature regulator with PID through the indicial response method of the furnace. Taking into consideration the experimental knowledge necessity of the furnace constructive functional characteristics it was made the first experiment to determine its indicial response. The gradual command of heating power was realized by using thyristor commanded in phase angle. In this case the relation between power and command angle Ψ is (Ciochina & Negrescu., 1999):

$$P = \frac{U_s^2}{R}\left(1 - \frac{\psi}{\pi} + \frac{\sin 2\psi}{2\pi}\right) \quad (1)$$

The variation of command angle of π radians corresponds to a variation of U_{com} command tension from the exit of digital-analogical converter of 10 V thus, U_{com} = 0 V corresponds to the angle $\psi = \pi$ (rad), and U_{com} = 10 V corresponds to the angle $\psi = 0$ (rad). Hence there is a relation:

$$\psi = \pi - \frac{U_{com}}{10}\pi \quad (2)$$

or

$$\frac{\psi}{\pi} = 1 - \frac{U_{com}}{10} \tag{3}$$

$$2\psi = 2\pi - U_{com}\frac{\pi}{5} \tag{4}$$

It results the relation:

$$P = \frac{U_s^2}{R}\left(\frac{U_{com}}{10} + \frac{\sin\left(\frac{\pi U_{com}}{5}\right)}{2\pi}\right) \tag{5}$$

The relation between variator theme U_{com} and the number of bitts applied to digital - analogical converter on eight bitts is:
U_{com} = 10 V - corresponds to a number of 256 bitts
U_{com} = 0 V - corresponds to a number of zero bitts
It results that at an U_{com} tension N bitts will correspond after the formula:

$$N = \frac{U_{com}.256}{10}(biți) \quad sau \quad Ucom = \frac{10N}{256} \tag{6}$$

To angle ψ=0 will correspond the power $P = \frac{U_s^2}{R} = P_{maximă}$, and to angle ψ = π will correspond power P=0. Hence we can write that:

$$P = P_{MAX}\left(1 - \frac{\psi}{\pi} + \frac{\sin 2\psi}{2\pi}\right) \tag{7}$$

Replacing ψ we can write:

$$P = P_{MAX}\left(\frac{U_{com}}{10} + \frac{\sin\left(\frac{\pi U_{com}}{5}\right)}{2\pi}\right) \tag{8}$$

Expressed with the help of a bitts number:

$$P = P_{MAX}\left(\frac{N}{256} + \frac{\sin\left(\frac{2\pi N}{256}\right)}{2\pi}\right) \tag{9}$$

The program is based on a logical scheme forwards presented in figure 8.

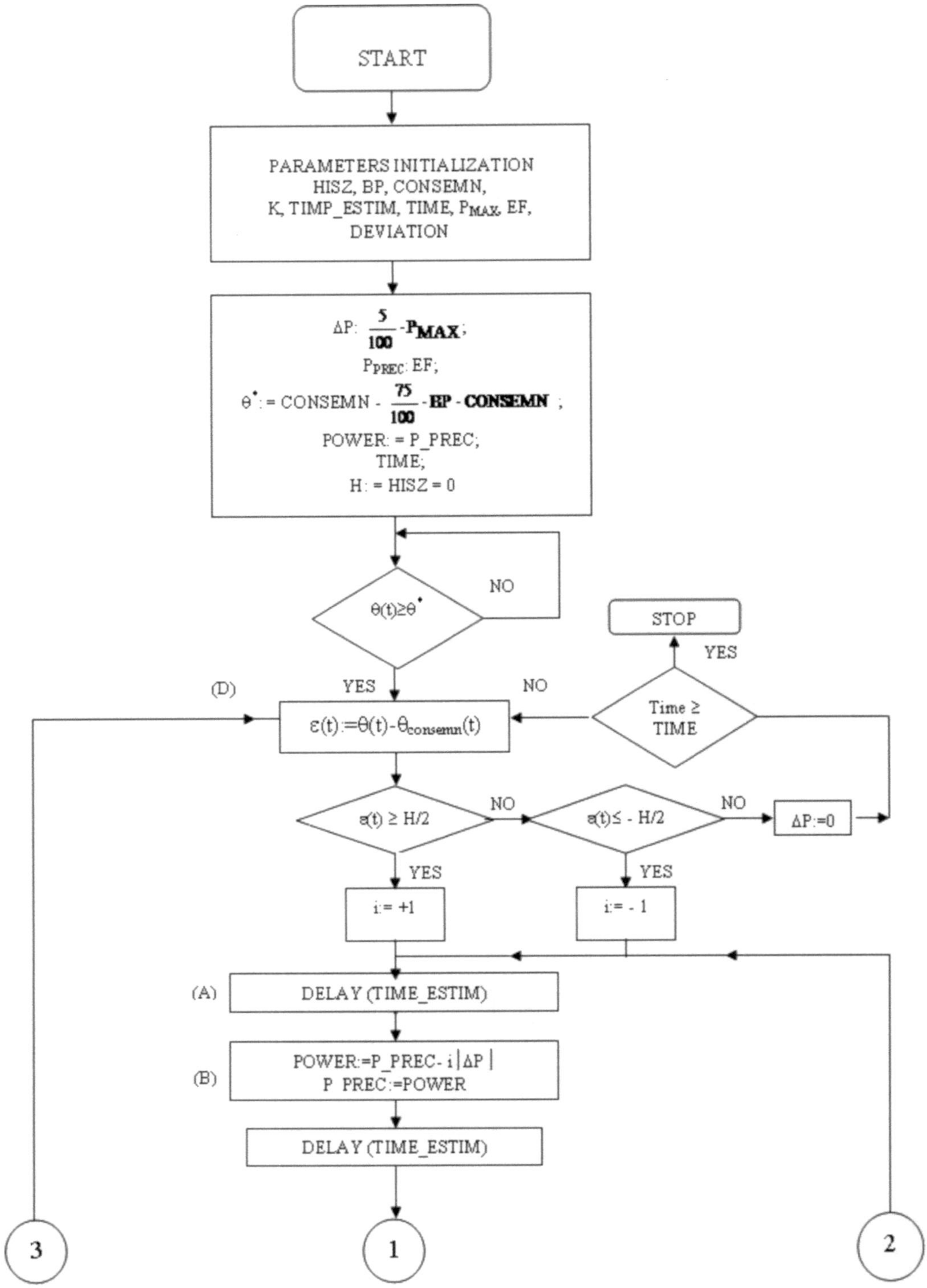
START
PARAMETERS INITIALIZATION
HISZ, BP, CONSEMN,
K, TIMP_ESTIM, TIME, P_MAX, EF,
DEVIATION
ΔP: 5/100 · P_MAX;
P_PREC: EF;
θ*: = CONSEMN - 75/100 · BP · CONSEMN ;
POWER: = P_PREC;
TIME;
H: = HISZ = 0
θ(t)≥θ*
NO
YES
STOP
YES
Time ≥ TIME
NO
(D)
ε(t):=θ(t)-θ_consemn(t)
ε(t) ≥ H/2
NO
ε(t)≤ - H/2
NO
ΔP:=0
YES
YES
i:= +1
i:= - 1
(A)
DELAY (TIME_ESTIM)
(B)
POWER:=P_PREC- i |ΔP |
P_PREC:=POWER
DELAY (TIME_ESTIM)
3
1
2

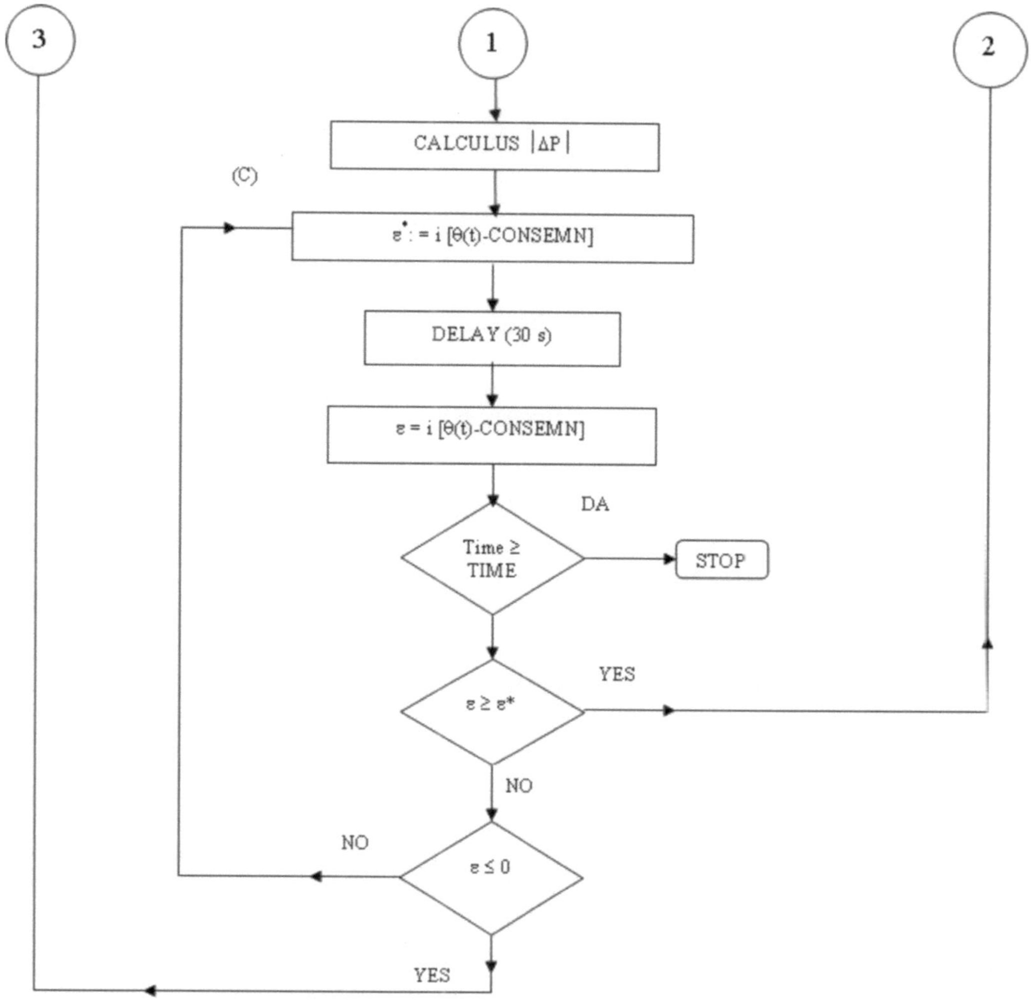

Fig. 8. Logical scheme of the expert system programming.

Mathematical model correspnd to to following steps:
I. Parameters initialization:
1°. Consign temperature (CONSEMN) (°C)
2°. Proportionality band (BP) (%): 5% ... 40%
3°. Hysteresis (HISZ) meaning max $|\theta_{measured}(t) - \theta_{programmed}(t)|$): 2°C ... 5°C
4°. Initial power applied to furnace (EF) (%): (60 ...80) x $P_{MAX}/100$
5°. Time (TIME), (min)
6°. Sampling quantum (K): 10 ... 15 seconds
7°. Estimate time (TIME_ESTIM) of T_u and V_{MAX} parameters: 3 ... 4 min
8°. Admitted maximum deviation (ABATERE) meaning:

$$\max|\theta_{măsurat}(t) - \theta_{estimat}(t)|: 1...3°C$$

II. The furnace is at ambient temperature thus we apply an initial power equal to that which was adjusted at aforementioned point 4° (EF).

III. When the furnace temperature θ(t) has the value:

$$\theta(t) \geq CONSEMN - \frac{75}{100}\, x\ BP\ x\ CONSEMN \tag{10}$$

We will verify the Hysteresis condition:

$$\left|CONSEMN - \theta(t)\right| \leq \frac{HISZ}{2} \tag{11}$$

If temperature respects this condition the power must not be modified (ΔP=0).
If the measured temperature does not respect this condition it should be applied a supplementary power step after the following algorithm:
1°. Sampling quantum (expressed in seconds) is K and sampling time (TIMP_ESTIM) (expressed in minutes) it will result a quanta number:

$$number = \frac{TIMP\_ESTIM\ x\ 60}{K} \tag{12}$$

In time range TIMP_ESTIM we will memorize the temperatures values measured at equal time intervals (K) in the rank:

$$TEMP\_TC_2[j]$$

where j index is varying from a maximum value of quanta number, aforementioned number (in logical scheme - see A block).
2°. It applies a supplementary power step to the furnace: 5/100 P_{MAX}.
Taking into consideration the approximate linear variations on small time intervals of 3-4 minutes order (TIMP_ESTIM) we could estimate the evolution of temperature in the furnace if it was not applied the above power step.
We note with (1) the variation of temperature in furnace measured in 0-T interval (T= TIMP_ESTIM) in figure 9. Without supplementary power step the temperature evolved in (T-2T) interval after curve (1), which we could approximate as AB line noted with (2) on a smaller time interval (T-3T/2). The line gradient (2) is calculated like this:
We trace a line 0A and measure it in moment T/2 as a difference:

$$\theta\left(\frac{T}{2}\right) - \frac{TEMP\_TC_2[0] + TEMP\_TC_2[T]}{2} = ECART \tag{13}$$

We prolong the line 0A until it meets C point where the ordinate value will be:

$$\text{DREAPTA}[2\text{T}] = 2x\,TEMP\_TC_2[2T] - TEMP\_TC_2[0] \tag{14}$$

We find B point by decreasing for five times the value of temperature range, value which is experimentally determined for temperature tangent variations not bigger than 1°C/min.
In order to estimate temperature I made the row:

$$BETA[q] = DREAPTA[numar] + \text{q x} \\ \left(\left(DREAPTA[2\ x\ numar] - 5\ x\ ECART\right) - DREAPTA[numar]\right) / \ numar \tag{15}$$

where q index is varying from 0 to a maximum value= number (in logical scheme see the B block).

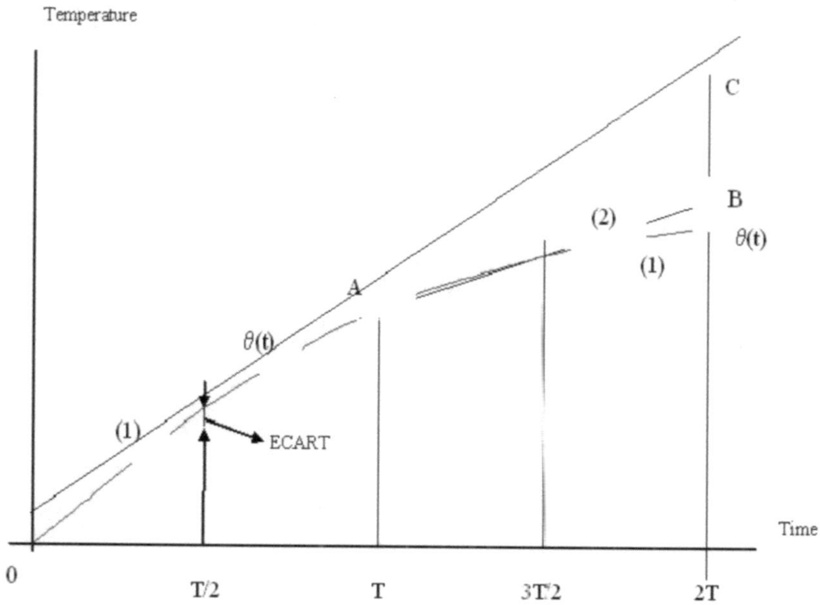

Fig. 9. Graphical representation of the estimation model of temperature evolution.

3°. In (T-2T) time interval we verify the condition:

$$TEMP\_TC_2[q] - BETA[q] \le ABATERE \tag{16}$$

For q=1 … number, meaning the maximum deviation between the measured value and the estimate one which should not excel the adjusted value.
The last index q that satisfies the above condition will give us T_u into a first estimation:

$$T_u = q \times K$$

4°. At the end of T period we can calculate $tg\alpha_{max}=V_{max}$, according to figure 10. which graphically represent the determination method of calculus parameters implied in the calculus of PID continuous regulator.

$$V_{max} = \frac{\theta(T) - \theta(i \cdot K)}{T - i \cdot K}, \tag{17}$$

where $i \cdot K = T_u$, the one from the first estimation (point 3°).
But V_{max} can be also expressed as:

$$V_{max} = \frac{\theta(i \cdot K)}{i \cdot K - t_m} \tag{18}$$

This will let us recalculate the time T_u:

$$T_u = t_m = i \cdot K - \frac{\theta(i \cdot K)}{V_{max}} \tag{19}$$

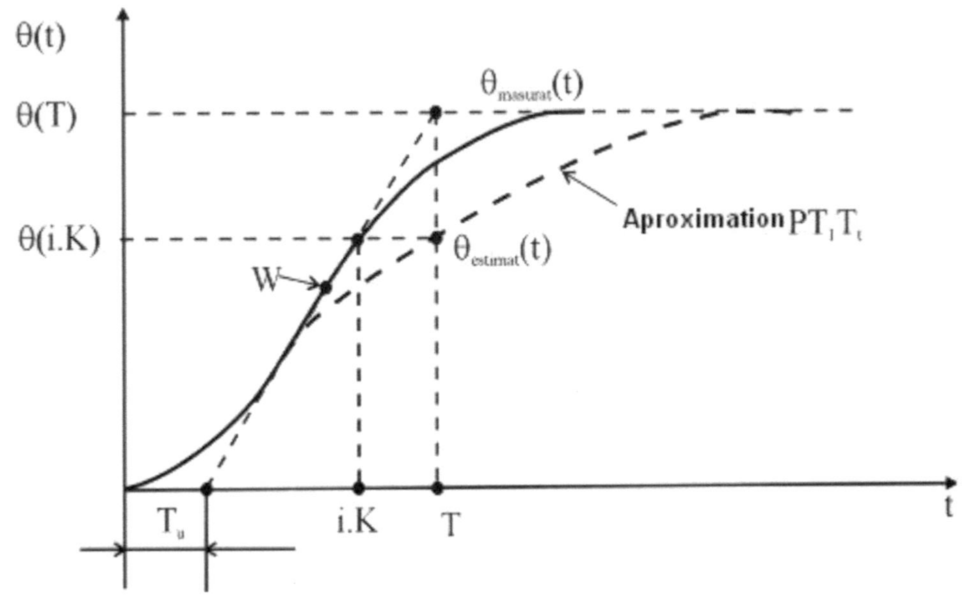

Fig. 10. Graphical calculus model used in determining the parameters of continuous PID regulator

IV. At the end of T period we could calculate:

$$\int_0^T \theta_{masurat}(t)dt \quad \text{şi} \quad \int_0^T \theta_{estimat}(t)dt.$$

$$\Delta W = K_R\left(\int_0^T \theta_{masurat}(t)dt - \int_0^T \theta_{estimat}(t)dt\right) \tag{20}$$

$$\frac{\Delta W}{T} = P(T) - P(0) \tag{21}$$

In relation (21) P (0) represents the old power step and P (T) the new power applied to the furnace. It results:

$$K_R = \frac{T\left[P(T) - P(0)\right]}{\int_0^T \theta_{masurat}(t)dt - \int_0^T \theta_{estimat}(t)dt} \tag{22}$$

Now we know the nest parameters at the end of T period: T_u, V_{max} and K_R, which are essential to recalculate the parameters K_P, T_I and T_D in the case of a continuous PID regulator.

V. In order to reach the desired temperature $\theta_{consemn}$ it will be necessary to apply a power step:

$$\Delta P = K_R \cdot \left[K_P\left(\theta_{consemn} - \theta(T)\right) + \frac{1}{T_i} \cdot \int_0^T \left(\theta_{consemn} - \theta(t)\right)dt + T_d \cdot \frac{d(\theta_{consemn} - \theta(t)}{dt}\right] \tag{23}$$

where K_P, T_I and T_D will be calculated accordingly to the next empirical rules deducted by applying Ziegler-Nichols method (the method of indicial response):

$$K_P = \frac{\theta_{consemn}}{1{,}7 \cdot V_{max} \cdot T_u \cdot 100}, \quad T_I = 2T_u, T_D = 2T_u$$

It results:

$$\Delta P = K_R \cdot \left[\frac{\theta_{consemn}}{1{,}7 \cdot V_{max} \cdot T_u \cdot 100} \left(\theta_{consemn} - \theta(T) \right) + \frac{1}{2T_u} \cdot \frac{\theta(0) - \theta(T)}{2} T + 2T_u \frac{\theta(0) - \theta(T)}{T} \right] \quad (24)$$

VI. After calculating the power step ΔP necessary for reaching the prescribed consign temperature (CONSEMN) we will measure a difference ε*=θ(t)-CONSEMN and after a period of 30 seconds we will measure again:

$$\varepsilon=\theta(t)\text{-CONSEMN} \quad (25)$$

If the time (time) overcomes the adjusted value TIME, the adjusting process ends (block STOP from logical scheme). If not, we will continue testing if it takes place a diminishing of the distance between measured and prescribed temperature in these 30 seconds (CONSEMN), $\varepsilon \geq \varepsilon^*$.

If the distance increases is obvious that we should recalculate the power step ΔP.

If the distance decreases ($\varepsilon < \varepsilon^*$), but $\varepsilon > 0$, we will recalculate ε* and ε (back to block (C) from logical scheme).

If, this time, $\varepsilon \leq 0$ it is moment to resume testing the Hysteresis interval (block (D) in logical scheme).

According to research methodology presented the constructive-functional improvement of heat treatments installations for copper alloys realized on determination base through experimental methods of theoretical mathematical models parameters. These demonstrate the complexity of the construction and functioning of these installations. This expert system assures the accuracy and uniformity of temperature within charge.

The experimental researches were made at Faculty of Materials Science and Engineering, The "Gh. Asachi" Technical University of Iasi, within the department of Plastic Processing and Heat Treatments, at S.C. "COMES" S.A. Savinesti, Neamt and at S.C. "PETROTUB" S.A Roman, Neamt, Romania.

The installation used for experiments was a CE 10-6.6.4 electric furnace made by „Independenta" Sibiu, Romania and having a command, adjust and control panel made once with the furnace by the same productive firm. This type of installation can be found in the use of many heat treatments departments of the firms from the entire country not only in machine constructions domain or metallurgical one.

5. Conclusion

In order to obtain the precision of temperature (imposed by the technological demands) it was replaced the panel within the furnace with an original leading system and the uniformity of temperature in charge was realized an auxiliary heating device closed muffle type where the pieces were placed. The necessity of using an auxiliary heating device came

from the conclusions of the experiments made with the initial heat treatment installation no-load and on load that showed the existence of some high temperature differences unallowable for copper alloys especially at the furnace arch and base of hearth.
Choice criteria for muffle form and material start from the phenomena of the complex heat transfer within the furnace, the furnace construction (useful space and heating elements disposal), the treated charge type (alloy, shape and dimensions for the pieces, pieces laying in the auxiliary heating device), the characteristics of used metallic materials (high alloyed refractory steels) such as mechanical strength at high temperatures, resistance to creep, refractoriness, thermal conductivity.
There of it was used the auxiliary heating device of T20CrNi370 austenitic alloy – SR-EN 6855-98.
From the dependency analysis between the view factors value between two parallel surfaces where there exist heat transfer through radiation and the distance size between that surfaces it results that the muffle walls must be as closer as possible to the heating elements (mounted in the walls).
From the conclusions of thermal fields in closed metallic muffle cubic and cuboids (presented in the fourth chapter of the paper) we chosen the cubic form with the dimensions 450x450x450 [mm] for the auxiliary heating device. The construction was welded in closed variant without cover sealing.
The expert system contains a hard structure and a specialized soft. Both were realized by taking into consideration the specific of the used installation (furnace power, thermocouples type, the indicial response of the furnace) and they form an „ON-LINE" self adaptive leading system in closed circuit with PID temperature adjusting.

6. References

Bhadeshia, H.K.D.H., (1999) *Neural network in materials science*, ISIJ International, vol. 39.

Ciochină, S., Negrescu, C., (1999) *Sisteme adaptive*, Colecția Comunicații, 352 p.

Dima, A., Vizureanu, P., (1997) About Software and Hardware Control on the Heat Processing Furnaces, *IVth International Conference Measurement and Control in Complex Systems*, Vinnytsia, p. 222-225.

Dumitrescu, D., (1999) *Principiile inteligenței artificiale*, Ed. Albastră, Cluj-Napoca.

Edenhofer, B., (1990) La flexibilité en traitement thermique grâce aux méthodes modernes de contrôle, *Revue de Traitement Thermique*, Nr. 241, p.20-27.

Garnearek, Z., (1992) Degree of heterogenity of thermal: a method of evaluation, *Heat and Mass Transfer* Nr. 11, p. 30-36.

Hallday, W., (1998) Model computerizat pentru controlul cuptoarelor de recoacere, *Steel Times International*, Anglia, vol. 12, nr. 6, decembrie 1998, p. 22-23.

Hatasescu, O., (1998) *Indreptar de metalurgie*, Editura Tehnică, Bucuresti, Romania.

He Jian-jun, Yu Shou-yi, (2005) Temperature Intelligent Control System of Large-Scale Standing Quench Furnace, *Journal of Electronic Science and Technology of China*, Vol.3 No.1, Mar. 2005.

Henrik A., (2005) *Simulation of Welding and Heat Treatment Modelling and Validation*, Doctoral Thesis:33 ISSN: 1402-1544, ISRN: LTU-DT - -05/33 -SE.

Higuchi, S., Allen, G., W. Bencze, R. Byer, A. Dang, D. B. DeBra, D. Lauben, S. Dorlybounxou, J., Hanson, L., Huffman, F., Sabur, K. Sun, R. Tavernetti, L. Rolih, R. VanPatten, Wallace, J. Williams, S. (2006) High-stability temperature control for ST-

7/LISA Pathfinder gravitational reference sensor ground verification testing, *Journal of Physics: Conference Series* 32 125–131.

Kang, J., Rong, Y., Wang, W. (2004) Numerical simulation of heat transfer in loaded heat treatment furnaces, *Journal of Physics*, Vol. 4, France, No. 120, pp. 545-553.

Lalam, Sree Harsha, (2000) *Modelling of Mechanical Properties of Ferritic Stell Weld Metals*, University of Cambridge, UK.

Lilantha S. (2003) *Distributed Control of Electric Drives via Ethernet*, TRITA-ETS-2003-09, ISSN 1650{674xISRN KTH/EME/R 0305-SE}, Stockholm 2003.

Lazăr, C., Păstrăvanu, O., Poli, E., Schonberger, F., (1996) *Conducerea asistată de calculator a proceselor tehnice*, Editura Matrix Rom, Bucureşti.

Mackay, David J.C., (1995) Bayesian No-Linear Modelling with Neural Networks, *University of Cambridge, Programme for Industry*, March 6, UK.

Malinov, S., Sha, W., (2003) Software products for modelling and simulation in materials science, *Computational Materials Science* 28, 179-198.

Nicolae, A., Predescu, C., (2001) *Bazele teoretice ale agregatelor termotehnologice din industria materialelor metalice*, Editura Printech, Bucureşti.

Nilsson, N., (2001) *Introduction to Machine Learning*, http://robotics.stanford.edu/people/nilsson/mlbook.html.

Partridge, D., Hussain, K.M., (1995) *Knowledge Based Information Systems*, Mc Graw-Hill Book Company Europe, London.

Singh S.B. et al., (1999) Neural Network Analysis of Steel Plate Processing, *Iron making and Steel making*, vol. 25, no. 5, p. 355-365.

Sourabh C., (2006) Transformation in TRIP-assisted Stells : Microstructure and Proprieties, *PhD Thesis, University of Cambridge*, UK.

Ştefan, M., Bădărău, Gh., Ioniţă, I., Vizureanu, P., Răileanu, T., Baciu, C., Manole, V., Mihai, D., (2007) *Conducerea automată şi informatizată în procesarea materialelor metalice*, Editura Tehnopress, Iaşi, 372 pg., ISBN 978-973-702-438-1

Ştefan, M., Vizureanu, P., Bejinariu, C., Manole, V., (2008) *Baze de date şi sisteme expert în selecţia şi proiectarea materialelor*, vol. I, Editura Tehnopress, Iaşi, 298 pg., ISBN 978-973-702-514-2

Vermesan, G., (1987) *Tratamente termice*, Editura Dacia, Cluj, Romania.

Veronesi M. (2003) Performance Improvement of Smith Predictor Through Automatic Computation of Dead Time, *Yokogawa Technical Report English Edition*, No. 35.

Vizureanu, P., (1998) Modern System for Heat Treatment Assisted by Computer, *Modelling and Optimisation in the Machines Buil Field*, Romanian Academy, p.137-141.

Vizureanu, P., (2005) Process Control Strategy on Industrial Furnaces, *37th International Conference on Mining and Metallurgy, Proceedings*, Bor, 3-6.10.2005, Serbia, p. 376-379.

Vizureanu, P., (2006) *Experimental Programming in Materials Science*, Mirea Publishing House, Moscow, 2006, 116 pg., ISBN 5-7339-0601-4

Vizureanu, P., Andreescu, A., Iftimie, N., Savin, A., Steigmann, R., Leiţoiu, S., Grimberg, R., (2007) Neuro-fuzzy expert systems for prediction of mechanical properties induced by thermal treatments, *Buletin I.P.Iaşi*, tom LIII (LVII), fasc. 2, secţia Ştiinţa şi Ingineria Materialelor, 2007, pg. 45-52.

Vizureanu, P., Ştefan, M., Baciu, C., Ioniţă, I., (2008) *Baze de date şi sisteme expert în selecţia şi proiectarea materialelor*, vol. II, Editura Tehnopress, Iaşi, 2008, 262 pg. (40 rânduri/pg.) ISBN 978-973-702-515-9

Vizureanu, P., (2009) *Echipamente şi instalaţii de încălzire,* Editura PIM, Iaşi, 2009, 316pg., ISBN 978-606-520-349-5.

Wang, D. M., (1993) An approximate solution for the dynamic response of wall transfer probes, *Heat and Mass Transfer* nr. 18, p.12-17.

Xu Xiaoli, Wu Guoxin and Shi Yongchao, (2005) Development of intelligent system of thermal analysis Instrument, *Journal of Physics: Conference Series* 13 59–62.

Yescas, M.A., (2001) Modelling the Properties of Austempered Ductile Cast Iron, *PhD Thesis, University of Cambridge,* UK.

Zang, X., (1993) *Les perturbations génerées par les gradateurs alimentant des Charges resistives et inductives constants et solutions,* EDF.

***, *Heat Treating of Copper Alloys,* Heat Treatment, v.4, ASM International, (1994), p.821-889.

***, *Standards: EN 10028,* EN 10137, EN 10113.

5

Expert System for Sintering Process Control

Xiaohui Fan, Xuling Chen and Yi Wang
Central South University
China

1. Introduction

Sintering is a method that makes powdered materials (such as fine ore or preparation concentrate) into block mass under conditions involving incomplete fusion by heating to high temperature. Its production is sinter which is irregular and porous (FU et al., 1996).
The following parts are usually included in sintering process: acceptance and storage of iron-containing raw materials, fuel and flux; crushing and screening of raw materials, fuel and flux; batching, mix-granulation, feeding, ignition and sintering of mix material; crushing, screening, cooling and size-stabilization of sinter. The flowchart is shown in Fig. 1.

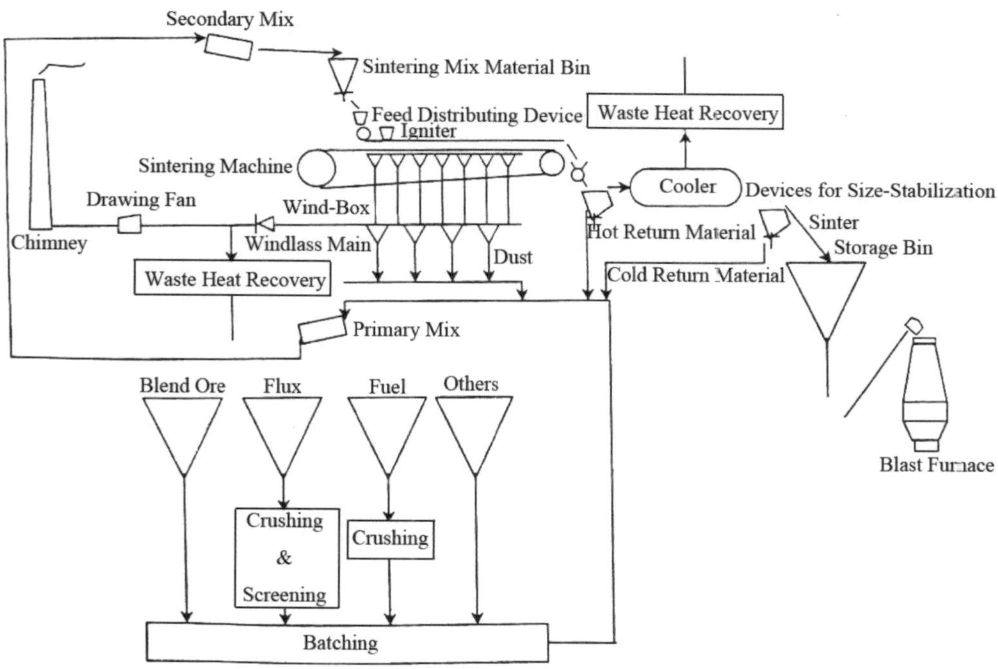

Fig. 1. Flowchart of sintering process

The purpose of computer control of sintering process is improving labor productivity, getting sinter with high yield and good quality, as well as saving energy. Application of computer control technology is a main reason for production improvement of sintering.

Effect of computer control technique on sintering process becomes increasingly remarkable along with the scaling-up of sintering equipment and requirement upgrade of sinter quality by blast furnace.

Computer control technology for sintering process developed along with sintering technology. Computers began to be used for detecting, alarming, recording, printing, etc. in sintering process in the early 1960s in America and European countries represent by France and Belgium. Later, computers were used for open and closed loop control step by step. The developing center of computer control for sintering process gradually shifted to Japan in the 1970s. Many mathematical models and control systems, as well as advanced testing equipments like material level instrument, device for continuous measurement of permeability, infrared moisture analyzer, etc. were developed successively by large-scale iron and steel enterprises represented by Nippon Steel Corporation, Kawasaki Steel, NKK and Kobe Steel. These companies focused on the overall management automation later, to achieve third-level computer control by combination of management information system automation and manufacturing process automation. Meanwhile, Distributed Control System (DCS) was built up. DCS was applied in Japanese factories such as Mizushima Factory and Chiba Factory of Kawasaki Steel, as well as Muroran Factory and Nagoya Factory of Nippon Steel Corporation (Ma, 2005).

Third-level computer control system includes Digital Control System, Process Computer System (PCS) and Central Computer System (CCS). Its function rating is shown in Fig. 2 (Unaki et al., 1986).

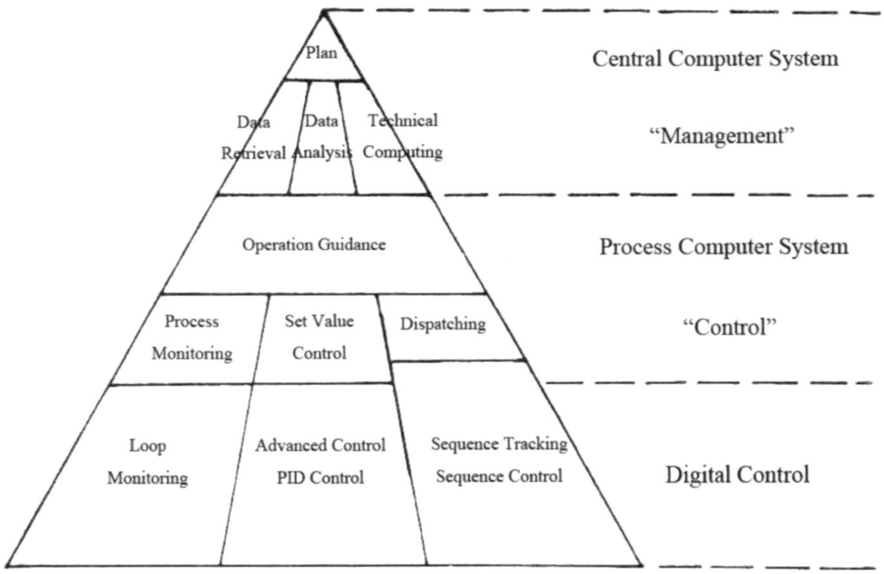

Fig. 2. Function diagram of third-level control system of sintering process

Digital control system is an integrated monitoring and control system. It includes direct digital control computers, sensors and transmission devices. It gives local loop control and advanced control of process with a standard of set value of process computer. Moreover, it takes real-time monitoring on sintering process based on sensor information as exhaust gas temperature, air displacement, etc.

The functions of sintering process computer system is collecting and processing data sent by digital control system, increasing the operation efficiency of equipments, realizing set value control and comprehensive operation guidance of sintering process based on the operation plan made by central computer.

Central computer locates on the top level of the system. It possesses databases of the whole ironmaking system. Central computer is in charge of collection and stockage of information sent by subordinate computers. It gives material purchasing and production planning, makes production report and technical analysis of production data.

This control system can overcome the obstacles of unicity and limitation of analog instrumentation, and avoid fatalness of highly concentrated computer control. It has flexibility structure, facilitative expansion and high reliability. It is a significant trend in the development of large-scale computer control system (CHEN, 1990).

From the mid-1980s, artificial intelligence technologies, especially expert system were applied into sintering, preceding by Kawasaki Steel in Japan. Thus control reliability and precision were greatly improved. During this time, America and Canada put a lot of effort into the development of measure equipment and mathematical model, and great progress was made.

With the application of third-level control system in Kawasaki Steel of Japan, human resources were saved, operation costs were reduced, and operation management level was increased (Unaki et al, 1986). NKK declared to have their No. 4 sintering machine in Fukuyama Factory to be the first unmanned operation sintering machine in the world. At present, Australia, Germany, France, England, Finland, Sweden, Italy and Korea have also reached great height of computer control level of sintering process.

A striking feature of the progress made by sintering process technology in China is the widespread use of computer control system since the 1980s. And artificial intelligence has been used in sintering production since the 1990s Researches and applications are mostly in expert system. At present, successful research results include expert systems for sintering process control developed by author in Anshan Iron & Steel, Wuhan Iron & Steel, Panzhihua Iron & Steel and Baosteel. This expert system consists of subsystems including expert system for chemical composition control of sinter, permeability control, thermal control and abnormity diagnosis of sintering process.

2. Characteristics and control schemes of sintering process

2.1 Characteristics of sintering process

The characteristics of sintering process resulting from characteristics of sintering technology and mechanisms of sintering process is as follow:

1. Large hysteresis

Raw materials to become sinter cake through batching, mix-granulation, feeding, ignition and sintering, and then Sinter production can be yield after procedures like hot crushing, hot screening, cooling and size-stabilization. And this process will take about two hours. Moreover, sinter yield and quality can be acquired by testing, which is usually taken out every 2 hours and last for about 1~2 hours in Chinese sintering plants.

Therefore, operating states of batching, mix and feeding before sintering can be reflected by sinter yield and quality after 3~5 hours. In other words, fluctuation of sinter yield and quality at present is caused by operations 3~5 hours ago. On the one hand, hysteresis of sintering process makes it hard to achieve accurate control; on the other hand, it causes fluctuations of sintering process. This is one of the key problems for accurate control of sintering production.

2. Complexity

① Complexity of mechanism

Sintering includes processes as combustion of fuel, heat exchange in sintering bed, evaporation and condensation of moisture, decomposition of chemical water, decomposition of carbonates, decomposition, reduction and reoxidation of oxides, solid state reaction, formation and condensation of liquid state during sintering process; theoretical foundation as thermodynamics, dynamics, heat transfer, hydrodynamics and crystalline-mineralogy, etc. Therefore, mechanism of sintering process is complex.

② Complexity of effect factors

From the process control point of view, sintering is a system as follow: certain material parameters and operating parameters act on device parameters (collectively referred to as "technological parameters"), then there are corresponding state parameters and index parameters. The model is shown in Fig. 3.

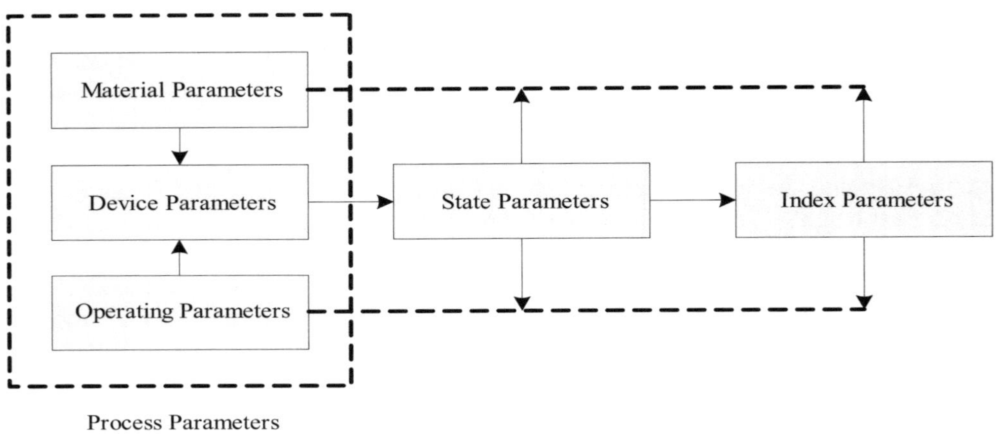

Fig. 3. Model diagram of sintering process

The complexity of effect factors of sintering process is reflected by the total amount of parameters in the five classes above and the correlation of them. Moreover, mutual restraint exists among effect factors of sintering process and quality indicators of sinter are closely related.

3. Dynamic time-varying

Sintering process is a complex industrial process which has the characteristics of continuity, nonlinear, time-varying and uncertainty besides complexity and large hysteresis.

2.2 Control schemes of sintering process

For a long time, sintering process is controlled with experience of operators to a large extent. The foundation of sintering process control is large amounts of real-time production data. Fluctuations of operation control which are adverse for production is inevitable because of hysteresis and fluctuations of data acquisition and detection, difference of operational knowledge, judgment-making ability, responsibility among operators, and other effect factors like physiological factors, psychological factors and environmental factors. This impact gets even bigger along with the scale-up of sintering machine. Meanwhile, it is hard to seize the opportunity to cut down the cost resulting from blind monitoring. Therefore, it is necessary to develop artificial intelligence control system of sintering process for the standardization and automation, further more, optimization of sinter production.

The necessity of index parameter prediction is decided by the large hysteresis of sintering process. For example, the large hysteresis of index parameters like chemical composition of sinter can be avoided by chemical composition prediction given by mathematical model of sinter chemical composition and material parameters, as material parameters are its main effect factors.

Applications of mathematical models in full-process control are limited because of the complexity of sintering process: mathematical models are useless in some parts and not accurate in some other parts; complex process models can not be used in online control, while simplified models bring in unstability, especially under abnormal circumstances. However, control by experience of operators may probably causes unstability of operation. Therefore, the problems which are hard to be solved by mathematical models can be figured out by artificial intelligence control system of sintering which is built using experience from sintering experts. Meanwhile, fluctuations of operation and production caused by artificial work can be avoided by standardization of operation, so that optimal control can be realized. Therefore, the combination of mathematical model and artificial intelligence is a condign method for sintering process control.

The complexity of sintering process results in the complexity of control system. However, high solving speed is necessary for real-time control system. Therefore, the general approach does some decomposition on complex control problems.

From the process control point of view, the purpose of sintering is getting optimal index parameters and state parameters by adjusting material parameters, operating parameters and device parameters. State parameters reflect the state of sintering process, while index parameters are indicators of sinter yield and quality. Quality indicators include chemical composition, physical properties and metallurgical properties, while physical and metallurgical properties are controlled by adjusting sintering process state and reducing the fluctuation of intermediate operation indicators. Factors affecting yield indicators are mainly permeability of sintering process, product yield and sintering pallet speed which are related to state control of sintering process. Energy consumption of sintering is connected with consumption of solid fuel, thereby related to thermal state. Therefore, sintering process control can be divided into sinter chemical composition control and sintering process state control as a whole. State control of sintering process mainly includes permeability state control and thermal state control.

3. Construction of sintering process expert system

3.1 Overall construction of expert system

Overall construction of sintering process control expert system is shown in Fig. 4.

Collect data required by system based on monitoring point of PLC, as well as data situation of distributed control system and factory LAN. After pre-processing, read these data in databases (multiple databases, easy to read and find). First, perform abnormity diagnosis: if it is only data exception, do optimal control after data processing; if it is production abnormity (including equipment overhaul, disorderly closedown, equipment failure, etc.), the system throws up alerts and corresponding suggestion. Then get into subsystems, and perform optimal control guidance at each of their own cycles.

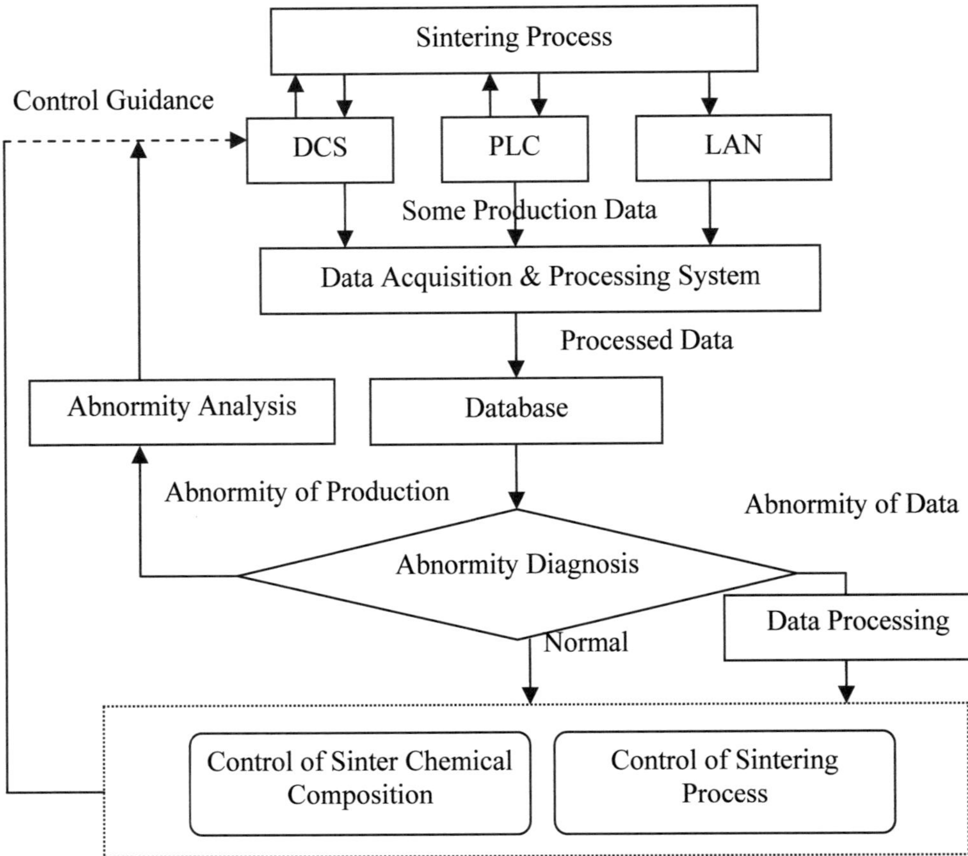

Fig. 4. Overall construction of sintering process expert system

3.2 Characteristics and description of sintering process knowledge

Knowledge of sintering process control includes five types: production data, facts, mathematical models, heuristic knowledge and meta-knowledge.

1. Production data

Production data is the starting point of sintering process control. In some reasoning process, such as basicity of sinter, burning through point, etc, production data of several moments is needed. While in some others, such as TFe, SiO_2 and CaO content of sinter, negative pressure of main pipeline, layer thickness, and production data in the present moment is the only requirement. Correspondingly, these two types of data can be defined as time-data and non-time-data. Predicate logic is used as a unified description:

predicate name (object 1, <…, object n>, <time>, value)

where: <…> is optional, followed the same.

2. Facts

Facts include dynamic facts which reflect production state, and static facts which reflect characteristics of technology, production requirements, and reasoning services for system. Among these dynamic and static facts, some of them are only qualitative or quantitative descriptions, like "limestone flow is heavy", "1-step of layer thickness adjustment is 10mm", etc; while some others also need to start certain process, some fact-description code or something. Therefore, facts are expressed in the unified form of predicate logic as follow:

predicate name (description 1, <..., description n>, <table>, <value>)

3. Mathematical models

Mathematical models are consists of time-invariant models with unchanged coefficient and time-varying models with time-changing coefficient. Whichever they are, they are descriptions of model solution which is a method of process representation. The reasoning process is efficient as in every single process, problem-solving is running into a fixed direction according to the order of embedded programs, and there is no need to match or select irrelevant knowledge. The efficiency is particularly outstanding for real-time identification needed time-varying models. Process expression of mathematical models is as follow:

process name (<code>, <variable>): — procedure body.

Other process can be called by procedure body.

Some quantitative calculation is required during inference process from time to time. Thus, model code is stored in heuristic knowledge rules. During solving process, appropriate model is adopted for quantitative calculation based on inference conditions.

4. Heuristic knowledge

Heuristic knowledge is a kind of empirical knowledge accumulated by sintering experts from long-term production practices. It is mainly used for state judgment, cause analysis and control guidance. The process of judgment, analysis and guidance is in the form of production rule, i.e. conclusions come from corresponding conditions. Thus, heuristic knowledge is mainly described by production rule. Heuristic knowledge has the following features: there are calls between rule and rule or rule and process; the condition part of rule includes both facts and production data; there are rules and code for other rules or process in the conclusion part. Therefore, heuristic knowledge is described by the combination of production rule, predicate logic and process. Its general form is as follow:

rule name (rule ID, condition part, conclusion part)

5. Meta-knowledge

Meta-knowledge is mainly used to decide the solve order of sub-tasks, and give out the solving strategy knowledge base names needed by each sub-task. Moreover, it is used to call the initial facts before solving sub-tasks and store the conclusions after that. The coordination of each sub-task is also accomplished by meta-knowledge. Process representation method is used for the description of meta-knowledge.

Diversity and complexity of sintering process control knowledge lead to the incompetence of single knowledge representation. Therefore, a hybrid knowledge representation model which is the combination of production rule, predicate logic and procedural representation is adopted. This hybrid system results in the multi base structure of knowledge base management.

3.3 Management of sintering process knowledge base

1. Multi-database structure

Knowledge base of sintering process has a structure of four-base-group which is consisted of data base, fact base, model base and rule base, which is shown in Fig. 5.

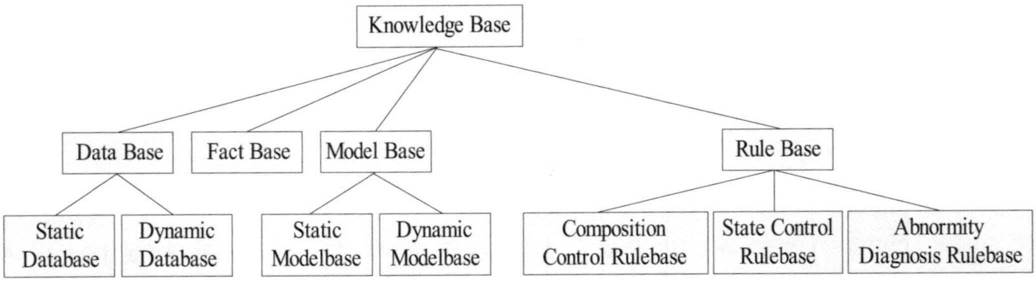

Fig. 5. Multi database structure of knowledge base

For relationship with time, production data and facts are divided into three types, real-time dynamic data and facts, slow-time-varying (i.e. data changes at regular intervals) and time-invariant static data and facts. Dynamic data and facts data are directly stored in internal dynamic database, i.e. blackboard, for the convenience of inference. While data of the other two types is stored in external database. Likely, there are two types of mathematical models, time-invariant model and time-varying model. They are stored in static model library and dynamic model library separately.

Rule base is used for the storage of heuristic knowledge. Sintering process control expert system is consisted of sub-systems such as composition control system, state control system, abnormity diagnosis system, etc. For the convenience of inference, corresponding rule base is divided.

2. Hierarchy of rule base

To narrow the search, and improve reasoning speed, groupings of rules in every rule base are established. For example, rules of process state control are divided into four groups based on the difference of tasks: group of state judgment rules, group of state prediction rules, group of cause analysis rules, group of control guidance rules. Expressed in the form of:

Rules for State Judgment: [data]→state judgment

Rules for State Prediction: [state 1, state 2, … , state n]→state prediction

Rules for Cause Analysis: [state 1, state 2, … , state n, <state prediction>]→cause analysis

Rules for Control Guidance: [cause, state] →control guidance

Layers are based on the group number of rules above. Rules which share the same group number are in the same layer. Provides that the smaller group number is, the higher layer is. Meanwhile, scheduling rules are designed in every group. These rules call corresponding rule blocks according to prerequisite. Expressed as follow:

[term 1, … , term n]→rule block

With applications of these rules, public use of condition part is realized, searching range is limited, and inference speed is accelerated.

3.4 Inference engine

Sintering process control expert system gives state judgments of parameters based on real-time production data; then analyzes their state and gives cause analysis; finally, gives control guidance based on these states and causes. Therefore, the reasoning process of sintering process control expert system is multi-level-objective.

Procedural inference is used for inference engine between three level targets: state judgment, cause analysis and control guidance. Inference engine prerequisites of each level are fully known and sufficient, thus forward inference is adopted. That means procedural

inference engine is adopted by overall target while forward inference engine is adopted by each level target.
Therefore, hybrid reasoning strategy which is a combination of forward reasoning and blackboard and procedural inference are adopted in this system. The inference engine structure is shown in Fig. 6.

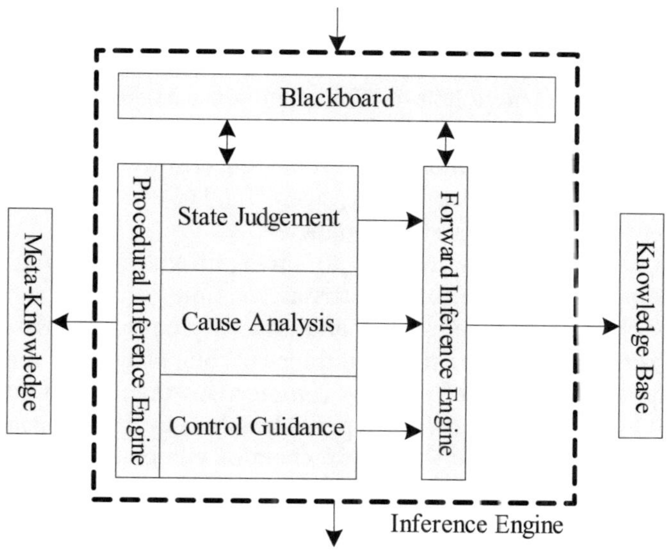

Fig. 6. Inference engine structure of sintering process control expert system

A new searching strategy is put forward according to the characteristics of the inference process. Characteristics of sintering process control inference are analyzed taking cause analysis of sinter chemical composition as an example.
Cause analyses of sinter chemical composition focus on R. R has five states, and it is in one state at each certain time. When R is in a certain state, TFe has five possible states. But TFe has only one state with specific production data at certain time. SiO_2, CaO, MgO and FeO are also the same. For example, the possible line of reasoning at certain time is as follow:

$$(R)_0 \rightarrow (TFe)_{-1} \rightarrow \cdots \rightarrow (MgO)_0 \rightarrow \text{Re}\mathit{ason}\ i$$

Characteristics of inference process are as follow:
1. All nodes at the same layer share the same characteristics. But they are mutually exclusive. When one node succeeds, the others are defaulted to be failed.
2. "Repeat search" never happens.

This study proposes a search strategy named Finite-Breadth-First-Search, based on the characteristics above. The searching process is as follow: firstly, searching nodes in the first layer. As long as there is one node succeeds, other nodes in the same layer are defaulted to be failed whether they have been searched or not. Moreover, all branches of these failed nodes are defaulted to be failed. Then searching nodes in the next layer, and limiting the range to the branch nodes of the successful upper layer nodes. Other layers are the same. This method is called limited-breadth-first search strategy as it is equal to searching every node in every layer with breadth-first search, but with limit in the breadth of node.

4. Chemical composition control of sinter

Chemical compositions of sinter include basicity (R), TFe, SiO_2, CaO, MgO, FeO, P, S, etc. Sticking point of chemical composition control of sinter is the stability of these compositions. Production practice home and abroad has proved that fluctuations of sinter chemical composition have great effect on blast furnace. When fluctuation of TFe content in sinter falls down from ±1.0% to ±0.5%, yield of blast furnace generally increases by 1%~3%. When fluctuation of R falls down from ±0.1 to ±0.075, yield of blast furnace increases by 1.5%, and coke ratio reduces by 0.8%. However, great fluctuation of sinter chemical composition is an outstanding issue of blast furnace both in China and abroad. Therefore, stability control of sinter chemical composition is significant.

Chemical composition control of sinter has the following characteristics:

① Stability of sinter chemical composition (except for FeO and S) is mostly affected by material parameters, while rarely by state parameters.

② It takes a few hours from raw material to sinter, till getting testing results of sinter chemical composition, i.e. there are great hysteresises in time.

③ Sintering process has dynamic complexity and time-varying characteristics.

④ There is great correlation between different chemical compositions of sinter.

⑤ Chemical composition control of sinter is complex. An unqualified composition is not necessarily caused by change of its own, but possibly solved by another aspect.

Therefore, neural network prediction model for chemical composition of sinter is developed using control method combined mathematical models with knowledge models. The flowchart is shown in Fig. 7, where u is input, y is output, u' is input after data processing, y' is output after data processing. y' is in a 2h cycle corresponding with testing cycle of sinter chemical composition.

4.1 Prediction models for chemical composition of sinter

It can avoid the complicated process of mathematical model development and realize nonlinear mapping of input parameters and prediction value of chemical composition by using artificial neural networks into prediction of sinter chemical composition. Dynamic changes of system can be tracked because of the adaptive character and self-learning ability of neural network.

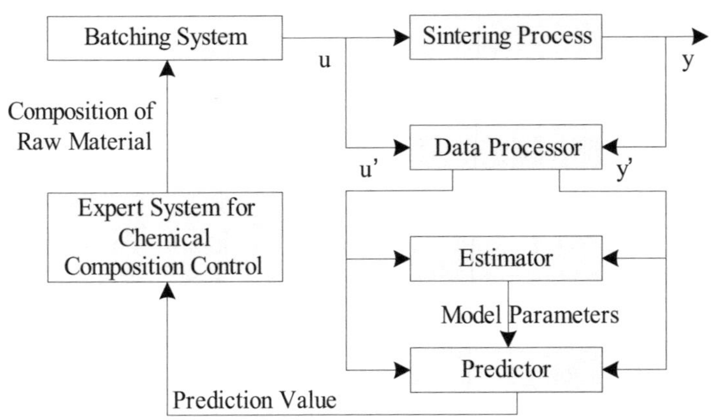

Fig. 7. Flowchart of chemical composition expert system based on prediction

Rapid BP algorithm with adaptive variable step-size via linear reinforcement is adopted based on research of neural network models and their algorithms:

$$\Delta\beta(t) = \varepsilon\lambda\beta(t-1) \tag{1}$$

Where $0 \le \varepsilon \le 1$ is constant, with a general value of $\varepsilon = 0.20 \sim 0.30$. And the definition of λ is as follow:

$$\lambda = \mathrm{sgn}\left(\frac{\partial E}{\partial W(t)} \bullet \frac{\partial E}{\partial W(t-1)}\right) \tag{2}$$

Then BP algorithm turns into the form below:

$$W(t+1) = W(t) - \beta(t)\frac{\partial E}{\partial W(t)} \tag{3}$$

Using Rapid BP Algorithm with Momentum Term and Adaptive Variable Step-Size:

$$W(t+1) = W(t) - \beta(t)Z(t) \tag{4}$$

$$Z(t) = \frac{\partial E}{\partial W(t)} + \alpha Z(t-1) \tag{5}$$

In this formula: $0 < \alpha < 1$ is momentum factor; $0 < \beta < 1$ is learning factor.

The neural network model above is available to predict after training for systems which are stable and non-time-varying. However, adaptive update of prediction model for sinter chemical composition is demanded during the process of using because sintering is a time-varying process. The most commonly used adaptive method is equal dimension and new information method which is adding latest data into training sample set, deleting the oldest sample, and keeping unchanged sample amount, i.e. adaptive update for one time. Training of neural network runs in the background.

Parameters of online learning are as follow: 80 groups of training samples; momentum factor α =0.30; initial rate of learning β =0.70; initial weight and initial threshold are both 0.50; excitation function is $f(x) = \frac{2}{1+e^{-x}} - 1$. Using Rapid BP Algorithm with Momentum Term and Adaptive Variable Step-Size via Linear Reinforcement, adjustment of weight moves towards the average at the bottom without great fluctuation. When the system is in the flat area of function surface, the error is really small, thus $\Delta W(t+1)$ is almost equal to $\Delta W(t)$ and the average of ΔW becomes $\Delta W \approx \frac{-\beta}{1-\alpha} \bullet \frac{\partial E}{\partial W}$, where $\frac{-\beta}{1-\alpha}$ gets more efficient that the adjustment can get out of saturation zone as soon as possible. The problem of low learning efficiency and easy to converge at local minimum can be solved. When the training step reaches 6000, training error of network is 0.000145 after online training the model on-site. Compared with general BP models, this model has faster rate of convergence which not only reduces the training time and guarantees the prediction accuracy, but also limits the oscillation and divergence. The error descending curves are compared in Fig. 8.

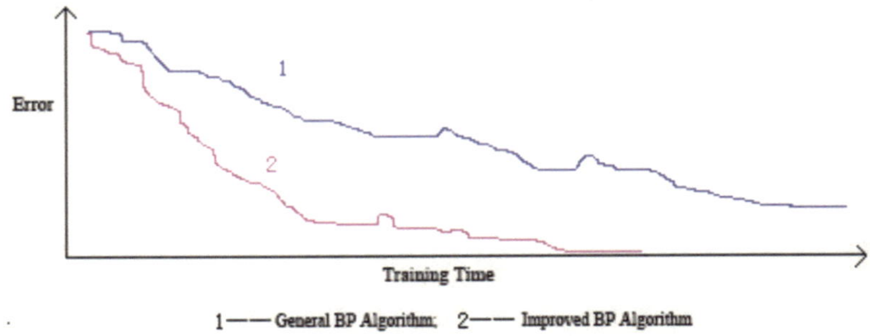

Fig. 8. Training error tendency of model

4.2 Expert system for chemical composition control of sinter

1. Control strategy of interval optimization

Point optimization which is unattainable because of characteristics of sintering process control is a control strategy aims at optimal point.

① Foundation of sintering process control is large amounts of real-time production data. Point optimization is hard to achieve because of the error between true value and detection value which is affected by noises and unmeasurable disturbances.

② Point optimization will result in frequent adjustment. Because of detection error and hysteresis of sintering process, frequent adjustments will cause large fluctuations of production. As a result, optimal control will be ruined as well as normal running of sintering process.

Relative to point optimization, interval optimization is a control strategy aims at optimal interval around optimal point. And interval optimization is a proper control strategy for sintering process control.

① Interval optimization aims at optimal interval. It can reduce inaccuracies caused by data measurement and avoid frequent adjustments of process control, so that stable operation of sintering process can be achieved.

② There are errors (within the allowable range) between prediction value and detection values of production parameters. Interval optimization can reduce misoperations caused by these errors.

Therefore, interval optimization is the control strategy adopted by this system.

Optimization of sintering process is based on normal running of sinter production, making judgments according to real-time detection value of production parameters. Therefore, values of production parameters can be divided into three intervals: optimal interval (marked as 0), feasible interval (interval between upper limit of optimal interval and upper limit of feasible interval is marked as +1, while interval between lower limit of optimal interval and lower limit of feasible interval is marked as -1), and abnormal interval (interval over upper limit of feasible interval is marked as +2, while interval under lower limit of feasible interval is marked as -2), shown in Fig. 9. The aim of interval optimization is getting optimal interval with feasible interval.

① Determination of Optimal Point

Optimal point is value of sintering process control object that meets requirement of process optimization. For sinter chemical composition, optimal point is standard of each

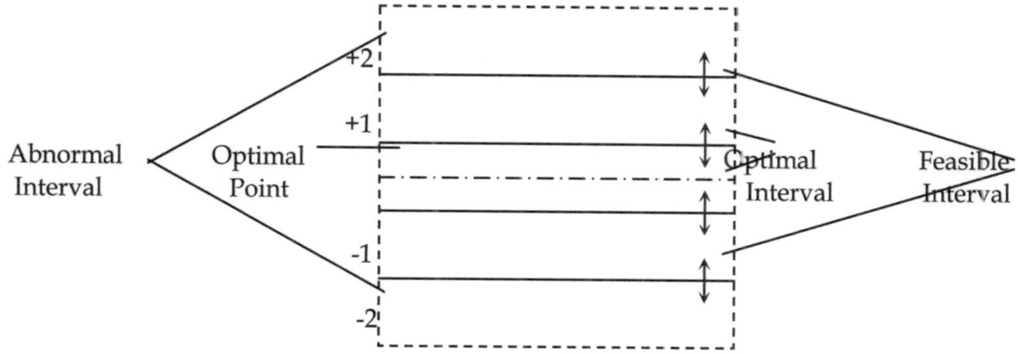

Fig. 9. Division chart of parameter interval
↔ variable boundary points

composition. For state parameters of sintering process, optimal point is determined according to the specific process and production conditions. For example, negative pressure of main pipeline is related to thickness of bed: the thicker bed is, the higher optimal value of main pipeline negative pressure is.

② Determination of Interval Boundary

Interval boundaries are critical points divided different intervals. Interval boundaries of sinter chemical compositions are based on the standards of first-grade, acceptable and defective products. For example: first-grade products specify TFe fluctuation in the range of ±0.50%; acceptable products specify TFe fluctuation in the range of ±0.75%; defective products specify TFe fluctuation in the range of ±0.75%. Therefore, interval boundaries of TFe are +0.5%, -0.5%, +0.75%, -0.75%.

③ Description of State Parameter

+1 and -1 represent two different production states while value of parameter is in feasible interval. Similarly, +2 and -2 are two production states as well. Divide each production parameter into 5 states in order to make production state judgment accurately with real-time data of production parameter, and realize interval optimization. Taking TFe as an example, its state descriptions are shown in Table 1.

Interval Code	+2	+1	0	-1	-2
State Description	too high	high	proper	low	too low
Interval Range	>+0.75	+0.75~+0.5	+0.5~-0.5	-0.5~-0.75	<-0.75

Table 1. State description of sinter chemical composition TFe

The purpose of interval optimization is realizing high-quality, high-yield and low-energy consumption by control of sintering process so that control variables are kept in optimal intervals.

2. Optimization strategy for sinter chemical composition

Synchronized optimization of each chemical compositions of sinter is optimal. However, the control strategy of "Synchronized Optimization" can hardly be achieved because of the great dependency of each chemical composition and randomicity of their changes. Therefore, sinter chemical composition control should lay emphasis on keystone.

Stableness of each composition is main point of sinter chemical composition control. The small fluctuation range is, the better. Chemical composition control of sinter focuses on R and TFe control, as their fluctuations can result in fluctuations of blast furnace state. As long as R and TFe meet the requirement, it is not necessary to make any adjustment, regardless of state of the other compositions. While adjustment must be made if R and TFe are unacceptable, even if requirements of the other composition are satisfied.

To realize the optimization of R and TFe, avoiding great fluctuations, as well as reducing the influence of prediction error, adjustments are made based on the state and changing tendency (past value, present value and future value) of R and TFe.

① R is too high (or too low) & TFe is too high (or too low): Adjust R and TFe regardless of state of the other compositions.

② R is too high (or too low) & TFe is high (or low): Focus on the adjustment of R. Adjustment of TFe is based on its changing tendency. If the prediction value, present value and past value share the same changing tendency, adjust TFe. Or else, do not make any adjustment temporarily.

③ R is too high (or too low) & TFe is proper: Focus on the adjustment of R.

④ R is high (or low) & TFe is too high (or too low): Focus on the adjustment of TFe. Adjustment of R is based on its changing tendency.

⑤ R is high (or low) & TFe is high (or low): Adjustments of R and TFe are based on their changing tendency, respectively.

⑥ R is high (or low) & TFe is proper: Adjustment of R is based on its changing tendency.

⑦ R is proper & TFe is too high (or too low): Focus on the adjustment of TFe.

⑧ R is proper & TFe is high (or low): Adjustment of TFe is based on its changing tendency.

⑨ R is proper & TFe is proper: Making no adjustment regardless of state of the other compositions.

5. Permeability control of sintering process

Permeability is the difficulty of gas passing through the solid bed. The fluctuation and change of gas are related to the processes of mass transfer, heat transfer and physicochemical reactions. Therefore, permeability of sintering bed plays a decisive role in smooth operation of sintering process, thus affects yield and quality of sinter.

Permeability is commonly referred to as permeability of mix bed and permeability of sintering process.

5.1 Permeability control of mix material

Permeability of mix material is the permeability of bed before ignition. It is decided by physical and chemical properties of raw materials, moisture, mix-granulation, feeding, etc. Therefore, permeability control of mix material is realized by feed-forward control of these factors above. And the key point is accurate detection.

Basic approach of continuous detection of permeability is blowing method, i.e. blowing compressed air into mix material and measuring the pressure and flow of it. Permeability J is calculated by the following equation:

$$J = KQ/\sqrt{p} \tag{6}$$

Where:

Q− −air flow, m^3/h;
p− −pressure of air, MPa;
K− −coefficient, $h \cdot m^{-3} \cdot (MPa)^{-\frac{1}{2}}$.

There are two specific methods. One method is as follow: hang a pipe to the feeding bin; blow compressed air into it; get permeability of mix material by testing the air flow (Fig. 10).

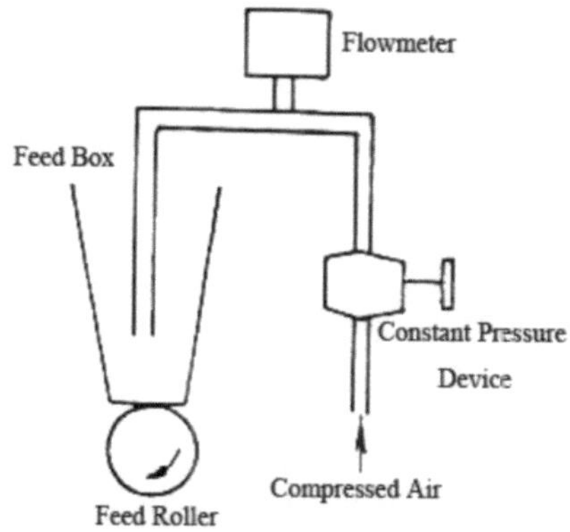

Fig. 10. Diagrammatic sketch of permeability detection

Another method is as follow: design a separate set of sampling devices; blow compressed air with constant pressure into a device full of mix material; measure the air flow; and the permeability is calculated based on the air flow. Compare two methods above, the former one has simple device structure, but with wind pipe easy to wear and clog. While the latter one has no wear and clog problems but its device structure is too complex.

In comprehensive simulation model of iron ore developed by Sumitomo Metals' Kashima Steel Works, permeability before sintering process is predicted by data of grain composition of raw material, granulation moisture, apparent density, etc (Takazo et al., 1987).

In process control model of sintering machine speed developed by Günther Straka from Austria, permeability of mix material can be calculated by the test data of waste gas flow, bed thickness and pressure difference in ignition hood. As well as the test data of air flow passing through bed (Straka, 1992).

5.2 Permeability control of sintering process

Permeability of sintering process is the permeability of bed after ignition. Along with sintering process, permeability of bed, which is one of the most important indicators for sintering operation, changes rapidly.

1. Operation Guidance System of sintering process

Kawasaki Steel Corporation in Japan developed Operation Guidance System for sintering process (OGS) in order to stable permeability of sintering process and sinter quality (Kazuma et al., 1987). Basic idea of OGS is shown in Fig. 11.

OGS consists of a main system and two subsystems. After inputting production data of sintering process into OGS, main system makes comprehensive assessment of permeability, sinter quality and productivity with decision making chart. And appropriate operation is chosen to meet the requirement of sinter yield and quality. One of these two subsystems is used to assess permeability, while the other is for auto-adjusting of the standard value for assessment.

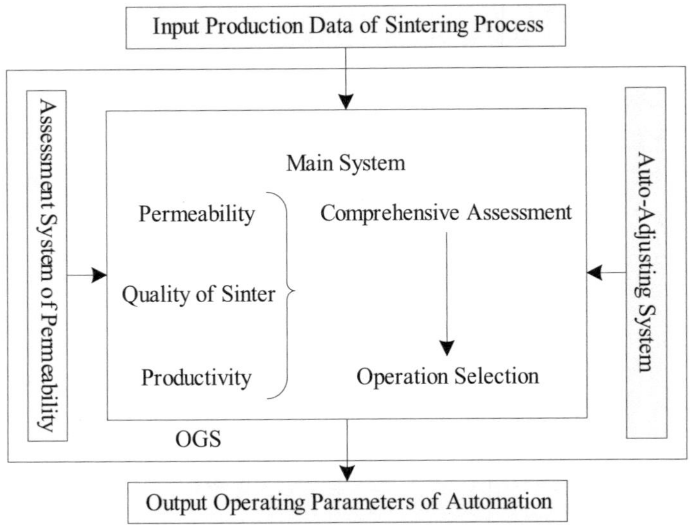

Fig. 11. Basic idea of OGS

Main system gives out the assessment by comparing 9 kinds of input data, such as permeability, productivity and quality, with the standard value of their 7 classes (0, ±1, ±2, ±3).

Some of these standard values for process data assessment require adjustment from "Auto-Adjusting System" every 30min. While other parameters, like main downdraught fan, which are not control objects, their standard values are from the average value, and their standard deviation is calculated by data collected in the past few hours.

$$\text{standard value} = f\left(\bar{x}, \sigma\right) \tag{7}$$

Where:

$\bar{x}$ — —average value of process data collected in the scheduled past few hours;

σ— —standard deviation of process data collected in the same period with $\bar{x}$.

Productivity and quality which are control objects not auto-adjusting, as they have their own standards. They are set by operators based on operating conditions.

In order to reduce unit coke consumption, return material ratio and unit coke consumption are measured as they are closely related. And standard value of return material ratio is calculated.

Permeability of bed varies with parameters. Therefore, pressure of main downdraught fan, maximum temperature of wind-box, and burning through point are predicted and used for the assessment of permeability. Though their impact factors are multiple, the most important one is raw material permeability (RP). Therefore, autoregression models of the relationship between raw material permeability and these three parameters are developed respectively for the prediction.

Optimization of productivity and quality by operation adjustment is the main function of OGS. A three-dimensional diagram is used to making decisions of operating variables and range based on the assessment of permeability, return material ratio and productivity. Experience-based operating variables (sintering pallet speed, density of raw bed, and coke proportion) as well as 7-level operating range from -3 to +3 are set.

2. Expert system for sintering process control centered on permeability

Fluctuations of sintering process are mainly caused by fluctuations of permeability. The state of permeability affects the stability of burning through point: with a too good permeability, burning through point is ahead of time; with a too bad permeability, burning through point is hysteretic. Thus stable and improve permeability of bed is the necessary way to stable burning through point, so that stability of sintering process can be achieved. Therefore, control of sintering process should center on permeability. Permeability-centered control strategy is as follow: when permeability is good, stable burning through point; when permeability is bad, improve permeability first, then consider keeping burning through point stable.

① Judging Method for Permeability of Sintering Process

Material parameters and operating parameters affect permeability of sintering process, while state parameters reflect it. When permeability is good, air is easy to pass through bed, so that air flow (Q), vertical sintering speed ($V_{\perp}$) and waste gas temperature (T) increase, burning through point is ahead of time, negative pressure of main pipeline (ΔP) falls down; the reverse is true. Therefore, Q, $V_{\perp}$, BTP, T and ΔP reflect permeability from different aspects and are capable for the use of permeability assessment. However, Q is affected by air leakage rates beside permeability; fluctuation of T is mainly affected by BTP, as well as air leakage rates, season and carbon proportion. Therefore, they are not suitable parameters for permeability assessment.

BTP as a evaluation parameters of permeability has hysteresis in time, which is definitely going to affect the accurate judge of permeability and optimal control of sintering process. Therefore, prediction of BTP is necessary. Long-term production practices have proved that when sintering process is normal, BTP is stable, inflection point of wind-box temperature curve (called normal inflection point) located in a certain wind-box, and temperature of this wind-box (called normal inflection point temperature) is in a certain range; when BTP changes, normal inflection point temperature changes with it. Therefore, BTP prediction can be realized based on normal inflection point temperature and BTP state.

According to experience, permeability is good when vertical sintering speed ($V_{\perp}$) is high, prediction value of burning through point (BTP) is ahead of time, and negative pressure of main pipeline (ΔP) is low; while it is bad on the contrary. Rule base for permeability comprehensive assessment with prediction values of $V_{\perp}$, BTP, and ΔP is developed based on this basic idea.

② Control Principle for Permeability of Sintering Process

With good permeability condition, burning through point is stabled by adjustment of sintering pallet speed and bed thickness. While with bad permeability condition, on the one hand, permeability has to be improved by controls of mix material moisture, mix material temperature, ignition temperature and coke proportion; on the other hand, burning through point has to be stabled by adjustment of sintering pallet speed and bed thickness.

Adjustment rules of sintering pallet speed and bed thickness are as follow: Focus on sintering pallet speed. Bed thickness has to be adjusted only if there are great changes for raw material and equipments.

6. Thermal control of sintering process

Temperature changes in sinter bed are the impetus of physical and chemical changes. Therefore, thermal state affects sintering process.

6.1 Thermal control based on BRP

1. Calculation of BRP

Burning through point (BTP) is calculated with exhaust gas temperature of wind-boxes along the length of sintering machine. However, the accuracy of taking BTP as thermal state index is affected by air leak caused by shrinkage cracks of material bed and from discharge end of sinter machine. Therefore, a new index for thermal state of sintering process - BRP (Fig. 6-1) is brought forward by Keihin Steelworks of NKK (Michnori et al., 1992). It can be calculated by formula below:

$$Gt_k = Ax_k^2 + Bx_k + C \quad (\text{k=1~3}) \tag{8}$$

$$A \cdot BRP_t^2 + B \cdot BRP_t + C = t \tag{9}$$

Where:
BRP_t—Burning Rising Point;
x—number of wind-box;
Gt—exhaust gas temperature below sintering pallet, °C;
A, B, C—coefficient of exhaust gas temperature below sintering pallet along the length of sintering machine described by conic section;
K—code of wind-box along the length of sintering machine (when K=1, it is No. 18 wind-box; when K=2, it is No. 20 wind-box; when K=3, it is No. 22 wind-box);
t —set temperature used for BRP calculation, °C, set temperature t is the temperature of the center of temperature measuring position, i.e. almost equals to exhaust gas temperature of No. 20 wind-box, t=250 °C.

Fitting conic sections to exhaust gas temperature of the last a few wind-boxes (except the very last one). The position corresponding to a certain temperature on the curve is chosen as BRP. BRP is considered as target parameter of burning through point control so that effect of air leak at discharge end of sinter machine on exhaust gas temperature can be avoided.

Speed of sintering pallet is controlled by relation between sintering pallet speed and vertical position of BRP_t, so that position of BRP_t along the length of sintering machine is stable.

2. Proposition and calculation of TRP

Exhaust gas temperature in wind-boxes from head to tail of sintering machine is studied. It is found that exhaust gas temperature curve is consistent with cyclic-n polynomial, as formula (6-3). And there is a strong-tie between temperature rising position and highest position. Therefore, Temperature Rising Position (TRP) is brought forward which is the position where temperature of exhaust gas in wind-boxes begins to rise (Fig. 12), as well as the position when mix material zone completely disappears. TRP is usually located at the mid-back part of sintering machine. There are not significant changes of exhaust gas temperature in the wind-boxes at the front part. And exhaust gas temperature rises rapidly after that.

$$T_g = a_0+a_1X+a_2X^2+\ldots\ldots + a_nX^n \tag{10}$$

Where:
T_g — exhaust gas temperature, °C;
X — measuring position of exhaust gas temperature, m;
n, a—coefficients of polynomial.

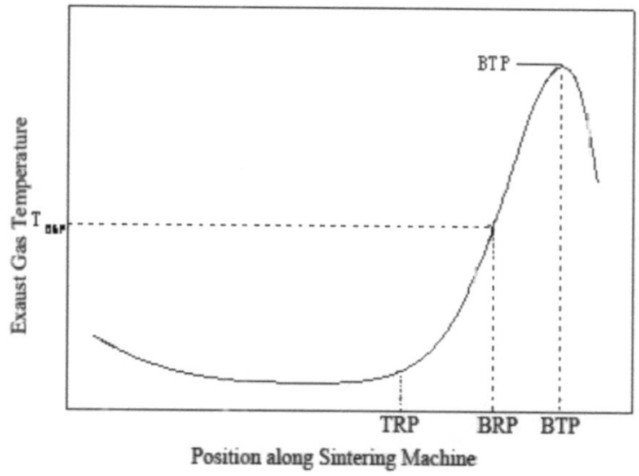

Fig. 12. Typical diagram of exhaust gas temperature curve

Measuring point data used for curve fitting is selected to avoid the effect of air leak at discharge end on exhaust gas temperature. Judgments of middle measuring point temperatures are made. If T (X_2) - $T(X_1) < T_c$, and $T(X_3)$ - $T(X_2) > T_c$, X_2 is centered; temperatures of 2 measuring points each side are taken; fit curve with these 5 temperature data; then real solution when slope of curve is 5 is considered as TRP temperature. T_c is decided according to the condition of production, and it is generally 10~20°C. Calculating range is set in $[X_1, X_3]$ according to the judgments above to get the TRP value fitting reality.

Stability of BTP can be realized by stability of TRP, which is achieved by adjustment of sintering machine speed, with predictive fuzzy control method, making use of the relation between sintering machine speed and TRP position.

6.2 BTP control based on combustion zone model

1. Combustion zone model

BTP is decided by vertical velocity of combustion zone and horizontal velocity of sintering pallet in sintering process. And the main influencing factors of combustion zone are negative pressure of main downdraught fan and resistance of mix material (Fig.13). Therefore, combustion zone model (Straka, 1994) is as follow:

$$\frac{d^2x(t)}{dt^2} = -A + Bx(t) \tag{11}$$

$$x(0) = H \tag{12}$$

$$\frac{dx(0)}{dt} = 0 \tag{13}$$

Where:

x(t) – position of combustion zone;

t – time (t=0 is the initial time);

A – pressure caused by main downdraught fan, which can be expressed by total flow of exhaust gas;

B—internal resistance of mix material, which is defined as a function of mix material permeability;
H— —thickness of bed.

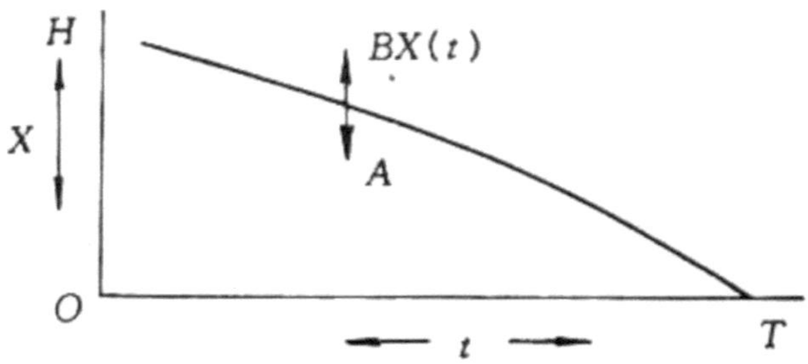

Fig. 13. Relation of combustion zone and time

2. Control model of sintering pallet speed
Control model of sintering pallet speed (Straka, 1994) is shown in Fig. 14.

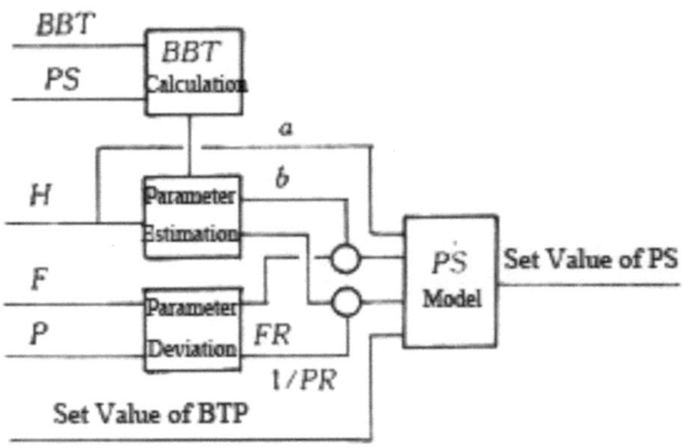

Fig. 14. Control model of sintering pallet speed

Burning through time (BTT) is calculated with BTP (which is calculated with detection value of exhaust gas temperature of wind-boxes) and sintering pallet speed (PS). Parameter a and b are estimated online according to stable condition. Parameter deviation FR and PR are constant or slowly changing average. Calculate BTT of mix material just passed by ignitor. And set value of pallet speed can be calculated with the precalculated BTT and set value of BTP.

6.3 Fuzzy control of BTP based on prediction

1. Prediction of BTP
Estimate BTP with exhaust gas temperatures of the last few wind-boxes is time-lagging. And stability control of BTP, even the entire sintering process will be affected. Therefore, BTP prediction is necessary.
① Input parameters of prediction model
BTP prediction includes long-term prediction (about 30min) and short-term prediction (about 10min). Long-term prediction is BTP prediction based on permeability of raw material. And great external disturbance of raw material system such as changes of material

proportion, segregation in material bins, changes of mix material moisture are the main considerations. Short-term prediction is BTP prediction based on temperature of BRP wind-box. It has the qualities of short feedback time and high accuracy. Thus it is used when there are little external disturbance.

② Methods for modeling

Least-Squares Identification Method and BP Algorithm have their advantages and disadvantages over data processing of dynamic system. After these two methods were compared with large amount of industrial production data, Least-Squares Identification Method (FANG & XIAO, 1988) is adopted by BTP predictions with short cycle. Initial values of model parameters are calculated by using 250 sets of production data. Then adaptiveness of model parameters is realized with recursive algorithm. Given the same confidence to former and latter data, data grows with time, information given by new data will be flooded by former data. Thus identification ability of the algorithm is lost, and "data saturation" happens. To solve this problem, identification algorithm is modified with method combines both ideas of forgetting factor and limited memory. Data length of identification keeps the same and forgetting factors are added to former data. The recurrence equation is shown in Formula (6-7). Forgetting factor μ is 0.98.

$$\begin{aligned}
&\hat{\theta}(k+1,k+L)=\hat{\theta}(k,k+L)-K(k+1,k+L)[y(k)-h^{\tau}(k)\hat{\theta}(k,k+L)]\\
&K(k+1,k+L)=P(k,k+L)h(k)[\mu^{-L}-h^{\tau}(k)P(k,k+L)h(k)]^{-1}\\
&P(k+1,k+L)=\mu^{L}[I+K(k+1,k+L)h^{\tau}(k)]P(k,k+L)\\
&\hat{\theta}(k,k+L)=\hat{\theta}(k,k+L-1)+K(k,k+L)[y(k+L)-h^{\tau}(k+L)\hat{\theta}(,k+L-1)]\\
&K(k,k+L)=P(k,k+L-1)h(k+L)[\mu+h^{\tau}(k+L)P(k,k+L-1)h(k+L)]^{-1}\\
&P(k,k+L)=\frac{1}{\mu}[I-K(k,k+L)h^{\tau}(k+L)]P(k,k+L-1)
\end{aligned} \tag{14}$$

2. Fuzzy control of Burning Through Point

Sintering process is a complicated nonlinear system. Fuzzy control method which includes fuzzification, fuzzy inference and defuzzification is adopted. Deviation and deviation change of prediction position and set position of burning through point are considered as inputs while speed of sintering machine is output for the control of burning through point. The input and output are represented by 7 fuzzy variables expressed as { NB, NM, NS, ZR, PS, PM, PB }, and the numeral expression is {-3, -2, -1, 0, 1, 2, 3}. The ranges of fuzzy variables are all in [-6, 6] in order to insure that fuzzy set can cover the whole range. The membership function is isosceles triangle, and distributes symmetrically in the whole range. It is showed in Fig. 15.

Commonly used fuzzy inference methods at present include Max-Min Method and Maximum Product Method, etc. For fuzzy control rule R_i, total satisfaction of conditions is the minimum of sub-condition membership, as the sub-conditions are connected by "and" operator. In fuzzy logic, "if - then" relation can be expressed by cross product of conditions and conclusions. If the minimum value of conditions and conclusions membership function is taken for cross product membership function, it is Max-Min Method; if product of conditions and conclusions membership function is taken for cross product membership function, it is Maximum Product Method. Final output fuzzy variables are the summation of membership functions inferred by all the rules because the connecting operator between rule and rule is "or". And it shapes as a polygon.

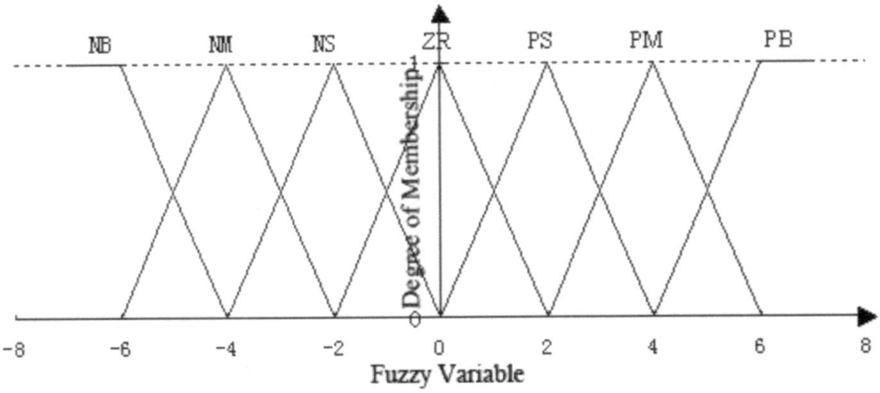

Fig. 15. Membership function of fuzzy controller

Defuzzification methods in common use include Maximum of Membership (MoM), Center of Gravity (CoG) and Center of Area (CoA). Values of MoM is relatively unilateral; calculation of CoA is more cumbersome, not easy-programming; while CoG covers all the possible values of output variables and is easy-programming. CoG also called as Weighted Average Method is similar to the calculation of gravity center (GUO et al., 1999). When the range is discrete:

$$Z_0 = \frac{\sum_{i=1}^{n} z_i \mu_{c'}(z_i)}{\sum_{i=1}^{n} \mu_{c'}(z_i)} \tag{15}$$

Sintering is a time-varying process. Change of raw material structure will result in change of optimal range for sintering process parameters, as well as change of control object. Therefore, fuzzy control algorithm should be adaptive, track changes of system automatically, and makes corresponding adjustment. Control effect depends on number of fuzzy set, membership function and control rules after the input and output variables of fuzzy control algorithm as well as fuzzy inference and defuzzification method are determined. In author's research, non-linear quantitative curve and adaptive control rules are used to realized the adaptiveness of control algorithm.

6.4 Control of BTP based on expert experience

Control of BTP is included in Diagnosis Expert System of Sintering Operation developed by Mizushima factory of Kawasaki Steel (Fukagawa, et al. 1991). It consists of management of normal BTP and management of abnormal BTP.

1. Management of normal BTP

Management of normal BTP includes management of real BTP and management of predicted BTP. Predicted BTP is usually used for BTP management. Management of real BTP is required for control adjustment when real BTP is beyond the normal management range for reasons like sudden external interference. Prediction of BTP consists of long-term prediction and short-term prediction. And autoregression model is their common prediction method. When long-term prediction value of BTP is over upper limit of requirement, immediate operation to slow down pallet speed is demanded, in order to avoid not burning through caused by operation delay. When long-term prediction value of BTP is under upper limit of requirement, firing state is judged by short-term prediction value and real BTP. The judgments are expressed in 11 grades. In conclusion, changing sintering pallet speed is the measure that taken when BTP is in abnormal state.

2. Management of abnormal BTP

Equipments are protected from breakage and burn with process value monitoring. Diagnoses of operation state of cooling temperature, EP temperature and negative pressure of main fan are taken out by management of abnormal BTP in a 1min cycle. When they are beyond the ratings, emergency measures of changing pallet speed or opening of main fan gate are taken. Then cause analyses of abnormities and operation guidance are given out. Opening of exhaust fan gate and pallet speed are back to normal according to real BTP state after eliminating the abnormities. Then it goes back to BTP management function.

6.5 Control of thermal state based on energy consumption of sintering

With certain mix material chemical composition, granularity and metallurgical properties, permeability of raw material is decided by mix material moisture, while permeability of sintering process which affects thermal state is decided by fuel ratio. Moreover, fuel ratio decides energy consumption of sintering process as well. Chiba Factory of Kawasaki Steel developed Sintering energy consumption control system (SECOS) (Sasaki, 1987) on No. 3 and No. 4 sintering machine. SECOS estimates energy fluctuations with RC and HZR, so that automatic control of coke ratio is achieved.

1. Calculation of RC

RC is equal to the carbon content calculated by concentration of CO and CO_2 in exhaust gas and flow of exhaust gas, minus CO_2 content produced by combustion of mixed-gas and decomposition of carbonate, then convert it into coke ratio, i.e.:

$$RC = \left[V_{ex} \cdot (CO + CO_2) - V_{CaCO_3} - V_{Dolo} - V_{MG}\right] \times \frac{13}{22.4} \times \frac{1}{M \times FC} \times 100\% \tag{16}$$

Where:

V_{ex}—flow of exhaust gas (dry), m^3/h;

V_{MG}—CO_2 amount produced by combustion of mixed-gas, m^3/h;

CO, CO_2—concentration of CO and CO_2 in exhaust gas; Sampling pipes are set at exhaust gas fan exit, considering the adverse effect of bias in gas collector and dust in exhaust gas.

V_{DOLO}, V_{CaCO_3} —CO_2 amount produced by thermal decomposition of dolomite and limestone, m^3/h; There is about 30min of time lag from mix material discharges from material bins to testing results of exhaust gas composition is given out. Therefore, track time is required before using amount of dolomite and limestone in calculation.

FC— —content of free carbon in coke, %;

M— —mix material consumption, t/h.

$$M = PS \times H \times W \times \rho \times 60 \tag{17}$$

Where:

PS— —detection value of sintering machine speed, m/min;

H— —detection value of sintering material thickness, m;

W— —width of sintering pallet, m;

ρ— —calculated value of mix material density on sintering machine, m^3/h.

2. Detection of HZR

Cross section of sinter cake which is about to falling is shot by monitor of industrial television (ITV) set at the discharge end of sintering machine. Image signals from the camera are presented on color monitor according to their temperatures after processed by image processing device and color simulation device. Meanwhile, hot zone (over 600°C) area ratio (HZR) is isolated by image processing device. HZR is calculated with the unit of 1 second. Maximum value of each pallet is considered as the control value. And index selection processing is carried out with superior process computer.

3. Status evaluation and control of RC and HZR

RC and HZR are calculated every 5min. And sintering state is estimated by 7 grade (0~±3) according to the deviation between calculated value and target value. Comprehensive evaluation of sintering heat level is given out based on separate evaluation results of RC and HZR. Amount and direction of coke adjustment is described by comprehensive evaluation 0~±3. Adjusted value is adopted only if there are deviations for both RC and HZR. Suitable value of coke ratio is calculated based on result of comprehensive evaluation. And it is used as set value of coke supply of lower DDC.

7. Conclusion

Optimal control for sintering process can be divided into two types, based on mathematic model and artificial intelligence, by control methods. As it is too hard to describe the complicated mechanism of sintering process, Japan and some other countries with advanced iron & steel industry made energetic efforts to develop artificial intelligence based control for sintering process and got some remarkable achievement in the late 1980s. In the late 1990s, advanced intelligent control systems are imported from abroad by some domestic large and medium-size iron & steel enterprises in China. However, these systems did not yield desirable results for a variety of reasons. Therefore, it is significant to develop an expert system for sintering process conforming to the complicated raw material structure and imperfect basic automation system of iron & steel enterprises in China.

Sintering process is a dynamic system with complex mechanism, multi-effect-factors, strong coupling and great lag. It is hard to develop precise mathematical models for control. Using artificial intelligence which simulates judgment and thinking of human being in process control is a powerful tool for control of this kind of complex systems. Therefore, the combination of mathematical model and artificial intelligence is a condign method for sintering process control.

Knowledge of sintering process control includes five types: production data, facts, mathematical models, heuristic knowledge and meta-knowledge. Diversity and complexity of sintering process control knowledge lead to the incompetence of single knowledge representation. Therefore, a hybrid knowledge representation model which is the combination of production rule, predicate logic and procedural representation is adopted. This hybrid system results in the multi base structure of knowledge base management, which is consisted of data base, fact base, model base and rule base. And the reasoning process of sintering process control expert system is multi-level-objective. A limited breadth first search strategy was put forward.

Since the early 1990s, funded by National Natural Science Foundation, National Research Project and some iron & steel enterprises, chemical composition control of sinter, permeability control of sintering process, thermal control of sintering process, abnormity diagnosis of sintering process, etc. have been studied, based on the target and characteristics of sintering process control, and expert system for sintering process was developed and successfully applied in iron & steel enterprises around China.

A neural network prediction model for chemical composition of sinter was developed using control method combined mathematical models with knowledge models. Rapid BP algorithm with adaptive variable step-size via linear reinforcement is adopted based on research of neural network models and their algorithms. Interval optimization is the control strategy adopted by this system. The control strategy of "Synchronized Optimization" can hardly be achieved because of the great dependency of each chemical composition and randomicity of their changes. Therefore, sinter chemical composition control should lay emphasis on keystone. Chemical composition control of sinter focuses on R and TFe control. Fluctuations of sintering process are mainly caused by fluctuations of permeability. Therefore, control of sintering process should center on permeability. Permeability-centered control strategy is as follow: when permeability is good, stable burning through point; when permeability is bad, improve permeability first, then consider keeping burning through point stable. Exhaust gas temperature in wind-boxes from head to tail of sintering machine is studied. Temperature Rising Position (TRP) is brought forward which is the position where temperature of exhaust gas in wind-boxes begins to rise. Stability of BTP can be realized by stability of TRP, which is achieved by adjustment of sintering machine speed, with predictive fuzzy control method, making use of the relation between sintering machine speed and TRP position.

8. References

CHEN Jinjiao. (1990). *Computer Control Technology*, Central South University of Technology Press, ISBN 7810203053, Changsha.

FANG Chongzhi, XIAO Deyun. (1988). Process Identification, Tsinghua University Press, ISBN 9787302002291, Beijing.

FU Juying, JIANG Tao, et al. (1996). *Sintering and Pelletizing*, Central South University of Technology Press, ISBN 7810208403, Changsha.

Fukagawa M, lyama Shunji, et al. (1991). Sinter Operation Control System with Artificial Intelligence. *Kavasaki Steel Technical Report*, Vol. 2, No. 3, (1991) 203-209, ISSN 0368-7236.

GUO Daiyi, LEI Wenyu, LIANG Shan. (1999). Fuzzy Control Technology and Its Applications in Metallurgy Industry, Chongqing University Press, ISBN 7562418926, Chongqing.

Kazuma N, et al. (1987). Sintering Process Control with "OGS". *Sintering and Pelletizing*, Vol. 12, No. 6 (1987) 41-48, ISSN 1000-8764.

MA Zhuwu. (2005). *Automation for Ironmaking*, Metallurgy Industry Press, ISBN 7-5024-3639-1, Beijing.

Michnori Hattori, Hiroshi Fukuyo, et al. (1992). Development of Uniform and stable Sintering Technology in Keihin Sintering Plant. *NKK Technical Report*, No. 138 (1992) 8-15, ISSN 0468-2815.

Sasaki Fuka, et al. (1987). Development of Sintering Energy Consumption Control System (SECOS). *Kavasaki Steel Technical Report*, Vol. 19, No. 26, (1987) 21-25, ISSN 0368-7236.

Straka G. (1992). Process Control Model for Sinter Machine Speed. *Metallurgical Plant and Technology International*, Vol. 15, No. 5, (1992) 78-80, ISSN 0935-7254.

Takazo K, Mayumi Y, et al. (1987). Development and Application of an Integrated Simulation Model for Iron Ore Sintering. *Ironmaking Proceedings*, No. 46, (1987) 99-106, ISSN 1528-5669

Unaki H, Miki K, et al. (1986). New Control System of Sinter Plants at Chiba Works, IFAC Automation in Mining, Mineral and Metal Processing, pp. 209-216, Tokyo, Japan, 1986.

6

Expert System Applications in Sheet Metal Forming

R. Ganesh Narayanan
Department of Mechanical Engineering, IIT Guwahati, Guwahati 781039
India

1. Introduction

Expert system can be defined as an intelligent computer program, a repository of knowledge, a set of rules, like a human consultant, all aiming at delivering accurate solutions/suggestions to a problem at any level, say during plan, design, manufacture, and quality control. Some of the important definitions are quoted here.

"An expert system is a computer system used to distribute the expertise of a human or group of humans throughout a group of users" (Wang et al., 1991)

"Expert systems (ES) are a branch of applied artificial intelligence involving that expertise, which is the vast body of task-specific knowledge, is transferred from a human to a computer. This knowledge is then stored in the computer and users call upon the computer for specific advice as needed" (Liao, 2005)

"An expert system is one that has expert rules and avoids blind search, reasons by manipulating symbols, grasps fundamental domain principles, and has complete weaker reasoning methods to fall back on when expert rules fail and to use in producing explanations. It deals with difficult problems in a complex domain, can take a problem description in lay terms and convert it to an internal representation appropriate for processing with its expert rules, and it can reason about its own knowledge (or lack thereof), especially to reconstruct inference paths rationally for explanation and self-justification" (Dym, 1985)

The general structure of an expert system is shown in Fig. 1 (Dym, 1985; Tisza, 1995). The components of the expert system include - *input/output facilities*, which allow the user to communicate with the expert system and to use and create a database for a specific problem under investigation; *an inference engine*, which contains rules or reasoning methods, that acts upon the input query and knowledge base, data base, to provide solution and justification to the problem stated. This is like an executive that runs the expert system. It fires existing rules according to the problem stated that not only acts on the knowledge/data base to generate solution, but also updates the knowledge/data base by adding new knowledge/data to it; *a knowledge base*, containing the basic knowledge about the field including the facts, beliefs, procedures, expert opinion etc.; *a knowledge acquisition system*, which does the job of acquiring knowledge automatically from varied resources like libraries, experts, other data bases and so on; *a data base*, which is similar to knowledge base, where in quantified data (e.g., material properties, tool conditions, forming machine parameters etc.) pertaining to that field are located that will be used by the inference engine during solution generation; *a data base generation system*, which collects the input given by expert and from other resources so that data base can be developed and updated at any stage of expert system. Both the expert and user are linked to each other so that data, knowledge can be easily updated at the development stage of expert system itself. The inference engine and knowledge/data base are not considered always as entirely separate components and there is a lot of overlap between the concepts of both the components (Dym, 1985). *A knowledge engineer*, expert in artificial intelligent techniques, is the one who structures the expert's knowledge, which will be shared by the user. Sometimes the expert himself acts as a knowledge engineer. However in this case, there are two practical dangers worth noting. One is that the domain experts developing their own expert system must learn a lot about knowledge/data representation. This will become clearer in due course, and should not underestimate the immensity of the task. On the other hand, though knowledge engineers learn a lot about the field on which the expert system is built, they should remember that they are not field experts and hence should remain as talented amateur in that field and efficient knowledge base builders (Dym, 1985).

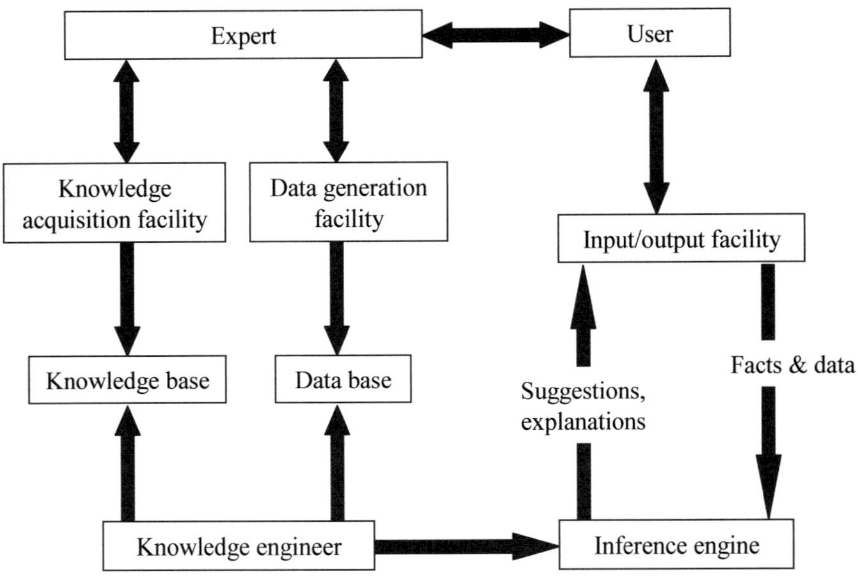

Fig. 1. Basic structure of an expert system (Dym, 1985; Tisza, 1995)

Expert system incorporates three types of knowledge: factual or data oriented knowledge, rule based knowledge, and procedural knowledge (Wang et al., 1991) embodied within a model base. The trend at present is to exploit the convergence of all the three kinds of knowledge representation in a single system. The knowledge base is contained in a set of rules or conditions and a secondary data base. Each production rule represents knowledge about a field, expressed in antecedent-consequent form and a knowledge base may contain hundreds of rules. For example, typical knowledge base can have some 700 rules on maximum load required for forming, press requirements and material properties. There are other ways of knowledge base representation like semantic networks, frame system etc. (Dym, 1985). In semantic network, there are set of *nodes* that represent objects, concepts, events etc. (say engines, hydraulic presses, die, burning) and *links* that connect the nodes and represent their interrelation (say function of, subset of, part of, in process). Frames are data structures where in, instead of symbols, declarative statements about the objects are included in pre-defined slots. The information can include material properties, engine names, manufacture name, applicable names etc. One can exploit the advantage of each of the representation ideas to have an efficient expert system (Dym, 1985). For instance, production rules, simplify the generation of explanation and prompts the user as it is easy to change antecedent-consequent "IF-THEN" form or rules into a questionnaire. In a rule that states "IF the effective strain rate in the notch to bulk is greater than or equal to 4 THEN the sheet material fails" can be seen as an explanation – "The effective strain rate in the notch to bulk greater than or equal to 4 indicates sheet material failure" or as a question – "Is the effective strain rate in the notch to bulk greater than 4?". Thus an expert system might combine semantic network to relate objects to each other, a frame system that exposes the features of individual objects, and production rules to uncover the properties of individual objects.

Inference engine basically work on inference rules that tries to derive answers from a knowledge base. Backward chaining and forward chaining are the two main methods of reasoning when using inference rules. Forward chaining is data driven, and backward chaining is goal driven. An inference engine using forward chaining searches the inference rules until it finds one in which the 'IF' clause is 'true'. It then concludes the 'THEN' clause and adds this information to its data. It would continue to perform this operation until a goal is attained. An inference engine using backward chaining would search the inference rules until it finds one which has a 'THEN' clause that closely matches a prescribed goal. If the 'IF' clause of that inference rule is not true, then it is added to the list of goals. The selection of inference engine is important and is coupled to the nature of task the system is intended to perform. The selection of inference engine depends mainly on memory allocation for solving the problem, solution space required, tentative reasoning about the domain, and whether or not the data are noisy and varying with time. Initially LISP, the list processing language; Prolog, a logic oriented language are used, but an important trend in the expert system market is the evolution of systems towards more performance oriented programming languages like C, Pascal, Fortran etc. The reason for such a shift is two fold. Not only the inference engines run faster (100 times faster than older LISP based), but also promote ease of integration with other software applications. Nowadays various methodologies are available to construct expert systems in any chosen field. Expert systems can be developed based on rules, knowledge systems, neural networks, fuzzy system, object oriented methodology, case based reasoning, system modeling, intelligent agents, database methodology etc. (Liao, 2005).

Sheet metal forming is one of the important manufacturing processes used predominantly in automotive, aerospace, electronics, electrical, house-hold appliances, and building sectors. This process involves plastic deformation of metallic sheet materials to make sheet metal components for any application. Typical applications can be seen in cars, washing machines, air plane wings, house-hold appliances like gas cylinders, beverage cans, and building roofs. The sheet metal forming processes include deep drawing, stamping, bending, rolling, spinning, cutting, and blanking. Generally the sheet components are made by any one of the mentioned process or combination of processes. Most of the sheet forming processes requires a sheet material to be formed; tools like die, punch, sheet holder, draw bead, mandrel and machines to perform the operation. The material properties like chemical composition, microstructure, texture; mechanical properties viz., yield strength, ultimate tensile strength, elongation; formability factors like strain hardening exponent, anisotropy index, strain path; process parameters like friction conditions between sheet and tools, working temperature, strain rate, blank holding force, draw bead restraining force; and finally tool (die, punch) geometry influence the sheet forming behavior in a compounding fashion.

In industrial practice, the sheet forming engineer should be aware of the process sequence, tool design aspect, process parameter design, sheet material behavior, blank design, and machine usage for successful fabrication of sheet parts. For example, the process sequence required for single stage and multi-stage components are different. Similarly the tool design requirements for making a sheet product made of un-welded blank and tailor welded blanks (two or more sheets of different thickness, grades etc. welded before forming) are not same because of the presence of different thickness, grade sheets, and weld line movement. The properties and behavior of the sheet material play a vital role in deciding its applicability in making a sheet part. The material behavior requirement will differ from product to product and hence knowledge on materials used is essential.

It is known that the parameters mentioned above determine the sheet formability in a synergistic manner. Designing sheet product for a typical application will be successful only by knowing the appropriate material behavior, process parameter design, process sequence, tool and machine design, and specific issues pertaining to advances in material and forming technology. Predicting these sheet stamping parameters in advance will be helpful in determining the formability of any sheet part. In order to fulfill this requirement, one has to perform lot of simulation trials and experiments separately for each of the cases which is time consuming and resource intensive. Automotive sheet forming designers will greatly benefit if 'expert systems' are available for sheet stamping that can deliver its forming behavior for varied material, process and tool conditions. Developing an expert system or knowledge based system, especially in fields like material forming and deformation behavior, die design, casting design, machining processes, metallurgy etc. is of interest to manufacturing and design engineers. In this chapter, the expert system and its application to predict the sheet metal formability in terms of tool, process and material design will be discussed through published literature. The expert system based analyses in sheet process design, process planning, strip layout design, tool design, material forming will be focused. The various techniques used to develop expert systems will be presented. The available expert systems and their applicability in sheet forming field will be highlighted. Finally an expert system research scheme that is being developed to predict the formability of Tailor Welded Blanks (TWB) will be discussed with case study results.

2. Process design

The sheet forming process includes operations like cup drawing, stamping, stretching, bending, ironing, spinning etc. that can be performed by many forming techniques using die, punch, blank holder and other tools. The purpose of process design is to predict and design the sheet forming process at the 'design stage' of a component manufacturing. For instance, the number of stages required and amount of cup drawing that is possible in each stage of a multi stage deep drawing process can be predicted at the design stage itself for successful completion of the sheet product. Similarly an intelligent process design would include closed loop control of blank holding force for changing friction conditions during forming. There are many expert systems (ES)/knowledge based systems (KBS) available for sheet process design. The sheet forming processes and techniques by which process design is performed is described here.

Mostly bending, deep drawing, and general stamping (say industrial sheet parts) are concerned for ES development. The applicability of expert system in enhancing the bending process design was demonstrated by Lin and Peing (Lin & Peing, 1994). In this, a prototype of sheet metal bending expert system is developed. This ES is capable of predicting the pressure, width of die shoulder, minimum flange length and product inner radius for a given set of bending and material input. With this data, the punch and die numbers are inferred and their drawings are given as result using the graphic mechanism in the ES. This is presented with an example of V-bending (Lin & Peing, 1994), where the bend angle and material of the sheet were given as input. The predictions are based on 'IF-THEN' rules within the ES that are constructed with the help of lot of qualitative data base and experience based knowledge base. Here PC/AT was chosen as the computer hardware and artificial intelligence language LISP (LISt Processing), which has a powerful symbol processing ability, was used as system construction language. Like wise, an Intelligent Design Environment (IDE) which is a knowledge based system, was developed (Palani et al., 1994) that provides a method of integration, automation and optimization of sheet metal forming. IDE integrates knowledge base, finite element analysis and geometric modelers in AI framework. For the inputs like geometry of the sheet and material, process constraints given to the system, the outputs like optimized die geometry, material and process parameters for successful forming operation will be delivered. This was demonstrated in their work (Palani et al., 1994) by analyzing automotive inner panel. In this, 'IF-THEN' rules like "IF strain distributions should be uniform, THEN increase the critical radius, AND change the lubrication; OR change the blank size and shape" were used and their IDE can diagnose 'splitting' failure. It can effect changes in material properties including thickness, friction, BHF, drawbead geometry, blank size for evaluating the optimum forming operation. In the case of automotive inner panel, the final decision on modifying sharp corners improved the strain distribution and die geometry. A knowledge based process layout system (CAPP) based on decision tables (Sing & Rao, 1997) was constructed for axi-symmetrical deep drawn cup which can deliver a set of highest feasible process parameters for die design purpose for which the final deep drawn product is required as input. In this CAPP system, the knowledge base is represented by 'production rules' and 'frames'. The production rules are based on popular 'IF-THEN' rules like "IF First Draw of mild steels THEN the maximum drawing ratio is 2.2". These rules are represented as decision tables, which makes it very different from other KBS, where in the user can suggest 'Yes', 'No' or 'Don't care' for many rules corresponding to 'condition stubs' entries. The condition stub mainly includes the final cup description like Horizontal elements included, Vertical elements more than one, Concave elements included and many more. Similarly the 'action stub' contains different types of drawn cups like flanged cup, hemispherical cup etc. for which once again 'Yes', 'No' or 'Don't care' entries are suggested for various rules. This system has fuzzy inference like "R1: IF thickness is T_i THEN drawability is M_i, for i = 1…n" which relates drawability and thickness range. Here 'R1' is a fuzzy relation mapping thickness (T_i) and drawability (M_i). 'T_i' and 'M_i' are subsets of sets A (thickness range) and B (drawability) on U and V universe, respectively. These fuzzy inferences are also represented as decision tables containing 'condition stubs' like thickness range, cup without flange and 'action stubs' like drawing rate. These decision tables are made from 'frames', having drawing rates for different types of cups. This system is tested with a 'flanged cup' that is given as input. The system basically evaluates, through analytical models and rules, the blank development, blank layout design, number of draws, clearance, air vent hole, tool radii, and BHF and delivers as output (Sing & Rao, 1997). A component check KBS was made (Shailendra Kumar et al., 2006) which is once again based on 'IF-THEN' rules made from details available with designers, manufacturers, and hand books that can suggest the feature based outputs based on inputs registered about the sheet material and product. This system makes use of Auto LISP and Auto CAD for data representation. An intelligent design system for multi stage deep drawing is also available (Choi et al., 2002). The capability of the system was illustrated with the help of single stage deep drawing, three step deep drawing, and deep drawing with embossing. A user friendly, menu driven decision support system (DSS) was also developed by Faura et al. for sheet metal blanking operation (Faura et al., 2001). The DSS consists of relational database having technical-economic information and collection of processing algorithms created to apply the know-how to the model. The technical knowledge is based on many experiments relating empirically the blanking clearance with edge draw-in, the penetration depth of cracks, and burr height. By providing dialog boxes to facilitate data input and display of output results, it is possible to predict the impact of blanking parameters on the cost and quality (Faura et al., 2001).

Other than the ES described above, there are expert systems that are helpful for web based manufacturing. These ES are generated and used through World Wide Web (WWW) for part and process design. The user can virtually sit in a remote place performing simulations and analyses and finally design the process and part as per their requirement. A virtual design system (VDS) for sheet forming was developed by Hindman and Ousterhout (Hindman & Ousterhout, 1998). This system has web based interface in 'fill out forms' where the user can input the details of forming like material properties, bend allowance, bend radius etc. The forms are framed by html programming and submitted by the user for further processing. The user can also transfer a part to remote shop through file transfer protocol (FTP) for fabrication with worry-free transfer of sensitive data indicating standard security. The VDS is not only demonstrated for 'bending' where final die design is performed, but also for spring back and deep drawing. The system works not only on equations, but also has space for real time simulations of the manufacturing processes. An interesting and efficient Distributed Multi Agent expert System (DMAS) was developed for sheet forming by Karayel and Ozkan (Karayel & Ozkan, 2006). DMAS is a system that operates in an integrated manner with all agents to realize a common objective. Each agent is an expert system containing rules and knowledge base that are at distant places connected through internet. The model proposed consists of knowledge management agent (KMA), product description agent (PDA), calculating and dimensioning agent (CDA), artificial intelligence agent (AIA), die design agent (DDA), assembly and disassembly agent (ADA), operation planning and cost agent (OPCA), validation and verification agent (VVA) and design mediator (DM), all are connected and have specific tasks. For example, the job of PDA is to describe sheet metal component geometry when the design is realized using multi agent system. The sheet metal parts are represented and stored as complete geometric and topological solid in 3D. Such a representation is suitable for display and any engineering analyses and simulation can be performed. The PDA also takes care of feature representation like holes, curvatures, bends, flanges, notches etc. Similarly the purpose of

VVA is to observe any faults and discrepancies in the manufacturing lot and notifies them to KMA. This agent prepares a global report on all faults and their degrees as well. Similarly all other agents are meant for specific purpose. This system will be implemented fully for efficient running of the sheet metal expert system (Karayel & Ozkan, 2006).
There are expert systems/knowledge based systems based on neural network that control the sheet forming processes. One best example would be the adaptive control system developed for controlling the deep drawing process (Manabe et al., 1998) where in neural network is used for initial process parameter identification. In this, chosen input parameters are trained with optimized network architecture and output material properties like strain hardening exponent (n), plastic coefficient (F), anisotropy coefficient (R) are identified. The predicted n, F, R values is used to evaluate the friction coefficient, fracture/wrinkle limit Blank Holder Forces (BHFs) using available equations.. The BHF is optimized for varying friction conditions during the drawing process by in-process sensing information. Corresponding to the current frictional condition, the fracture and wrinkle limit BHFs are modified and the BHF path scheme can be optimized accordingly. This adaptive system, where the BHF is updated continuously with changing friction conditions, was demonstrated by monitoring thinning distribution of wall region of the cup and comparing it with the constant BHF case. The thinning behavior is found to be improved in the case of adaptive deep drawing system (Manabe et al., 1998). Summing up one can say that, deep drawing, bending and stamping of industrial sheet parts are generally modeled using expert system for planning and controlling the sheet forming process. Also the expert systems used for process design are mainly based on production rules (IF-THEN rules), web based process control strategies, and neural network based data modeling and process control or a combination of different techniques. In the case of ES based on rules, predominantly AutoLISP is used for data handling, in conjunction with AutoCAD for graphics representation. One can also refer the state of the art report by Duflou et al. (Duflou et al., 2005) on computer aided process planning for sheet bending.

3. Process planning and process sequence design

Table 1 shows the details of process planning and sequence design in sheet forming. Most of the literature suggests that 'IF-THEN' variety is used for knowledge base implementation, while few of them are based on specified algorithms, design rules, fuzzy set theory etc. The sheet operations considered are axi-symmetric forming (like drawing), blanking, bending, general stamping sequence, and specific sheet parts like rotor and stator. The KBS developed are validated with industrial shop floor trials having simple to complex geometries.

4. Strip layout design

The strip layout design exercise is like a tailor's job. Here the tailor maps the different parts of the shirt and makes a layout as per the customer's choice, efficient cloth utilization and fashion. Later the layout is used for stitching shirts. Similarly strip layout involves laying out the material strip that is passed through the press in order to produce stamping, exactly as it will appear after all operations have been performed on its parts (Ann & Kai, 1994). The strip layout design is an art by itself, wherein the experience and practice in the light of reality decides the quality of the stamped sheet product. In early days, the strip layout was done manually. The trial and error method followed resulted in maximum material

S. No.	Publication details	Process details in expert system	Purpose of expert system	Technique used for developing expert system	Knowledge generation modes	System deliverables	Illustrations (if any)
1	Ong et al., 1997	Brake forming; tools having punch, flat sheet, bend sheet, die, finger stops	CAPP system for process sequence design	Fuzzy set theory	--	Bending process sequence	A complex part is used here and the system suggests two different bending sequences with six stages in each sequence
2	Sitaraman et al., 1991	Axi-symmetric sheet forming	Knowledge based system for process sequence design	IF-THEN rules variety like "If the input object geometry is axi-symmetric, then the blank is circular"; Knowledge base & inference engine in Prolog, Analysis module in Fortran	Literature, industrial brochure, industrial visits, experts opinion etc.	Process sequence with intermediate product geometry	Flanged shell having two diameters, tapering concave shell, Reverse geometry; System analyzes the process based on product geometry (1st pass) and product formability (2nd pass) details
3	Uzsoy et al., 1991	General sheet parts giving importance to bending & hole punching	Process planning for sheet forming operations – binding & hole making	Rule based KBS, IF-THEN variety like "If there is a hole on a bent edge, then do the hole before the bend"; implemented using Turbo prolog	Discussion with die designers & process planners, die design & forming handbooks	Bending & hole making sequence with die number in which the process occurs	A simple sheet part with total of eight features; four holes with two holes of radius 2 units, two holes of radius 1 unit, & four bends
4	Gupta et al., 1998	Bending operations	Automated process planning for robotic sheet metal bending press brakes; system contains central operation planner, tooling & set up planner, grasping planner, motion planner	State-space search formulation based on A* algorithm; sequence decision is based on cheapest total time (total time = execution time + repositioning time + set up time); specific modules are based on rules & constraints; Implemented using C++	--	Operation sequence, tools & robot grippers needed, tool layout grasp positions, gage, robot motion plans for product making	Separate illustrations are given for each of the modules for different operations; Presently sheet with 23 bends can be addressed for its process planning & other sequences.

5	Park et al., 1998	Axi-symmetric deep-drawing products based on G&TR strategy	Computer aided process planning design system – Pro_Deep, having four modules – input, geometrical design, test & rectification & user modification	IF-THEN rules based system; Implemented in AutoLISP on the AutoCAD	Plasticity theories, handbooks, experimental results & knowledge of field experts	Process sequence with intermediate object geometry, process parameters - drawing load, BHF, clearance, cup-drawing coefficients	Flanged shell with two diameters, stepped cup, motor housing
6	Choi & Kim, 2001	Making rotor and stator parts with blanking operation	CAD/CAM system having nine modules – input and shape treatment, flat pattern layout, production feasibility check, blank layout, strip layout, die layout, data conversion, modeling, post processing	Design rules for blanking or piercing like 'If holes to be pierced are close to each other or are not related to function, the holes are distributed for many processes' and formulae like $P_{face} = F_d / L_{Shear}\ t\ BLR$	Plasticity theories, experimental results & knowledge of field experts	Generating automatically NC data to match tooling requirements by checking dimensions according to the drawings of the die layout module	Stator and Rotor parts
7	Rajender Singh & Sekhon, 2005	Sheet metal operations like piercing, blanking, notching, forming, cropping, shearing, trimming, clipping, parting, slitting, perforating, bending & drawing	Process planning for small and medium scale sheet metal industries based on rules (150 nos.) implemented in AutoLISP on AutoCAD	IF-THEN rules like 'If, 0.01 < minimum accuracy needed on part in mm< 2.0; and feature required on part = Line cut then, required operation=slitting'	Knowledge of process planners, die designers, Handbooks, monographs, journals, & industrial brochures	Optimal process plan for sheet metal operations	Sheet parts used in Indian telephone industries, India (blanking, plating) & Indo-Asian Fuse Gear Ltd., India (piercing, blanking, & plating)
8	Ciurana et al., 2006	Meant for drawing operations in sheet forming	Computer aided process planning in sheet forming based on activity model	Based on design rules implemented in visual basic with GUI, & application development environment	Discussion wit process planners, scientific community, enterprises	Drawing process steps, dimensions of steps, route selection, lay out die definition	An industrial part is simulated for validation

Table 1. Details of expert systems for process sequence and planning design in sheet forming

utilization and is still followed in many small and medium scale industries. Nowadays there are many computer aided systems that takes care of the strip layout design even in complex parts. A knowledge based system for strip layout design was presented by Ann and Kai (Ann & Kai, 1994), includes two important modules viz., part orientation module and sequence of operation module. The part orientation module is meant for providing recommendations about the appropriate 'part orientation' in the parent strip, while the sequence of operation module is mainly to suggest the proper design in terms of strip layout in each of the four operations of the progressive die - piercing, blanking, bending and trimming. The 'part orientation module' has few sub-modules like *customer's specification*, where the user can opt for any strip orientation; *material optimization*, in which the KBS will decide the appropriate orientation, part-to-part and part-to-edge distances, space for pilot hole and their locations; *type of end product removal method*, where the rules are meant for checking the type of end-product removal methods employed to remove the final stamped part from the scrap strip; *smooth strip movement through the die*, contains rules to check whether the strip is rigid enough to move through the die smoothly without any obstruction due to collapsing of the strip. Subsequently, it will inform the user to orientate the strip in a compromised orientation. In such cases, the part-to-part and part-to-edge gaps will have to be increased for more strip rigidity at the cost of increased material wastage. The four forming operations in the 'sequence of operation module' contain many phases in each of them. In the case of 'blanking', the phases - shape of blanking portion, location tolerance of two blanking portions, distance between nearer edges of two blanking portions, dimension tolerance, and strip movement through the die are present. The other forming operations also contain similar phases. Both the modules work as per the rules framed through 'decision tables' (Ann & Kai, 1994). Finally the applicability of the knowledge based system is demonstrated with an example. A strip layout design for sheet metal on progressive die (Kumar & Singh, 2008) is also based on 'IF-THEN' rules. In this, many rules for strip layout design and conditions for piloting operations are listed. The rules are coded in AutoLISP and interfaced with AutoCAD for layout modeling. Finally the expert system is tested for brass sheet metal for its validity. An interesting work was conducted (Nye, 2000) which is aimed to design strip layout for optimal raw material utilization based on the '*Minkowski sum*'. According to this concept, if two blanks are considered, 'A' and 'B', they will overlap only if $A \oplus (-B)$ contains the origin. To avoid overlapping between blanks, they need to be translated relative to each other. This relative translation causes a similar translation of the Minkowski sum, and when the Minkowski sum no longer contains the origin, the blank overlap is eliminated. This property leads to the mapping of '*strip pitch*' - distance to the edge of the Minkowski sum, and '*strip width*' - maximum perpendicular distance between the strip longitudinal axis (through the origin) and the perimeter of $A \oplus (-B)$. The material utilization can be easily calculated as a function of blank orientation, once the Minkowski sum is generated (Nye, 2000). The strip orientation in the parent sheet is represented by 'sweepline' vector, which sweeps through a range of orientations and is anchored at the origin. The raw material utilization, strip width and pitch were evaluated with the help of expressions derived. This concept of strip layout design is demonstrated by T-shaped blank, for which the optimal blank orientation occurs at θ = 18.43° and 161.56°, with a corresponding material utilization of 53.3% (Nye, 2000). The metal stamping layouts using analytic hierarchy process method is also an important contribution for strip nesting design (Rao, 2004). To explain briefly, this method necessitates the decision makers to develop a hierarchical structure for the factors and to provide judgments about the relative significance of each of these factors and specifying a preference for each decision alternative with respect to each factor. It provides a ranking order indicating the overall preference for each of the decision alternatives (Rao, 2004). This method is helpful in selecting suitable strip layout from a large number of available strip-layouts for a given metal stamping operation. From the above references, it can be said that 'IF-THEN' rules based strip layout design system are predominantly used, while stand alone efficient algorithms for strip nesting are also developed to improve the skill set of stamping designers.

5. Tool design

This section focuses on the development of expert system or knowledge based system for designing the press tools (like punch, die etc.) used for sheet stamping operation. Emphasis is given on the input-output details of the system, structure and design methodology used in the system and case study illustrations. It is observed from the selected references that progressive die design involving varied forming operations, tool design for bending, drawing die design and specific applications like industrial parts, roll forming etc. are dealt with extensively. An attempt has been made to automate the progressive metal stamping die design through knowledge base approach (Cheok et al., 1994). The main input to the system is the 3D representation of a product and the system delivers the die to transform the strip into the stamped (or final) product. Some of the crucial issues to be addressed while automating the die design are work shape representation, die components representation, punch shape recognition and decomposition, staging and assembly of die components, operation simulation of various die operations. In the work shape representation, using existing CAD/CAM system, a 2D drawing of the strip layout can be obtained. In order to convert this data into useful information like detailing the topological relations of the various features of the work shape, semantic network based Constructive Solid Geometry (CSG) representation of the workpiece is considered in the KBES. In CSG, the external profile and internal features of the workpiece are represented as 'nodes' where the geometry details about the work shape is stored. There are other decisions pertaining to die design like holes that can be punched in same or different stations are registered as 'slots' like Box515, Cyl516 etc. It can be understood that the CSG tree of a workpiece provides a wealth of topological information that can be processed by declarative knowledge statements in a KBES to guide the synthesis of a die. In the case of punch profile recognition, the KBES contains twelve different geometric features that are used to select the usable punch profiles for internal profiles. If a suitable match cannot be achieved, the system will decompose the profile of the internal feature into a combination of the pre-defined shapes using a 'divide and match' approach. This is achieved by dividing the original punch profiles into a combination of smaller profiles of standard dimensions that can be included in the twelve punch shapes available in the KBES. The 'divide and match' approach is guided by number of condition statements in the KBES. Similarly the selection of punches for external profiles is also governed by few rules and procedures. In order to represent the die components, model based reasoning (MBR) approach is followed. MBR requires die components to be represented in such a way that their geometrical modeling information, their parametric dimensions – stored in database, and the algorithmic mathematical functions for design can interact with declarative knowledge statements governing the synthesis of these components. The standard die components can be represented by part identification and parametric dimensions. The data on its location and orientation is also provided when inserting into the die assembly. The non-standard die components are complex and hence need more information to describe them that depends on other components in the sub-assembly too. As an example, the topology of a punch plate depends on the size and location of the punches it carries, their mounting arrangements, and the size and location of the fasteners and dowels. In this, rules and functions are defined that require resolution of conflict and that do not require resolution of conflict (Cheok et al., 1994). The staging of punch operations and selection of pilot holes are based on IF-THEN rules. Finally all the different components of the KBES are implemented on a PC that uses AutoCAD extension modeling for solid modeling and Kappa PC to provide the object oriented programming capabilities. The routines that convert geometries into features are written in C++ for efficient working. Similarly 'logic programming' has been used to plan the process in sheet forming with progressive dies (George-Christoper et al., 2005). The product category targeted is U-shaped with bending and cutting operation predominantly. This expert system consists of three modules like *part design, process planning, and tool design*. The data gathered is introduced into the system in the form of IF-THEN rules. Questions are posed to the customer to obtain all necessary information, related to geometry, machine tool characteristics, etc. Clarifications, explanations, intermediate results and prompts for corrections are in a textual format, and the user is also supported by information from files and figures in order to answer system questions. The code is developed in Amzi Prolog and consists of about 3000 lines. The logic programming using Prolog is a declarative language. A program consists of Predicates, each containing a functor (name) and a number of components (arguments). Each predicate is defined by a clause which can be a fact or a rule. A Prolog program is initiated by a high-level question, which triggers some predicates, which in turn may trigger more, thus propagating the question to deeper levels. In order to obtain a solution to the question asked, a path leading from deeper levels to the highest level should be proven to be valid. This path spans several predicates involved in providing the high level solution. The process of finding a solution is a searching process, which needs to be conducted efficiently and smartly. In part design module, there are about 16 main rules that govern the design process. These generic rules are used to evaluate the important parameters like part thickness, type of material, bending tolerance, flanged hole characteristics etc. that determine the manufacturability. A clause reads 'If the actual distance is above 3 mm and greater than 1.5 times the sheet thickness, then there is no problem' for steel material in the case of minimum distance between any features. In process planning module, there are similar rules that guide the entire process. The knowledge representation is based on predicates that contain information about the part state and the list of processes that have to be performed. Similar to part design, tool design module also functions with the help of rules like 'For processes executed on the vertical plane, side cam mechanisms should be used'. They are executed by 'facts' which contains the query like 'How large is the die?' with choices of 'small, medium, or large' (George-Christoper et al., 2005). This system is illustrated with an industrial example of forming strip in progressive die and the design correlates well with the actual design.

Bending tool design is another important issue to be discussed. There are expert systems based on 'rules' for bending tool design. There are few based on neural network too. Neural network based bending tool design (Lin & Chang, 1996) based on back propagation network requiring machine inputs like pressure capacity of the bending machine, the bending length of the product, the open height of the die, and the punch stroke, is efficient in designing the final tooling for bending using pattern classification capability of the BP neural network. The ANN modeling is performed under digital and conditional attributes mode. For the inputs specified, the output of the system is the bending machine code containing information like pressure capacity, maximum stroke, bending speed, motor power, number of cylinders. Esche (Esche et al., 1996) developed a process and die design methodology for multi step forming (say deep drawing) of round cups. ASFEX - Axisymmetric Sequence Forming Expert System was developed initially in MPROLOG. Later this was transferred to C/C++ environment on UNIX platform. The main aim of the system is to develop the process sequence, especially for multi step forming operation, and tool configuration for the whole forming process. In process sequence design, both geometry and formability based decisions will be taken. The process is then analyzed by finite element simulation to check the feasibility of the production. Later tooling for each stage of forming operation will be decided. There are standard steps and rules to evaluate the forming sequence in the system. The system is demonstrated through a sample simulation of round cup made of Aluminium alloy material and compared with experiments. The radial strain and thickness are also compared with experiments and the results are found to be satisfactory (Esche et al., 1996). Similar expert system for drawing dies is seen in (Lin et al., 2008) also, except that the design is based on parametric design system. The efficiency of the system to improve the design quality is demonstrated through inner wheel housing part.

Roll forming is a continuous bending operation, in which the ductile sheets are passed through consecutive set of rolls, or stands, each performing only incremental, prescribed bending operation, till the actual cross-section profile is obtained. This process is particularly suitable for long strips of large quantities, with minimum material handling. Expert systems are available for roll forming pass design that are based on neural network and shape element idea. In the case of neural network based ES (Downes & Hartley, 2006), Radial Basis Function (RBF) is used for training the input data. The example taken for study has four bends and three parallel surfaces connected by slanting sides. The four bends are quantified by four angles φ_1, φ_2, φ_3, and φ_4 that forms input for ANN. The ANN system predicts the output which is the location of the design data. There are almost 63 different locations for the design data that are present with the industrial collaborator. Classification of the data depends on a number of section parameters, such as the total number of bends, sheet thickness and sheet width prior to forming. The system developed in this project searches the 63 storage locations to find integral shapes. If a similar shape is identified it will have the same number of bends, and each corresponding bend angle φ_1, φ_2, φ_3, and φ_4 will have a similar value (Downes & Hartley, 2006). In the case of shape element idea (Shen et al., 2003), the roll formed part is visualized as combination of forming of each part. The relationship of space geometry is relatively fixed and the forming steps of these parts are almost same. These parts are called as 'shape element'. The validity of the system is presented with few examples like roll forming with symmetrical section, non-symmetrical section, welded pipe, and complex shape of steel window section (Shen et al., 2003). There are expert systems for press selection (Singh & Sekhon, 1999) also. The press selection expert system belongs to IF-THEN variety following forward chaining method. The rules are based on information obtained from experienced designers, shop floor engineers, handbooks, journals, monographs and industrial brochures. This system suggests the press tonnage, recommended presses, optimum press and unit manufacturing cost for the posed inputs or queries (Singh & Sekhon, 1999). There are expert systems for specific applications like die design for automotive parts (Lin & Kuo, 2008), progressive die design for electron gun grid parts (Park, 1999) etc. A fully integrated CAD/CAM/CAE system was developed (Lin & Kuo, 2008) for stamping dies of automotive sheet parts that functions with the help of high end softwares like CATIA for layout diagram design and die structure analysis, STRIM software for die face design, DYNAFORM for formability analysis and CADCEUS for tooling path generation and simulation. Finally the stamping die development is illustrated for the 'trunk lid outer panel' (Lin & Kuo, 2008).

6. Material forming

Table 2 details the expert/knowledge base system (or models) to predict the material forming behavior like flow stress, shear strength, material failure, mechanical properties, residual stress etc. The materials considered are steel, Al alloys, Zircaloy, welds, and processes like rolling practice, shot peening are modeled. Most of the techniques used are ANN based and few others are based on design rules, specific theories and algorithms. ANN is found to reproduce the results with maximum accuracy showing its efficiency over rule based systems. The material behavior thus predicted is of academic importance and industrial practice as well. TENSALUM, an expert system used to predict the stress-strain data of Al alloys, implemented in industries, shortened the testing time by approximately 300-400% in comparison with other programs in market (Emri & Kovacic, 1997). Similarly the KBS for materials management developed by Trethewey et al. (Trethewey et al., 1998) which is demonstrated for the selection of coating for marine applications is of practical importance. More details on the KBS for material forming are given in table 2.

7. Expert system for tailor welded blanks (TWB) forming

Tailor Welded Blanks (TWB) are blanks of similar or dissimilar thicknesses, materials, coatings etc. welded in a single plane before forming. This welded blank is then formed like un-welded blanks to manufacture automotive components, with appropriate tooling and forming conditions. Applications of TWB include car door inner panel, deck lids, bumper, side frame rails etc. in the automotive sector.

Some of the advantages of using TWBs in the automotive sector are: (1) weight reduction and hence savings in fuel consumption, (2) distribution of material thickness and properties resulting in part consolidation which results in cost reduction and better quality, stiffness and tolerances, (3) greater flexibility in component design, (4) re-usage of scrap materials to have new stamped products and, (5) improved corrosion resistance and product quality. (Ganesh & Narasimhan, 2008). The forming behavior of TWBs is critically influenced by thickness and material combinations of the blanks welded; weld conditions like weld orientation, weld location, and weld properties in a synergistic fashion. Designing TWB for a typical application will be successful only by knowing the appropriate thickness, strength combinations, weld line location and profile, number of welds, weld orientation and weld zone properties. Predicting these TWB parameters in advance will be helpful in determining the formability of TWB part in comparison to that of un-welded base materials. In order to fulfill this requirement, one has to perform lot of simulation, experimental trials separately for each of the cases which are time consuming and resource intensive. This can be avoided if an 'expert system' is available for TWBs that can deliver its forming behavior for varied weld and blank conditions.

S. No.	Publication details	Purpose of expert/knowledge base system	Material details	Technique used	Testing method & data base details	System deliverables
1	Emri & Kovacic, 1997	To test the mechanical properties of Al and Al alloys. The ES is called as TENSALUM	Mainly for Al and Al alloy sheets; Can be updated for materials like polymers, wood, textile fabrics & leather	--	Tensile testing is performed based on the data base including test conditions, material, product form, elongation, temper condition, mechanical property limits made from various resources	Stress-strain data is measured from the testing machine for the inputs provided. The tedious procedure of comparing the values of mechanical properties that the tested material should meet with the standards during manual experiments is completely avoided when the ES is used.
2	Qiang et al, 2006	ES named as IndBASEweb-HT is an intelligent database web tool system of simulation for heat treatment process. This system is capable of performing Metallo-thermo-mechanical coupled analyses.	Meant for metallic materials suitable for heat treating conditions	Data mining technology is used to analyze the data from different aspects and finding correlations or patterns among dozens of fields in large relational database.	Database is developed through technical references & experiments	Phase transformation physical properties, heat physical properties, mechanics physical properties, mechanical properties, retrieve element and standard of the material, and display the characteristic chart of each material.
3	Trethewey et al., 1998	Generic model of the knowledge structure of materials performance, viz., materials selection and failure analysis, has been developed	--	Certainty theory is used to judge exact inferences. Certainty factor is defined as a measure of belief and disbelief based on evidence is used as decision making index. Visual Basic is used to create inference engine and microsoft Access for the database.	Data base contains material performance knowledge & corrosion details. The data retrieval is done through case based reasoning. The data generated is obtained from domain expert, knowledge engineer and transferred to computer through expertise elicitation shell.	The system identifies failure modes & material, geometric properties. The failure modes like corrosion, creep, deformation, fatigue, fracture, surface damage and wear erosion will be identified, after diagnoses. Properties include melting point, yield strength, bond strength etc.

4	Calcaterra et al., 2000	Prediction of mechanical properties of spheroidal cast iron	Spheroidal cast iron was made for different chemical composition and other casting parameters that has become input for the model	Neural network is used to build the model. The NN with different hidden layers and neurons were evaluated for investigation.	Many test samples were made using varied chemical composition and casting parameters and tensile tested for UTS evaluation. This forms the data for validating the ANN model	UTS of the sample obtained through tensile test. This is compared with the reference value for checking the adequacy.
5	Rao & Prasad, 1995	Flow stress prediction during hot deformation	Medium carbon steels tested under different strain, strain-rate and temperatures	ANN based on back propagation network with two hidden layers and 40 hidden neurons	Experimental data was used to train the network; Strain, strain-rate & temperature were input parameters for predicting the flow stress (σ)	Flow stress of the material as function of T, $\dot{\varepsilon}$, & ε
6	Shashi Kumar et al., 2007	Flow stress prediction during hot deformation	Different carbon steels with varying carbon equivalent at different strain, strain-rate and temperature	ANN based on recurrent self-organizing neuro fuzzy networks	Experimental runs varied in the range of 1000-20000; Strain, strain-rate & temperature were input parameters for predicting the flow stress (σ)	$\sigma = f(\varepsilon, \dot{\varepsilon}, T, \%C)$
7	Karatas et al., 2009	Study the impact of shot peening on residual stresses and predicting the same	Shot peened steel sample of C-1020 material	ANN based on back propagation learning algorithm with one hidden layer having four neurons;	Experimental results were used as training data set; Shot peening and depth of surface as inputs & residual stress as output	Residual stress as a function of depth from surface & shot peening
8	Vasudevan et al., 2005	Predicting the shear strength of stainless steel & Zr-2 welds	Austenitic stainless steel welds and Zr-4 welds	Multilayer preceptron based ANN is adopted to model the system; 6-20-2 architecture with 20 neurons in hidden layer	AE signals generated during the spacer pad welding were used as input for ANN	Shear strength of stainless steel & Zr-2 welds

Table 2. Details of expert systems in material forming

The main objective of the present research work is to develop an 'expert system' for welded blanks that can predict their tensile, deep drawing, forming behavior under varied base material and weld conditions using different formability tests, material models, and formability criteria. It is decided to develop the expert system in conjunction with Artificial Neural Network (ANN). The data required for the expert system development is obtained through simulations only. PAM STAMP 2G a finite element code is used to generate data for varied base material and TWB conditions. The proposed expert system design for TWB forming is shown in Fig. 2 (Veera Babu et al., 2009). This expert system is expected to involve three different phases. All the three phases have a design mode of operation where an initial expert system is created and put in place. The created expert system is then operated in use and update mode.

In Phase 1, while the expert system is designed, a range of material properties and TWB conditions are defined within which ANN models are developed to predict the results as discussed in the earlier sections. The same phase while operated in the usage mode, the user selects base material properties and TWB conditions within the chosen range for application and prediction of formability. In this phase, user can select different material models viz., strain hardening laws and yield theories to predict the forming behavior. There is no single strain hardening law and yield theory that can predict the forming behavior of TWBs made of varied sheet materials accurately. Hence in the design mode, ANN models will be developed to predict the forming behavior using different material models. As a result, in the usage mode of the expert system, the user can opt for desired material models to predict the forming characteristics.

Phase 2 involves selecting the forming behavior to be predicted for chosen base material and weld conditions. In the design mode, tensile behavior, formability characteristics, deep drawability of welded blanks will be simulated by standard formability tests. Different category of industrial sheet parts will be simulated and expert system will be developed to predict their forming behavior. The global tensile behavior of TWB viz., stress-strain curve, yield strength, ultimate tensile strength, elongation, strain hardening exponent and strength co-efficient will be monitored. Formability properties like forming limit curve, percentage thinning, dome height at failure, failure location will be predicted by Limit Dome Height (LDH) test and in-plane stretching tests using different limit strain criteria (say M-K analysis, thickness gradient based necking criterion, effective strain rate criterion, semi empirical approach etc.). Cup deep drawability response like draw depth, weld line movement, punch force, failure location, earing and draw-in profile can be predicted. Also it is planned to develop ANN model and expert system for predicting the formability of application (or industry) specific sheet parts made of welded blanks. In the usage mode, the user selects the type of test results that is required to be predicted.

In phase 3 the training, testing, usage and updating the ANN predictions with simulation results will be performed. In the design mode operation, various ANNs are created and validated for predicting the forming behavior (enumerated in Phase 2) for various combination of material properties and TWB conditions and constitutive behavior (enumerated in Phase 1). In the usage mode, the user predicts the required forming behavior for an initially chosen material, TWB condition and constitutive behavior. If the forming behavior predicted is not indicative of a good stamped product, the user changes the above said conditions till he gets satisfactory results. In the absence of this expert system, the user will have to run time consuming and resource intensive simulation for this iterative stage. In

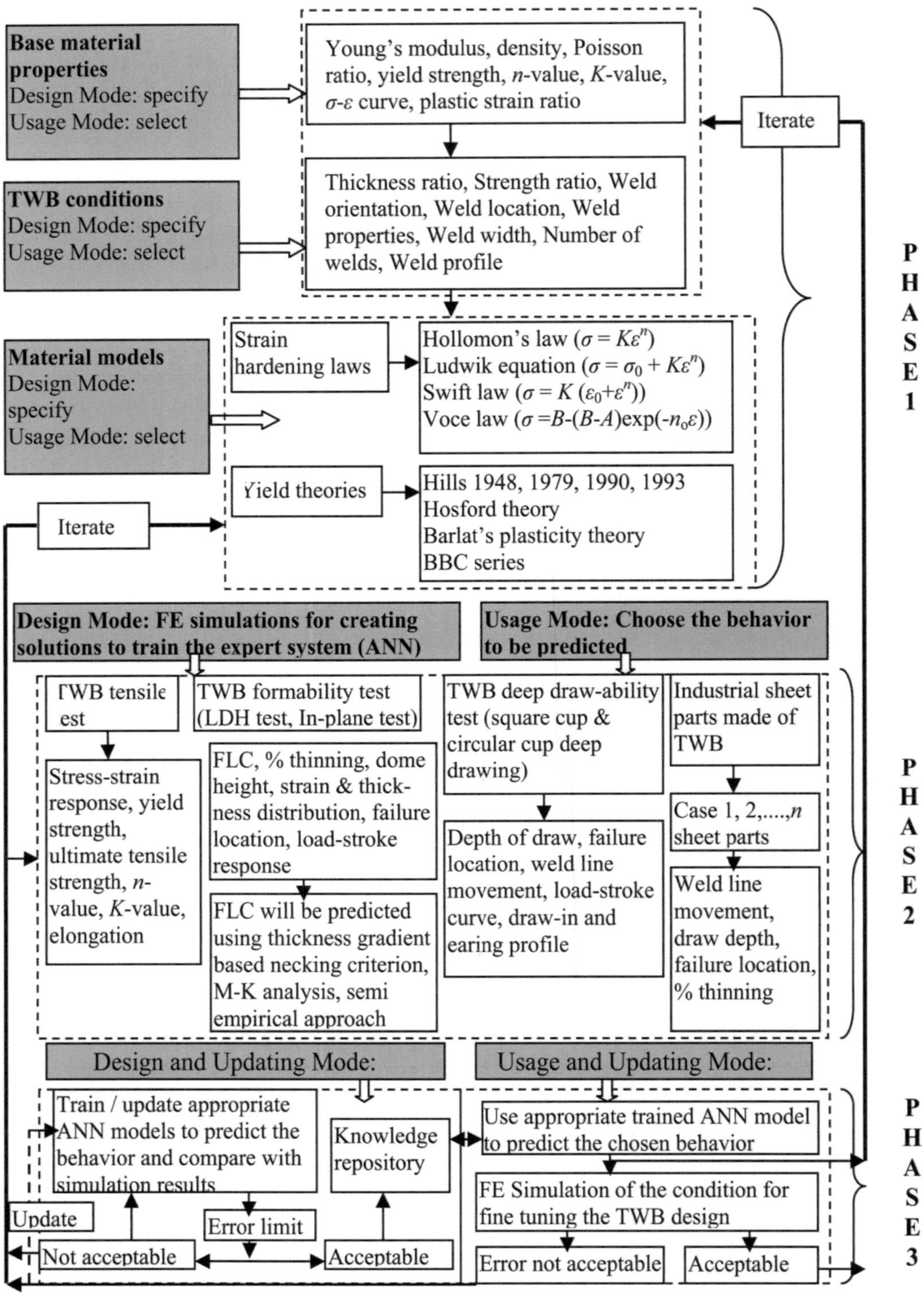

Fig. 2. Expert system proposed for TWB forming (Veera Babu et al., 2009)

the usage mode, if the results are not with in the expected error limit, the user will have the choice of selecting different material models for predicting the required forming behavior as described earlier and/or the expert system is updated with the specific case by updating the ANN models to predict the case within acceptable error limits. In this way, the expert system also learns form the application cases, enhancing the range and success rate of predictions.

In this chapter, some representative expert system prediction like the stress-strain behavior, draw-in profile during cup deep drawing, and forming limit curve are presented. The tools required for tensile test, deep drawing test, Limit dome height test simulation and modeling details can be obtained from (Veera Babu et al., 2009; Siva Krishna, 2009). The six different input parameters are varied at three different levels (decided from literature) and simulation trials were conducted as per L27 Taguchi's orthogonal array. The various ANN parameters like number of hidden layers, neurons, and transfer functions are optimized based on many trials to predict the outputs within the normalized error limit of 10^{-4}. Various network structures with one and two hidden layers with varying number of neurons in each layer are examined. Finally the architecture which yielded better performance is used for modeling. In all the cases, a feed forward back propagation algorithm is selected to train the network in Matlab programming environment. Here the scaled conjugate gradient algorithm is used to minimize the error. From the available simulation data sets, 27 data sets are used to train and two intermediate data sets are utilized for testing the ANN model/expert system. The comparison between ANN predicted true stress-strain behavior and simulation results are shown in Fig. 3. The strain hardening exponent (n) and strength co-efficient (K) values obtained from ANN models are incorporated into Hollomon's equation ($\sigma = K\,\varepsilon^n$) for TWB made of steel and aluminium alloy base materials and true stress-strain curves are obtained. It should be noted that even though Hollomon's strain hardening law is not accurate to predict the tensile behavior of aluminium alloy base material, ANN predictions are quite accurate in predicting the same. Similarly, the comparison between ANN/expert system and simulation results of draw-in profile during square cup deep drawing is presented in Fig. 4. At different TWB conditions, the draw-in profile predicted by ANN model/expert system is well matched with the simulation results for both steel and Al alloy TWBs. In the case of LDH test, the FLC is predicted by thickness gradient based necking criterion

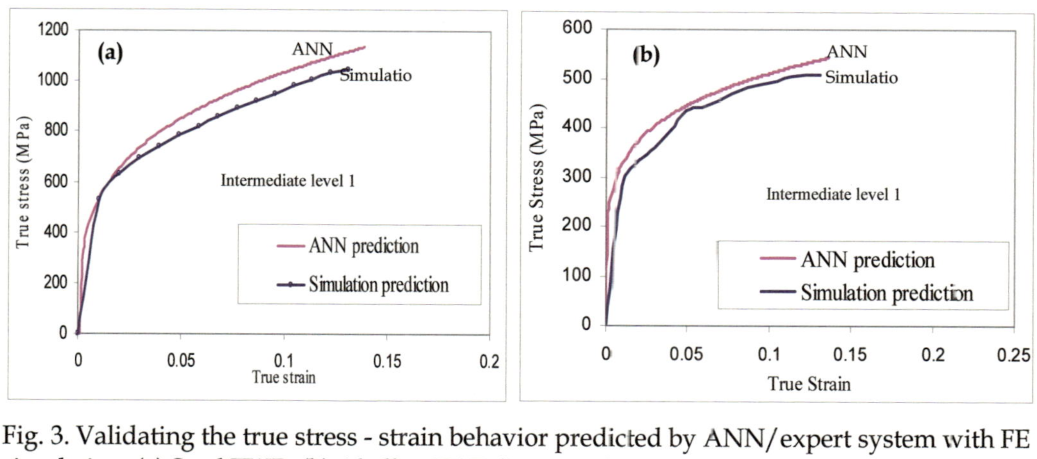

Fig. 3. Validating the true stress - strain behavior predicted by ANN/expert system with FE simulation; (a) Steel TWB, (b) Al alloy TWB (Veera Babu et al., 2009)

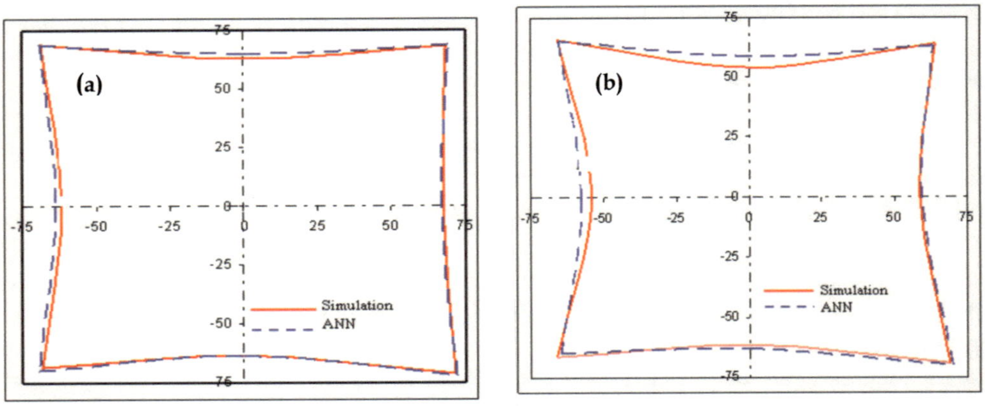

Fig. 4. Comparison of cup draw-in profile between ANN prediction and FE simulation; (a) Steel TWB, (b) Al alloy TWB (Veera Babu et al., 2009)

(TGNC). The ANN/expert system prediction is found to show excellent correlation with FLC from the criterion (Fig. 5 a-c) for steel TWB. It is also found (Siva Krishna, 2009) that the FLCs predicted from other failure criteria - effective strain rate, major strain rate based necking criteria, both the original and modified ones (Fig. 5 a-c), are comparing satisfactorily with the expert system results. A slight deviation in the plane strain and stretching modes of deformation is seen in both the intermediate TWB conditions.

The proposed ANN based expert system for TWB is in rudimentary stage of development. The suitability of the system is problem specific. A sheet forming engineer who wants to develop an expert system for some industrial TWB sheet part can just make it as part of

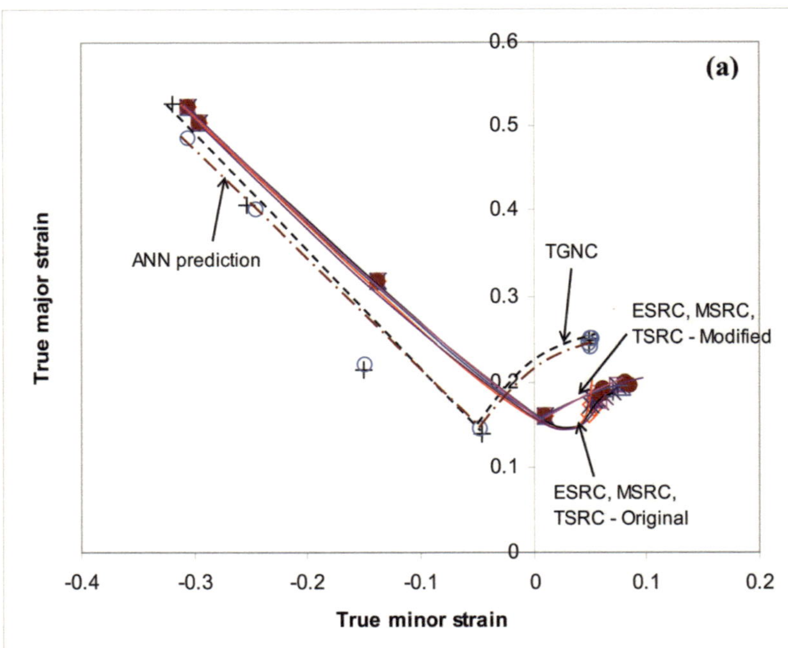

Fig. 5. Comparison of ANN prediction with TGNC and other failure prediction (continued)

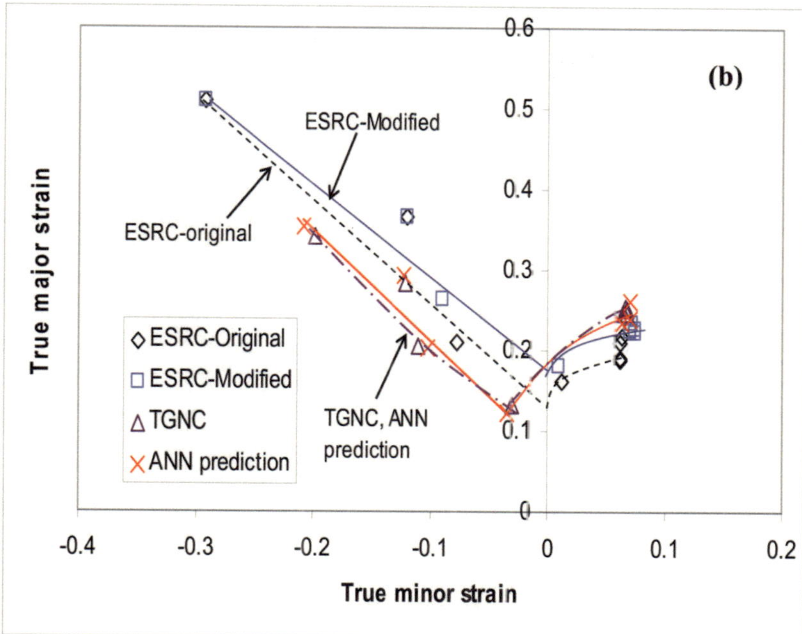

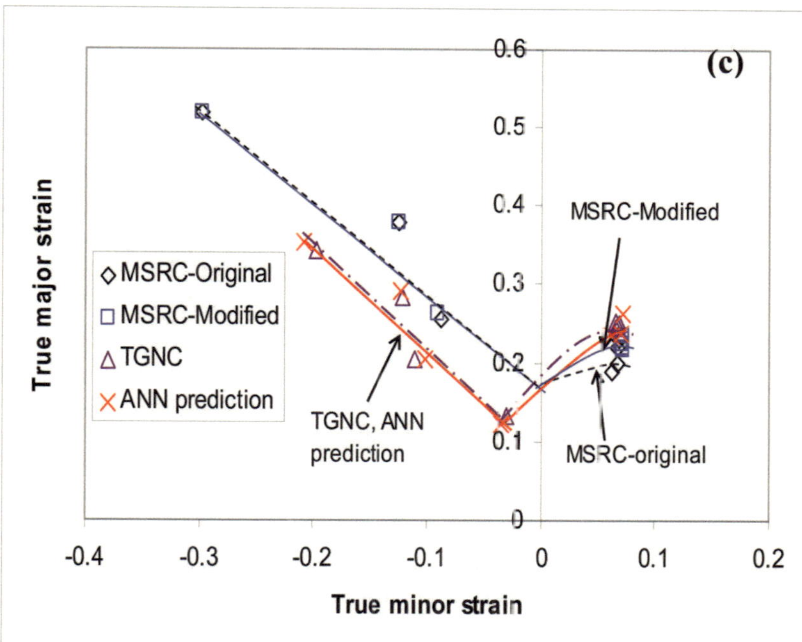

Fig. 5. Comparison of ANN prediction with TGNC and other failure prediction - (a) intermediate level 1, ESRC, MSRC, TSRC comparison; (b) intermediate level 2, ESRC; (c) intermediate level 2, MSRC (Siva Krishna, 2009)

existing system framework in the same line of thought, with out introducing new rules and conditions. This way the expert system is also expanded, becomes more efficient in solving realistic TWB forming conditions. The relations between TWB inputs and outputs are nonlinear in nature and hence it is complex to explicitly state rules for making expert system. But these complex relationships can be easily handled by ANN. In fact, it is not mandatory that the user should know about the input-output relations in TWB. Since this expert system is ANN based, it can potentially become a learning system as the problem solved by the system can also become a part of training examples for customers. Though the expert system can not reason out the decisions/results unlike rule based systems, one can interpret the results by comparing the outputs of two different input conditions quantitatively with minimum knowledge in TWB forming behavior. The ANN learning and fixing optimum architecture takes time and are problem specific, which can be sorted out by practice. The expert system developed in this work is applicable within the range of input and base material properties specified by Veera Babu et al. (Veera Babu et al., 2009). Though this is true, the range specified is large enough to include usable TWB conditions. It is worth to study the applicability of the present expert system outside the range and for many new sheet materials including high strength steels.

8. Summary

In this chapter, the expert system applications in designing, planning, and manufacturing of sheet parts is discussed. Emphasis is given for process design, process sequence and planning, strip layout plan, and tool design. The use of expert system in material forming is also highlighted. Finally an expert system that is being developed to predict the TWB forming behavior is presented. The expert systems play a vital role in designing the sheet forming processes and acts like a 'brain' in taking decisions and suggesting the optimum conditions for better sheet formability. In TWB, the expert system can predict the weld line movement for the given input properties, by which the blank holding force can be varied suitably to minimize the weld line movement. Most of the expert/knowledge based systems belong to IF-THEN variety which has interpretation power and updating ability. Some of the systems are neural network based that are capable of handling non-linear relationships in a better fashion and are independent of existing design rules. The only disadvantage is that they can not interpret the results, unlike IF-THEN rule based systems. The strength of ANN based system is that any new material, forming process, process parameter, and industrial parts can be included into the model without formalizing new rules, except that one needs to train and test the network whenever it is updated for new prediction work. The IF-THEN variety systems are based on data obtained from experts, industries, handbooks, journals etc. while ANN are based on data from experiments and simulations. Also it looks like most of the systems are developed as per industrial requirements, rather than for academic research. There are ES for deep drawability, bending, and blanking that are quantified by 'geometric parameters' like cup height, bending angles etc. and hardly any expert system is found to design the sheet forming based on 'forming limit diagram (FLD)' which is quantified by strain or stress developed during the forming operation. The ES based on FLDs will give more insight into the sheet design aspects. In this case, one has to follow some forming limit criteria to predict the limit strains under varied TWB conditions, as depicted earlier in TWB expert system.

In future, expert systems to design and predict, (a) the sheet formability of new materials like high strength steels, advanced high strength steels; new processes like hydro forming, micro forming etc.; (b) the ability of allied processes like friction stir welding, laser welding to manufacture sheet parts are expected. For instance, expert system can be developed for tailor welded blanks made of dual phase steel, friction stir welded blanks made of Al alloy sheets, hydro forming of dual phase steel, spring back and bending of high strength steels that are of practical importance and can be used efficiently in industries. Efficient expert systems that can predict the microstructural, fatigue, and high temperature behavior of many automotive and constructional materials should be developed in future. ANN model developed by Hosseini et al. (Hosseini et al., 2004) to predict the tensile strength and elongation of TRIP steels is an example of this kind. One can also develop hybrid expert systems that integrate different methods of expert system development like ANN and Genetic Algorithm (GA) to predict the sheet forming behavior. The best example for this is the spring back prediction work done by Liu et al. (Liu et al., 2007) using integrated ANN and GA, in which GA is used to optimize the weights during ANN modeling.

9. References

Ann, B. N. K., Kai, C. C. (1994). A knowledge-based system for strip layout design, *Computers in Industry*, Vol. 25, No. 1, 31-44, 01663615

Calcaterra, S., Campana, G., Tomesani, L. (2000). Prediction of mechanical properties in spheroidal cast iron by neural networks, *Journal of Materials Processing Technology*, Vol. 104, No. 1-2, 74-80, 09240136

Cheok, B. T., Foong. K. Y, Nee. A. Y. C., Teng, C. H. (1994). Some aspects of a knowledge-based approach for automating progressive metal stamping die design, *Computers in Industry*, Vol. 24, No. 1, 81-96, 01663615

Choi, J. C., Kim, C. (2001). A compact and practical CAD/CAM system for the blanking or piercing of irregular shaped-sheet metal products for progressive working, *Journal of Materials Processing Technology*, Vol. 110, No. 1, 36-46, 09240136

Choi, T. H., Choi, S., Na, K. H., Bae, H. S., Chung, W. J. (2002). Application of intelligent design support system for multi-step deep drawing process, *Journal of Materials Processing Technology*, Vol. 130-131, 76-88, 09240136

Ciurana, J., Ferrer, I., Gao, J. X. (2006). Activity model and computer aided system for defining sheet metal process planning, *Journal of Materials Processing Technology*, Vol. 173, No. 2, 213-222, 09240136

Downes, A., Hartley, P. (2006). Using an artificial neural network to assist roll design in cold roll-forming processes, *Journal of Materials Processing Technology*, Vol. 177, No. 1-3, 319-322, 09240136

Duflou, J. R., Vancza, J., Aerens, R. (2005). Computer aided process planning for sheet metal bending: A state of the art, *Computers in Industry*, Vol. 56, No. 7, 747-771, 01663615

Dym, C. L. (1985). EXPERT SYSTEMS: New Approaches to Computer-aided Engineering, *Engineering with Computers*, Vol. 1, No. 1, 9-25, 14355663

Emri, I., Kovacic, D. (1997). Expert system for testing mechanical properties of Aluminium and Aluminium parts, *Expert Systems With Applications*, Vol. 12, No. 4, 473-482, 09574174

Esche, S. K., Khamitkar, S., Kinzel, G. L., Altan. T. (1996), Process and die design for multi step forming of round parts from sheet metal, *Journal of Materials Processing Technology*, Vol. 59, No. 1-2, 24-33, 09240136

Faura, F., Sebastián, M. A., Zamora, R. (2001). A decision support system for sheet metal blanking process parameters selection, *Journal of Materials Processing Technology*, Vol. 118, No. 1-3, 371-376, 09240136

Ganesh Narayanan, R., Narasimhan, K., (2008). Predicting the forming limit strains of tailor welded blanks, *Journal of Strain Analysis for Engineering Design*, Vol. 43, No. 7, 551-563, 03093247

George-Christopher, V., Segredou, I., Giannakakis, T. (2005). Logic programming for process planning in the domain of sheet metal forming with progressive dies, *Journal of Intelligent manufacturing*, Vol. 16, No. 4-5, 479-497, 15728145

Gupta, S. K., Bourne, D. A., Kim, K. H., Krishnan, S. S. (1998). Automated process planning for sheet metal bending operations, *Journal of Manufacturing Systems,* Vol. 17, No. 5, 338-360, 02786125

Hindman, C., Ousterhout, K. B. (1998). A virtual design system for sheet metal forming, *Journal of Materials Processing Technology*, Vol. 84, No. 1-3, 107-116, 09240136

Hosseini, S. M. K., Zarei-Hanzaki, A., Panah, M. J. Y., Yue, S. (2004). ANN model for prediction of the effects of composition and process parameters on tensile strength and percent elongation of Si–Mn TRIP steels, *Materials Science and Engineering A,* Vol. 374, No. 1-2, 122–128, 09215093

Karatas, C., Sozen, A., Dulek, E. (2009), Modelling of residual stresses in the shot peened material C-1020 by artificial neural network, *Expert System With Applications,* Vol. 36, No. 2, Part 2, 3514-3521, 09574174

Karayel, D., Ozkan, S. S. (2006). Distributed multi-agent system approach for sheet metal forming, *Journal of Materials Processing Technology,* Vol. 177, No. 1-3, 327-330, 09240136

Kumar, S., Singh, R. (2008). Automation of strip-layout design for sheet metal work on progressive die, *Journal of Materials Processing Technology,* Vol. 195, No. 1-3, 94-100, 09240136

Liao, S. H. (2005). Expert system methodologies and applications—a decade review from 1995 to 2004, *Expert Systems with Applications,* Vol. 28, No. 1, 93–103, 09574174

Lin, Z. C., Peing, G. J. (1994). An investigation of an expert system for sheet metal bending design, *Journal of Materials Processing Technology,* Vol. 43, No. 2-4, 165-176, 09240136

Lin, Z. C., Chang, D. Y. (1996). Application of neural network machine learning model in the selection system of sheet metal bending tooling, *Artificial intelligence in Engineering,* Vol. 10, No. 1, 21-37, 09541810

Lin, B. T., Chan, C. K., Wang, J. C. (2008). A knowledge based parametric design system for drawing dies, *International Journal of Advanced Manufacturing Technology,* Vol. 36, No. 7-8, 671-680, 14333015

Lin, B. T., Kuo, C. C. (2008). Application of an integrated CAD/CAM/CAE system for stamping dies for automobiles, *International Journal of Advanced Manufacturing Technology*, Vol. 35, No. 9-10, 1000-1013, 14333015

Liu, W., Liu, Q., Ruan, F., Liang, Z., Qiu, H. (2007). Springback prediction for sheet metal forming based on GA-ANN technology, *Journal of Materials Processing Technology,* Vol. 187–188, 227–231, 09240136

Manabe, K., Yang, M., Yoshihara, S. (1998). Artificial intelligence identification of process parameters and adaptive control system for deep-drawing process, *Journal of Materials Processing Technology,* Vol. 80-81, 421-426, 09240136

Nye, T. J. (2000). Stamping strip layout for optimal raw material utilization, *Journal of Manufacturing Systems,* Vol. 19, No. 4, 239-248, 02786125

Ong, S. K., De Vin, L. J., Nee, A. Y. C., Kals, H. J. J. (1997). Fuzzy set theory applied to bend sequencing for sheet metal bending, *Journal of Materials Processing Technology*, Vol. 69, No. 1-3, 29-36, 09240136

Palani, R., Wagoner, R. H., Narasimhan, K. (1994). Intelligent design environment: A knowledge based simulations approach for sheet metal forming, *Journal of Materials Processing Technology*, Vol. 45, No. 1-4, 703-708, 09240136

Park, S. B., Choi, Y., Kim, B. M., Choi, J. C. (1998). A study of a computer-aided process design system for axi-symmetric deep-drawing products, *Journal of Materials Processing Technology*, Vol. 75, No. 1-3, 17-26, 09240136

Park, S. B. (1999). An expert system of progressive die design for electron gun grid parts, *Journal of Materials Processing Technology*, Vol. 88, No. 1-3, 216-221, 09240136

Qiang, GU, Rui, Z., Dong-ying, JU. (2006). Development of materials database system for CAE system of heat treatment based on data mining technology, *Trans. Nonferrous Met. Soc. China*, Vol. 16, No. 2, s572-s576

Rajender Singh, Sekhon, G. S. (2005). PROPLAN: an expert system for optimal planning of sheet metal operations, *Journal of Materials Processing Technology*, Vol. 166, No. 2, 307-312, 09240136

Rao, K. P., Prasad, Y. K. D. V. (1995). Neural network approach to flow stress evaluation in hot deformation, *Journal of Materials Processing Technology*, Vol. 53, No. 3-4, 552-566, 09240136

Rao, R. V. (2004). Evaluation of metal stamping layouts using an analytic hierarchy process method, *Journal of Materials Processing Technology*, Vol. 152, No. 1, 71–76, 09240136

Shailendra Kumar, Rajender Singh, Sekhon, G. S. (2006). CCKBS: A component check knowledge-based system for assessing manufacturability of sheet metal parts, *Journal of Materials Processing Technology*, Vol. 172, No. 1, 64-69, 09240136

Shashi Kumar, Kumar, S., Prakash, Shakar, R., Tiwari, M. K., Kumar, S. B. (2007). Prediction of flow stress for carbon steels using recurrent self-organizing neuro fuzzy networks, *Expert Systems With Applications*, Vol. 32, No. 3, 777-788, 09574174

Shen, X., Liu, J., Wang, X., Huang, C. C. (2003). Development of an applied roll forming pass design expert system based on the shape element idea, *Journal of Materials Processing Technology*, Vol. 140, No. 1-3, 505-508, 09240136

Sing, W. M., Rao, K. P. (1997). Knowledge-based process layout system for axi-symmetrical deep drawing using decision tables, *Computers and Industrial Engineering*, Vol. 32, No. 2, 299-319, 03608352

Singh, R., Sekhon, G. S. (1999). An expert system for optimal selection of press for a sheet metal, *Journal of Materials Processing Technology*, Vol. 86, No. 1-3, 131-138, 09240136

Sitaraman, S. K., Kinzel, G. L., Altan. T. (1991). A knowledge-based system for process-sequence design in axi-symmetric sheet-metal forming, *Journal of Materials Processing Technology*, Vol. 25, No. 3, 247-271, 09240136

Siva Krishna, K. (2009). An expert system to predict the forming limit of tailor welded blanks, *M. Tech. thesis*, IIT Guwahati, India.

Tisza, M. (1995). Expert systems for metal forming, *Journal of Materials Processing Technology*, Vol. 53, No. 1-2, 423-432, 09240136

Tretheway, K. R., Wood, R. J. K., Puget, Y., Roberge, P. R. (1998). Development of a knowledge-based system for materials management, *Materials and Design*, Vol. 19, No. 1-2, 39-56, 02613069

Uzsoy, R., Ramcharan, D. J., Martin-Vega, L. A. (1991). An experimental expert system for process planning of sheet-metal parts, *Computers and Industrial Engineering,* Vol. 20, No. 1, 59-69, 03608352

Vasudevan, M., Rao, B. P. C., Venkatraman, B., Jayakumar, T., Raj., B. (2005). Artificial neural network modelling for evaluating austenitic stainless steel and Zircaloy-2 welds, *Journal of Materials Processing Technology,* Vol. 169, No. 3, 396-400, 09240136

Veera Babu, K., Ganesh Narayanan, R., Saravana Kumar, G. (2009). An expert system based on artificial neural network for predicting the tensile behavior of tailor welded blanks, *Expert System With Applications,* Vol. 36, No. 7, 10683-10695, 09574174

Wang, L., Porter, A. L., Cunningham, S. (1991). Expert Systems: Present and Future, *Expert Systems with Applications,* Vol. 3, No. 4, 383-396, 09574174

7

Expert Systems Controlling the Iron Making Process in Closed Loop Operation

Angelika Klinger, Thomas Kronberger, Martin Schaler, Bernhard Schürz and Klaus Stohl
Siemens VAI
Turmstrasse 4, 4031 Linz,
Austria

1. Introduction

1.1 Iron making

Since heavy industry is often big in physical size, loud and dirty, it is often considered as low technology. This applies also for the iron and steel industry, and here especially for the early phases of the production chain: Iron making, the process of turning solid iron bearing materials into liquid hot metal (typically 1500°C, 94.5% Fe, 4.7% C, 0.6% Si, some additional trace elements), is a process, which is known in its earliest form since thousands of years. It was improved over the centuries and builds still the starting point for about 65% of the world's steel production.

An average blast furnace, which is the predominant production unit for liquid hot metal, has an inner volume of about 3500 m³ and produces about 8000 t of hot metal per day, thus consuming about 12000 t of iron bearing material and 4000 t of coke per day. In many plants one or two blast furnaces feed the processes down stream. Therefore, any problems immediately have consequences on the whole plant. The furnace should operate continuously 24 hours a day. Restarts after shutdowns are technically challenging and very costly.

Controlling a blast furnace is very difficult, because the properties of the used materials are not known exactly and are not stable over time. Control actions regarding the charged materials, the so called burden, take several hours before a reaction can be experienced. Moreover, such reactions are often overshadowed by other effects. Therefore, operating a blast furnace was for a long time considered somewhere between art and magic, and was entirely based on experience, but – as we will show in this paper – was turned over the last few decades into science.

Blast furnaces are fed alternating with layers of coke, produced in a coke plant, and iron bearing materials like lump ore, pellets or sinter. For the latter two special production units, namely pelletizing plants and sinter plants are required.

Coal cannot be charged into a blast furnace because it does not have enough physical strength to withstand the conditions inside of the furnace. Also, it is not possible to charge too many fine materials, because this would lead to a blockage of flow of the reducing gas. Therefore sinter plants are required to convert a mixture of iron carrier fines, coke and some additive materials into solid chunks of material with a Fe content of more than 60%.

An alternative to the production route described above is the COREX® process. It produces liquid hot metal, just like a blast furnace, but can be charged with coal instead of coke, thus eliminating the need for a coke plant. Sinter is not required either, because lump ore or pellets are used as iron carrier feed material.

1.2 Automation systems

After starting of the automation age, blast furnaces were soon equipped with so called basic automation systems, in order to automatically control more and more parts of the furnace operation (sequence logic). However, the operational setpoints were determined by experienced engineers. Soon, the need was felt to take away the "magic" of determining setpoints and replace it with science.

So, one of the first such applications were charge models, which calculate - under the assumption that all input and output streams are known - based on material balance calculations, which materials have to be charged by which amount, to get the desired results, which are hot metal and slag with a certain chemical composition.

Following this example more and more process models were developed, initially used only offline in some computer centres, and then with the advent of cheaper and more powerful personal computers more and more online.

However, there was still a lot of art in controlling the blast furnaces, because it was not possible to find proper algorithms for the problems at hand, and so the experience of the operators and the engineers still had a major impact on the performance of a blast furnace.

In the 1970's and 80's artificial intelligence techniques were slowly finding their way from universities and research centres into the "real world". Rule based expert systems and later fuzzy logic based systems were the leaders of this development. Neural networks and other data based techniques soon followed. Steel producers were not shy to experiment with these technologies and investigated whether they can benefit from them (Gottlob & Nejdl, 1990).

1. 3 Expert systems

Medical diagnosis systems were developed to support doctors in their work (e.g. MYCIN, Buchanan & Shortliffe, 1984). The underlying ideas were adopted by the iron making industry and similar systems were developed by several different suppliers and researchers (Hörl et al 2006, Inkala et al 1994, Sato et al 1988, Sun et al, 2002) throughout the world.

Although they used different techniques and tools, they all shared the same goals, which are

- establish a diagnosis of the status of the blast furnace
- suggest corrective actions if needed (therapy)
- explain the reasoning behind diagnosis and therapy

When we look at all existing blast furnace expert systems we can see that there are three different types, which also comply with the historical development of these systems.

- Intelligent alarming and forecasting expert systems: Such a system uses the measured process data, evaluates them, combines different values to form more complex diagnoses, forecasts certain blast furnace events, gives an alarm to the operator and is able to explain its results (diagnosis).

  However, such a system could not lead to measurable changes in the blast furnace process stability, was not fully accepted by the operators and - most important - could not decrease the operation costs.

- Advisory expert systems: Almost any blast furnace expert system found in literature belongs to this group. Such a system goes one step further as the one mentioned before. In addition to just establishing a diagnosis, it also suggests control actions to be performed by the operator, but still the last decision is with the operator. Such advisory systems were very well accepted and gave useful suggestions, lead to a uniform control philosophy over all shifts, but could not decrease the operation costs significantly.

  Closed-Loop expert systems: The main difference to an advisory system is the automatic and simultaneous execution of corrective actions when necessary. E.g., when the coke rate has to be changed this also influences the Silicon content in the hot metal. Therefore such a change requires simultaneously a change in the burden basicity. Such combined actions, especially when the system is fine-tuning the process and performs many corrections, cannot be handled by the interaction between operator and advisory system.

  Only with a closed-loop expert system, a significant reduction of the production costs can be proven.

The systems, which are described further in this chapter are all of the third group. The product family is called SIMETAL^{CIS} VAiron. SIMETAL^{CIS} BF VAiron is the system dedicated to the blast furnace. Product names for the other iron making production units follow the same pattern. In this paper, the name VAiron is used for short.

1.4 State of the art

Although the starting point was establishment of diagnoses, it turned out that diagnosis is nice and interesting, but the real question is "what do I have to do to stabilize and further optimize the production?". Only answering this question allows the producers to save money and of course this is the ultimate driving force and justification of any such developments. Consequently, modern systems should be referred to as Therapy Systems instead of Diagnosis Systems.

Starting with simple if-then-else rules, blast furnace expert systems were enhanced step by step to increase their capabilities:

- Fuzzy logic rules were added because it was felt that this kind of reasoning is closer to the way how people think. Also, it is possible to express the vague, heuristic knowledge in a much more natural way.
- As mentioned in the beginning of this chapter a wide variety of process models were developed. These models can be used by human operators, but they can also be used directly by an expert system, thus turning a rule based system into a model based (or better model enhanced) system.
- Neural networks or also other learning techniques are common applications in the current automation field. Expert systems can for example call such a neural network to interpret patterns in data and then use the returned information for the further reasoning process.
- Optimising the blast furnace process does not necessarily mean that the overall production site is at an optimum as well (local optimum, i.e. blast furnace only, versus global optimum, whole ironmaking area). Therefore is important that production units upstream and downstream of the blast furnace are also considered. This is described in more detail in chapter 4 of this paper.

1.5 VAiron expert system

The VAiron expert system is fully integrated into the online process optimization package, which is now installed on many iron making production units world wide, thus being involved in more than 10% of the world's hot metal production.

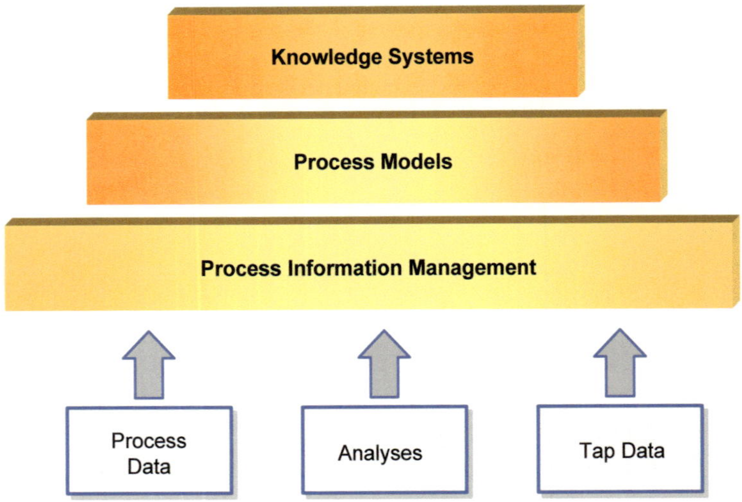

Fig. 1. VAiron Overall Structure

The top component "Knowledge Systems" is described in the following chapter.

2. VAiron expert system main modules

2.1 Data evaluation and preprocessing

2.1.1 Data handling modules

The purpose of the data handling modules of the VAiron expert system are to

- collect data from the different data sources, the main sources are continuous measurements , charging data (charging matrix setpoints and actual weights), cast data (timing information, hot metal temperature data, consumables, etc.), chemical analysis information for burden materials and hot metal and slag as well as plant status information (on/off conditions of the blast furnace and auxiliary plants)
- check whether used data are valid and provide substitutions if necessary and possible
- perform some auxiliary calculations

2.1.2 Data collection

Data used by the VAiron expert system are mainly measured values like temperatures, pressures or flows but also calculated tags like the gas utilization degree or the flame temperature. The measured values are read from the basic automation system with different scan rates which are corresponding to the rates of change of the underlying data points. The calculated tags are generated by various auxiliary modules of the VAiron system based on actual values and the history of process data.

The VAiron expert system needs actual values and the history of process data. Actual process data are taken taken from the memory of a dedicated VAiron system process. History data that are kept in the VAiron process database are read into memory of the expert system whenever necessary. Target values are also stored in the VAiron database and may be maintained through graphical user interfaces at any time.

Charging data, cast data and plant status information are collected, processed and stored in the VAiron process database by dedicated VAiron system processes. These system functions are triggered by events generated in the basic automation system. Due to mechanical and operational reasons the handling of these data in the Level-1 system is different for every blast furnace but the final data structures in the process database which are accessed by the VAiron expert system remain the same.

Chemical analysis information for burden materials and blast furnace products (hot metal and slag) are important inputs to the VAiron blast furnace models and the expert system. The chemical analyses are either read from external systems (like Level-3, raw material handling, laboratory) whenever new samples are available or manually entered in the VAiron system through a graphical user interface. Again dedicated VAiron system processes for data handling guarantee that the final data structures in the process database which are accessed by the VAiron expert system remain the same for every VAiron installation.

2.1.3 Data validation

Data Validation methods are used by the VAiron expert system to find out if the raw values of process variables may be used in the expert system without further processing.

Data are checked whether they are up to date and whether they are reasonable from the process point of view. Such checks can be limit checks, rate of change calculations or the evaluation of simple formulas.

For example data which are checked whether they are up to date are the hot metal and slag chemical analyses because these data are used for thermal and quality control of hot metal and slag and have to be available for the VAiron expert system at least some time after the last cast is closed. A typical example for a consistency check based on simple formulas is the comparison between measured and calculated (based on blast volume and steam addition flow) blast humidity, and only the validated blast humidity is used for the blast moisture control module of the VAiron expert system.

In case missing or invalid data is detected, a message will be generated and displayed on the main screen of the user interface of the VAiron expert system.

In general the diagnosis and corrective actions of the VAiron expert system use different input data and need different quality of data. The decision whether all required input data for a diagnosis or corrective action are available and valid is made inside the diagnosis or corrective action. If data is missing or invalid for a diagnosis or corrective action the missing or invalid data and the violated checks are listed in the process overview log window, which is updated cyclically by the VAiron expert system.

The data validation checks of the VAiron expert system are highly configurable by using parameters for all relevant limits which can be maintained through graphical user interfaces.

2.1.4 Data preprocessing

Some diagnosis and corrective action modules of the VAiron blast furnace expert system require special auxiliary calculations. These calculation methods can be classified into the following groups:

- Time based statistics over arbitrary time spans (trends, mean values, standard deviations, minimum and maximum limits, etc.)
- Other statistics which combines different tags (for example mean values or arithmetic combinations of different tags)
- Additional calculations of high complexity which are provisional results of the respective expert system modules

For example the water leakage diagnosis of the VAiron expert system is interested not only in the actual values of the top gas H_2 analysis but also in the mean values, trends and minimum and maximum limits over some specific time spans. These calculations are provisional results of the water leakage diagnosis and thus can be performed by the diagnosis itself and do not have to be made available as tags for access by other modules of the VAiron system.

Another example for an additional calculation of high complexity is the computation of the change of SiO_2 content in the slag due to a change in hot metal temperature which is an intermediate result of the slag basicity corrective action of the VAiron blast furnace expert system.

2.2 Diagnosis calculation

2.2.1 Introduction

Diagnoses are established using fuzzy logic and conventional expert system (rule based) technology. The validated and preprocessed input data are fed to the fuzzy logic rule sets to establish an initial value for each diagnosis. Then additional process knowledge like actual actions of the operators or special situations are used to establish the final diagnosis results.

Usually the result of the diagnosis is in the range [-1,…,+1] using arbitrary units. The results of the diagnoses are visualized graphically on the main screen of the VAiron expert system using a kind of traffic light system with red, yellow and green zones for the diagnosis result ranges very low and very high, low and high and normal respectively. Additionally, a detailed description of the input data and results of each diagnosis are contained in the process overview log window of the VAiron expert system as part of the overall explanation.

The diagnosis rules are implemented relative to a configurable, and therefore easy modifiable, target value; absolute values are avoided at any time.

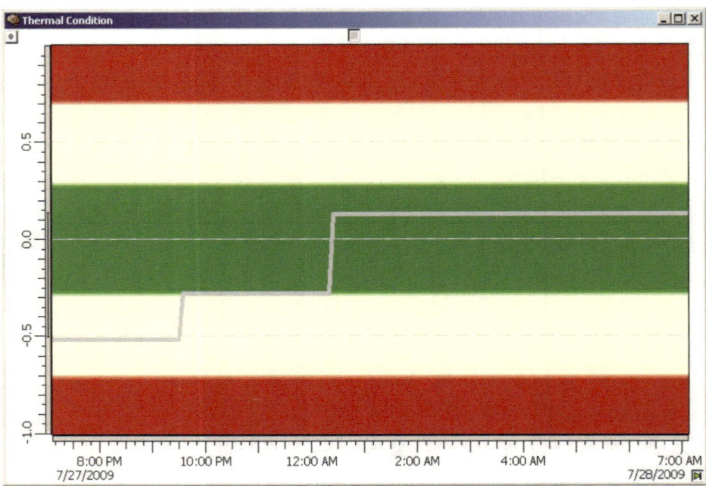

Fig. 2. Graphical Display of Diagnosis Result

2.2.2 Example of blast furnace scaffolding diagnosis

Scaffold build-up and removal (peeling) are permanent processes even in a smoothly running stable blast furnace. Whenever the build-up of scaffolds in a certain area exceeds a maximum limit for a longer time, the operators in the blast furnace control room have to pay attention on this phenomenon because a sudden removal of large scaffolds might have negative impact on the thermal level of the hot metal.

The scaffolding diagnosis of the VAiron expert system gives the operator a visual indication of the scaffold build-up and removal tendencies.

Initially two individual diagnoses are established, one for scaffold formation and one for scaffold removal, which are then combined into one diagnosis, which is displayed in the HMI. Depending on the cooling system of the blast furnace such diagnoses can be established separately for various sections of the furnace. Following is a list of input data. Note, that as described above, there are measured as well as calculated values used.

- Average heat flux over different time spans
- Normalized trend of the heat flux different time
- Average of the top gas utilization over different time spans
- Number of hot blast furnace cooling elements in the considered section, which is the result of a different diagnosis

The figure below shows the user interface screen which combines the scaffolding diagnosis results of all sections of the blast furnace which gives the control room operator an immediate overview of the ongoing build-up and removal activities and simplifies the identification of critical areas of the plant. When this screen dump was taken, the furnace was in a quite critical state, heavy scaffold formation was taking place in all sectors for several hours.

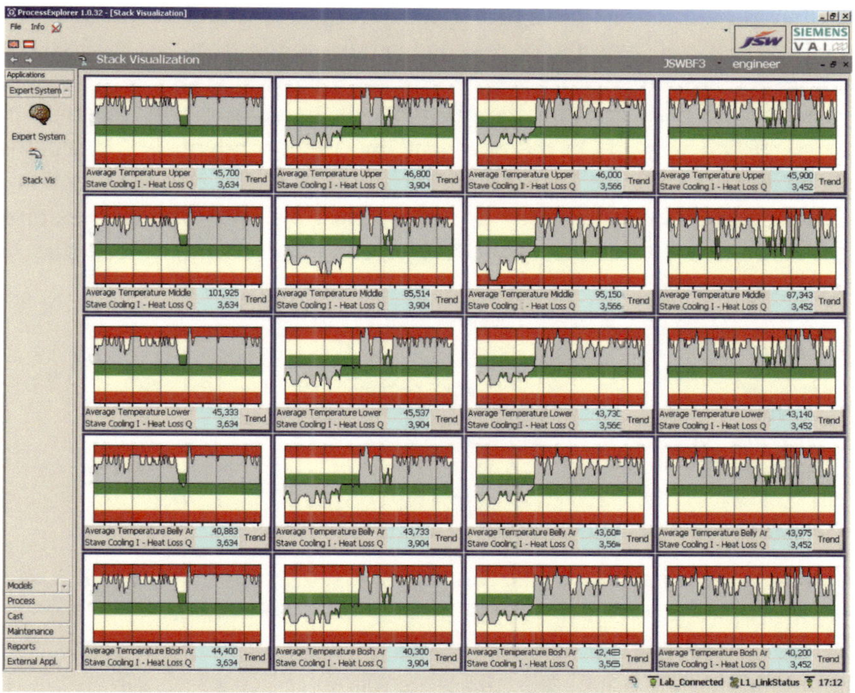

Fig. 3. Example Stack Visualization

The process overview log window of the VAiron blast furnace expert system contains the following explanation of the scaffolding diagnosis for a certain section:

```
Scaffolding - Middle Stack Quadrant 4: Peeling
 Heatfluxes: 7.01 [MW] Average: 6.86 [MW]  Trend: -0.01 [MW/h]
 Number of hot staves:          57.1[%]
 Top Gas Utilization:           47.21 [%]    Average:  47.08 [%]
```

2.3 Evaluation of corrective actions

2.3.1 Introduction

Corrective actions are proposals for the operating personnel to change some process parameters (setpoints). The VAiron expert system suggests one or more corrective actions out of a set of possible ones. Some of the corrective actions are provided qualitatively, that means the VAiron expert system suggests an increase or decrease of some process parameters instead of giving exact values to the user. Other corrective actions (e.g. fuel rate or slag basicity) are suggested quantitatively, that means the new process setpoints are calculated by the VAiron expert system.

Internally, the process of suggesting a corrective action is a two step procedure. First the actual situation is analyzed independently from other actions and also independently from the past. In a second step the history of the operation as well as of the process is taken into account. An example of such a post-processing step for the evaluation of the new setpoint for the coke rate is to take into account actual changes to the coke rate that were executed in the recent past shorter than the throughput time of the blast furnace.

Based on the configuration in the process database some corrective actions have to be acknowledged by the operators. The operators have to input a reason into the graphical user interface if they do not follow the expert systems suggestions and this corrective action is not executed. The entered reasons for rejecting certain suggestions are the basis for offline tuning of the expert system.

Explanations provide guidelines for the operators to understand why a certain corrective action was suggested or not. On the one hand the process overview log window of the VAiron expert system contains the status information for each corrective action and it is refreshed automatically every time the expert system runs. The following example shows the status information for the slag basicity corrective action and we see that finally no correction was required.

```
-- Rule 2: Slag Basicity
The slag basicity B2 of the previous tap {1568} was 1.154
(corr. value: 1.120 setpoint: 0.975 trend +0.0669 [1/h]
corr. trend +0.0669 [1/h]).
The HM temperature was 1534 [°C]
(corr. value: 1537 [Â°C] setpoint 1500 [°C]).
This results in a suggested change of -0.060.

From the previous basicity changes -0.017 are still active.
Therefore it is suggested to change the basicity by -0.043,
(maximum suggested basicity change is +/-0.050).

Because the tap number has not changed since the last suggestion,
NO suggestion is made.
```

Each explanation consists of two parts. The first one shows the current values of the most important process values involved in establishing the decision and the second shows the actions to be taken by the operators.

The following figure shows the graphical user interface for presenting a corrective action to the control room personnel. We see the detailed explanation of the suggested slag basicity change and the user has the possibility to reject the proposal of the VAiron expert system and enter a reason for this decision into the text box on the bottom of the screen. All data are stored in the process database and can be accessed offline for report generation and tuning purposes.

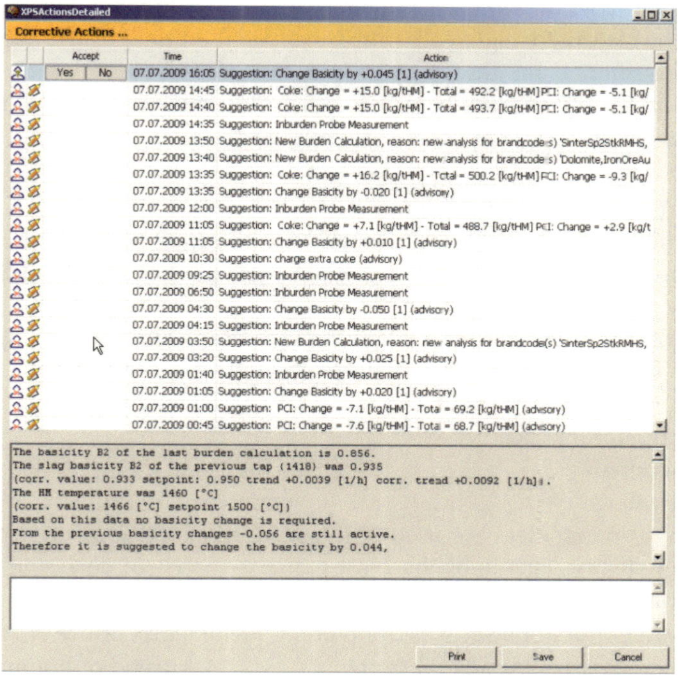

Fig. 4. Display Corrective Actions

The VAiron expert system knows two operation modes for a corrective action:

Advisory Mode (Semi-Automatic)

Closed Loop Mode

For operational safety and acceptance by the operators, all suggestions are displayed in the HMI. There is a configurable time span (typically 1 - 30 minutes) during which the operator can either confirm or reject the proposal. When the operator neither confirms or rejects, the action will be carries out if the setting of this action is closed loop, and it will be suspended if the setting is advisory mode.

For understanding of the two examples of the corrective actions suggested by the VAiron expert system we have to define what we mean by *active amount* of fuel or slag basicity. The *active amount* of a certain process variable is the sum of all changes of the process variable, which did not have time yet to produce a reaction of the blast furnace. Mathematically spoken it is a weighted sum of all changes of the process variable (i.e. changes of specific fuel rates in kg per ton of hot metal or changes of slag basicity) within the activation time span of the process variable.

The activation time span is different for different process variables. For example a change of the specific coke rate which is charged into the furnace from the top needs 5 to 8 hours to become metallurgically active whereas a change of the specific coal rate which is injected into the blast furnace tuyeres becomes metallurgically active within 1.5 to 3 hours. Therefore the VAiron expert system has to sum up the coke rate changes within the previous 5 to 8 hours and the coal rate changes within the previous 1.5 to 3 hours in order to compute the coke and coal active amounts respectively.
The question that remains is how the VAiron expert system knows the actual specific coke rate, the actual specific coal rate and the actual slag basicity at any time. This is done by the VAiron *Burden Control Model* which is triggered automatically when a new charging matrix which contains the material weight setpoints is activated on the Level-1 automation system. The result of this model are the specific (per ton of hot metal) rates of all materials (including coke and coal) and the complete hot metal and slag chemistry (especially the analysis elements which appear in the slag basicity definition).

2.3.2 Example of hot metal thermal control

The thermal stability of hot metal is an important objective of blast furnace ironmaking because it determines among other quality parameters the hot metal Sulphur content and the alkali balance.
The *Hot Metal Thermal Control* corrective action of the VAiron expert system calculates setpoints for the specific coke rate and the specific rates for the injected fuels through the tuyeres (coal, oil, gas) in order to keep the key quality parameters

- hot metal temperature and
- hot metal Si content

close to its target values.
The following input parameters are used by the VAiron expert system, in this example we assume that the reducing agents of the blast furnace consist of coke and injected coal (it could also be natural gas, oil or shredded plastics):

- Hot metal temperature of last casts, trend of hot metal temperature of last casts
- Hot metal chemistry (especially Si) content of last casts, trend of hot metal chemistry of last casts
- Target hot metal temperature
- Target hot metal chemistry
- History of the specific coke rate and the specific coal rate which are calculated by the VAiron burden control model

After the initial "calculation" of the required change of the specific fuel rate, we have to consider the active amounts of coke and. Then we have to split up the change of the specific fuel rate into changes of the specific coke rate and the specific coal rate. These changes are finally applied to the actual specific coke and coal rate in order to compute the new setpoints for the specific coke and coal rates.
All these intermediate calculation steps are presented to the operator through the graphical user interface of the VAiron expert system as we see in the following example:

Suggestion: Coal: Change = +6.1 - Total = 128.5 [kg/tHM] - 481.3 [g/Nm^3] (advisory)

```
The current fuel rate is 565.5 [kg/tHM] (coke equivalent)
(coke=445.0 [kg/tHM] PCI=122.4 [kg/tHM])
The HM temperature of the last tap {1619} is 1460 [°C]
```

```
(setpoint: 1500[°C] avg 1473[°C] trend -13.0 [K/h]).
The HM silicon of last tap is 0.373 [%]
(setpoint: 0.700 avg 0.436 trend -0.1175 [%/h]).
Based on the thermal condition a fuel rate change of +5.0 [kg/tHM]
is suggested.
Based on the HM silicon a fuel rate change of +5.0 [kg/tHM] is
suggested.
This leads to a suggested fuel rate change of +5.0 [kg/tHM].
(combination factors: 70.0 [%] temperature + 30.0 [%] silicon)

Since -1.9 [kg/tHM] from the previous changes are still active
(coke -1.9[kg/tHM],PCI 0.0 [kg/tHM], maximum total +/-15.0 [kg/tHM]),
a fuel rate change of 5.9 [kg/tHM] is suggested
(maximum suggested fuel rate change is +/-10.0 [kg/tHM]).

The following changes are suggested:
PCI: Change = +6.1 - Total = 128.5 [kg/tHM] - 481.3 [g/Nm³]
```

The VAiron blast furnace expert system automatically calculates a new charging matrix using the VAiron burden control model and sends the material weight setpoints to the Level-1 automation system. In other words the VAiron expert system prepares the new charging pattern automatically without further operator interaction.

2.3.3 Example of slag basicity control

The blast furnace slag basicity (defined as ratio of chemical compounds CaO/SiO_2, $(CaO+MgO)/SiO_2$ or $(CaO+MgO)/(SiO_2+Al_2O_3)$ depending on the raw material quality) has to be closely observed and controlled in order to keep the slag viscosity below a certain limit and to guarantee that the alkali compounds Na_2O and K_2O leave the blast furnace with the slag.

The *Slag Basicity Control* corrective action of the VAiron blast furnace expert system calculates setpoints for the charged material weights in order to keep the key quality parameters slag basicity close to its target value.

The following input parameters are used by the VAiron blast furnace expert system:

- Slag basicity of last casts, trend of slag basicity of last casts
- Target slag basicity
- History of the slag basicity which is calculated by the VAiron burden control model
- Target hot metal temperature and Si content as also used by the *Hot Metal Thermal Control* corrective action

The steps of execution are the same as in the thermal control described above. After the determination of the initial results, the active amount is considered to fine tune the expert system's proposal. Results are displayed in the HMI and also an explanation is provided. Triggering the VAiron burden control model a new charging matrix (and thus weight setpoints for the level 1 automation) is prepared and downloaded to level 1, where it can be used without any further operator interaction required.

It is important to mention that thermal level and the slag basicity influence each other which makes it difficult for the operator to keep control of these quality parameter because the hot metal temperature measurements and the results of the hot metal and slag chemical analysis for a certain cast are available at different times. The VAiron expert system has the ability to keep this overview and suggest the required corrective actions on time.

3. Savings and benefits

3.1 General benefits

3.1.1 Increase of operator know how

The VAiron Expert System generates textual explanations for the diagnoses and suggestions, allowing the operator to understand the situation in detail. Additionally, the user interfaces of the VAiron Expert Systems provide graphical information allowing for understanding the situation in brief. This combination of explanation facilities avoids the potential problem of high sophisticated automation solutions: the operational personnel looses its skills and get more and more dependent on the system. But permanent understanding the background of the system is more like an additional training for the operational staff, and even increases the skills of the operators.

3.1.2 Smooth plant operation

The earlier deviations from optimum conditions are detected, the earlier counter actions can be initiated. Moreover, this allows to apply small corrective actions instead of heavy ones. In a typical cycle time of five minutes, the VAiron Expert System checks:

- Several hundred measurement points from the Level-1 automation, and
- Related model calculations for internal process states which cannot be measured directly.

Even a high experienced human operator is not able to cope with this flood of information and therefore cannot identify process deviations as fast as the VAiron Expert System can do this. Also, no operator in the world can be constantly alert, but of course the expert system never gets tired.

In consequence, the main difference between manual operation and operation supported by the VAiron Expert System is that the later is characterized by more frequent, but smaller control actions. The resulting smooth operation of the blast furnace or the sinter plant avoiding heavy control actions and critical process situations leads to:

- Extended availability of equipment,
- Longer lifetime of equipment, and
- Reduced maintenance efforts and costs

3.1.3 Eliminating the human factor

Installing the VAiron expert system at a customer's plant goes in several phases. In a first phase the customer specific situation (raw materials, furnace geometry, equipment, operation philosophy, ...) is analysed. Then the rules are adapted to the specific situation. Finally, during commissioning the rules are fine-tuned together with the customer.

This procedure has the following advantages

- High acceptance of the system, it is understood as their tool and not so much as some software which tells them what to do
- The customer's operation philosophy is followed 24 hours a day, 7 days a week.
- Consistent operation over all shifts, resulting again in a smoother operation

3.2. Specific benefits of VAiron blast furnace expert system

The general benefits mentioned in the previous section have long term character. An immediate advantage is not measureable, because reduced maintenance costs due to less wear and extended equipment lifetime appear only after years of operation with the system.

On the other hand, the VAiron Blast furnace Expert System gives also immediate benefits where the system pays back the investment costs starting on the first day of operation. The three main beneficial points in this respect are:

- Reduced specific fuel consumption and reduction of emissions.
- Increased productivity of the blast furnace.
- Stable hot metal quality even under usage of cheaper, low graded raw materials.

3.2.1 Reduced fuel consumption

A reduction of the fuel consumption leads to significant cost reductions for the blast furnace operating company and hand in hand to a reduction of emissions, especially of carbon dioxide. Depending on the original situation, and the magnitude of cooperation between the customer, voestalpine Stahl (GmbH) and Siemens VAI, the typical reduction of fuel consumption is between 5 and 15 kg fuel (mainly coke) per ton of hot metal. The following figure shows an example from a South African customer, where about 15 kg/t of hot metal have been achieved. The main factor for this excellent result was a very intensive cooperation between all parties:

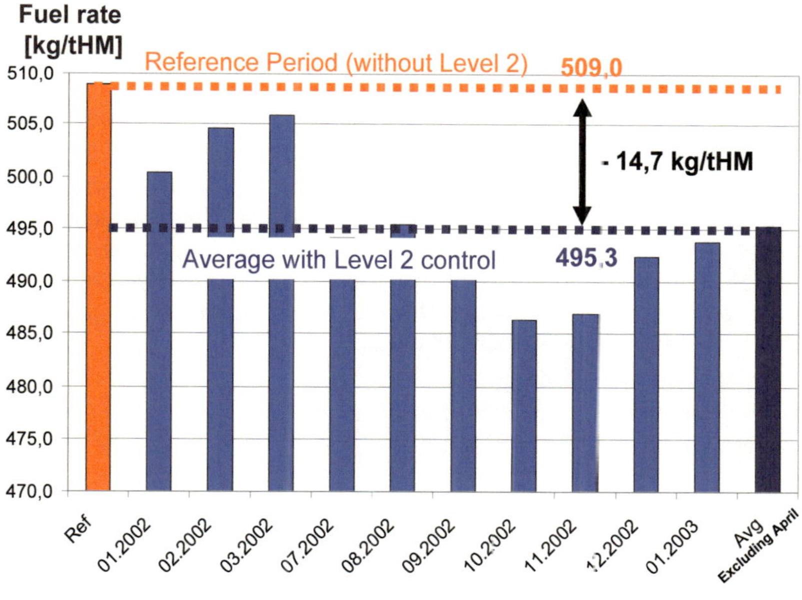

Fig. 5. Fuel Rate Savings Over Time

A severe incident in blast furnace operation is a freezing hearth. Therefore, operators tend to run a furnace warmer than required, giving them more safety in case of problems. By doing that, valuable coke is wasted. A closed loop expert system allows operating the furnace closer to its limits, therefore saving coke but still maintaining high operational safety.
Also, operators typically do not react immediately on incoming process data. If further data confirm the need of corrective action, quit significant corrective actions might be required. An expert system reacts earlier, and this allows typically smaller corrective actions.
15 kg/t of hot metal seem not to be a big saving, but considering a yearly production of 2 million tons of hot metal, the saving amounts to 30000 t of coke per year. With an average coke price of 200 €/t we end up with savings of 6 mill € per year!

3.2.2 Increase of blast furnace productivity

A further advantage of VAiron Blast furnace Expert System operation is an increase of productivity mainly resulting from stable operation avoiding process disturbances like e.g. hanging of the burden leading to reduced charging into the furnace, and therefore to reduced production. Additionally, the permeability control ensures optimum gas flow through the blast furnace, which also is a main factor for good productivity.

3.2.3 Stable hot metal quality

The VAiron Blast furnace Expert System receives the raw material and product analyses immediately from the laboratory. It reacts to deviations from optimum hot metal and slag analysis, and performs control actions to bring the quality parameters back to the setpoints. Fluctuations in raw material analyses are considered as soon as they are detected and the new optimum burden composition is calculated to avoid quality deviations in advance.
The control of fuel rate is keeping the thermal condition in the blast furnace hearth stable leading to stable hot metal temperature. Since there is a strong relationship between temperature and distribution of Silicon in hot metal and slag, the stable hot metal temperature implies stable Silicon content in the hot metal, which is an important requirement of the hot metal consumer, i.e. the steel plant.

3.3 Specific benefits of VAiron sinter expert system

Environmental regulations are rather tough in Western Europe and especially in Austria. To avoid problems due to exceeding emission thresholds, a special environmental diagnosis was introduced in the VAiron Sinter Expert System for voestalpine Stahl (GmbH) in Linz and Donawitz. This diagnosis warns the operational personnel as soon as the concentrations of dust or any other pollutant in the waste gas stack is approaching the threshold.
As in the case of the blast furnace system, the general benefits of the VAiron Sinter Expert System cannot be measured immediately. But the following specific benefits of the system allow for short term pay back of investment costs:

- Increased productivity of sinter plant.
- Reduced fuel consumption and emissions.
- Stable sinter quality.

3.3.1 Increase of sinter plant productivity

The usage of a higher percentage of sinter with stable quality in the blast furnace burden results in a further reduction of the blast furnace fuel consumption. Therefore, the increase of productivity of the sinter plant is a very important benefit of the VAiron Sinter Expert System. Typically, values between 2% and 5% can be achieved.
The VAiron Sinter Expert System was based on a former set of independent controllers for burn through point (BTP), return fines proportioning, coke addition, and for sinter basicity. The advantage of combining these controllers into a comprehensive expert system is the more general approach. The controllers do not act independently anymore, but their actions are connected by the system of rules. Additionally, the VAiron Sinter Expert System takes many more parameters into consideration, than the old controllers did. For example, while controlling the position of the burn through point parameters like harmonic diameter of sinter, actual return fines ratio, raw material mix, waste gas temperature, temperature on the cooler, etc. are also considered to prevent from short-sighted control actions, which would be done if only the actual position of the BTP is taken into account.

The gain in sinter plant productivity is mainly achieved by the rules and control loop controlling the BTP together with the optimum coke rate. Two independent control loops deal with BTP:

- The Classical (Longitudinal) BTP Controller, and
- The Transversal BTP Controller.

The classical, or longitudinal, BTP controller is basically watching the actual BTP position and adjusts the sinter strand speed in order to keep this point at the setpoint. The optimum position of the BTP (the setpoint) depends upon the specific plant. It is the optimum point balancing two phenomena: if the BTP is too close to the end of the sinter strand (the sinter machine speed is too fast), the sinter process is not yet completed, and a higher amount of return fines reduces the net production of the sinter plant. If the BTP is too far away from the end of the sinter strand (the machine speed is too low), then an increase of speed leads to an increase of sinter production.

Sinter plant productivity is a very good example for the interaction of human knowledge (customer and voestalpine Stahl (GmbH) process engineer evaluate the optimum position of the BTP) and artificial intelligence (the expert system takes care that the actual BTP is really at the optimum position).

The actual BTP is calculated from the average waste gas temperature in the wind boxes beyond the sinter pallet cars. It defines the mean position of the flame front. Since a sinter plant can be several meters in width, it is not clear, that the flame front is homogeneous, i.e. at the same position along transversal direction. A second control loop, the Transversal BTP Controller considers this situation. The following figure shows an inhomogeneous flame front at the left and a homogeneous one on the right.

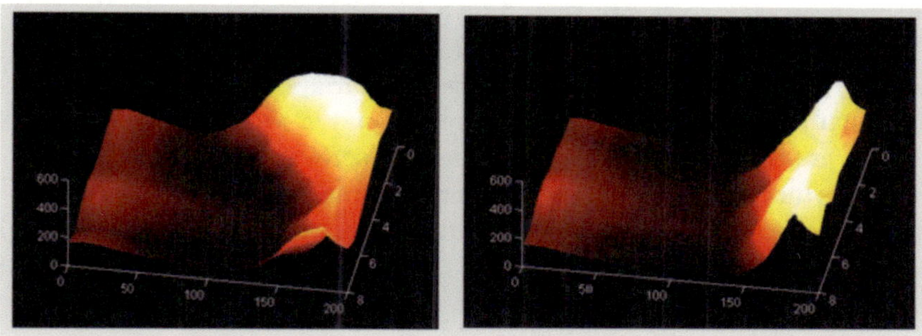

Fig. 6. Burn Through Point Position

3.3.2 Reduced fuel consumption

Similar to the VAiron Blast furnace Expert System, the VAiron Sinter Expert System reduces the fuel consumption of the process. Besides the immediate monetary benefit for the customer due to less expense for fuel, the positive environmental effect of less carbon dioxide emission is important. In the future this carbon dioxide effect will be an economical issue as well.

3.3.3 Stable sinter quality

The stable sinter quality is achieved by special quality controllers considering incoming sinter analyses from laboratory and performing counter actions, if deviations in one of the following quality parameters from the setpoint are detected:

- Harmonic diameter of sinter
- Sinter basicity
- Sinter SiO_2 content
- Total sinter Fe content

Additionally, fluctuations in raw material analyses are detected and the new optimum raw mix composition is calculated immediately, downloaded to the level 1 automation system and executed there. Obviously this is much faster than waiting to see effects in the produced sinter.

4. The next step: VAiron productivity control system

The VAiron Productivity Control System is a new development started by Siemens VAI together with voestalpine Stahl (GmbH). Target is the implementation of a powerful automated production control system for the various plants involved in the iron making process (i.e. coke oven plants, raw material yard, sinter plants, blast furnaces)

A superimposed expert system ensures a fully automatic linkage of the interacting plants. Thus an overall optimization of the complete plant network is realized instead of independent optimizations of the single plants which often do not represent the best solution.

This approach features essential benefits:

- Transparent and traceable production decisions
- Optimization of the complete plant network instead of independent single optimizations
- Reduction of costs and increase of production

4.1 Basic situation

At voestalpine Stahl (GmbH) hot metal is produced by three blast furnaces. Sinter and coke, which are input materials for the blast furnaces are produced in a sinter and a coke oven plant. Additionally other external material brands may also be bought in if needed. The involved plants are equipped with enhanced level 2 software automation system based on advanced process models and closed-loop expert systems.

Yet, there was the requirement for a superimposed system integrating the complete plant network. This missing overall link was the reason for the development of the VAiron Productivity Control System:

- Production control was done offline, decentralized and manually
- The necessary information were retrieved from different sources
- The executed measures were not fully traceable in the sense of quality assurance

4.2 Target situation

Target was a coordinated production control and an automated execution of the plan data by specifying setpoints which are sent directly to the level 2 automation systems of the involved plants.

The coordination of the production control is by an expert system considering actual deviations and evaluating production, resulting in optimized production setpoints.

The following targets were defined:

- Transparent and traceable plan data and planning decisions based on a clear identification and storage of all production plan data.
- Implementation of an authorization concept

- Automated production control with optimized production increase and cost reduction
- Control of the produced amounts and qualities in particular for the sinter plant, the blast furnaces and the coke oven plant

4.3 Implementation

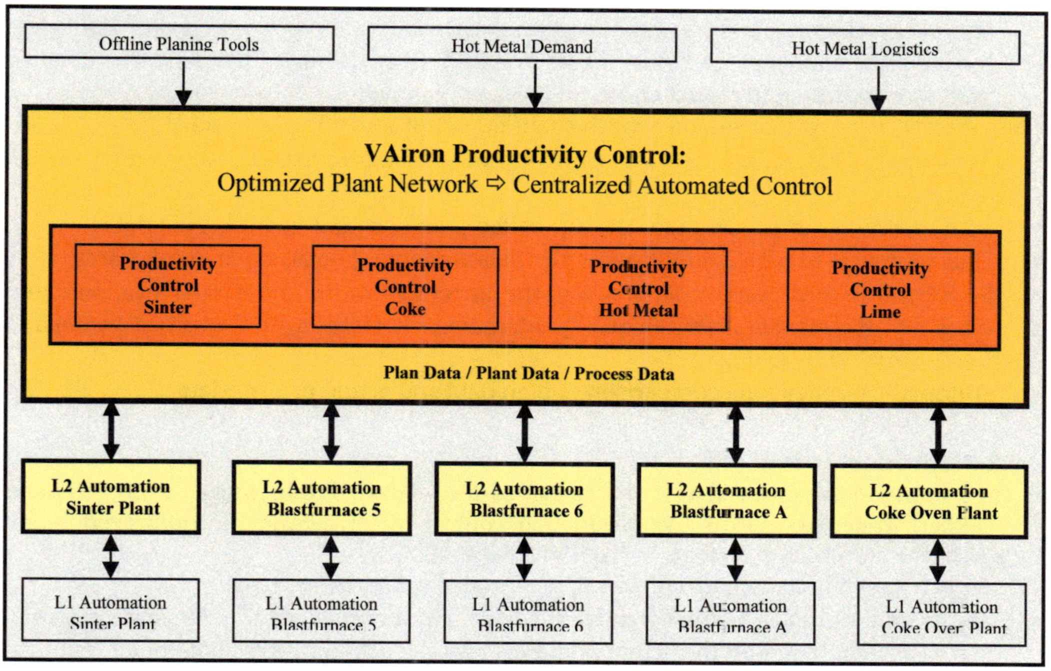

Fig. 7. VAiron Productivity Control System Concept

To meet the requirements the concept for a integrated solution package was defined (refer to Figure 7).

- A superimposed expert system ensures the overall optimization of the complete plant network and a centralized automated control
- The actual plan data provide the framework for this expert system
- The actual plant status data and the process data of the involved plants provide the input data for this expert system
- Fully automated interfaces between all interacting automation systems allow the exchange of all necessary data in all directions
- The optimized measures evaluated by the superimposed expert system are executed online by specifying setpoints which are sent directly to the level 2 automation systems of the involved plants. There, these setpoints are processed by local expert systems.
- Based on the measures finally resulting from the local expert systems, setpoints for the level 1 automation systems are preset and executed.

4.3.1 Production plan data

The actual production plan data provide the framework for evaluation of the optimized figures by the expert system. Therefore the recording, administration and implementation of the plan data is an integrative part of the system:

Annual plan data:
Planning done once per year for the next financial year.
Operation plan data:
Deviations from the annual plan data during operation are recorded separately in the system.
Detailed plan data:
Short-term deviations from the operation plan data resulting from current influences (actual plant status, process data ...) are handled using detailed plan data. The detailed plan data represent the latest and most binding plan data.
The system covers various features for the handling of production plan data:

- Recording of the actual plan data using a process database and a graded authorization concept
- Administration of annual plan data, operation plan data and detailed plan data
- Data exchange of plan data figures with other systems using automated interfaces
- Supply of up-to-date information about the currently needed and available amount and quality of the burden materials using automated interfaces to the involved plants and the raw material yard
- Automatic target-actual comparison of plan data and actual process data

4.3.2 Production control

A superimposed expert system is the kernel of the VAiron Productivity Control System. This expert system performs the production control by presetting the optimized target figures to the automation systems of the involved plants.
The expert system is charactarized by fully automated online processing:

- The overall optimized target figures are evaluated automatically by the superimposed expert system based on the actual plan data and the actual process data of all involved plants.
- These setpoints are preset directly to the level 2 automation systems of the involved plants.
- Local expert systems included in the level 2 automation systems apply the setpoints recieved from the VAiron Productivity Control System to evaluate detailed corrective measures.
- The setpoints resulting from the evaluation of the local expert systems are finally preset to the level 1 automation systems of the single plants.

A modular structure allows to extend the system in defined steps during the further development. Two modules are already integrated in the superimposed expert system, the production control of the sinter and the production control of the coke.
Target of the production control of sinter is the coordination between the sinter production in the sinter plant and the sinter consumption by the blast furnaces.
Basically for the operation plan the material mix of the sinter burden und the blast furnaces burden is calculated so that the produced amount of sinter minus process losses equals the sinter amount consumed by the blast furnaces. Anyway in real operation there are deviations of the sinter production as well as of the sinter consumption. These deviations are buffered by the sinter stock.
To ensure an operation with a defined sinter stock level a control of the sinter consumption of the blast furnaces is implemented by evaluating and presetting the target sinter basicity figure for the sinter plant.

Target of the production control of coke is a defined stock level of coke produced in the coke oven plant in Linz. Therefore this module evaluates the optimum ratio of the coke brands charged at the blast furnace and readjusts the setpoint.

4.4 Further actions

A first version of the VAiron Productivity Control System implemented with the described functionality is in use at voestalpine Stahl (GmbH). At the moment the actually implemented modules are fine-tuned and optimized.
For the future the gradual integration of further modules in the existing expert system is planed. Ideas are e.g. an optimized distribution of the available oxygen between the blast furnaces, the control of the slag quality for better utilization or the control of the hot metal amount.

5. Conclusions and outlook

It was shown that a powerful automation system based on expert system technology, ensures that the know-how and experience of the best operators and engineers are executed 24 hours a day, can lead to tremendous cost savings. These savings by far outnumber the costs of such a system.
Although reduction of costs is the predominant reason for installing such systems, there are also other benefits, that can not be quantified, but are worth mentioning, as there are for example

- Fewer process disturbances
- Smooth consistent operation in all shifts
- Early detection and therefore early reaction on any process changes or upcoming problems

Basically all developments were driven to reduce the final cost of the hot metal. It has been shown in more than 100 references that Blast Furnace and Sinterplant expert systems can significantly contribute to reduce the production costs. As the next step to further optimize the complete Ironmaking process, we are confident that the VAiron productivity control expert system will give us the desired result.

6. References

Buchanan, Shortliffe (eds.) (1984) Rule-Based Expert Systems: The MYCIN, The Addison-Wesley Series in Artificial Intelligence

Gottlob, G., Nejdl, W. (eds) (1990) Expert Systems in Engineering - Principles and Applications, Springer Verlag

Hörl, J., Schaler, M., Stohl, K., Piirainen, I. Ritamäki, O. (2006), Blast furnace Optimization – The Next Generation, Procedings of AISTech 2006, Cleveland, USA, May 1-4-, 2006

Inkala, P., Seppänen, M., Säily, S. (1994). The Rautaruukki-Kawasaki Blast furnace Expert System, Proceedings of 12th Hungarian Pig Iron and Steel Making Conference, Balatonszeplak, Hungary, Sepetmber 7-9, 1994

Sato, M. Kiguchi, M, Senoo, Y., Iida, O (1988), Development of Advanced Go-Stop System and its Application to Mizushima No. 4 Blast furnace, Steels&Metals Magazine, Vol. 26, No 10

Sun Wendong, Bettinger, D, Straka, G., Stohl, K. (2002), Sinter Plant Automation on a New Level!, Proceedings of AISE Annual Convention, Nashville, USA, Sep 30 - Oct 2, 2002

8

Design of Demand Forecasting Expert System for Dynamic Supply Chains

Hanaa E. Sayed, Hossam A. Gabbar and Shigeji Miyazaki
Okayama University
Japan

1. Introduction

When distributors and wholesalers seek help with issues relating to inventory management, they are usually concerned about an increasing level of out-of-stocks or over stocking. Out of stocks are leading to sales loss and customer service complaints. Over-stocks are resulting in slow inventory turnover and a buildup of dead inventory. In fact, out-of-stocks and over-stocks are actually a flip side of the same inventory management coin. Any effective initiative to resolve these issues must address core structural causes of these inventory management problems. Superior inventory management begins with timely, accurate, detailed demand forecasts.

Over last decade demand forecasting has played a prominent role in the corporations worldwide. Corporate executives have spent millions of dollars and invested thousands of man-hours trying to improve methods used & complicate it more. In each case little attention was paid to the integration between drivers, inputs and demand forecast (Harrison & Qizhong, 1993). In the face of all these advancements in hardware and software forecast error still remain high.

The inaccuracy in the forecast is due to previous researchers focused on statistical methods and their improvements only. There was no effort on the modeling of the problem and how to build an expert system to interact properly with the dynamic changes of the supply chain (Ajoy & Dobrivoje, 2005). The forecasting model is not treated as enterprise system has its specifications and constraints which are modeled and simulated.

In this research we propose a design of expert demand forecast system which is designed after deep understanding of demand cycle within dynamic supply chain and interaction between different parameters within the supply chain. It is utilizing Bayesian vector auto regression, restricted vector auto regression, and kernel fisher discriminant analysis (Scholkopf & Smola, 1998), (Scholkopf et al., 1999) with improved genetic algorithm to filter, analyze inputs and factors affecting demand along with demand history and then generate baseline and operational forecasts. This model proposes new mathematical and expert modeling methodology to generate forecasts. We used a practical case study from international FMCG (Fast Moving Consumer Goods) industry using over 1000 product types and results show that a significant forecast accuracy and other supply chain key performance indicators improvements over one year months rolling.

The proposed model is composed of the integration between statistical and intelligent methods with expert input to generate more accurate demand forecasts. The inputs to the model are history demand time series, demand factors history series and the expert inputs. The process starts with calculating the effects of demand factors on the demand series, which is followed by eliminating the effects of these factors. The next step is to perform the forecasting of raw or baseline demand. Finally, perform the estimation of the best collection of factors and activities in future based on history and expert inputs or using the judgmental input to adjust the activities collection. The outcome of this process is final operational forecast.

2. The detailed framework

The framework of the proposed demand planning model consists of three sub models; the first sub model is called "Factors Classifying Model". Its inputs are history demand series and demand factors. The model outputs are cleaned history demand and Regular Factors Matrix (RFM) of possible factors on the demand series. The first model is responsible for the following consecutive steps: (1) evaluating real demand by eliminating the effects of the unavailability; (2) calculating the effects of demand factors on the cleaned sales using multiple regression models; (3) establishing the knowledge base which is updated after each run of the model; and (4) classifying input factors based on effect on demand.

The second sub model is called "Intelligent Time Series Model". Its inputs are the cleaned history demand series, RFM. It is responsible for calculating time series components (trend, seasonality, and cycles) of the real demand and calculating raw or baseline forecast which represents demand without the effects of demand factors. Baseline is calculated by combining selected statistical methods (Bovas & Johannes, 1983): simple exponential smoothing, winter's additive and winter's multiplicative methods, other techniques can be found in (Allan, 2005). The best combination is obtained by calculating the best set of weights for each method using genetic algorithm which minimizes MSE.

Finally, the last sub model is the "Intelligent Combining Model". Its inputs are the generated baseline forecast, RFM. And its output is the final forecast including forecast factors. The model compares factors using genetic algorithm, which minimizes the cost and increases the profit of forecast.

The final outcome of the model is the final demand forecast (Operational Forecast) and activities which maximize profit. Operational forecast is the summation of baseline forecast and activities forecast. The model can be further tuned using opinions of experienced people, which can change any of the activities followed by recalculation of the forecast model based on the new suggested parameters by experts. The proposed model is shown in Fig.1.

The following sections explain the construction of domain knowledge for demand factors which is used throughout the model. This is followed by the explanations of the first sub model (i.e. factors classifying model) in details. Then the second sub model (i.e. intelligent times series model) is explained along with the different statistical methods. And then the proposed genetic algorithm is explained using selected case study.

3. The domain knowledge & data structure

As explained in the introduction, the model inputs are divided into three categories: demand series, demand factors, and setup parameters. Demand series is the history demand time series which is considered as numbers exist in a time frame. Demand factors such as

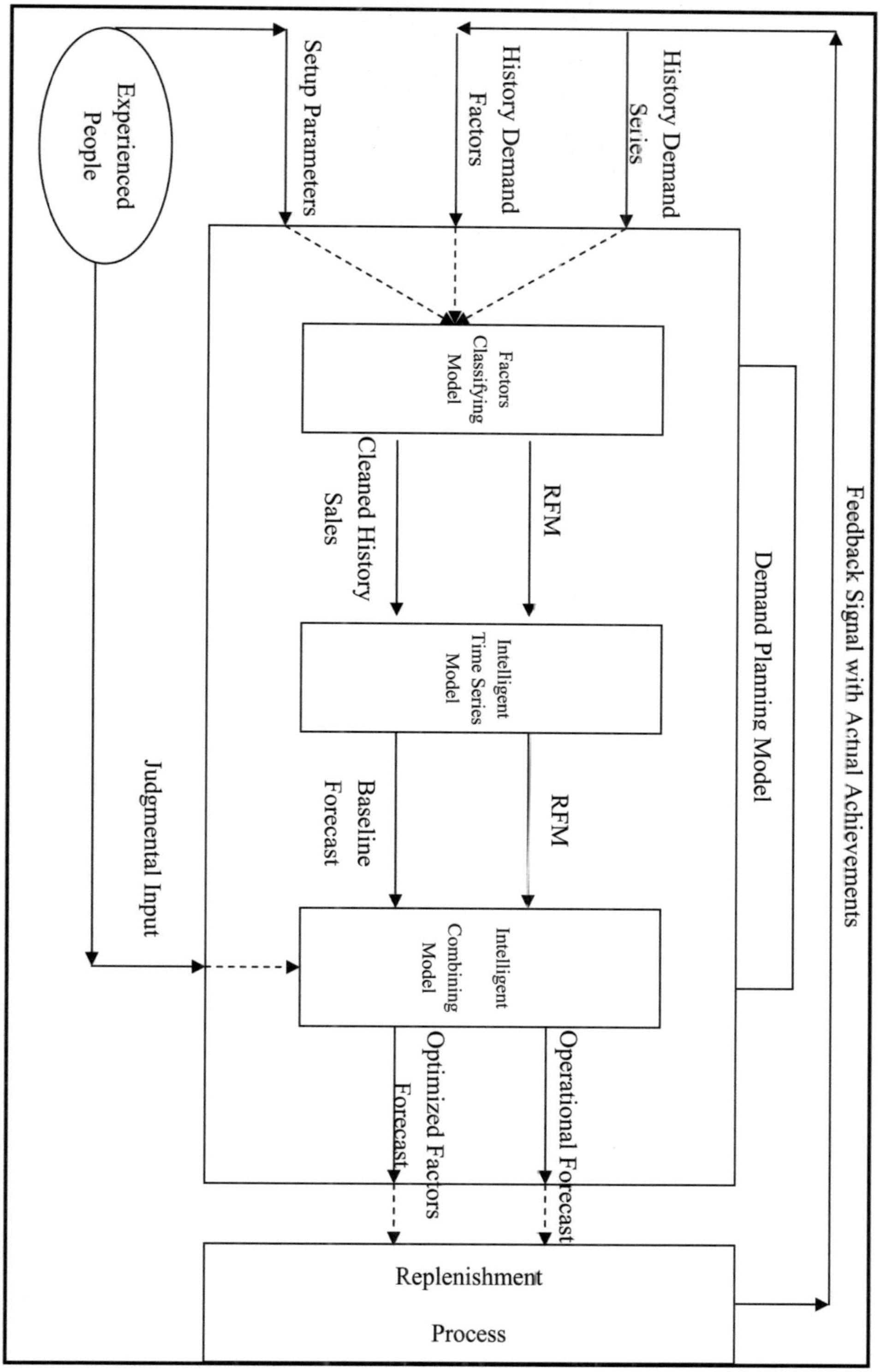

Fig. 1. Demand Forecast Model

activities or temperature. Set up parameters such as forecast horizon and history time buckets.
To ensure clear structuring of demand factors, it is needed to construct knowledge base, which is based on consumer products industry. It can be further tuned to fit another industry.
The following are the advantages behind the proposed knowledge base:
1. Explicitly define suitable structure of possible demand factors;
2. Enable the reuse of domain knowledge;
3. Clearly explain the different assumptions and intentions of model parameters;
4. Facilitate the analysis of domain knowledge.

3.2 "Demand Factors" classes

The classes of the demand factors domain knowledge are divided based on how they will be handled and analyzed in the model. Detailed explanations about the different demand factors with examples can be found in (Flores & Olson, 1992). Demand factors are divided into controllable and uncontrollable as shown in Fig.2.

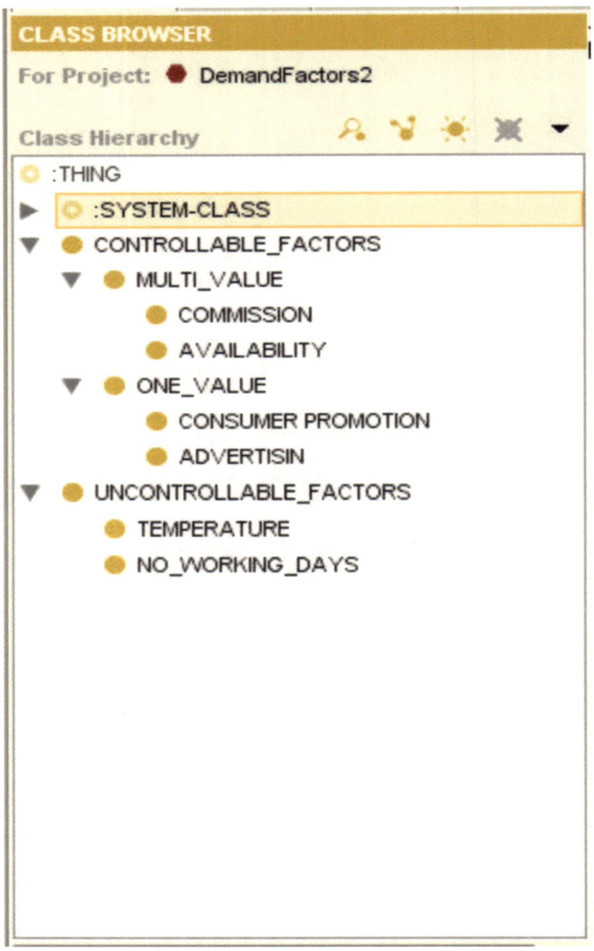

Fig. 2. Knowledge Base Classes for the Demand Factors

3.2 Controllable factors

Controllable factors are those that expert can control their timing and amount. During the forecast process, the proposed model calculates their effect percentages on demand series using multiple regression methods then forecast their time and amount which maximizes the profit.

Controllable factors are divided into multi value and one value. Multiple values mean its values are ranged from multiple numbers like percentage of discount, e.g. 2%, 4%, or any other value. One value means it occurs or not, it can be explained by ON / OFF, where ON is mapped to 1 and OFF is mapped to 0.

Multi value division is divided into:

1. Commission (CM): which indicates percentage of price discount given for certain period, and it can be maximum 100% and minimum 0%
2. Availability (AV): which indicated percentage of product availability, its maximum limit is 100% and its minimum limit is 0%.

One value division is divided into:

1. Consumer Promotion (CP): which are the promotions done to the consumers, like "chance to win" so its value is done or not done.
2. Advertising (AD): Like TV or radio advertising, or street shows, also its value is done or not done.

3.3 Uncontrollable factors

Uncontrollable factors means we can't control their time nor amount. In order to predict them in future, the proposed model forecasts them using time series analysis method like linear regression.

Uncontrollable factors are divided into:

Temperature (T): This represents the temperature degree for each period, so it can be varied under long range. The temperature is represented qualitatively based on ranges of the degrees as shown in Table 1.

No_Of_Working_Days (WD): Number of working days per period. It gives an indication of the strength of each period in terms of number of days they can produce and sell the product. WD is represented into two values small, and Normal as shown in Table 2.

Range	Quantitative
T< 10	VL (Very Low)
10 <= T < 20	L (Low)
20 <= T < 30	M (Moderate)
30 <= T < 35	H (High)
35 <= T	VH (Very High)

Table 1. Temperature Degree

Range	Quantitative
WD < 26	Small
WD > = 26	Normal

Table 2. Distribution of Number of Working Days

4. Factors classifying model

Factors Classifying model is the first sub model in the solution framework. The inputs to the sub model are the history demand series which is coming from sales history, the demand factors, products prices, and the setup parameters. The outcomes of that model are RFM and cleaned history demand series (Raw History Demand).
First module is using domain knowledge rule. Inputs are categorized and inserted into the predefined factors parameters which are used throughout the model. This division is useful where it facilitates the utilization of rules and constraints. It is easy to add additional factors in future where system can adapt itself automatically, without changing the model structure.
The second module, real demand calculation, is used to eliminate the effects of availability factor from regular series and promotion series to generate real history regular demand and real history promotion series.
Final module is activity analysis & cleaning. Its inputs are real history demand series and real history factors series. The outcome of the factors classifying model is the cleaned regular and promotion series, and the regular factors matrix and the promotion factors matrix. The term cleaned means that it represents the real demand without any effect of the demand factors. Multiple regression method is used to calculate the effects of demand factors on demand series. The framework of the cause & effect model is shown in Fig.3.

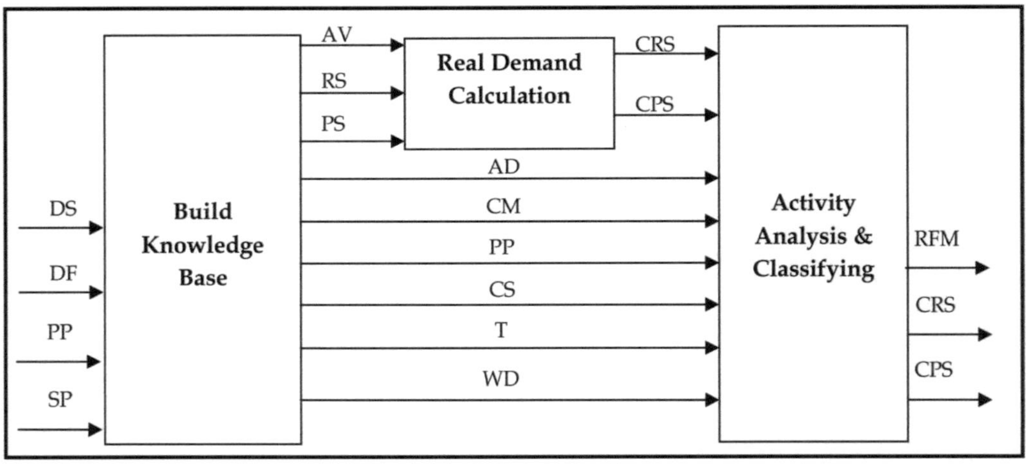

Fig. 3. Factors Classifying Model

4.1 Build knowledge base

Objectives:
This module is used to prepare and maintain the required data sets to perform the following tasks:
1. Calculate the data Series;
2. Calculate the activities costs;
3. Use the rules identified.

Inputs:

DS: represents the time series of the volumes of the demand and the time is the period buckets such as weeks or months.

DF: the history demand factors and activities and it consist of the following series:

P: series of the consumer promotions types and cost per month
CM: represents series of the price reduction percentage per month
AD: represents the series of the advertising types and cost per month
T: the temperature degrees per month series
WD: represents the series of number of working days per month
AV: availability % parameter
PP: represents the series of the product price history per month, this series is used to calculate the cost of the activities

Outputs:

RS: the time series of the regular demand (actual sales without the consumer promotions)
PS: the times series of the promotional demand.
AD: time series of one value either ON or OFF whether there was ad or not.
CM: the percentage of the price reduction.
CS: the series of the cost for all activities

```
For All History i, i is the monthly periods {

    IF (P_i > 0) Then {  PS_i = DS_i

                         RS_i = 0

    } else {   PS_i = o

               RS_i = DS_i

    } END IF

    CS_CP_i = PS_i * P_PC_i

    CS_CM_i = ( RS_i + PS_i ) * PP_i * CM_i

    CS_AD_i = AD_CC_i

    IF (T_i < 10) Then T_i = "VL"

    Else IF (10<= T_i < 20) Then T_i = "L"

    Else IF (20<= T_i < 30) Then T_i = "M"

    Else IF (30<= T_i < 35) Then T_i = "H"

    Else T_i = "VH"

    END IF

    IF (WD_i < 26) Then WD_i = "Small"

                  Else WD_i = "Normal"

    END IF  }
```

Fig. 4. Knowledge Base Algorithm

T: temperature series is a divided into ranges in order to enable analyzing them and forecasting them.

WD: number of working days, which affects the number of visits to the consumer, and hence the sales.

Constraints:

$RS \cap PS = \Phi$

AD = 1 or 0

4.2 Real demand calculation

Objective:

1. Obtain the real demand by removing the effect of the availability parameter on the sales:

$$\text{Loss} = 0, \text{ if availability} = 100\%$$

$$= [RS * (100 - \text{availability})] / \text{availability}, \text{ if availability} < 100\%$$

2. Removing the effect of promotion volumes on regular sales (For all RS = 0, RS = average (3 previous PS)

Constraints:

Availability <= 100%

```
For All History {
        IF (AV_i = 100) Then LS_i = 0
        Else LS_i = [(RS_i * (100 - AV_i))/AV_i]+[(PS_i*(100 - AV_i))/AV_i]
      END IF
        IF ( RS_i = 0 ) Then
                CPS_i = PS_i - LS_i
        Else    CRS_i = RS_i - Ls_i
        END IF
}
For All History {
        IF (CRS_i = 0) Then
                CRS_i = Average (CRS_i-2, CRS_i-1, CRS_i+1, CRS_i+2)
        END IF
}
```

Fig. 5. Real Demand Calculation Algorithm

4.3 Activity analysis & classifying

Objective:

1. Calculate the effect of the CP & AD & CM & CPS on the regular series using multiple regression statistical method for each uncontrollable pair (T, WD) to construct RFM;
2. Clean the regular series by removing the effect of the AD, CM and recalculate RS at PS > 0;
3. Classify the input factors based on effect using KFDA and improved genetic algorithm.

T	WD	CP (%)	CM (%)	AD (%)
VL	S	20	2	12
VL	N	23	3	14
L	S	27	5	18
L	N	35	7	19
M	S	40	8	25
M	N	46	10	27
H	S	52	11	29
H	N	60	12	31
VH	S	84	15	34
VH	N	95	17	36

Table 3. RFM Example

In the previous example, for raw one it indicates that when temperature is very low and #of working days is small then the effect of consumer promotion on the regular sales is 20%, the effect of 1% commission is 2%, and the effect of the advertising is 12%.

```
For Each Row in RFM {
        -- To calculate the CP%, AD%, CM% for the RFM_i
        Multiple_Regression (RFM_i)
}
-- Removing the effect of the AD & CM from the sales
FOR All History {
        AD_i% = GET_AD_RFM (T_i, WD_i)
        CM_i% = GET_CM_RFM (T_i, WD_i)
        CRS_i = CRS_i - AD_i% * CRS_i - CM_i% * CRS_i
}
FOR All History {
        IF (CPS_i >0) Then
        CRS_i = Average( CRS_i-2, CRS_i-1, CRS_i+1, CRS_i+2)
        END IF
}
G_KFDA (RFM);
```

Fig. 6. Activity Analysis & Classifying Algorithm

5. Intelligent time series model

After cleaned regular sales are calculated, using previous module, the history sales will be analyzed using statistical and computational methods. At this model three types of methods are used: SES, additive winter's method and multiplicative winter's method (Armstrong, 1998). Then the genetic algorithm is used to calculate the best weights between the three methods to give the least error and generate baseline forecast using optimum weights.

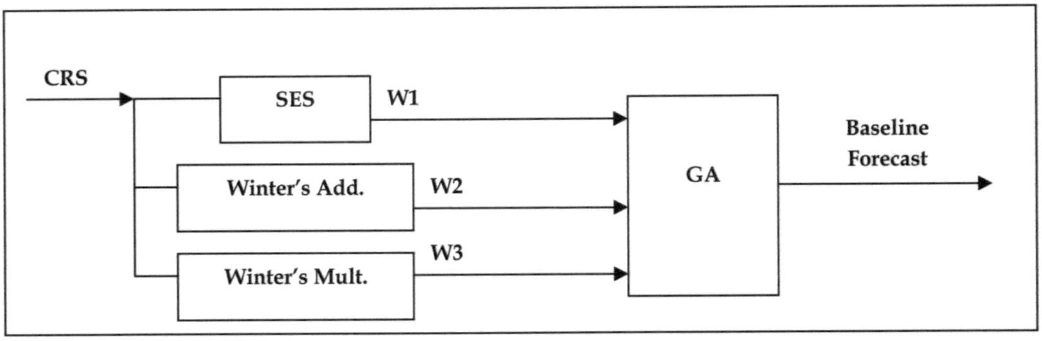

Fig. 7. Intelligent Time Series Model

5.1 Simple exponential smoothing

SES is used to forecast non seasonal Time series. The assumption is that the means moves slowly over time. Heuristically, in such a case it would be reasonable to give more weight to the most recent observations and less to the observations in the distant past.

A = CRS
Y = Forecast
K = number of history periods
$Y_n = \alpha A_n + (1 - \alpha) Y_{n-1}$
α is the smoothing constant and it is usually chosen between 0.05 and 0.30
Initial value of Y_0:
Through repeated equation of the SES, it can be shown that:

$$Y_n = \alpha [A_n + (1 - \alpha) A_{n-1} + (1 - \alpha)^2 A_{n-2} + \ldots + (1 - \alpha)^{n-1} A_1] + (1- \alpha)^n Y_0$$

Thus the influence of Y_0 on Y_n is negligible, provided that n is moderately large and $(1 - \alpha)$ is smaller than 1. We take the simple average of the available history data (A_1, A_2, $A_3, \ldots,$ A_n) as the initial estimate of Y.

Choosing the smoothing constant α

The best value is between 0.05 and 0.30 so by simulating the result by calculating the MSE for each α. and estimating α which gives least MSE is the optimum one.

5.2 Winters' methods

Winters (1960) considers linear trend model with seasonal indicators. The seasonal and the trend components can be either additive or multiplicative. More details about the methods equations are introduced in chapter 2.

$Y_0 = (1/K) \sum_{0<n<=k} (Y_n)$

For $\alpha = 0.05$ to 0.30 Do

  For $n = 1$ to K Do

    $Y_n = \alpha A_n + (1 - \alpha) Y_{n-1}$

  End For

  $MSE = (1/12) \sum_{k-12<n<=k} (A_n - Y_n)^2$

  Find least MSE

  Get Optimum α

  Obtain best Y

End For

Fig. 8. SES Algorithm

To make initialization, it is needed one complete cycle of data, i.e. s values. Then set

$$L_s = \frac{1}{s}(Y_1 + Y_2 + ... + Y_s)$$

To initialize trend, it is used s + k time periods

$$b_s = \frac{1}{k}\left[\frac{Y_{s+1} - Y_1}{s} + \frac{Y_{s+2} - Y_2}{s} - ... + \frac{Y - Y}{s}\right]$$

As long as the series is long enough, so it is used here k=s so that two completed cycles are used.
Initial seasonal indices can be taken as

$$S_k = \frac{Y_k}{L_s} \qquad k = 1,2,...,s$$

The parameters γ, β, and α must lie in the interval [0, 1[, and they are selected to optimize the MSE.

5.3 Proposed genetic algorithm

Objective:

The objective of GA is to calculate the optimum weights W = (W1, W2, W3) which minimize the MSE in the training set to get the best forecast.

W1 is the weight of the SES method
W2 is the weight of the winter's additive method
W3 is the weight of the winter's multiplicative method

GA elements:

Fitness function = min (MSE)

$MSE(Y) = (1/12) \sum_{k-12<n<=k} (A_n - Y_n)^2$

$Y_{final} = W_1 Y_1 + W_2 Y_2 + W_3 Y_3$

Constraints:

$0 <= W < 1$

$\sum W's = 1$

Representation:

Our variables are the weights of the different statistical methods.

First, we need to encode decision variables into binary strings. The length of the string depends on the required precision. In this case the domain of the variable w_j is $[a_j, b_j[$and the required precision is two places after the decimal point.

The required bits, denoted by m_j, for the variable is calculated as follows:

$$2^{mj-1} < (b_j - a_j) * 10^2 <= 2^{mj}$$

The mapping from a binary string to a real number for variable w is completed as follows:

$$W_j = a_j + \text{decimal (substring)} * (b_j - a_j)/(2^{mj} - 1)$$

Where the decimal (substring) represents the decimal value of substring_j for decimal variable w_j.

To calculate the number of digits needed to represent the weight:

$$(1 - 0) *100 = 100$$

$$2^{mj-1} < 100 <= 2^{mj}$$

$$(Mj -1) \log 2 < \log 100 <= Mj \log 2$$

$$Mj -1 < 6.6 <= Mj$$

$$Mj < 7.6$$

$$Mj >= 6.6$$

$$Mj = 7$$

Then number of digits needed for each weight is 7 digits. So the total length of the chromosome is 3 * 7 = 21 digits

Example of calculating the Weights:

W: 0011010 → its decimal number = 26

$W= 0 + 26 * 1/(2^7 - 1) = 0.20$

GA Procedure:

- Initialization of the population

The initial population is selected randomly. The population is consisting of 10 solutions as follows:

V1 = [00100110110101010110111]
V2 = [11001010001100000 1100]
V3 = [00001001001101010111 0]
V4 = [110010000100100001000]
V5 = [000000111110100000100]
V6 = [011111100110010100110]
V7 = [010001010011100001111]
V8 = [000000011101000001010]
V9 = [001010101010011000001]
V10= [111100000000000000111]

The corresponding decimals:

V1 = [w1, w2, w3] = [0.15, 0.42, 0.43]
V2 = [w1, w2, w3] = [0.80, 0.10, 0.10]
V3 = [w1, w2, w3] = [0.03, 0.61, 0.36]
V4 = [w1, w2, w3] = [0.79, 0.14, 0.07]
V5 = [w1, w2, w3] = [0.01, 0.96, 0.03]
V6 = [w1, w2, w3] = [0.50, 0.20, 0.30]
V7 = [w1, w2, w3] = [0.27, 0.61, 0.12]
V8 = [w1, w2, w3] = [0.00, 0.91, 0.09]
V9 = [w1, w2, w3] = [0.17, 0.32, 0.51]
V10= [w1, w2, w3] = [0.94, 0.00, 0.06]

Evaluation:

The process of evaluation the fitness of a chromosome consists of the following three steps

Evaluation Procedure:

Step 1. Convert the chromosome's genotype to its phenotype. This means converting binary string into relative real values, which is happened above.

Step 2. Evaluate the objective function f (w^k).

Step 3. Convert the value of objective function into fitness. For the minimization problem, the fitness is simple equal to the value of objective function eval (v_k) = f (w^k), k=1, 2..., pop_size

$$\text{eval}(v_k) = \text{MSE}(Y)$$

$$Y = w1 * Y1 + w2 * Y2 + w3 * Y3$$

It is clear that chromosome V_7 is the best result and that chromosome V_{10} is the weakest result.

Selection:

Its target to choose which solutions will remain in the new population and which solutions will be changed. By doing the following steps:

1. Get the least MSE from the original methods which is MSE
2. Arrange the solutions ascending based on their evaluation function
3. Compare the eval function for each solution by the MSE_{best}. The first one which is less than MSE_{best} will be taken to the new population. And the rest of the solutions will be changed.

Actual	SES	ADD	Multi
11.58	29.86	12.57	10.48
29.19	29.86	18.59	9.44
26.14	29.86	29.97	23.45
29.07	29.86	16.73	17.15
37.63	29.86	40.70	36.50
33.82	29.86	13.65	25.00
65.61	29.86	70.12	61.11
14.40	29.86	14.23	25.49
24.14	29.86	25.34	22.01
21.26	29.86	21.17	15.79
	24.00	67.04	81.78
	24.00	16.84	22.59
	24.00	19.10	15.19
	24.00	41.95	23.28
	24.00	39.55	22.64
	24.00	45.41	21.95
	24.00	48.45	26.02
	24.00	43.67	26.61
	24.00	63.10	42.92
	24.00	8.67	16.86
	24.00	15.02	19.22
	24.00	11.08	21.21

				weights			V1	
				W1	W2	W3	Forecast	Error
11.58	29.86	12.57	10.48	0.15	0.42	0.43	14.3	7.1
29.19	29.86	18.59	9.44	0.80	0.10	0.10	16.3	165.7
26.14	29.86	29.97	23.45	0.03	0.61	0.36	27.1	1.0
29.07	29.86	16.73	17.15	0.79	0.14	0.07	18.9	103.9
37.63	29.86	40.70	36.50	0.01	0.96	0.03	37.3	0.1
33.82	29.86	13.65	25.00	0.50	0.20	0.30	21.0	164.5
65.61	29.86	70.12	61.11	0.27	0.61	0.12	60.2	29.3
14.40	29.86	14.23	25.49	0.00	0.91	0.09	21.4	49.6
24.14	29.86	25.34	22.01	0.17	0.32	0.51	24.6	0.2
21.26	29.86	21.17	15.79	0.94	0.00	0.06	20.1	1.3
MSE	204	72	80				MSE	52.3

V2		V3		V4		V5		V6	
Forecast	Error	Forecast	Error	Forecast	Error	Forecast	Error	Forecast	Error
26.2	213.6	12.4	0.6	26.0	209.0	12.6	1.1	20.6	81.2
26.7	6.2	15.6	183.8	26.8	5.6	18.4	116.6	21.5	59.4
29.2	9.5	27.6	2.1	29.4	10.8	29.8	13.1	28.0	3.3
27.3	3.2	17.3	138.6	27.1	3.9	16.8	149.3	23.4	31.9
31.6	36.2	38.8	1.5	31.9	33.2	40.5	8.1	34.0	13.0
27.8	36.7	18.3	241.6	27.2	43.5	14.1	387.4	25.2	74.9
37.0	817.8	65.6	0.0	37.8	774.3	69.5	15.3	47.3	335.7
27.9	181.1	18.8	19.3	27.3	167.3	14.7	0.1	25.4	121.4
28.6	20.1	24.3	0.0	28.7	20.5	25.3	1.3	26.6	6.1
27.6	40.0	19.5	3.1	27.6	40.6	21.1	0.0	23.9	7.0
MSE	136.5		59.1		130.9		69.2		73.4

V7		V8		V9		V10	
Forecast	Error	Forecast	Error	Forecast	Error	Forecast	Error
17.0	28.9	12.4	0.7	14.4	7.7	28.8	296.3
20.5	75.0	17.8	129.8	15.8	180.0	28.7	0.2
29.2	9.2	29.4	10.7	26.6	0.2	29.5	11.3
20.3	77.0	16.8	151.3	19.1	99.0	29.2	0.0
37.3	0.1	40.3	7.3	36.8	0.8	30.2	54.8
19.3	209.8	14.6	368.0	22.1	136.3	29.6	17.8
58.3	53.8	69.3	13.9	58.9	45.7	31.6	1157.7
19.7	28.5	15.2	0.6	22.6	66.8	29.6	231.6
26.2	4.1	25.0	0.8	24.4	0.1	29.4	28.0
22.9	2.6	20.7	0.3	19.9	2.0	29.1	61.2
MSE	48.9		68.3		53.9		185.9

Table 4. Test Sets

Implementing on our example:
Eval (V1) = 52
Eval (V2) = 136
Eval (V3) = 59
Eval (V4) = 131
Eval (V5) = 69
Eval (V6) = 73
Eval (V7) = 49
Eval (V8) = 68
Eval (V9) = 54
Eval (V10) = 186

Arranging the solutions based on the evaluation function:

V7	49
V1	52
V9	54
V3	59
V8	68
V5	69
V6	73
V4	131
V2	136
V10	186

Table 5. Ordered Solution

The MSE_{best} = MSE(V7) = 72
Then V7 will stay in the new population and the rest of the solutions will be changed.

Crossover:

Crossover used here is one-cut-point method, which randomly selects one cut-point and exchanges the right parts of two parents to generate offspring.
The probability of crossover is set as p_c = 0.25, so we expect that, on average, 25% of chromosomes undergo crossover. Crossover is performed in the following way:

```
Begin
        k ← 2;
        While (k<= 9) do
                R ← random number from [0, 1[;
                If (rk < 0.25) then
                        Select Vk as one parent for crossover;
                End
                k ← k+1;
        End
End
```

Fig. 9. Crossover Procedure

Assume that the sequence of random numbers is:

0.266 0.288 0.295 0.163 0.567 0.0859 0.392 0.770 0.548 0.337

This means that the chromosome v4 and v6 were selected for crossover. Then we generate random number pos from the range [1, 20] (because 21 is the total length of a chromosome) as cutting point or in other words, the position of the crossover point. Assume that the generated number pos equals 3, the two chromosomes are cut after the first bit, and offspring are generated by exchange the right parts of them as follow:

V4 = [000000111110100000100]
V6 = [010001010011100001111]
| |
V
V4' = [010000111110100000100]
V6' = [000001010011100001111]

Mutation:

Mutation alters one or more genes with a probability equal to the mutation rate. The probability of mutation is set as $p_m = 0.01$, so we expect that, on average, 1% of total bit of population would undergo mutation. There are m * pop_size = 21 * 10 = 210 bits in the whole population; we expect 2.1 mutations per generation. Every bit has an equal chance to be mutated. Thus we need to generate a sequence of random numbers r_k (k=1,2,…,210) from the range [0,1]. Assume that the following genes will go through mutation:

Bit_pos	Chrom_num	bit_no	random_num
50	2	8	0.00987
62	2	20	0.00311
110	5	5	0.00128

After Mutation:

V_2 = [110010100011000001100]
V'_2 = [110010110011000001110]
V_5 = [000000111110100000100]
V'_5 = [000010111110100000100]
After the mutation & the crossover, the new generation is:
V'_1 = [001001101101010110111]
V'_2 = [110010110011000001110]
V'_3 = [000010010011010101110]
V'_4 = [010000111110100000100]
V'_5 = [000010111110100000100]
V'_6 = [000001010011100001111]
V'_7 = [010001010011100001111]
V'_8 = [000000011101000001010]

V'_9 = [001010101010011000001]
V'_{10} = [111100000000000000111]

We continue the iterations until the termination condition happened. The termination condition is that when doing 10 consecutive iterations without generating any new solution which is giving better evaluation function than the best previous one. Then we stop and the best solution with the optimum weights will be the last better evaluation function solution we obtained.

6. Intelligent combining model

The objective from this module is to calculate the optimum choices of the activities in the future periods which maximize the profit. So using this genetic algorithm module we can choose the best time we can do the activity and the best timing.
The first step is to forecast the uncontrollable factors for the required periods. T and WD are forecasted using the intelligent time series model at Fig.10. Then to calculate what is the best combination of the controllable factors (AD, CP, and CM) timings using the genetic algorithm and the values are calculated using RFM from the values of forecasted T & WD corresponding to the time point.

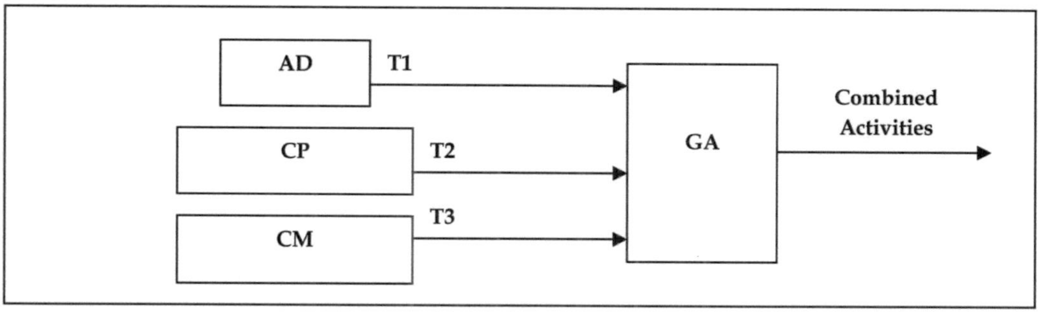

Fig. 10. Intelligent Combining Model

GA Elements:

Fitness function = Max (Profit)
Profit = Sales - Cost

Constraints:

Cost <= Limited_Cost

Assumptions:

Periods = 12 periods

Representation:

There are three variables:
The timing of the CP for the coming 12 periods
The timing of the CM for the coming 12 periods
The timing of the AD for the coming 12 periods

To encode the above variables into binary digits so each variable will be consisting of 12 genes or bits representing the 12 periods. And if the bit is 0 that means there is no activity at this period, if the bit is 1 that means there is an activity at this period.
Total number of genes at each chromosome will equal 12 * 3 = 36.

GA Procedure:

Initialization of the population:

The initial population is selected randomly. The population is consisting of 10 solutions. Example of initial population:

V1 = [101101011101010010010101001010101010]
V2 = [001010101010101010001111100101010100]
V3 = [111010001100101001011111000100001010]
V4 = [010101010000111010101000011100101010]
V5 = [101010101010000001010101110010101011]
V6 = [010101010110101010010000111001010111]
V7 = [110101011011001010001110101000101011]
V8 = [111010010101001010010101001000010111]
V9 = [110110010100010101010100011100010110]
V10 = [010000101001010101010100010001100011]

After calculating their real values:

V1 ➔ CP will happen in future in periods: 1, 3, 4, 6, 8, 9, 10, and 12
CM will happen in future in periods: 2, 5, 8, 10, and 12
AD will happen in future in periods: 3, 5, 7, 9, and 11
And so on

Evaluation:

Objective function = Max (Sales – cost)
CP_i ➔ If at point i there is CP then it is 1, else it is 0
AD_i ➔ If at point i there is CP then it is 1, else it is 0
CM_i ➔ If at point i there is CP then it is 1, else it is 0
$CP\_Volume_i = CP_i * Y_i * GET\_CP\_RFM (T_i, WD_i)$
$AD\_Volume_i = AD_i * Y_i * GET\_AD\_RFM (T_i, WD_i)$
$CM\_Volume_i = CM_i * Y_i * GET\_CM\_RFM (T_i, WD_i)$
$Sales = \sum_{i=1to12} PP * [Y_i + (CP\_Volume_i + AD\_Volume_i + CM\_Volume_i)]$
$CP\_Cost_i = Average (P\_PC_i) * CP\_Volume_I$
$AD\_Cost_i = AD_i * Average (CS\_AD_i)$
$CM\_Cost_i = Average (PP_i) * CM\_Volume_I$
$Cost = \sum_{i=1to12} (CP\_Cost_i + AD\_Cost_i + CM\_Cost_i)$

For maximization problem, the fitness is simply equal to the value of the objective function

$eval(v_k) = f(x^k), k=1, 2, \ldots pop\_size.$

In this case we have three x's: x_1 represents the CP timing through the future 12 periods. x_2 is represents the CM timing through the future 12 periods and x_3 represents the AD timing through the future 12 periods.

CP_Effect, AD_Effect and CM_Effect are calculated through getting the value of the % from the RFM table.

Selection:

In most practices, a roulette wheel approach is adopted as the selection procedure; it belongs to the fitness-propotional selection and can select a new population with respect to the probability distribution based on fitness values. We constructed the roulette wheel as follows:

Calculate the fitness value $eval(v_k)$ for each chromosome v:

$$Eval(v_k) = f(x^k) \qquad k=1, 2,\ldots,pop\_size$$

Calculate the total fitness for the population:

$$F = \sum_{k=1 \text{ to pop-size}} eval(v_k)$$

Calculate selection probability p for each chromosome v_k:

$$p_k = eval(v_k) \,/\, F, \qquad k=1, 2,\ldots,pop\_size$$

Calculate cumulative probability for each chromosome v_k:

$$q_k = \sum_{j=1 \text{ to } k} p_j, \qquad k=1, 2,\ldots,pop\_size$$

This selection process begins by spinning the roulette wheel pop_size times; each time, a single chromosome is selected for a new population in the following way:

Selection Procedure:

Step 1. Generate a random number r from the range [0,1].
Step 2. If $r<=q_1$, then select the first chromosome v_k; otherwise, select the kth chromosome v_k ($2 <= k <= pop\_size$) such that $q_{k-1} < r <= q_k$.

Crossover & mutation will be implemented as explained in GA model. A detailed case study will be explained in the next chapter.

7. Results

In this session, there is a comparison between traditional statistical methods and the proposed model results. The comparison is based on the forecasting accuracy measure which is MSE. By running it on different types of products time series patterns and showing the difference between the two scenarios, it is shown that for all different types of times series the proposed model is giving better results than any traditional statistical method. Other examples are shown also in (Fred & Scott, 1992).

The model is run for 6 consequent months. And after each month the results are compared between the traditional statistical methods and the proposed model. And the following graphs are showing how improvements have done. A comparison between the models MSE is also shown. That proofs that the proposed model is improving forecasting accuracy for different types of times series. We will find too that each statistical method is giving better forecasting accuracy for some types of time series. That shows that complicating or using a standalone statistical method is not the best case to improve the forecasting accuracy.

No trend no seasonality

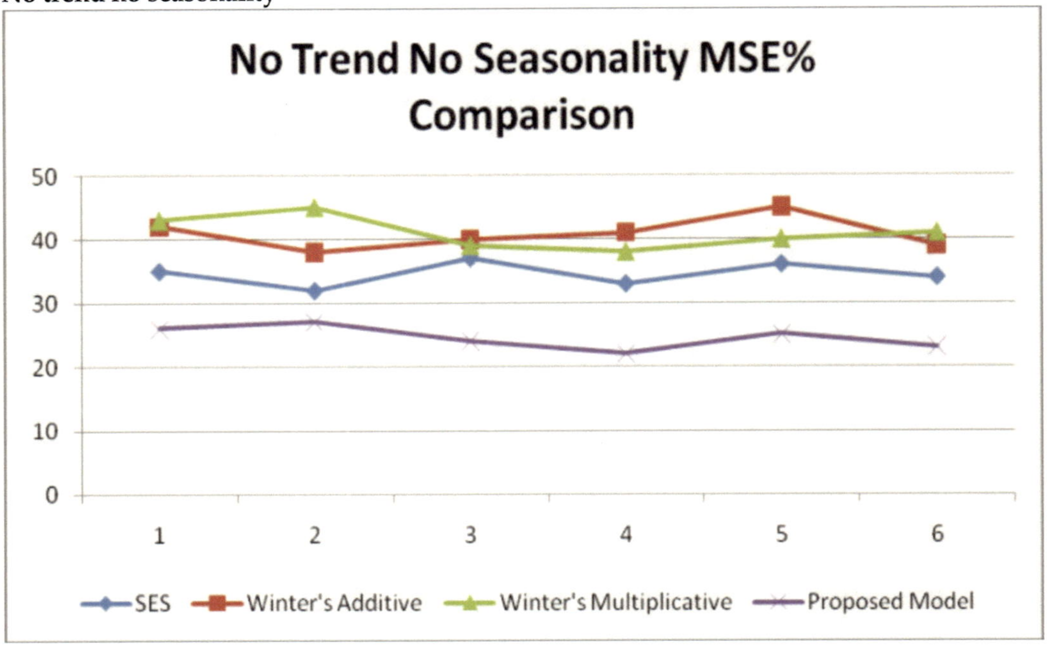

Fig. 11. Comparison of MSE% for No Trend No Seasonality Time Series

No trend linear seasonality

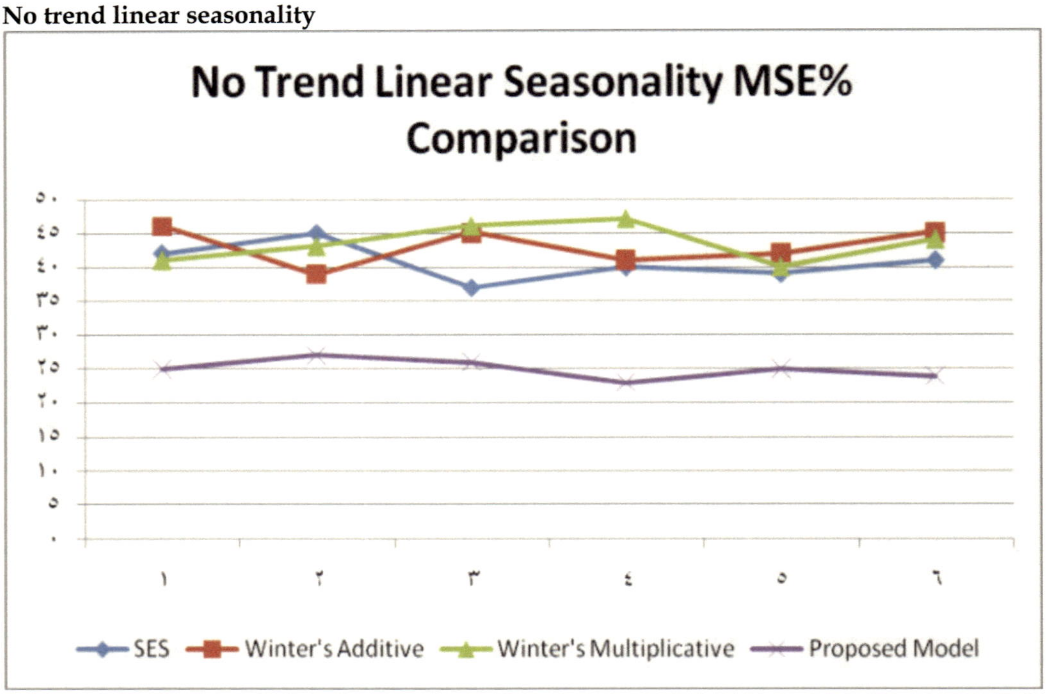

Fig. 12. Comparison of MSE% for No Trend Linear Seasonality Time Series

Linear trend linear seasonality

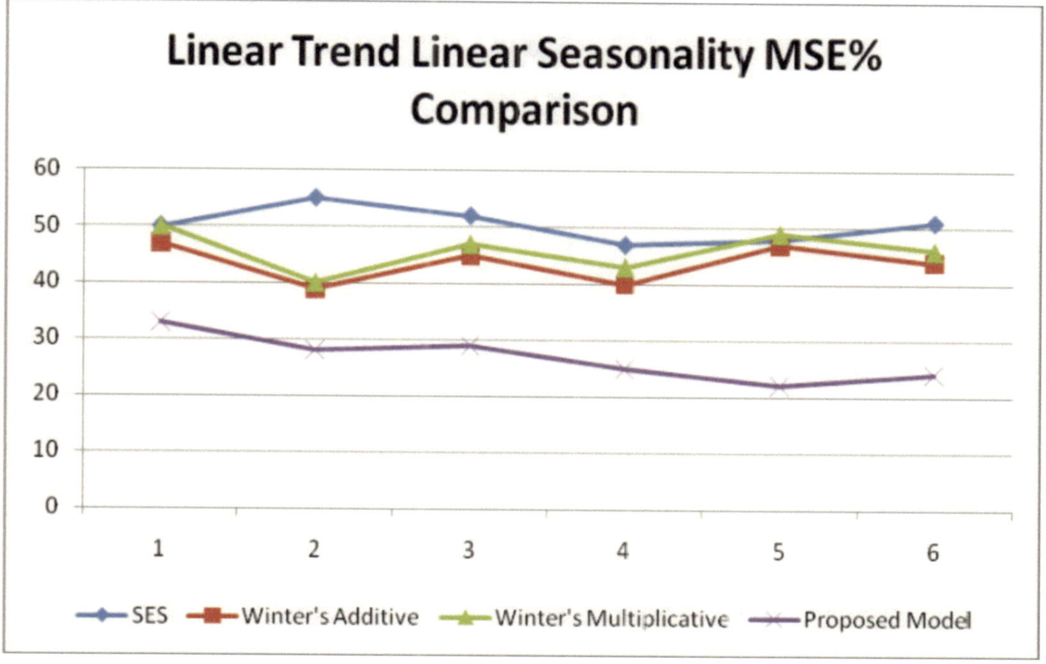

Fig. 13. Comparison of MSE% for Linear Trend Linear Seasonality Time Series

Linear trend exponential seasonality

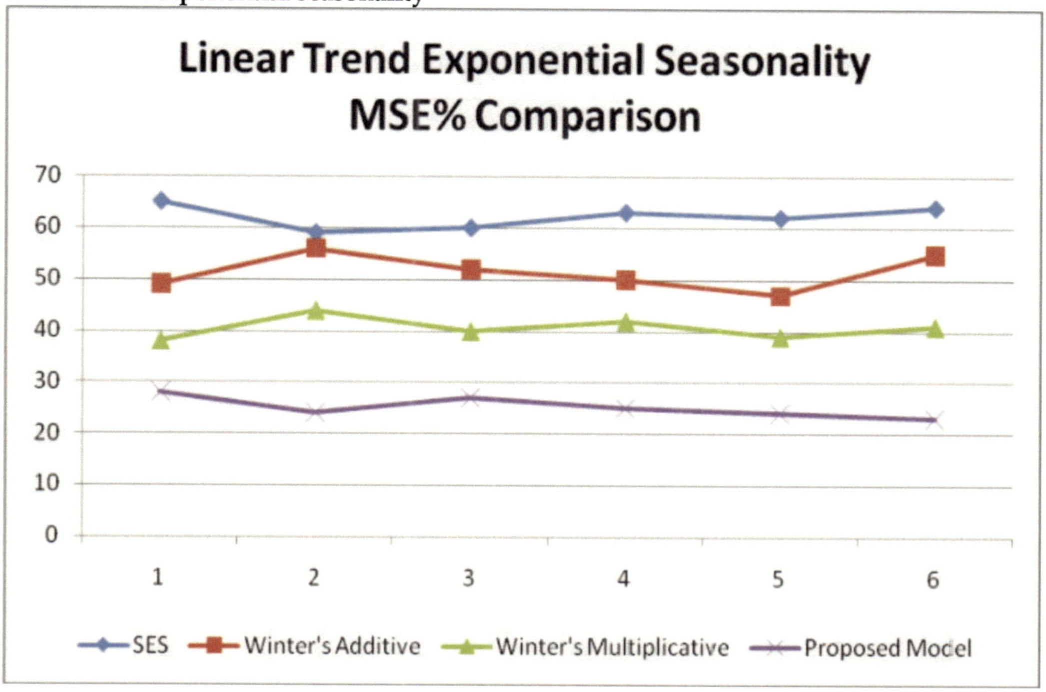

Fig. 14. Comparison of MSE% for Linear Trend Exponential Seasonality Time Series

Exponential trend linear seasonality

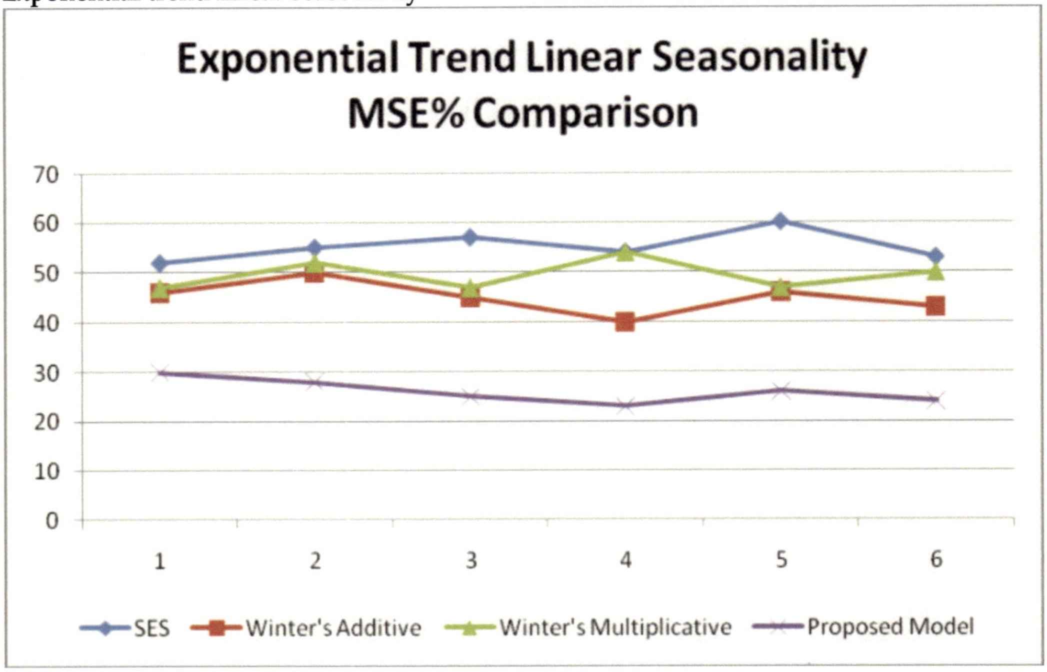

Fig. 15. Comparison of MSE% for Exponential Trend Linear Seasonality Time Series

Exponential trend exponential seasonality

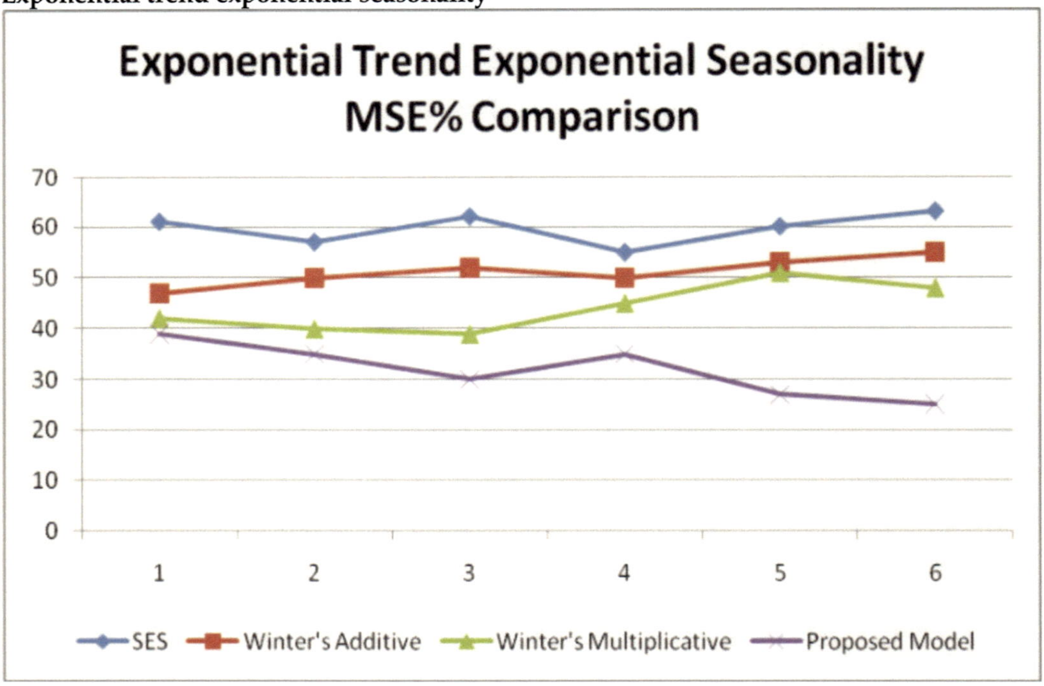

Fig. 16. Comparison of MSE% for Exponential Trend Exponential Seasonality Time Series

8. Conclusions & future work

Forecasting using single statistical method showed limitations in providing accurate forecasting. The use of a combined intelligent model is needed for providing accurate forecasting specially for complex environments which have different demand factors. As described in this chapter, the use of a new genetic algorithm is proposed to combine statistical methods and for combining activities with the baseline forecast, which suggests forecasts that are more accurate. First, the genetic algorithm searches for the best combination of weights between the methods, which minimizes MSE error. Then, genetic algorithm searches between the activities timing to choose the best timing, which increases the profit. Forecast methods are chosen so that they can cover different types of times series. Comparison of the obtained results shows better accuracy than that obtained using traditional methods. Other combinations of forecast methods can be included in the proposed solution for better forecast accuracy. Further improvement to the forecast model is obtainable by changing the crossover, mutation in the genetic algorithm, or by changing the initial population. As future work, it is recommended to try to add some neural techniques to the proposed model as it showed improving the forecasting capabilities.

9. References

Ajoy K. Palit and Dobrivoje Popovic, 2005, Computational Intelligence in Time Series Forecasting theory and engineering applications, Springer.

Allan Timmermann, 2005, Forecast Combinations, UCSD.

B. Scholkopf, A.J. Smola, 1998. Nonlinear component analysis as a kernel eigenvalue problem. *Neural Computation,* 10:1299-1319. [Online]. Available from: http://www.mitpressjournals.org/doi/abs/10.1162/089976698300017467. DOI: 10.1162/089976698300017467.

B. Scholkopf, S. Mika, C.J.C. Burges, P. Knisch, K.R. Muller, G. Ratsch. 1999. Input space versus feature space in kernel based methods. *IEEE Transactions on Neural Networks,* 10:1000-1017. DOI: 10.1109/72.788641.

Bovas Abraham, Johannes Ledolter, 1983, Statistical Methods for Forecasting, Wiley.

Flores, B.E., Olson, B.L. & Wolfe, C., 1992, Judgmental adjustment of forecasts: a comparison of methods. International Journal of Forecasting, 7, 421-433.

Fred Collopy, J. Scott Armstrong, 1992, Rule-Based Forecasting: Development and Validation of an Expert Systems Approach to Combining Time Series Extrapolations, Management Science, 38 (10), 1394-1414.

H.C.Harrison, Gong Qizhong, 1993, "An intelligent business forecasting system", ACM Annual Computer Science Conference, Pages: 229 - 236.

J. Scott Armstrong, 1998, "Integration of Statistical Methods and Judgment for Time Series Forecasting: Principles from Empirical Research", University of

Pennsylvania, Philadelphia, PA Fred Collopy Case Western Reserve University, Cleveland, OH.

9

A Multi-Agent Expert System for Steel Grade Classification Using Adaptive Neuro-fuzzy Systems

Mohammad Hossein Fazel Zarandi[1], Milad Avazbeigi[1], Mohammad Hassan Anssari[2] and Behnam Ganji[1]
[1]*Amirkabir University of Technology,*
[2]*University of Tehran*
Iran

1. Introduction

Iron and steel industry is a crucial basic section for most of the industrial activities. This industry provides the primary materials for construction, automobile, machinery and many other businesses. Furthermore, the iron and steel manufacturing is highly energy consuming. The influence of an efficient process control on the cost and energy reduction and environmental effects in iron and steel industry makes the process control one of the main issues of this industry.

Iron and steel industry should mainly rely on the new integrated production processes to improve productivity, reduce energy consumption, and maintain competitiveness in the market. Without rational process controlling systems, the potential benefits of new production processes can't be fully realized. Process control is the key function in the production management. Furthermore, a high degree of real-time operation and dynamic adjustment capabilities is required. In particular, the coordination of different production stages must be considered so as to achieve overall goals of the entire production processes.

In most steel companies, the principal production planning and scheduling techniques have been essentially manual techniques with little computerized decision support. These manual techniques are mainly based on the know-how and the experiences of those experts who have worked in a plant for years. Considering the above mentioned characteristics of a steel manufacturing, some important characteristics of this area can be summarized as:

- Steel manufacturing is a multi-stage process, logically and geographically distributed, involving a variety of production processes (Ouelhadj et al., 2004);
- In a steel grade classification, an operator has to determine the amount of additive materials in steel-making process. This is mainly based on the know-how and the professional experience of experts who have worked in the plant for years;
- A high degree of real-time operation and dynamic adjustment capabilities is required;
- The output of some stages is usually the input of some other stages, so integration is mandatory;
- The percentage of elements in steel-making usually has a fuzzy nature

According to the above characteristics of the steel manufacturing, a steel automation system is needed to represent distribution and integration existing in this industry. A fuzzy multi-agent expert system can provide such capabilities.

In the literature, there are only a few scientific papers and technical reports which are related directly to the design and development of intelligent expert systems for iron and steel industry. Perez De La Cruz et al. (1994) presents an expert system which is designed for the problem of identifying a steel or cast iron from a microphotograph. However, the essential aim of the implemented system is to help metallography students in the task of learning the concepts relevant for identifying and classifying steels and cast irons. Kim et al. (1998) presents an application of neural networks to the supervisory control of a reheating furnace in the steel industry. Also there are some papers concentrating on the scheduling of different steel making processes like casting, rolling, scrap charge using fuzzy multi-agent systems (Cowling et al., 2003; Cowling et al., 2004; Lahdelma & Rong, 2006; Ouelhadj et al., 2004). Finally, Fazel Zarandi and Ahmadpour (2009) present a fuzzy multi-agent system for steel making process. Each process of electric arc furnace steel making is assigned to be an agent, which works independently whilst coordinates and cooperates with other acquaintance agents. Adaptive neuro-fuzzy inference system (ANFIS) is used to generate agents' knowledge bases.

Most of the previous researches are related to the scheduling and coordination of steel making processes while our attempt is mainly about the steel grade classification. This chapter presents a new multi-agent expert system based on adaptive neuro-fuzzy inference system to help an operator to determine the amount of additive materials in steel-making process. Since the percentage of elements in steel-making usually has a fuzzy nature, the fuzzy rule sets and adaptive neuro-fuzzy systems are more accurate and robust to model this complex problem.

In the design of the adaptive neuro-fuzzy systems, determination of the appropriate number of the rules is critical. In other words, large number of rules increases the complexity of the systems exponentially. In this research, to estimate the optimal number of rules, first a clustering algorithm is presented based on the historical data of steel grade process. Moreover, appropriate values for the parameters of clustering algorithm including the number of rules and membership functions of fuzzy rule set are determined using an iterative procedure.

Here, an agent named "Clustering Agent" carries clustering procedure using the initial random membership functions obtained by another agent named "Initiator Agent".

The output of the "Clustering Agent" is cluster centers and the initial values of membership functions in fuzzy rule set. This output is used as the input to the adaptive neuro-fuzzy agents. These agents apply ANFIS to tune the obtained fuzzy rule set generated by clustering agent. ANFIS combines the advantages of fuzzy rule sets and neural networks capability of learning and hence provide a powerful tool of modeling fuzzy systems. In the proposed multi-agent system, five agents are responsible for implementation of ANFIS for different additives, each of which is responsible for each additive.

The cooperation of agents forms a fuzzy expert system which can help the operator to determine the suitable amount of additive materials in steel-making process.

The multi-agent expert system is programmed and simulated using Matlab. For three grade of steel including CK45, C67 and 70CR2 historical data are applied first for extraction of fuzzy rules using the "Clustering Agent" and "Initiator Agent", and then for tuning the ANFIS agents.

2. Steel making process

Iron and steel plants and their components are usually large-scale and very complex. In order to improve quality and productivity, many techniques have been developed combining the computer system and control theory and expert system. To overcome the complexity, the problem can be divided into some small sub-problems. In this chapter a model for steel grade classification in pneumatic steel making method (converter) is proposed. In this section, first the steel making process is briefly presented and then, in the next sections our proposed model is explained.
The steel manufacturing involves many processing stages and diverse technologies. In Fig. 1 the sub-processes of steel making process are shown (Council on Wage and Price Stability, 1977).

- **Coke production:** Coke is produced independently and is charged to blast furnace as one of the raw materials.
- **Sintering plant:** Iron ore is roasted with coke and limestone to produce a clinker.
- **Blast Furnace:** In the blast furnace the sintered ore is converted into the pig iron. With blowing hot air and fuel from bottom of furnace and charging sintered iron ore, and coke from top of furnace pig iron produce in the bottom of furnace. Pig iron transported in open ladles to metal mixers.
- **Steel Production:** Pig iron is smelted to steel. Steel in LD steel works. The steelmaking processes consist of three stages: steel-making, refining, and continuous casting.

In steel making stage, carbon, sulphur, silicon, and other impurity contents of molten iron are reduced to desirable levels by burning with oxygen in a converter or Electric Arc Furnace. The output from the stage is molten steel with the main alloy elements. To obtain the different grades of steel, some materials are charged in LD or EAF. These materials are called additives of alloying metals. These alloying metals tune the percentage of the elements such as carbon, manganese, aluminium, and etc. For fine-tuning the molten steel from the steel-making process is poured into ladle furnace (LF) by a crane. The operator at this stage further refines the chemicals and eliminates impurities in molten steel or adds the required alloy ingredients.
After refining, molten steel is poured into a tandish for casting. In the casting stage, molten steel flows down from a hole at the bottom of the tandish into the crystallizer. The last process is rolling.
Alloying in steel-making process and grade classification is a very important stage. In order to omitting human errors, an expert system is proposed to help an operator to determine the amount of additives.

3. Proposed multi-agent system

The proposed multi agent system has three types of agents including:

- Initiator agent which provides the input for the clustering agents. The output of the initiator agent is a set of the initial membership functions generated randomly.
- Clustering agent which carries clustering procedure using the initial random membership functions obtained by another agent named initiator agent.
- ANFIS agents apply ANFIS to tune the obtained fuzzy rule set generated by clustering agent. ANFIS combines the advantages of fuzzy rule sets and neural networks capability of learning and hence provide a powerful tool of modeling fuzzy systems. In the proposed multi-agent system, five agents are responsible for implementation of ANFIS for different additives, each of which is responsible for each additive.

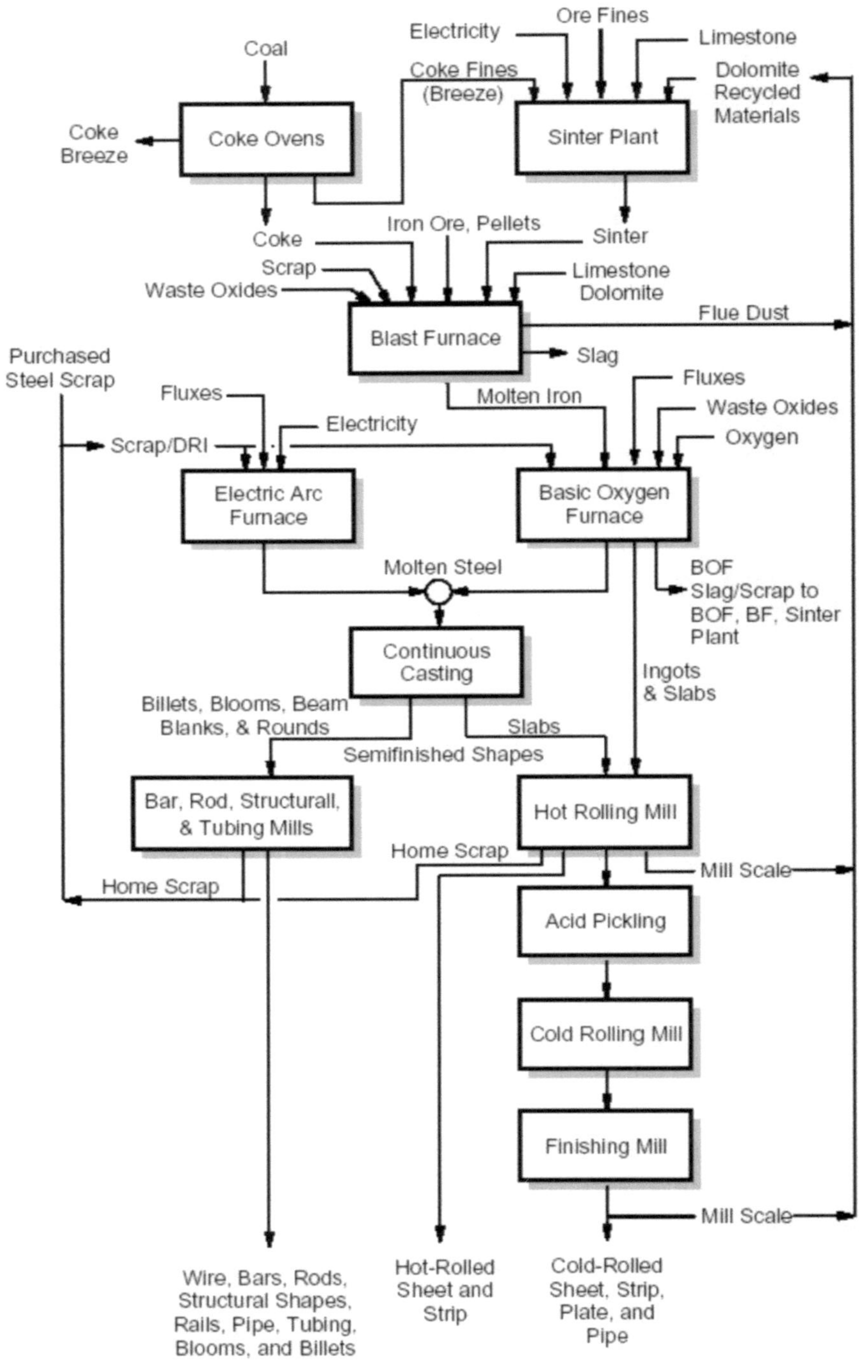

Source: Adapted from U.S. Council on Wage and Price Stability, *Report to the President on Prices and Costs in the United States Steel Industry, 1977* (COWPS, October 1977).

Fig. 1. Overview of steel making Process

The cooperation of agents forms a fuzzy expert system which can help the operator to determine the suitable amount of additive materials in steel-making process.

3.1 Initiator and clustering agents

The basic objective of the cluster analysis is to partition optimally the n unlabeled data points into c clusters base on a similarity measure. In crisp clustering, the separation of the clusters is sharp. However, in the real world problems, the separation of the clusters is usually fuzzy. Fuzzy clustering analysis has been extensively studied by many researchers (Bezdek & Pal, 1992; Huntsberger et Al., 1993; Moghaddam Zadeh & Bourbakis, 1997; Nguyen & Cohen, 1997; Pal & Ghosh, 1992). The most commonly used fuzzy clustering algorithm is fuzzy C-means (FCM), developed by Bezdek (1993). The objective function of FCM is defined as:

$$J(U,V;X) = \sum_{i=1}^{c} u_{ij}^{m} d_{ij}^{2} \quad (1)$$

where, u_{ij} is membership function of element j in cluster i:

$$\sum_{i=1}^{c} u_{ij} = 1, \forall j = 1,..., n \tag{2}$$

where, V_i is the cluster center of fuzzy cluster i, $d_{ij} = \left\| x_j - v_i \right\|$ is the Euclidean distance between i-th cluster center and j-th data point; and m is a weighting exponent that determines the degree of fuzziness. The necessary conditions for equation (1) to reach its minimum are:

$$v_i = \frac{\sum_{i=1}^{n} u_{ij}^{m} x_j}{\sum_{j=1}^{n} u_{ij}^{m}} \tag{3}$$

$$u_{ij} = \left[\sum_{k=1}^{c} \left(\frac{d_{ij}}{d_{kj}}\right)^{2/(m-1)} \right]^{-1} \tag{4}$$

In a batch-mode operation, FCM determines the cluster center v_i and the membership matrix U using the following steps (Bezdek, 1993):
Step 1: Initialize the membership matrix U with random values between 0 and 1 such that the constraints in Equation (2) are satisfied.
Step 2: Calculate c fuzzy cluster center v_i, i=1,…,c, using Equation (3).
Step 3: Compute the Cost Function according to Equation (1).
Stop if either it is below a certain tolerance value or its improvement over previous iteration.

Step 4: Compute a new U using Equation (4). Go to step 2.
FCM suffers from some challenging problems such as unknown number of clusters, noise contaminated data and supervisory determining the u:

- The first is that the number c of clusters must be pre-defined and the resulting structure for the specified number of clusters is assumed to be the best. This is seldom the case in practice. Thus, the difficult problem encountered is the cluster validity, which is required to evaluate the quality of the c-partitions resulting from the algorithms.
- The second is that the FCM algorithm is sensitive to noise in the data. To solving this problem in many algorithms based on FCM, the m parameter is fixed in a predefined value (Bezdek, 1993).

To improve the performance of clustering various clustering validity indices have been proposed. However, most of them focus on improving robustness or extending the function of FCM (Krishnapuram & Keller, 1993; Pedrycz, 1996; Nasraoui & Krishnapuram, 1996; Fazel Zarandi et al., 2009). In this book chapter, an unsupervised clustering is proposed which allows initializing the u, automatic setting of optimal cluster number, and finding the most appropriate m.
The objective function of penalized Fuzzy c-means proposed by Yang and Su (1994) is defined as follows:

$$J = \frac{1}{2}\sum_{i=1}^{c}\sum_{j=1}^{n}(u_{ij})^m d_{ij}^2 - \frac{1}{2}v\sum_{i=1}^{c}\sum_{j=1}^{n}(u_{ij})^m Ln\alpha_i \tag{5}$$

where u_{ij} is the membership degree of the *j-th* data point Xj in the *i-th* cluster, d_{ij} is their distance, N is the total number of data and c the number of clusters to be found, α_i is a proportional constant for class j and v >= 0 is a constant. When v equals zero, we will have J_{FCM}.
Now consider the problem of minimizing J with respect to u_{ij} fuzzy, subject to m>1 and the constraints (2).
As we know:

$$0 \le u_{ij} \le 1 \tag{6}$$

and this constraint many be eliminated by setting $u_{ij} = S_{ij}^2$ with S_{ij} real. We adjoin the constraints (2) and (6) to J with a set of Lagrange multipliers (λ_i) to give:

$$J = \sum_{i=1}^{c}\sum_{j=1}^{n}(u_{ij})^m d_{ij} - v\sum_{j=1}^{c}\sum_{j=1}(u_{ij})^m \ln\alpha_i + \sum_{j=1}^{n}\lambda_i(\sum_{i=1}^{c}u_{ij}-1) \tag{7}$$

$u_{ij} = S_{ij}^2$ then:

$$\frac{\partial J}{\partial S_{ij}} = 2m(d_{ij} - v\ln\alpha_i)S_{ij}^{2m-1} + 2S_{ij}\lambda_i \tag{8}$$

$$\frac{\partial J}{\partial S_{ij}} = 0 \qquad then: \quad S_{ij}{}^{2(m-1)} = \frac{-\lambda i}{m(d_{ij} - v\ln\alpha_i)} \tag{9}$$

By summing over j and using (2) the necessary conditions for Equation (7) to reach its minimum are:

$$\alpha_i = \frac{\sum_{j=1}^{n} u_{ij}^{m}}{\sum_{i=1}^{c}\sum_{j=1}^{n} u_{ij}^{m}} \tag{10}$$

$$v_i = \frac{\sum_{j=1}^{n} u_{ij}^{m} x_j}{\sum_{j=1}^{n} u_{ij}^{m}} \tag{11}$$

$$u_{ij} = \left[\sum_{l=1}^{c} \frac{(d_{ij}^2 - vLn\alpha_i)^{1/(m-1)}}{(d_{il}^2 - vLn\alpha_l)^{1/(m-1)}} \right]^{-1} \tag{12}$$

The objective function (5) has two main components. The first component is similar to the FCM objective function and has a global minimum when each data point is in a separate cluster. The global minimum of the second component can be achieved when all points are in the same cluster such that it controls the number of clusters.

According to (10), (11), (12) an iterative procedure is proposed for obtaining the optimal cluster centers. In this procedure, an unsupervised method is used for finding the membership matrix *U*, *m* and v. The program for finding the initial *U* is shown in Fig. 2.

Clusters can be found easier and with less number of iterations using the initial agent's program. The pseudocode of the clustering agent combining the initial agent's program is also shown in Fig. 3.

```
u=zeros(c, n);
sum = 0;
for j=1:n
  for i=1:c
    b(I) = rand;
sum= sum+ b(i);
end
for i=1:c
  u (i, j)=b(i)/sum;
end
sum=0;
end
```

Fig. 2. Pseudocode of the initial agent's program

Step 1: Set the initial values in the parameter of the algorithm, for instance P=0.0001, ν=0 and m=1.001.
Step 2: Find the membership matrix, *U* with initial agent.
Step 3: Calculate α and *V* vectors by the Equations (10), (11).
Step 4: Find the distance matrix, *D* as follows:

$$d_{ij} = |x_j - v_i| \quad j = 1.....,n \qquad i = 1.....,c \tag{13}$$

Step 5: Calculate the cost function *J* from Equation (5).
Step 6: If $|J - P| \leq \varepsilon$ go to step 11 Else go to step 7.
Step 7: *P=J*.
Step 8: From Equation (12) up to date the membership matrix, *U*.
Step 9: Keep the values of *v, u, m, ν,* and α in new symbols.
Step 10: Go to step 3.
Step 11: *m=m*+0.001, and ν=ν+0.001.
Step 12: Compute *J, D, α,* and *V* from Equations of (5), (13), (10), and (11).
Step 13: If $|J - P| \leq \varepsilon$ stop. Else go to step 14.
Step 14: Keep the values of *v, u, m, ν,* and α in new symbols.
Step 15: Go to step 3.

Fig. 3. Pseudocode of the clustering agent's program

So from algorithm we can find the cluster centers with optimal location and number. After running the algorithm we can merge some cluster center that they are the same or very near each other, but in our model we want to use these cluster centers for training, so we don't eliminate any of them and train our model with some repetitive data.

3.2 ANFIS agents

Neuro-fuzzy models have played an important role in the design of the fuzzy expert systems. However in most situations, the proper selection of the number, the type, and the parameters of the fuzzy membership function and rules are crucial for achieving the desired performance. The desired performance has yet been achieved through the trial and error. This fact highlights the significance of tuning of the fuzzy systems.
ANFIS is a fuzzy Sugeno network in the framework of adaptive systems facilitating learning and adaptation. Such a framework makes models more systematic and less relying on expert knowledge. To understand the ANFIS architecture, consider the following fuzzy system which has two rules and is a first order Sugeno model:
Rule 1:

$$if\ (x\ is\ A_1)\ and\ (y\ is\ B_1)\ then\ (f_1 = p_1 x + q_1 y + r_1) \tag{14}$$

Rule 2:

$$if\ (x\ is\ A_2)\ and\ (y\ is\ B_2)\ then\ (f_2 = p_2 x + q_2 y + r_2) \tag{15}$$

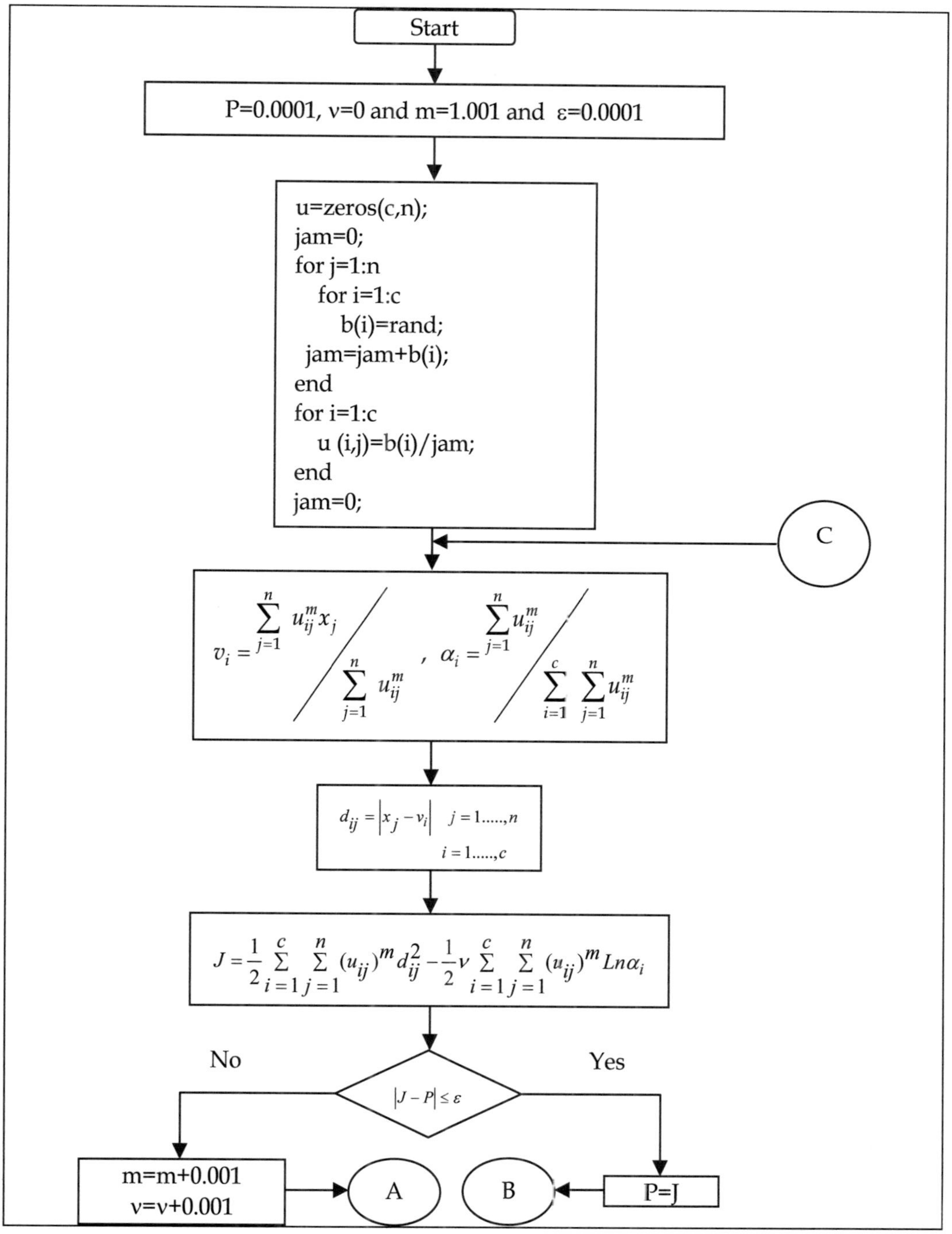

Fig. 4. Flowchart of the initiator and clustering agents' procedures (part I)

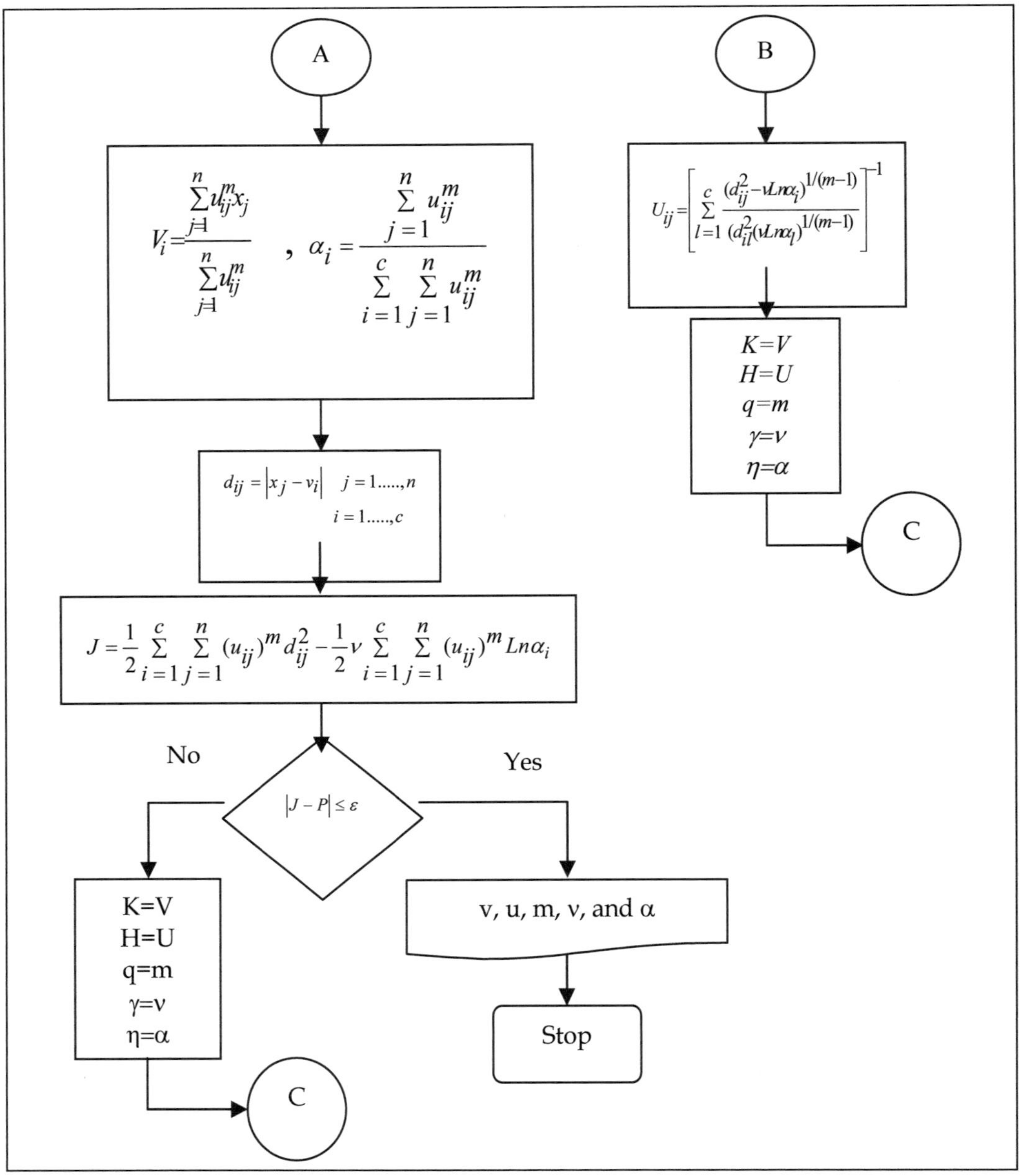

Fig. 4. Flowchart of the initiator and clustering agents' procedures (part II)

Several types of fuzzy reasoning have been proposed in the literature (Lee, 1990a and 1990b). Depending on the type of fuzzy reasoning and fuzzy if-then rules employed, most fuzzy inference systems can be classified into three types:

- The overall output is the weighted average of each rule's crisp output induced by the rule's firing strength (the product or minimum of the degrees of match with the premise part) and output membership functions. The output membership functions used in this scheme must be monotonic functions (Tsukamoto, 1979).

- The overall fuzzy output is derived by applying "max" operation to the qualified fuzzy outputs (each of which is equal to the minimum of firing strength and the output membership function of each rule). Various schemes have been proposed to choose the final crisp output based on the overall fuzzy output; some of them are centroid of area, bisector of area, mean of max, maximum criterion, etc (Lee, 1990a and 1990b).
- Takagi and Sugeno's fuzzy if-the rules are used (Sugeno, 1985; Takagi and Sugeno, 1985). The output of each rule is a linear combination of input variables plus a constant term, and the final output is the weighted average of each rule's output. A possible ANFIS architecture to implement these two rules is shown in Fig. 5. Note that a Circle indicates a fixed node whereas a square indicates an adaptive node (the parameters are changed during training). Here, O_{li} denotes the output of node i in layer l.

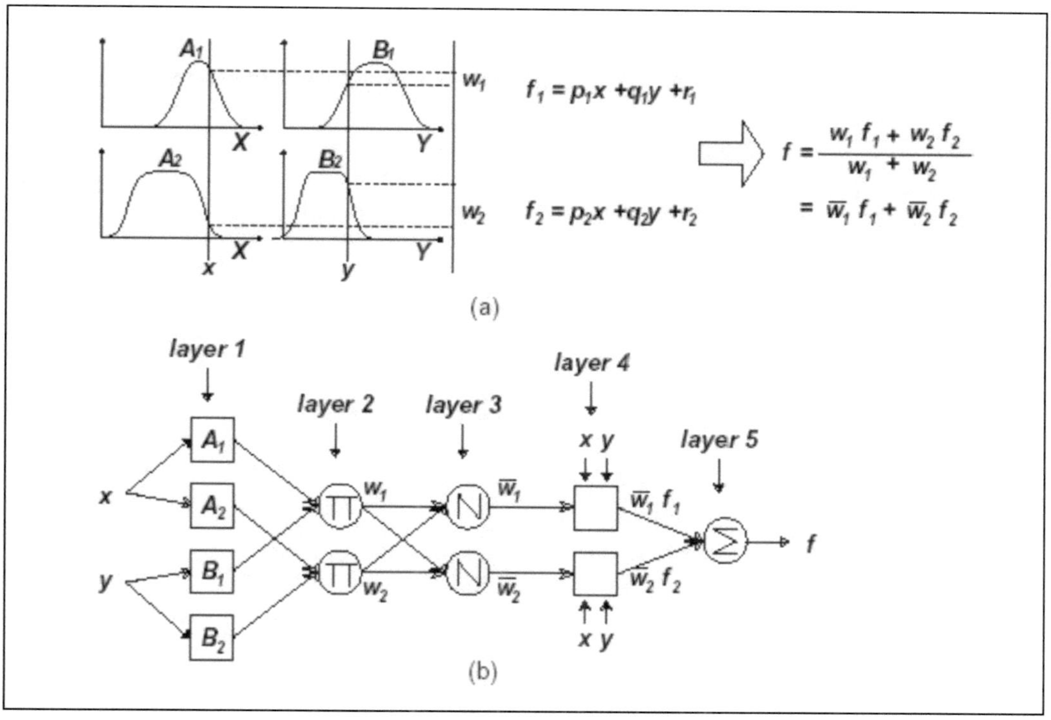

Fig. 5. ANFIS architecture

The explanation of the layers of ANFIS is as follows:

Layer 1: All the nodes in this layer are adaptive nodes. The output of each node is the degree of membership of the input of the fuzzy membership functions represented by the node:

$$O_{1,i} = \mu_{A_i}(x) \quad i = 1,2 \tag{16}$$

$$O_{1,i} = \mu_{B_i}(x) \quad i = 3,4 \tag{17}$$

where, A_i and B_i are any appropriate fuzzy sets in parametric form, and $O_{1,i}$ is the output of the node in the ith layer. This study uses bell shape membership functions. A bell shape membership function can be shown as follows:

$$\mu_{A_i}(x) = \frac{1}{1 + \left[\left(\frac{x - c_i}{a_i} \right)^2 \right]^{b_i}} \tag{18}$$

Here, a_i, b_i and c_i are the parameter for the membership functions.
Layer 2: The nodes in this layer are fixed (not adaptive). They are labelled by M to indicate that they play the role of a simple multiplier. The outputs of these nodes are given by:

$$O_{2,i} = w_i = \mu_{Ai}(x)\mu_{Bi}(y) \quad i = 1,2 \tag{19}$$

The output of each node in this layer represents the firing strength of the rule.
Layer 3: Nodes in this layer are also fixed nodes. They are labelled by N to indicate that they perform a normalization of the firing strength from the previous layer. The Output of each node in this layer is given by:

$$O_{3,i} = \overline{W_i} = \frac{W_i}{W_1 + W_2} \qquad i = 1,2 \tag{20}$$

Layer 4: All the nodes in this layer are adaptive nodes. The output of each node in this layer is simply the product of the normalized firing strength and a first order polynomial (for first order Sugeno model):

$$O_{4,i} = \overline{W}_i f_i = \overline{W}_i (P_i x + q_i y + r_i) \quad i = 1,2 \tag{21}$$

where p_i, q_i and r_i are design parameters (referred to as consequent parameters since they deal with the then-part of the fuzzy rule).
Layer 5: This layer has only one node labelled by S to indicate that it performs the function of a simple summation. The output of this single node is given by:

$$O_{5,i} = \sum_i \overline{W}_i f_i = \frac{\sum_i W_i f_i}{\sum_i W_i} \qquad i = 1,2 \tag{22}$$

The ANFIS architecture is not unique. Some layers can be combined and still produce the same output. In this ANFIS architecture, there are two adaptive layers (Layers 1 and 4). Layer 1 has three modifiable parameters (a_i, b_i and C_i) pertaining to the input MFs. These parameters are called premise parameters. Layer 4 has also three modifiable parameters (p_i, q_i and r_i) pertaining to the first order polynomial. These parameters are consequent parameters.
The task of the training or learning algorithm for this architecture is to tune all the modifiable parameters to make the ANFIS output match the training data. It should be noted that a_i, b_i and c_i describe the sigma, slope and center of the bell shape membership functions. If these parameters are fixed, the output of the network becomes:

$$
\begin{aligned}
f &= \frac{W_1}{W_1+W_2} f_1 + \frac{W_2}{W_1+W_2} f_2 \\
&= \overline{W}_1 f_1 + \overline{W}_2 f_2 = \overline{W}_1 (P_1 x + q_1 y + r_1) + \overline{W}_2 (P_2 x + q_2 y + r_2) \\
&= (\overline{W}_1 x +) P_1 + (\overline{W}_1 y) q_1 (\overline{W}_1) r_1 + (\overline{W}_2 x) P_2 + (\overline{W}_2 y) q_2 + (\overline{W}_2) r_2
\end{aligned}
\tag{23}
$$

which is a linear combination of modifiable parameters. Therefore, a combination of gradient descent and the least-squares method (hybrid learning rule as in Jang, 1991) can easily identify the optimal values for the parameters p_i, q_i are r_1. If the membership functions are not fixed and are allowed to vary, the search space becomes large and consequently, the convergence of the training algorithm becomes slower.

3.3 Merging ANFIS with clustering

Clustering techniques are primarily used in conjunction with radial basis function or fuzzy modeling to determine the initial location of the radial bases functions or fuzzy if-then rules. For this purpose, clustering techniques are validated on the basis of two assumptions:

- The similar inputs to the target system which have to be modeled should produce the similar outputs.
- These similar input-output pairs are bundled into clusters in the training data set.

First assumption states that the target system to be modeled should be a smooth input-output mapping; this is generally true for the real-world systems. Second assumption requires that the data set has to conform to some specific type of statistical distribution functions. However, this is not always true and therefore clustering techniques used for structure identification in neural networks or fuzzy modelings are highly heuristic. That's why heuristic methods are widely used to overcome the problem.

Fuzzy or neuro-fuzzy systems define a rule for every inputs and outputs. For instance, in an ANFIS model with 10 inputs which every input is mapped to two membership functions, 2^10=1024 rules can be formed, and with further inputs, and mapping to further MFs the number of rules increases exponentially. Hence, a data set can be partitioned into several groups with the similar properties and later these groups can be used as the training data for ANFIS. In our case we could develop a model with fewer rules than ANFIS.

4. Implementation, verification and validation of the multi-agent expert system for the steel grade classification problem

The basic oxygen process is characterized by three things:

- The use of gaseous oxygen as the sole refining agent.
- A metallic charge composed largely of blast furnace iron in a molten condition, thus greatly reducing the thermal requirements of the process.
- Chemical reactions that proceed quite in bath of comparatively low surface -to-volume ratio, thus minimizing external heat losses.

A schematic representation of progress of refining in top-blown vessel is shown in figure Fig. 6.

As the Fig. 6 shows the percent of elements are not crisp and they can be better modelled using fuzzy numbers. This is also valid for the final steel. That's why in this research the fuzzy methods are used for the clustering. The cluster centers are then used for training the ANFIS model.

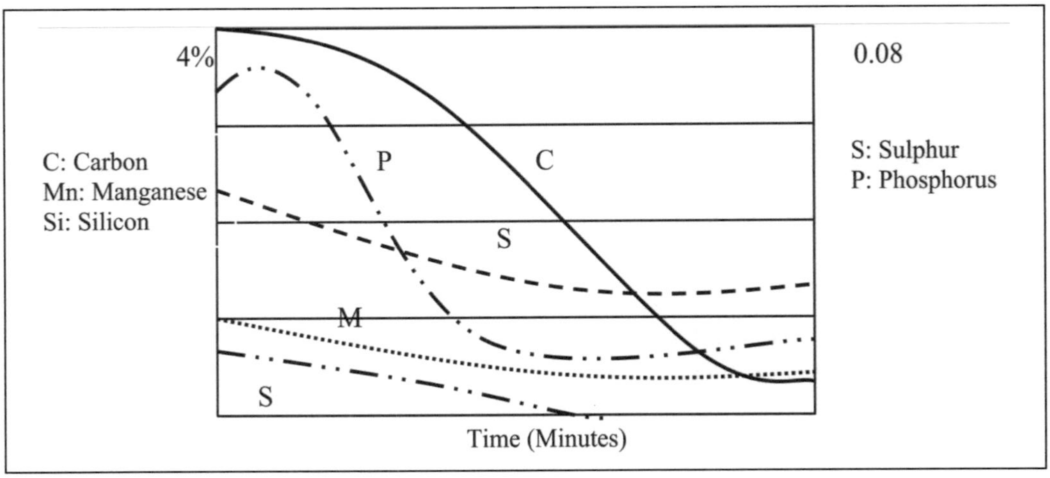

Fig. 6. Schematic representation of the progress of refining in top-blown vessel

About 200 data were collected in a matrix, named with the mark of steel. A sample of the collected data is shown bellow:

Steel Analyze in LD				*Steel Analyze in LF*						*Amount of Additives*				
C% *100	Mn% *100	P% *1000	Temp.	C% *100	Mn% *100	Si% *1000	P% *1000	S% *1000	Temp.	FeMn Kg	FeSi Kg	Al Kg	Granol Kg	SiCa Kg
12	37	31	1675	45	63	16	20	16	1670	770	290	06	590	190
16	20	24	1680	46	67	30	28	25	1675	850	539	15	540	440
14	23	26	1670	44	70	33	32	28	1665	845	593	18	540	490
12	19	28	1673	68	73	37	30	24	1670	970	665	14	650	565
15	25	26	1682	47	55	20	28	24	1678	540	360	14	580	260
11	21	28	1680	46	63	27	25	20	1675	760	485	10	630	385
09	21	27	1679	50	68	32	31	26	1674	845	575	16	740	475
10	21	24	1671	45	74	30	32	27	1668	953	540	17	700	440
08	15	28	1682	48	72	29	20	15	1677	1030	520	05	720	421
10	14	18	1677	43	53	25	21	17	1672	700	450	07	590	350
10	15	20	1673	47	58	28	27	20	1674	770	500	10	660	400
09	14	19	1674	45	62	22	28	22	1671	863	395	12	650	295
12	16	22	1670	44	67	33	29	21	1665	920	595	11	575	495
16	18	22	1680	46	69	38	30	30	1675	920	683	20	539	583
12	20	27	1671	50	73	20	32	18	1670	950	360	08	680	260
10	20	20	1679	49	72	21	30	19	1674	935	377	09	700	277

Table 1. Sample of collected data for CK45

According to the proposed algorithm the collected data are clustered and then the cluster centers (*C=10*) are saved in a matrix.

The values of the fuzzification parameters for 10 clusters are shown below. These parameters are related to the objective function of the clustering method.

m1	m2	m3	m4	m5	m6	m7	m8	m9	m10	m11	m12	m13	m14	m15
3.2	3.27	2.53	2.63	3.12	2.41	2.27	3.23	2.38	2.21	3.17	3.15	3.54	2.78	2.7

Table 2. Fuzzification parameters value

Vi ≈ .098, i=1,…,15.

All of these parameters are obtained by an unsupervised mode. If v equals zero, the cost function converts to Fuzzy c-mean's cost function. After the clustering, the cluster centers are used as the inputs for the ANFIS training. The number of rules in knowledge base and the running time decrease considerably by using the output of the clustering method as the input of the ANFIS.

C%	16.9959	15.0000	14.0000	16.9994	10.0091	9.0010	10.0005	14.8235	16.0000	16.9999
Mn%	20.9999	16.3357	21.0000	18.0000	14.0000	15.9940	16.0000	15.5730	15.0040	16.0000
P%	24.0020	28.0000	24.0000	29.8114	23.0002	28.2872	25.0000	30.0000	20.0128	25.0008
Temp.	73.0000	74.0003	78.7339	80.0000	80.0000	74.0047	73.4254	71.5233	74.0000	80.0000
C%	46.0120	42.0007	47.0000	48.9922	43.0278	44.9913	45.0000	43.0000	43.0000	48.0000
Mn%	73.0000	68.5728	65.8806	53.0642	69.0523	71.1385	71.4639	60.0000	66.0000	69.0000
Si%	27.0000	21.0000	30.0000	29.1963	20.0000	25.9769	21.0058	25.9270	23.0000	33.6949
P%	31.0000	30.9995	25.0000	29.8779	25.6069	24.0000	25.0000	25.0000	29.0000	26.0002
S%	28.0000	28.0000	27.0000	27.9538	28.0000	31.9940	25.0000	22.8422	22.1667	19.8773
Temp.	71.0000	74.9999	73.9558	70.0000	73.9979	70.0000	74.2199	77.4732	72.0974	72.0000
FeMn	92.4316	85.0000	85.0009	76.0001	82.9576	82.0001	95.0000	84.0000	86.4096	84.0000
FeSi	40.0000	54.0000	50.6572	53.9992	37.5990	58.1757	51.7653	49.6328	38.0000	53.9912
Al	20.0000	20.0000	6.2156	17.9602	23.9869	16.0000	18.0000	14.9998	3.0289	19.6295
Gran.	52.1006	63.9593	56.5167	66.0000	52.0000	55.5068	66.9999	69.9870	69.9992	61.3691
SiCa	26.0001	38.4433	58.2097	49.0000	49.0000	55.0000	31.6977	49.0000	40.6215	40.2289

Table 3. Input, Output, and Additive Elements Cluster matrix for CK45.

We use the training data in the following form:

$$
\begin{aligned}
y_1 = [F_eM_n], U = [\underbrace{C\%, Mn\%, P\%, T}_{\text{Steel Analyze in LF}}, \underbrace{C\%, Mn\%, Si\%, P\%, S\%, T}_{\text{Steel Analyze in LD}}] \\
y_2 = [F_eS_i], U \\
y_3 = [Al], U \\
y_4 = [Gramol], U \\
y_5 = [S_iC_a], U
\end{aligned}
\tag{24}
$$

U is the input and y_i (i=1… 5) are the outputs (Additives). For simplicity the model is designed in multi-input single-output form (see Fig. 7-11 ANFIS training and test for 5 additives).

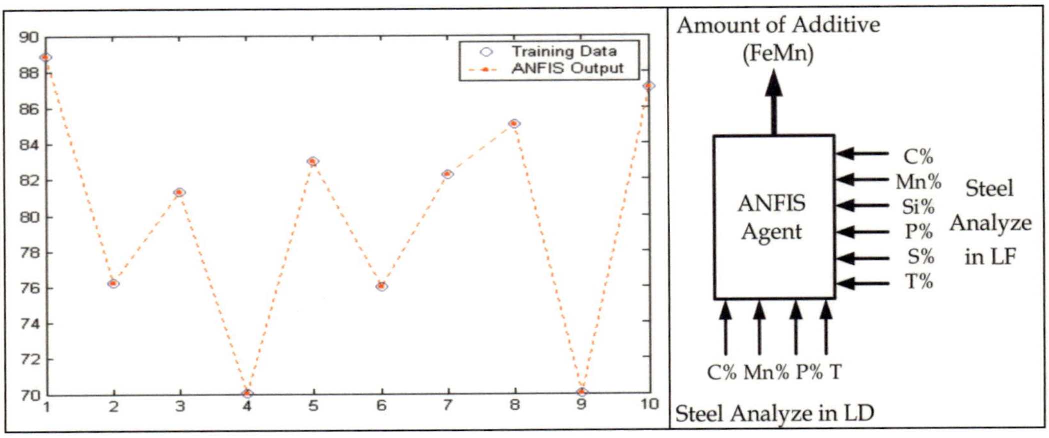

Fig. 7. Comparision of the training data output and the ANFIS Output and the architecture of the FeMn ANFIS agent

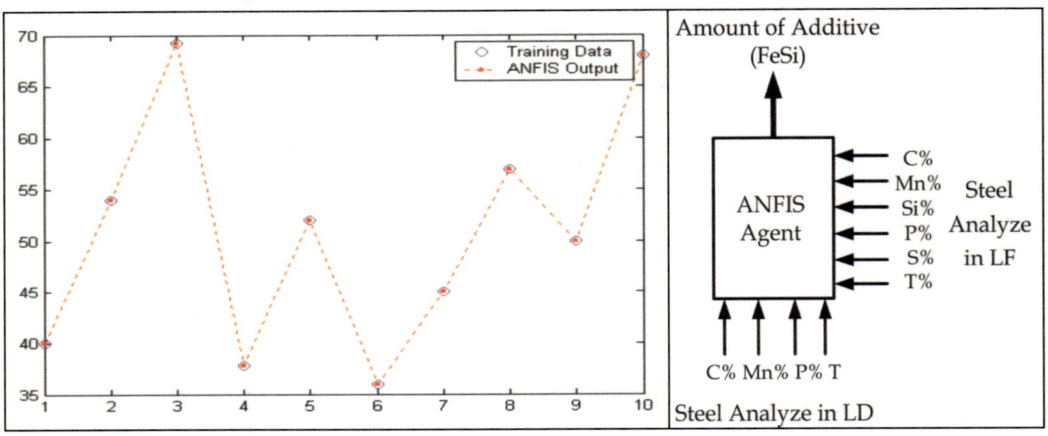

Fig. 8. Comparision of the training data output and the ANFIS Output and the architecture of the FeSi ANFIS agent

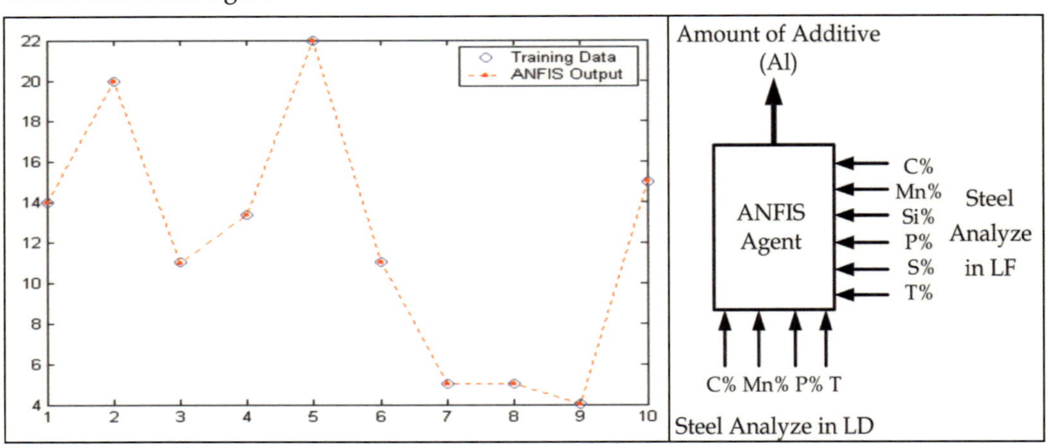

Fig. 9. Comparision of the training data output and the ANFIS Output and the architecture of the Al ANFIS agent

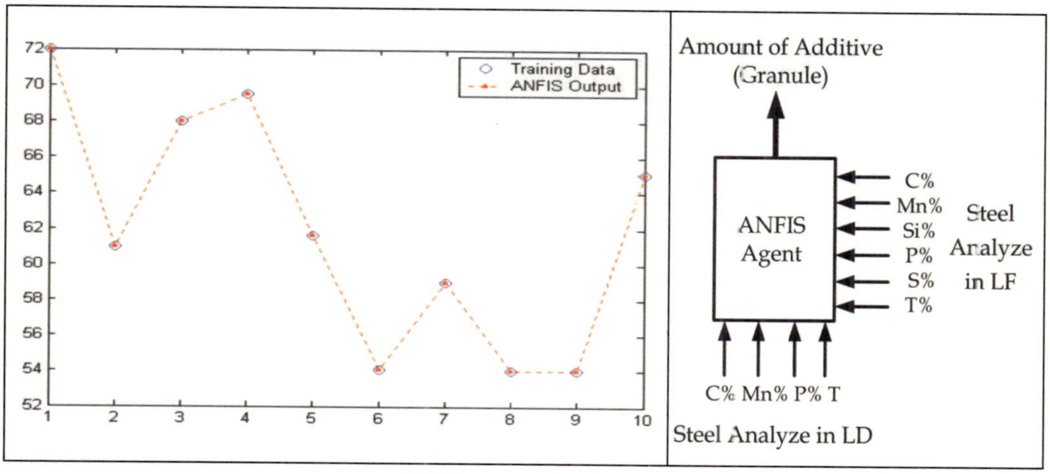

Fig. 10. Comparision of the training data output and the ANFIS Output and the architecture of the Granule ANFIS agent

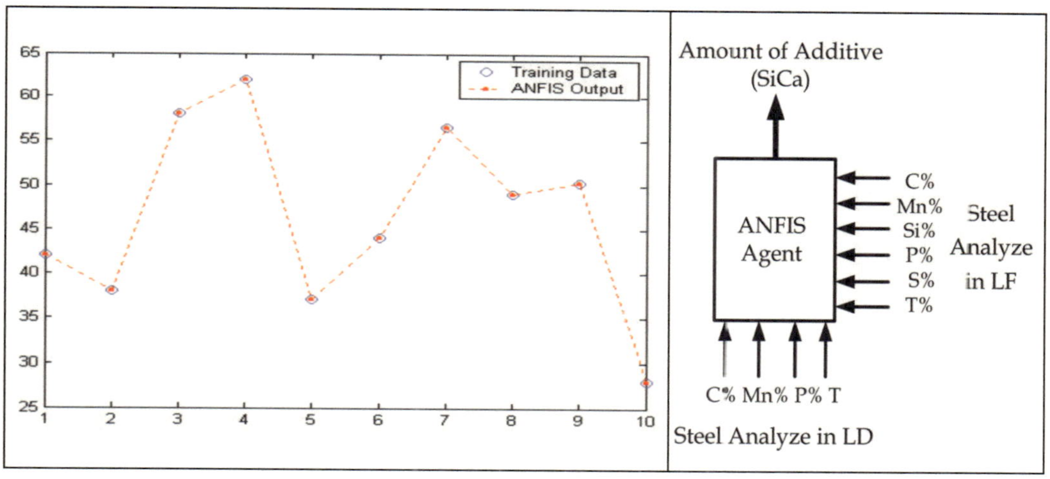

Fig. 11. Comparision of the training data output and the ANFIS Output and the architecture of the SiCa ANFIS agent

To show the performance of the designed multi-agent expert system, the system is applied to determine the value of the additives for CK45. The model has ten inputs according to table 4. As explained before, each additive amount is determined by a specialized agent. Each agent first uses the ouput of the initiator agent and the clustering agent to train its ANFIS. Then, it applies the trained ANFIS to determine the amount of the related additives. The Amounts of the additives are summarized in table 5.

C% *100	Mn% *100	P% *1000	Temp. -1600	C% *100	Mn% *100	Si% *1000	P% *1000	S% *1000	Temp. -1600
8.000	15.025	25.257	76.799	47.999	74.989	20.002	31.980	27.000	75.000

Table 4. Input parameters values for determintion the additives of CK45

FeMn Kg	FeSi Kg	Al Kg	Granule Kg	SiCa Kg
939.082	497.827	15.312	633.155	448.793

Table 5. Output values of the additives of CK45

5. Conclusion

Iron and steel manufacturing is a crucial basic industry for most of the industrial activities. The influence of an efficient process control on the cost and energy reduction has made the process control one of the main issues of this industry. Iron and steel manufacturing should mainly rely on the new integrated production processes to improve productivity, reduce energy consumption, and maintain competitiveness in the market.

In the most steel companies, the principal production planning and scheduling techniques are essentially manual techniques with little computerized decision support. These manual techniques are mainly based on the know-how and the experiences of those experts who have worked in the plant for years. Moreover, steel production is a multi-stage process, logically and geographically distributed, involving a variety of production processes. Also, in a steel grade classification, an operator has to determine the amount of additive materials in steel-making process. Because of the above reasons, a steel automation system is needed to represent distribution and integration existing in this industry. A fuzzy multi-agent expert system can enable such capabilities.

This chapter proposes a multi-agent expert system includes three different types of agents:

- Initiator Agent: Provides the initial membership functions and cluster centers for the clustering agent.
- Clustering Agent: Produces the initial cluster centers for training of the ANFIS agents
- ANFIS Agents: By using ANFIS we can refine fuzzy if-then rules obtained from human expert to describe the input-output behaviour of a complex system. However, if human expertise is not available we can still set up reasonable membership functions and start the learning process to generate a set up fuzzy if-then rules to approximate a desired data set.

The results show that the proposed system can identify the amounts of the additives for different classes of steel grade. Also the results show that the Multi-agent expert systems can be applied effectively in the steel-making.

6. References

Bezdek, J.C. (1993). *Fuzzy mathematics in pattern classification*, Ph.D. dissertation. Cornell University, Ithaca, NY.

Bezdek, J.C. and Pal, S.K. (1992). *Fuzzy Models for pattern Recognition*, IEEE press, New York.

Council on Wage and Price Stability (1977). Report to the President on Prices and Costs in the United States Steel Industry. October. Washington, D.C.: U.S. Government Printing Office.

Cowling, P. I., Ouelhadj, D., & Petrovic, S. (2004). Dynamic scheduling of steel casting and milling using multi-agents, *Production Planning and Control*, Vol. 15, page numbers 1–11.

Cowling, P. I., Ouelhadj, D., & Petrovic, S. (2003). A Multi-agent architecture for dynamic scheduling of steel hot rolling, *Journal of Intelligent Manufacturing*, Vol. 14, page numbers 457–470.

Fazel Zarandi, M.H., Ahmadpour, P. (2009). Fuzzy agent-based expert system for steel making process, *Expert Systems with Applications*, Vol. 36, page numbers 9539–9547.

Fazel Zarandi, M.H., Avazbeigi, M., Turksen, I.B. (2009). A new Fuzzy Noise-rejection Data Partitioning Algorithm with Revised Mahalanobis Distance, *proceeding of IFSA09*.

Huntsberger, T.L., Jacobs, C.L., and Cannon, R.L. (1993). Iterative fuzzy image segmentation, *Pattern Recognition*, Vol. 18, page numbers 131-138.

Jang, J.S.R. (1991). Fuzzy modeling using generalized neural networks and kalman filter algorithm, *Proceedings of Ninth Nat. conf-Artificial Intell. (AAAI-91)*, pp. 762-767.

Kim, Y.I., Moon, K.C., Kang, B.S., Han, C. and Chang, K.S. (1998). Application of neural network to the supervisory control of a reheating furnace in the steel industry, *Control Engineering Practice*, Vol. 6, page numbers 1009-1014.

Lahdelma, R., & Rong, A. (2006). Scrap charge optimization using fuzzy chance constrained linear programming, *In New developments in artificial intelligence and the semantic web proceedings of the 12th Finnish artificial intelligence conference STeP*.

Lee, C-C. (1990a). Fuzzy logic in control systems: Fuzzy logic controller-parti. *IEEE Trans. Syst. Man, cybern.*, Vol. 20, page numbers 404-418.

Lee, C-C. (1990b). Fuzzy logic in control systems: Fuzzy logic controller-parti. *IEEE Trans. Syst. Man, cybern.*, Vol. 20, page numbers 419-435.

Moghaddam Zadeh, A. and Bourbakis, N. (1997). A fuzzy region growing approach for segmentation of color images, *Pattern Recognition*, Vol. 30, page numbers 867-881.

Nasraoui, O. Krishnapuram, R. (1996). An improved possibilistic C-Means algorithm with finite rejection and robust scale estimation, *proceeding of NAFIPS Biennial Conference of the North American*.

Nguyen, H.H. and Cohen, P. (1993). Gibbs random field, fuzzy clustering and the unsupervised segmentation of textured images, *CVGIP Graphical Models Image Processing*, Vol. 55, page numbers 1-19.

Ouelhadj, D., Petrovic, S., Cowling, P. I., & Meisels, A. (2004). Inter-agent cooperation and communication for agent-based robust dynamic scheduling in steel production, *Advanced Engineering Informatics*, Vol. 18, page numbers 161–172.

Pal, S.K. and Ghosh, A. (1992). Image segmentation using fuzzy Correlation, *Inform. Sce.*, Vol. 62, page numbers 232-250.

Pedrycz, W. (1996). Conditional Fuzzy C - Means, *Pattern Recognition Letters*, 17, page numbers 625 - 632.

Perez De La Cruz, J.L., Marti, M.J., Conejo, R., Morales-Bueno, R. and Fernandez, T. (1994). An Expert System for Identifying Steels and Cast Irons, *Engng Applic. Artif. Intell.*, Vol. 7, No. 4, page numbers 455-459.

Sugeno, M. (1985). *Ed. Industrial Applications of Fuzzy control*, New York Elsevier.

Tsukamoto, Y. (1979). An approach to fuzzy reasoning method, In Madan M. Gupta, Rammohan K. Ragade and R. Yager edts. *Advances in fuzzy set theory and applications*, North-Holland, Amsterdam, page numbers 137-149.

Takagi, T., Sugeno, M. (1985). Fuzzy identification of system and its applications to modeling and control. *IEEE Trans. Syst., Man, Cybern.*, Vol. 15, page numbers 116-132.

Yang. M.-S., Su, C.F. (1994). On parameter estimation for normal mixtures based on fuzzy clustering algorithms, *Fuzzy sets and systems,* Vol. 68, page numbers 13-28.

Krishnapuram, R., Keller, J.M. (1993). A Possibilistic Approach to Clustering, *IEEE TRANSACTIONS ON FUZZY SYSTEMS,* VOL. 1, No. 2 .

10

Knowledge Based Expert Systems in Bioinformatics

Mohamed Radhouene Aniba and Julie D. Thompson
Laboratoire de Biologie et Génomique Intégrative, Institut de Génétique et de Biologie Moléculaire et Cellulaire (IGBMC)
France

1. Introduction

The recent revolution in genomics and bioinformatics has taken the world by storm. From company boardrooms to political summits, the issues surrounding the human genome, including the analysis of genetic variation, access to genetic information and the privacy of the individual have fuelled public debate and extended way beyond the scientific and technical literature. During the past few years, bioinformatics has become one of the most highly visible fields of modern science. Yet, this 'new' field has a long history, starting with the triumphs of molecular genetics and cell biology of the last century, where bioinformatics was used for the computational treatment and processing of molecular and genetic data.

Despite its widespread use, no single standard definition exists to describe bioinformatics. From the biologist's point of view, it is generally considered to be the use of computational methods and tools to handle large amounts of data and the application of information science principles and technologies to make the vast, diverse, and complex life sciences data more understandable and useful. On the other hand, a computational scientist will generally define bioinformatics as a direct application area of existing algorithms and tools and the use of mathematical and computational approaches to address theoretical and experimental questions in biology.

In July 2000, the NIH (National Institute of Health) released a working definition of bioinformatics as the research, development, or application of computational tools and approaches for expanding the use of biological, medical, behavioural or health data, including those to acquire, store, organize, archive, analyze, or visualize such data, where as computational biology was defined as the development and application of data-analytical and theoretical methods, mathematical modelling and computational simulation techniques to the study of biological, behavioural, and social systems.

2. « Omics » science and bioinformatics

In the last decade, the high throughput genome sequencing techniques and other large scale experimental protocols, have led not only to an exponential increase in the amount of biological data, but also to the diversification of molecular biology data, leading to a new biological research paradigm, one that is data-rich and data-driven. Many of the emerging areas of large-scale biology are designated by adding the suffix '-omics' to existing terms.

The most widely known omics sciences are genomics (the quantitative study of genes, regulatory and non-coding sequences), transcriptomics (RNA and gene expression), proteomics (proteins and their expression) and metabolomics (metabolites and metabolic networks). The importance to the life-science community as a whole of such large-scale approaches is reflected in the huge number of citations to many of the key papers in these areas, the human and mouse genome papers being the most obvious examples.

In the context of this huge flood of data, complex data management and integration systems are now being introduced to collect, store and curate all this heterogeneous information in ways that will allow its efficient retrieval and exploitation. These developments are opening up new possibilities for large scale bioinformatics projects, aimed at understanding how genetic data is translated into molecules, networks and pathways, all the way to physiology and even ecological systems.

3. Current challenges

The development of high-throughput biotechnologies and the subsequent omics studies is paving the way to exciting new routes of scientific exploration. Instead of being restricted to the analysis of a handful of genes or proteins per experiment, whole genomes and proteomes (the complete set of proteins encoded by an organism's genome) can be analyzed today. This allows biologists, with the help of bioinformaticians, to explore more complicated processes than were possible before (Carroll et al, 2006; Lein et al, 2007; Souchelnytskyi, 2005; Spellman et al, 1998; van Steensel, 2005). Nevertheless, the new data poses as many problems as it does opportunities. An obvious example is the human genome project where, once the technological limitations were lifted and the DNA sequence was obtained, the bottleneck rapidly shifted to its annotation, i.e. the identification of the genes encoded by the genome and their functions. As a consequence, in a similar way to the new biotechnologies, large bioinformatics projects have been initiated, with numerous research groups collaborating to tackle complex issues, such as the detailed annotation of the complete human genome (The ENCODE Project Consortium, 2004).

Thus, new layers of bioinformatics annotations and predictions are laid on top of the experimental omics data and are made available progressively through public web-accessible data stores, such as Ensembl (www.ensembl.org) or the UCSC Genome Browser (genome.ucsc.edu). The fact that the data is broadcast via the web leads to new issues of data management, maintenance and usage. Easy access is a crucial factor that will allow biologists to use the data as a rich source of information for *in silico* data integration experiments. Nevertheless, accessing these heterogeneous data sets across different databases is technically quite difficult, because one must find a way to extract information from a variety of search interfaces, web pages and APIs. To complicate matters, some databases periodically change their export formats, effectively breaking the tools that allow access to their data. At the same time, most omics databases do not yet provide computer-readable metadata and, when they do, it is not in a standard format. Hence, expert domain-specific knowledge is needed to understand what the data actually represents, before it can be used efficiently.

To further complicate matters, today's bioinformatics analyses require a combination of experimental, theoretical and computational approaches and data must be integrated from a large variety of different data resources, including genomic sequences, 3D structures, cellular localisations, phenotypes and other types of biologically pertinent data. However,

several problems related to the 'omics' data have been highlighted. For example, data emerging from 'omic' approaches are noisy (data can be missing due to false negatives, and data can be misleading due to false positives) and it has been proposed that some of the limitations can be overcome by comparing and integrating data obtained from two or more distinct approaches (Ge et al, 2003). In this context, a major challenge for bioinformaticians in the post-genomic era is clearly the collection, validation and analysis of this mass of experimental and predicted data, in order to identify pertinent biological patterns and to extract the hidden knowledge (Roos, 2001).
Important research efforts are now underway to address the problems of data collection and storage. One approach has been data warehousing, where all the relevant databases are stored locally in a unified format and mined through a uniform interface. SRS (Etzold et al, 1996) and Entrez (Sculer et al, 1996) are probably the most widely used database query and navigation systems for the life science community. Alternatively, broadcast systems implement software to access mixed databases that are dispersed over the internet and provide a query facility to access the data. Examples include IBM's DiscoveryLink (Haas et al, 2001), BioMOBY (Wilkinson et al, 2003). More recently, semantic web based methods have been introduced that are designed to add meaning to the raw data by using formal descriptions of the concepts, terms, and relationships encoded within the data. Many of these technologies are reviewed in more detail in (Romano, 2008).
Today's information-rich environment has also led to the growth of numerous software tools, designed to analyse and visualize the data. The tools can be merged using pipelines, or more recently workflow management systems (WMS), to provide powerful computational platforms for performing *in silico* experiments (Halling-Brown et al, 2008). However, the complexity and diversity of the available analysis tools mean that we now require automatic processing by 'intelligent' computer systems, capable of automatically selecting the most appropriate tools for a given task. In particular, one major insight gained from early work in intelligent problem solving and decision making was the importance of domain-specific knowledge.
Thus the field of bioinformatics has reached the end of its first phase, where it was mainly inspired by computer science and computational statistics. The motivation behind this chapter is to characterize the principles that may underlie the second phase of bioinformatics, incorporating artificial intelligence techniques. In this context, knowledge-based expert systems represent an ideal tool for an emerging research field, known as 'integrative systems biology'.

4. Expert systems in bioinformatics

Expert systems have been used in bioinformatics for many years, although some past and current projects have incorporated similar technologies without actually employing the term 'expert system'. The domains covered range from fundamental computational biology studies to medical research, forensic sciences and environmental protection research.
In this section we will describe some examples of expert system applications, highlighting the importance of knowledge based architectures and their impact on advanced research.

4.1 Medical diagnostics

One of the earliest direct applications of expert systems in a biological discipline was in medicine. This is a very data-rich domain and knowledge based expert systems (KBS) quickly became an essential tool for diagnostics and personalized treatments. KBS are widely used in domains where knowledge is more prevalent than data and that require heuristics and reasoning logic to derive new knowledge. The knowledge in a KBS is stored in a knowledge base that is separate from the control and inference programs and can be represented by various formalisms, such as frames, Bayesian networks, production rules, etc. In the medical field, a combination of domain knowledge and data are used for the detection, diagnosis, (interpretation) and treatment of diseases. Depending on the problem, the balance between data and knowledge varies and appropriate systems are identified and deployed, including knowledge biased computing models such as rule-based reasoning (RBR), model-based reasoning (MBR) and case-based reasoning (CBR).

In RBR, the knowledge is represented by symbolic rules (Ligeza, 2006) and inference in the system is performed by a process of chaining through rules recursively, either by reverse or forward reasoning (Patterson, 1990). In MBR, the knowledge base is represented as a set of models (satisfying assignments, examples) of the world rather than a logical formula describing it. In CBR, the knowledge is stored as a list of cases, where a case consists of a problem, its solution, and some information about how the solution was obtained. New problems are then solved by reusing the past cases.

Each of these approaches has advantages and disadvantages and as a result, many systems in the medical domain use a combined approach. One example is the BOLERO expert system (Lopez et al, 1997), which uses CBR to improve a RBR medical diagnosis based on the information available about the patient. The MIKAS system (Khan et al, 1997) also integrates CBR and RBR, with the goal of automatically providing a diet recommendation that is strongly tailored to the individual requirements and food preferences of a patient. Other systems incorporate a mixture of MBR and CBR, such as PROTOS (Porter et al, 1986), which uses knowledge acquisition for heuristic classifications in medical audiology, or CASEY (Koton, 1988) which uses CBR to improve the computational efficiency of a causal model of heart disease. Finally, T-IDDM (Montani et al, 2003) is a multi-modal reasoning system providing an accurate decision support tool for the diagnosis of type 1 diabetes, based on a mixture of RBR, MBR and CBR.

In cases where the translation of implicit knowledge into explicit rules is problematic, alternatives to the reasoning systems described above are intelligent computing systems (ICS) or statistical inference, such as that based on Bayes' theorem, which assigns a probability to each advised output (equivalent to a disease in the medical domain). Statistics-based approaches have been exploited in expert systems for the diagnosis and management of pacemaker-related problems (Bernstein et al, 1995) or other medical predictions (Dragulescu et al, 1995). While this type of expert system is suitable for reciprocally exclusive diseases and independent symptoms, they fail when some symptoms have the same cause (are connected) or when a patient can suffer from more than one disease. In this context, artificial neural networks (ANN) have been developed. ANNs have been widely utilized and are an accepted method for the diagnosis of data intensive applications. (Grossi et al, 2007) showed that ANN can improve the classification accuracy and survival prediction of a number of gastrointestinal diseases. ANN has also been used in many other fields, including radiology, urology, laboratory medicine and cardiology (Itchhaporia et al, 1996). Finally, ICS, like KBS, often rely on combined approaches or hybrid expert systems (HES). For example, (Brasil et al, 2001) developed a HES for the diagnosis of epileptic crises, where some of the problems inherent to ANNs were resolved using Genetic Algorithms.

4.2 DNA sequence analysis: Forensic science

An interesting application of expert systems is the analysis of DNA sequences in forensic science. We have all heard about forensics thanks to Hollywood movies and TV series, where a scientist simply inserts a tube into a machine and immediately recognizes the suspect. A lot of us think that this is somewhat exaggerated and unrealistic. Well this is not the case. Forensics is a very developed science and due to its importance, governments devote large budgets to research in this domain.

The processing of forensic DNA samples and the interpretation of DNA profile data is complex and requires important resources both in terms of equipment and in highly trained personnel. But the growth of robotic equipment to automate the extraction of DNA from forensic samples, to quantify and amplify the samples, together with multi-capillary electrophoresis instrumentation has shifted the emphasis to the data analysis stage. Traditionally, the analysis and interpretation of DNA profile data was performed manually by at least two independent highly trained, experienced human scientists. However, this is a time-consuming process and in recent years, DNA profiling interpretation has been automated by replacing the human workers with bioinformatics software and notably, expert systems.

The analysis begins with a sample of an individual's DNA, which is then processed to create a sample DNA profile. This stage is performed by two software packages: GeneScan and Genotyper (Applied Biosystems, Foster City, CA, USA), and includes a manual review step. The subsequent interpretation of the DNA profile involves the comparison of the sample DNA profile with another sample or a database to determine whether there is a genetic match. The interpretation is not a simple process since extremely high accuracy and consistency of forensic evidence is clearly necessary. Therefore, a hierarchy of decision rules has been produced to deal with a certain number of biological and technological artefacts and noise in the data. Once the artefacts have been removed, all remaining peaks are assumed to be "real" and can be assigned either to the individual in the case of single donor samples or can be treated by another set of complex decision rules, in the case of mixed donor samples.

A number of knowledge based expert systems have been developed in order to automate this part of the DNA analysis as much as possible, thus reducing the amount of time taken to analyse an important number of DNA profiles, e.g. GeneMapper ID (Applied Biosystems, Foster City, CA, USA), FaSTR DNA (Power et al, 2008) or FSS-i3 (The Forensic Science Service DNA Expert System Suite FSS-i3). In each of these expert systems, rules are activated when a DNA profile is not from a unique source or when the quality of the profile is substandard. The expert system then requests the analyst to manually re-examine the data and accept or reject the assignment made. The combined use of such automated systems has been shown to provide independent "expert" analyses, which increase consistency and save analysis time compared to manual processing.

4.3 DNA sequence analysis: Genome annotation

Since the completion of the human genome in 2003, a large number of genomes of other organisms have been sequenced. These genome sequences consist of strings of As, Ts, Cs, and Gs representing the base pairs that make up the DNA, and have lengths in the order of millions of characters. Without marking the locations of biologically important parts of the sequence such as the genes and their regulatory elements, this string of characters has little usefulness. A major challenge in the "post-genomic era" is therefore the localisation of the genes in each genome, their organization, structure and function. Two areas of genomic biology are dedicated to this task, namely structural and functional annotation. Structural

annotation refers to the task of identifying genes, their location on the genome sequence, their exon/intron structure and the prediction of the molecular sequences (RNA and proteins) that they encode. Functional annotation aims then to predict the biological function of the gene products: RNA and protein molecules.
Structural annotation methods can be classified into: (1) *ab initio* methods, based on codon usage to discriminate between coding and non-coding regions, and pattern searches for regulatory elements, (2) methods that use evolutionary conservation to infer gene localization and structure, (3) hybrid methods that combine these two approaches and usually present the best compromise in terms of sensibility and specificity in gene detection.
Computational methods for functional annotation are mainly split into two types: (1) similarity based approaches that infer a function based on the comparison of a given sequence with a sequence of known function and (2) phylogenomic inference approaches, based on evolutionary history and relationships between biological sequences. Phylogenomic methods avoid many of the false inference problems associated with the simpler similarity-based methods, although they require a high degree of biological expertise, are time consuming, complex, and are difficult to automate.
Both structural and functional annotations usually require the composite chaining of different algorithms, software and methods and expert biologists are often needed to make important decisions, modify the dataset and to compare intermediate results, which is labor intensive and can be error prone. In order to handle the large amounts of data produced by genome sequencing projects, automation of these pipelines is an absolute necessity. Diverse attempts have been made to develop annotation platforms automating some of these pipelines, particularly in the domain of structural annotation (e.g. the Ensembl pipeline (Hubbard et al, 2002). With regard to functional annotation, a number of platforms are available that can automate either the similarity-based approaches or the more complex phylogenomic approaches.
FIGENIX (Figure 1) (Gouret et al, 2005) is one example of an automated annotation platform featuring an expert system that models the biologists' expertise and is able to compare results from different methods, and to evaluate the significance of predictions. FIGENIX incorporates a number of different pipelines for structural and functional annotation, in particular, a structural annotation pipeline, which is a hybrid method combining *ab initio* and similarity-based approaches, and a functional annotation pipeline fully automating a complex phylogenomic inference method.

4.4 Protein sequence analysis

The complete sequencing of genomes for a number of organisms and their subsequent annotation has led to the definition of thousands of new proteins of unknown biological function. In order to investigate the biological activity of the proteins, the first step is to determine its primary structure, i.e. the ordered sequences of amino acids making up the protein. Knowledge of the amino acid sequence then allows predictions to be made about protein structure and the relationships between different proteins. Expert systems have been used to solve a number of different problems in such protein analyses.
The precise determination of amino acid sequences in proteins is a very important analytical task in biochemistry, and the most common type of instrumentation used for this employs Edman degradation (Edman, 1956). In this method, N-terminal amino acid residues are repeatedly labelled and cleaved from the protein. The amino acids are then identified as their phenylthiohydantoin (PTH) derivatives by high performance liquid chromatography

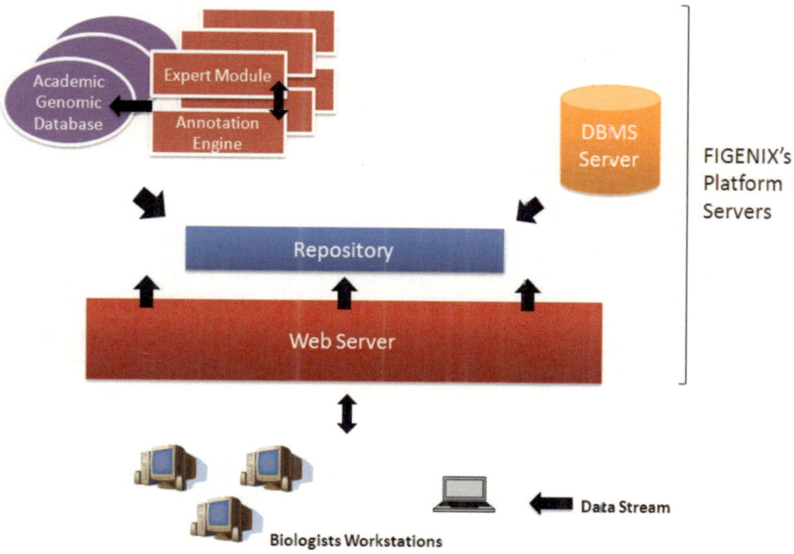

Fig. 1. Figenix architecture : "Annotation Engine" or "Expert System" servers can be cloned and distributed on several CPU.

(HPLC: a form of column chromatography used frequently in biochemistry and analytical chemistry to separate, identify, and quantify compounds). Interpretation of the HPLC data is often problematic due to unstable baselines (points of reference used to identify peak in the chromatograph), drifts in elution times of PTH-amino acids, and additional contamination effects which are a consequence of partial cleavage during Edman degradations and/or side reactions that occur during the cycles. Such problems may cause peak misidentification by onboard software programs on commercial sequencers, and visual interpretation of the HPLC data by a human expert is often required for successful interpretation of the chromatographic profile.

In this context (Hu et al, 1996) developed an expert system that uses heuristic rules built by human experts in protein sequencing. The system is applied to the chromatographic data of PTH-amino acids acquired from an automated sequencer. The peak intensities in the current cycle are compared with those in the previous cycle, while the calibration and succeeding cycles are used as ancillary recognition criteria when necessary. The retention time for each chromatographic peak in each cycle is then corrected by the corresponding peak in the calibration cycle at the same run. Such technologies have now been adapted by several biotechnology manufacturers and have been incorporated into their laboratory equipment to increase precision, making them more useful for experimentalists.

As another case study of an expert system application, (Praveen et al, 2005) reported an expert system for rapid recognition of metallothionein (MT) proteins. MT proteins are responsible for regulating the intracellular supply of biologically essential zinc and copper ions and play a role in protecting cells from the deleterious effects of high concentration metal ions. MT is generally induced when the organism experiences certain stress conditions and therefore, recognition of MT from tissues or from animal models is very important.

In order to develop an expert system for this task, the physical and chemical characteristics of MT proteins were derived based on a set of experiments conducted using animal models. The derived characteristics were broken into a set of rules, including (1) proteins with low molecular weight versus high molecular weight, (2) proteins with metal content versus no metal content, (3) the presence or absence of aromatic amino acids and (4) sulphur content versus no sulphur content. The derived rules (consisting of a series of attribute and value pairs, followed by a single conclusion that contains the class and the corresponding class value) were produced using the ID3 algorithm (Quinlan, 1986), and a minimum number of rules were selected using human expertise in order to maximize true positive recognition. The rules were then formulated as an IF - THEN - ELSE algorithm and translated into VISUAL BASIC language statements, providing an efficient software solution.

Another important application of expert systems in protein analysis is mass spectrometry (MS). MS is an analytical technique for the identification of the composition of a sample or molecule. It is also used for the determination of the chemical structures of molecules, such as peptides (parts of protein sequences) and other chemical compounds. The method begins with degradation of the proteins by an enzyme having high specificity and the resulting peptides are subject to analysis by MS. A computer algorithm is then used to compare the masses established for the resulting peptides with theoretical masses calculated for every sequence in a protein or DNA sequence database and the studied protein is identified based on the results of this comparison.

ProFound (Zhang et al, 2000) is an expert system which employs a Bayesian algorithm to identify proteins from protein databases using mass spectrometric peptide mapping data. Bayesian probability theory has been widely used to make scientific inference from incomplete information in various fields in bioinformatics, including sequence alignment and NMR spectral analysis. When the system under study is modelled properly, the Bayesian approach is believed to be among the most coherent, consistent, and efficient statistical methods. The ProFound system ranks protein candidates by taking into account individual properties of each protein in the database as well as other data relevant to the peptide mapping experiment, including data from multiple digestions, the amino acid content of individual peptides, and protein components in mixtures. The program consistently identifies the correct protein(s) even when the data quality is relatively low or when the sample consists of a simple mixture of proteins.

4.5 Comparative genomics and evolutionary studies

The annotation of a single genome provides important clues to the functions of the encoded genes, and how they work together in the complex networks that perform the essential processes of living organisms. However, in the famous words of Theodore Dobzhansky: "nothing makes sense in biology except in the light of evolution" and therefore, the field of comparative genomics (the comparison of genome sequences from two or more organisms) and the reconstruction of ancestral genomes are now playing essential roles in understanding the evolutionary processes that have shaped the biological complexity of living organisms.

An expert system, called CASSIOPE (Rascol et al, 2009), has been developed specifically to address the problem of ancestral genome reconstruction. CASSIOPE compares the organizational structure of genomic regions that have been conserved in a large number of informative species. Hypotheses can then be formulated to account for such conserved genomic regions: (1) the regions are due to chance and are not biologically important, (2) the regions result from a standard ancestral region through inheritance or (3) the regions are due to evolutionary convergence with possible selective pressure. The objective then is to select the most likely explanation for these conserved regions. CASSIOPE is able to reject the null hypothesis (conserved regions are due to chance) in favor of one of the two alternatives, although it cannot differentiate between them (ancestral regions or convergence). The system aims to automatically reproduce the chain of analyses and decisions performed by human experts and incorporates fundamental evolutionary biology-based concepts. First, orthologs (genes in different species that evolved from a common ancestral gene by speciation keeping the same functions) and paralogs (genes related by duplication within a genome, thus different functions) are detected via phylogenetic analysis. Second, the probability that the genomic regions from different species are inherited from a common ancestor is estimated based on the neutrality theory.

The process developed in CASSIOPE (Figure 2) involves various tasks, such as phylogenetic reconstruction or consulting web databases, and each task is independent from the others.

CASSIOPE deploys the following core tasks: (1) data processing: a modular system with various agents (virtual machines that work on specific tasks) deployed in conjunction with an expert system that communicates with every agent and takes rule-based decisions to answer initial biological questions, (2) data comparison: database searches can be performed for newly sequenced regions or genomes, (3) detection of orthologous genes by robust phylogenetic reconstruction, (4) statistical scoring to assess the significance of conserved regions and (5) a reverse-search feature making it possible to extend the initial searches.

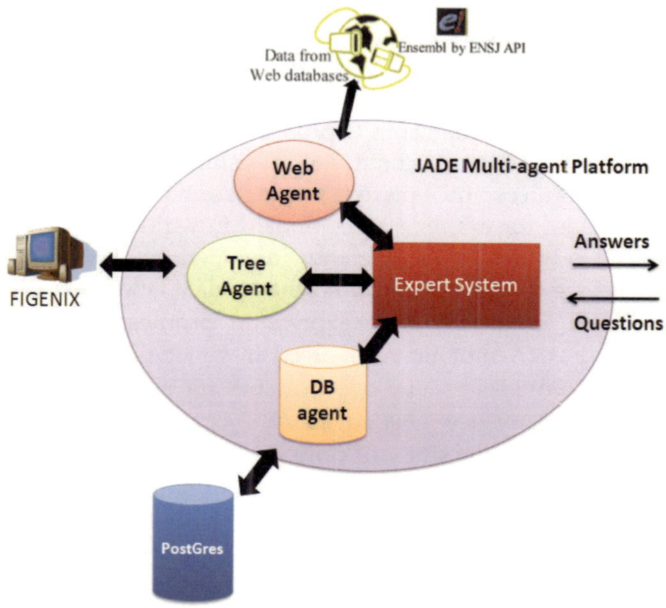

Fig. 2. CASSIOPE multi-agent system

The whole process is controlled by the expert system, which uses the other agents to obtain the data required. The expert system communicates with the different agents to answer questions, such as which genomic regions are significantly conserved? It receives queries and tries to find the necessary, pertinent data in the databases. The knowledge in the system is formulated in the form of an advanced rule set allowing decision-taking on the information received. For example, if data is partial, unavailable or outdated (> 1 month), the system deduces the agent interrogations it has to perform. The rule sets of the expert system can be updated, removed or added, just as a human scientist would.

5. Conclusion

Bioinformatics is a cross-disciplinary research field that is concerned with the efficient management and analysis of heterogeneous data and the extraction of valuable knowledge. Due to the exponential growth of the biological databases, especially in the so-called 'post-genomic era' since the human genome project, the task of extracting the hidden patterns underlying the data has become more and more difficult. The situation is further complicated by the complexity of biological data (numerous different types, sources, quality, etc.) and the creation of tools that can exploit the accumulated human expertise in this field is now crucial.

Thanks to recent developments in IT, the storage and the maintenance of the petabytes of data have been widely addressed and efficient solutions are being developed. Future challenges will concentrate less on how we can store the huge amount of data, and more on how we can explore the hidden knowledge. Success in this domain will have profound effects on fundamental research and our knowledge of the mechanisms involved in the complex networks that make up living beings. Bioinformatics is also playing an increasing important role in a wide range of applications, including medical diagnostics and treatment, pharmaceutics and drug discovery, agriculture and other biotechnologies.

The relatively simple task of annotating genes involves consulting various molecular, functional, disease and other databases to verify complete or partial annotations. Online data resources such as those furnished by the National Center for Biotechnology Information (NCBI), the Wellcome Trust Sanger Institute and many others, have become invaluable in helping annotators attribute putative functions to proteins based on computational results. The way in which biological information is stored, i.e. in distinct, heterogeneous data sources, means that data integration is an essential prerequisite to its annotation. Information regarding functional properties of genes for example is distributed in various online databases which were developed independently and do not inherently interoperate.

Today, new technologies are changing the bioinformatics data landscape and are providing new sources of raw data, including gene expression profiles, 3D structures, genetic networks, cellular images, DNA mutations involved in genetic diseases and many more. The current flood of data provides unique opportunities for systems-level studies. At the same time, it also poses as many new challenges. As a consequence, the field of systems biology has emerged, focusing on the study of complex biological systems, that exploits the new genomic data and the recent developments in bioinformatics. Systems biology studies biological systems by systematically perturbing them (biologically, genetically, or chemically); monitoring the gene, protein, and informational pathway responses; integrating these data; and ultimately, formulating mathematical models that describe the structure of the system and its response to individual perturbations (Ideker et al, 2001). Intelligent systems, such as the expert systems described in this chapter, will play an essential role in these studies, by integrating human expertise and computational and mathematical tools to highlight the knowledge underlying the data.

6. References

Bernstein, A.D.; Chiang, C.J. & Parsonnet, V. (1995). Diagnosis and management of pacemaker-related problems using and interactive expert system. IEEE 17th *Annual Conference on Engineering in Medicine and Biology Society*, 1, (701–702).

Brasil, L.M.; De Azevedo, F.M. & Barreto, J.M. (2001). Hybrid expert system for decision supporting in the medical area: complexity and cognitive computing International. *Journal of Medical Informatics*, 63, (19–30).

Carroll, J.S.; Meyer, C.A., Song, J., Li, W., Geistlinger, T.R., Eeckhoute, J., Brodsky, A.S., Keeton, E.K., Fertuck, K. C., Hall, G.F., Wang, Q., Bekiranov,S., Sementchenko, V., Fox, E.A., Silver, P.A., Gingeras, T.R., Liu, X.S. & Brown, M. (2006). Genome-wide analysis of estrogen receptor binding sites. *Nat. Genet.*, 38, (1289–1297).

Consortium, T.E.P. (2004). The ENCODE (ENCyclopedia Of DNA Elements) Project. *Science*, 306, 5696, (636-640).

Dragulescu, D. & Albu, A. (2007). Expert system for medical predictions. 4th International Symposium on Applied Computational Intelligence and Informatics, 13–18.

Edman, P. (1956). On the mechanism of the phenyl isothiocyanate degradation of peptides. *Ada Chim. Scand.*, 10, (761-768).

Etzold, T.; Ulyanov, A. & Argos, P. (1996). SRS: information retrieval system for molecular biology data banks. *Meth Enzymol*, 266, (114–128).

Ge, H.; Walhout, A.J.M. & Vidal, M. (2003). Integrating 'omic' information: a bridge between genomics and systems biology. *Trends in Genetics*, 19, (551-560).

Gouret, P.; Vitiello, V., Balandraud, N., Gilles, A., Pontarotti, P.& Danchin, E.G. (2005). FIGENIX: Intelligent automation of genomic annotation: expertise integration in a new software platform. *BMC Bioinformatics.*, 6, 198.

Grossi, E.; Mancini, A. & Buscema, M. (2007). International experience on the use of artificial neural networks in gastroenterology. *Digestive and Liver Disease*, 39, (278–285).

Halling-Brown, M. & Shepherd, A.J. (2008). Constructing computational pipelines. *Methods Mol Biol*, 453, (451-470).

Hass, L.; Schwartz, P., Kodali, P., Kotlar, E., Rice, J.& Swope, W. (2001). Discovery Link: a system for integrating life sciences data. *IBM Syst. J.*, 40, (489-511).

Hu, L.; Saulinskas, E.F., Johnson, P. & Harrington, P.B. (1996). Development of an expert system for amino acid sequence identification. *Comput Appl Biosci.*, 12, 4, (311-318).

Hubbard, T.; Barker, D., Birney, E., Cameron, G., Chen, Y., Clark, L., Cox, T., Cuff, J., Curwen, V., Down, T., Durbin, R., Eyras, E., Gilbert, J., Hammond, M., Huminiecki, L., Kasprzyk, A., Lehvaslaiho, H., Lijnzaad, P., Melsopp, C., Mongin, E., Pettett, R., Pocock, M., Potter, S., Rust, A., Schmidt, E., Searle, S., Slater, G., Smith, J., Spooner, W., Stabenau, A., Stalker, J., Stupka, E., Ureta-Vidal, A., Vastrik, I. & Clamp, M. (2002). The Ensembl genome database project. *Nucleic Acids Res.*, 30, 1, (38-41)

Ideker, T.; Galitski, T. & Hood, L. (2001). A new approach to decoding life: systems biology. *Annu Rev Genomics Hum Genet*, 2, (343-72).

Itchhaporia, D.; Snow, P.B., Almassy, R.J. & Oetgen, W.J. (1996). Artificial neural networks: current status in cardiovascular medicine. *Journal of the American College of Cardiology*, 28, 2, (515–521).

Khan, A.S. & Hoffmann, A. (2003). Building a case-based diet recommendation system without a knowledge engineer. *Artificial Intelligence in Medicine* 27, (155–179)

Koton, P. (1988). Reasoning about evidence in causal explanations. *Proceedings of the Seventh National Conference on Artificial Intelligence, AAI Press, Menlo Park, CA*, (256–263).

Lein, E.S.; Hawrylycz, M.J., Ao, N., Ayres, M., Bensinger, A., Bernard, A., Boe, A.F., Boguski, M.S., Brockway, K.S., Byrnes, E.J., Chen, L., Chen, L., Chen, T.M., Chin, M.C., Chong, J., Crook, B.E., Czaplinska, A., Dang, C.N., Datta, S., Dee, N.R., Desaki, A.L., Desta, T., Diep, E., Dolbeare, T.A., Donelan, M.J., Dong, H.W., Dougherty, J.G., Duncan, B.J., Ebbert, A.J., Eichele, G., Estin, L.K., Faber, C., Facer, B.A., Fields, R., Fischer, S.R., Fliss, T.P., Frensley, C., Gates, S.N., Glattfelder, K.J., Halverson, K.R., Hart, M.R.,

Hohmann, J.G., Howell, M.P., Jeung, D.P., Johnson, R.A., Karr, P.T., Kawal, R., Kidney, J.M., Knapik, R.H., Kuan, C.L., Lake, J.H., Laramee, A.R., Larsen, K.D., Lau, C., Lemon, T.A., Liang, A.J., Liu, Y., Luong, L.T., Michaels, J., Morgan, J.J., Morgan, R.J., Mortrud, M.T., Mosqueda, N.F., Ng L.L., Ng, R., Orta, G.J., Overly, C.C., Pak, T.H., Parry, S.E., Pathak, S.D., Pearson, O.C., Puchalski, R.B., Riley, Z.L., Rockett, H.R., Rowland, S.A., Royall, J.J., Ruiz, M.J., Sarno, N.R., Schaffnit, K., Shapovalova, N.V., Sivisay, T., Slaughterbeck, C.R., Smith, S.C., Smith, K.A., Smith, B.I., Sodt, A.J., Stewart, N.N., Stumpf, K.R., Sunkin, S.M., Sutram, M., Tam, A., Teemer, C.D., Thaller, C., Thompson, C.L., Varnam, L.R., Visel, A., Whitlock, R.M., Wohnoutka, P.E., Wolkey, C.K., Wong, V.Y., Wood, M., Yaylaoglu, M.B., Young, R.C., Youngstrom, B.L., Yuan, X.F., Zhang, B., Zwingman, T.A.& Jones, A.R. (2007). Genome-wide atlas of gene expression in the adult mouse brain. *Nature*, 445, (168-176).

Ligeza, A. (2006). Logical Foundations for Rule-Based Systems Studies in Computational Intelligence; Springer, Berlin. 11.

Lopez, B. & Plaza, E. (1997). Case-based learning of plans and medical diagnosis goal states. *Artificial Intelligence in Medicine*, 9, (29–60).

Montani, S.; Magni, P., Bellazzi, R., Larizza, C., Roudsari, A.V. & Carson, E.R. (2003). Integrating model-based decision support in a multi-modal reasoning system for managing type 1 diabetic patients. *Artificial Intelligence in Medicine*, 29, (131–151).

Patterson, D.W. (1990). Introduction to Artificial Intelligence and Expert System, *Prentice-Hall, Inc., Englewood Cliffs, NJ, USA* .

Porter, B.W. & Bareiss, E.R. (1986). PROTOS: an experiment in knowledge acquisition for heuristic classification tasks. *Proceedings of the First International Meeting on Advances in Learning (IMAL), Les Arcs, France*, (159–174).

Power, T.; McCabe, B. & Harbison, S.A. (2008). FaSTR DNA: a new expert system for forensic DNA analysis. *Forensic Sci Int Genet*, 2, 3, (159-165).

Praveen, B.; Vincent, S., Murty, U.S., Krishna, A.R. & Jamil, K. (2005). A rapid identification system for metallothionein proteins using expert system. *Bioinformation*, 1, 1, (14-15).

Quinlan, J.R. (1986). Induction of Decision Trees. *Readings in Machine Learning*, 1, 1, (81-106).

Rascol, V.L.; Levasseur, A., Chabrol, O., Grusea, S., Gouret, P., Danchin, E.G. & Pontarotti, P. (2009). CASSIOPE: An expert system for conserved regions searches. *BMC Bioinformatics*, 10, 284.

Romano, P. (2008). Automation of in-silico data analysis processes through workflow management systems. *Brief Bioinform*, 9, (57-68).

Roos, D.S. (2001). Computational biology. Bioinformatics--trying to swim in a sea of data. *Science*, 291, (1260-1261).

Schuler, G.D.; Epstein, J.A., Ohkawa, H. & Kans, J.A. (1996). Entrez: molecular biology database and retrieval system. *Methods Enzymol*, 266, (141-162).

Souchelnytskyi, S. (2005). Bridging proteomics and systems biology: what are theroads to be traveled? . *Proteomics*, 5, (4123–4137).

Spellman, P.T.; Sherlock, G., Zhang, M.Q., Iyer, V.R., Anders, K., Eisen, M.B., Brown, P.O., Botstein, D. & Futcher, B. (1998). Comprehensive identification of cell cycle-regulated genes of the yeast Saccharomyces cerevisiae by microarray hybridization. *Mol. Biol. Cell.*, 9, (3273–3297).

van Steensel, B. (2005). Mapping of genetic and epigenetic regulatory networks using microarrays. *Nat. Genet.*, 37, (18–24).

Wilkinson, M.D. & Links, M. (2002). BioMOBY: an open source biological web services proposal. *Brief Bioinform.*, 3, (331-341).

Zhang, W. & Chait, B.T. (2000). ProFound: an expert system for protein identification using mass spectrometric peptide mapping infocrmation. *Anal Chem.*, 72, 11, (2482-2489).

11

Web-Based Domain Specific Tool for Building Plant Protection Expert Systems

Ahmed Rafea
Computer Science and Engineering Department
American University in Cairo,
Egypt

1. Introduction

This work describes a tool that aids the development of a plant protection expert system (ES) for field crops. It is the result of accumulation of knowledge and expertise for building agricultural expert systems for about 20 years in the Central Laboratory for agricultural Expert Systems (CLAES). We have found out that all crop management tasks are candidate for using the ES technology to transfer expertise from highly qualified human experts to small farmers through intermediaries whom we call, extension workers in the agriculture domain. Plant protection tasks are part of crop management of any crop which need expertise that can be better represented in symbolic knowledge representation schemes rather than other tasks, like irrigation and fertilization which includes mathematical models more than symbolic knowledge. In addition to that annual yield losses due to pests are estimated to be in billions of dollars worldwide. Therefore, a decision has been taken to develop a plant protection expert systems building tool to expedite the development and maintenance processes of plant protection expert systems for field crops. Analyzing the plant protection task we come up with four sub tasks namely: variety selection, cultural practices, pest diagnosis, and pest control.

The second section will address the importance of building such tool. The third section will describe previous related work. The fourth section will describe the design and implementation of the tool, its web interfaces and its four main components corresponding to the four agricultural sub tasks : variety selection, cultural practices, pest diagnosis, and pest control. The fifth section will include our experience in developing the Barley expert system using this tool. The last section will conclude the chapter and propose new ideas for future research needed to enhance the tool.

2. Importance of building such tool

One of the most important problems that hinders the developing of expert system was the knowledge acquisition which is characterized in the literature as the bottle neck in building any expert system. Early research was concentrating on building generic problem solving shells like EMYCIN (van Melle, 1981) in which the problem solving method was an inference engine for rules knowledge base. Later on the frame paradigm was included with rules like the tools called KEE, LOOPS (Jackson, 1999) which allowed the behaviour of a frame to be represented in terms of a set of production rules. Other tools based on what is called second generation expert systems (David et. Al., 1993) was allowing a generic problem solving scheme like the generic task methodology proposed by Chndrasekaran (1988) and the KADS methodology which has been developed in an European project (Wielingaa et al., 1992). Those tools were never being commercialized on a large scale and stayed in the academic and research environment. All these tools were oriented toward general problem solving task not toward domain specific tasks. Our work concentrated on building domain specific problem solving tasks that could help in acquiring domain knowledge in specific format and consequently help knowledge engineers and domain experts in expediting the development of expert systems in a specific domain; in our case the domain is crop protection for plants.

3. Related work

In general the tools built for second generation expert systems for specific tasks like classifications, design and other tasks are related to what we are going to present in this chapter. The main difference is that we are more concentrating on the domain in addition to the tasks. Clancey(1993) introduced the heuristic classification task as he identified a wide range of expert systems in different domains which appear to function in more or less the same way. Ontology was recognized by many scientists as important component in an expert systems and some efforts were exerted to develop tools to assist users in building ontology and associated with it problem solving reusable methods. An example of these tools is PROTÉGÉ (Musen, 1989; Rothenfluh et al., 1994). Role limiting method is another method used to knowledge modelling (Studer et. al., 1998) but we are not aware of any tools developed to implement this method. The generic task (GT) methodology (Chndrasekaran, 1988) was introduced in the late eighties and some tools have been built for hierarchical classification and routine design task in academic and research institutions. The expertise model of CommonKADS methodology was also introduced for knowledge modelling using three layered approach domain knowledge layer, inference layer, and task layer (Wielingaa et al., 1992). Tools have been developed based on CommonKADS methodology for helping knowledge engineers in acquiring and analyzing knowledge such as the PC PACK tool which is developed by Epistemics company (www.epistemics.co.uk). Some other tools were developed in the early nineties but they were not used on a large scale.

In effect we have developed many expert systems using the GT methodology and CommonKADS methodology. The interested reader can search the following web site to get a lot of papers on the developed expert systems http://wwww.claes.sci.eg. In effect we were working on developing tools to help us in building expert systems using GT and CommonKADS methodology since long time. We started by developing tool similar to first generation rule based system tools augmented with objects on the top of Prolog to enable us in building the CommonKADS three layers better than commercial shells. This tool was called KROL (Shaalan et.al., 1998). We also developed a methodology for automatic KBS construction from reusable domain Specific components (Abdelhamid et.al., 1997). In 2003, we published a paper on automatic knowledge acquisition tool for irrigation and fertilization expert systems (Rafea et.al., 2003) in which we made use of the domain layer we have developed in irrigation and fertilization expert systems to develop an interactive tool to acquire knowledge from domain experts in these areas. This task was repeated for other tasks like diagnosis of plant disorders (El-Korany et. al, 2004). The accumulated experience enabled us to build the tool that we are going to present in this paper.

4. Design and implementation of the tool

The objective of building this tool was to expedite the knowledge acquisition process and implementation of plant protection tasks expert systems. The tool was availed on the web and allowed collaborative development of these expert systems on the web. It has an administration component that enables the tool administrator to: manage registrations of different types of users (administrator, expert, end user), manage the addition /deletion of expert systems projects, and assign users to projects. The tool contains also an ontology editor to help the user in building the plant protection ontology. This section describes the four task that comprise the plant protection expert system namely variety selection, cultural practice, pest identification, and pest control.

4.1 Variety selection task

The varietal selection task assists the user in identifying varieties that are resistant to certain pests and is suitable for cultivation according to other user requirements. The variety selection task is simply modelled in CommonKADS. The task layer uses a specially designed problem solving method called "select and assign". The inference layer contains two inference steps named "select" and "assign-value". The domain layer has two knowledge bases. The first knowledge bases is for selecting the appropriate variety based on input user requirements, and the second knowledge base is for assigning a value to an attributes like predicted yield based on environmental parameters like soil type or weather condition. The tool contains the task, and the inference steps, and the domain knowledge types, in this case the knowledge types are rules.

The knowledge acquisition mode works in a very a simple way such that a domain expert can use the tool. The user who may be a knowledge engineer or a domain expert can specify the varieties of the crop he will be using and add them to the ontology available with the tool which contains basic concepts and properties of any agricultural expert system. For each variety the user adds the features of the variety such as the pests it is resistant to, the environmental factor it is tolerant to, its expected yield, and other features. For each feature the user can decide whether this feature is an input or output feature of the variety selection task (rule schema for selecting the variety). If it is an output feature the tool acquire other factors that affect this feature (rule schema for assigning attribute value). For example the expected yield may change based on environmental factor and consequently the tool acquires these factors. Once the schema is defined the rule instances are acquired .The acquired knowledge is mapped into a suitable rule based knowledge representation scheme using XM L while the input/output features are represented in a presentation layer.

The consultation mode uses the built-in task layer to run on the acquired knowledge: This task starts by asking the users about the features of the variety they want, and run the inference mechanism to produce the recommended variety and then ask the user about the environmental parameters to determine the value of attributes that depend on these parameters.

4.2 Cultural practices task

The cultural practice task recommends cultural practices that should be done before and/or after cultivation to prevent disorder appearance. This task is modelled using routine design generic task. In the Routine Design Generic Task the problem is divided into a collection of specialists, and each a specialist is responsible for accomplishing a small part of the overall design. Following the Generic Task view, the specialist decides which of his plans should be carried out based on the plan constrains (Plan selector). Generally each specialist selects one of its plans. Each plan selected decides which tasks should be carried out based on the task constrains (Task selector), and each task has a number of steps that determine the detailed description for it. The cultural practices task has one specialist, six plans corresponding to the main pests categories: fungal diseases, viral diseases, insects, weeds, nematodes, and snail slugs, a number of tasks corresponding to practices types applied on each of the main pests categories under the plan handling each category, and steps under each task that assign values to the attributes describing the agricultural practices handled by the task. The generic task control that handles this knowledge representation scheme is a built-in module in the tool.

The knowledge acquisition mode: In the knowledge acquisition mode the tool acquires the cultural practices to protect the crop against certain pests given by the user. After providing the tool with the practices needed to protect the crop against a category of pests, the properties of each practice that are represented as steps of the task, and the factors that affect the decision for choosing a value for this property, the tool starts asking the user about the properties values of each practice and the factors that affect the selection of this value. For example if the practice is "spraying pesticides" and this operation has a property called pesticide name, and this pesticides depends on the soil type and the variety cultivated, the tool asks the user about the soil type and cultivated variety that are used to determine the pesticide name. It can acquire as many decision rules that relate pesticides protecting a crop against certain pest taking into consideration the factors affecting the selection. The acquired knowledge instantiates the routine design knowledge representation scheme using XM L while the input/output features are represented in a presentation layer.

The consultation mode uses the built-in task control to ask the users about the pest against which they want to protect their crops. Based on this pest and the attributes added to the presentation layer built during the knowledge acquisition of factors affecting the generation of the solution, the system generates a screen asking about the factors and then run the routine design task control that generates the recommended practices with their properties.

4.3 Pest identification task

The pest identification task assists the user in identifying the causes (disease, Insect, and others) of the user complains (Observation). The pest identification task is modelled in CommonKADS. The task layer uses a specially designed problem solving method called "generate and confirm". The task contains the sub task "generate" which is implemented using the problems solving method "identify and generate, and the inference step "confirm-hypothesis". The task "generate" has two inference steps" identify-observation" and" generate-hypothesis". The inference layer contains the subtask "generate" and the inference step "confirm-hypothesis". The domain layer has two knowledge bases. The first knowledge base is a tree where growth stages node is the root , and each growth stage is a child node of the root, plant parts that appear within this growth stage are children of this growth stage, and observation for each plant part are the leaves. The second knowledge base is a relation between primary and secondary observations and causes. The tool contains the task, the inference steps, and the domain knowledge types; in this case the knowledge types are tree together with its schema and rules.

The knowledge acquisition module acquires all diseases, insects and other pests affecting the underlying crop. For each cause the user adds its symptoms and the plant part on which this symptom appears (In effect the second knowledge base is built during this acquisition process). For each symptom the user can decide whether this symptom is a primary observation or not. It is also required to acquire first knowledge base by acquiring the growth stages of the underlying crop, the plant parts that are visible during each growth stage, and the primary observations on these parts. .The acquired knowledge is mapped into a suitable knowledge representation using XML while the input/output features are represented in a presentation layer.

The consultation mode uses the built-in task layer to run on the acquired knowledge: This task starts by running the subtask "generate" which asks the users about the growth stage, selects the primary observations that can be visible during this stage, generate a screen containing these primary observations, asks the user about primary observations, and generate suspected disorders. After generating the suspected disorder the pest identification asks the user whether they want to confirm the suspected disorders. If the user clicks yes the confirmation process starts by generating related observation which are generated from the rules that have partially matched. The inference steps "generate-hypothesis" and "confirm-hypothesis" use a specially designed inference method that partially match the condition part of the rule and come up with a certainty measure based on the number of premises matched in case of the confirmation process. Each time the users select an observation the confirmed causes appear with a certain degree of certainty. In effect there are two modes of confirmation process; one mode which diagnoses a single cause and another mode which diagnoses multi-causes. In the single cause diagnosis the confirmation process tries to satisfy the rule that diagnoses one cause by selecting this rule once the user chooses a certain observation while in the multi-causes diagnosis the confirmation process keeps the list of suspected disorders and just changes their certainty measures after each observation selection. The certainty measure ranges from 0.0 to 1.0.

4.4 Pest control task

The pest control module is similar to the cultural practice module. It is also based on the routine design generic task. It differs in that it assumes that the pest has appeared and needs to be controlled. So this task needs to acquire more inputs from the user during the knowledge acquisition phase such as the infestation level, and time to harvest.

5. Developing Barley Expert System

The development of Barley Expert System for plant protection was the first expert system developed using the tool presented in this paper. The effort in developing this expert system started in collaboration with International Centre for Agricultural Research in the Dray Areas (ICARDA) in 2003 and a paper documenting this collaboration was published (Abdul- Hadi et.al. 2006). CLAES continued working on this expert system and developed a new version containing the Egyptian expertise only (http://es.claes.sci.eg/barley/). The system contains the four tasks presented here above. The following sections describe briefly the four tasks as an example to of using the tool to clarify the concepts provided in section 4.

5.1 Variety selection module

The input parameters identified by the domain expert are plant height, row type, and the pests that the variety needs to be resistant to. Providing the system with the following data: plant height =tall, row type=6-Row, and the pest that the variety needed to be resistant to, is leaf rust, the system generated two varieties: Giza 123, and Giza 132. In this implementation the domain experts did not find that it is necessary to add the second knowledge base that determine some features based on environmental parameters. So the only output is the varieties selected. Clicking on the variety selected the features of the variety is displayed.

Fig. 1. Variety Selection Module

5.2 Cultural practice module

The cultural practice module covers 7 pest classes with a total of 38 pests. Once the user chooses certain pests the system responds by giving the cultural practices needed to be done as a preventive measure to inhibit their appearances. For example choosing cultural practices to prevent the appearance of Loose smut and Grasshoppers and click on cultural practices button produces the output shown in figure-2.

5.3 Pest identification module

The first thing that the system requests as input from the end user is the growth stage. The system covers the 8 growth stages of Barley. If the user chooses one stage, say flowering, the system displays a screen that contains primary observation on plant, leaf, and grain. Entering the primary observation, say dead plants, and clicking on diagnosis using single cause

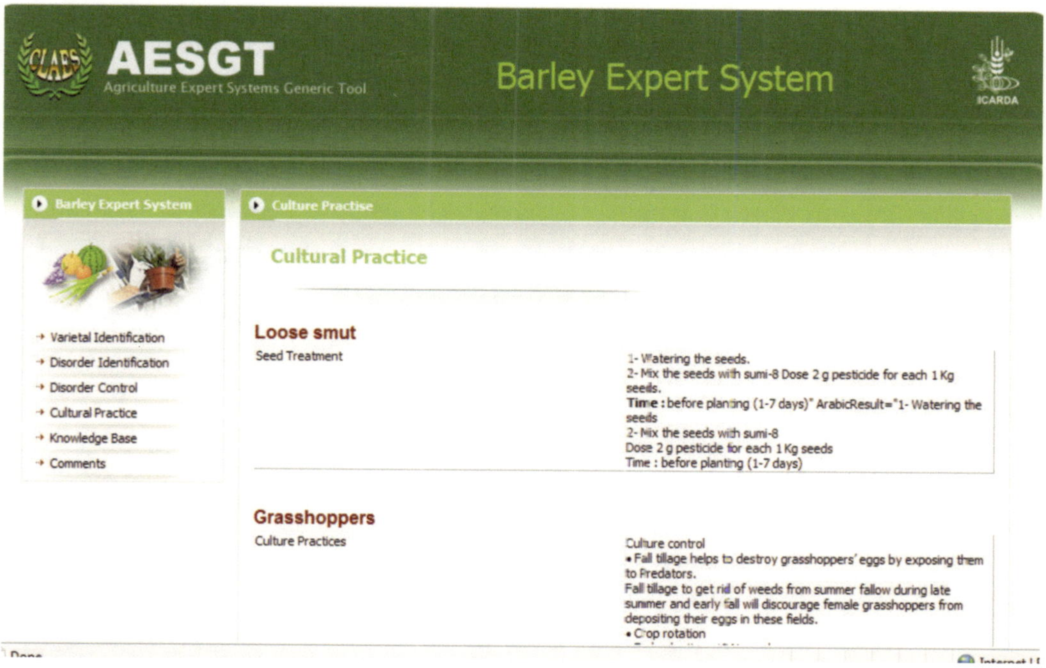

Fig. 2. Cultural Practices Module

Fig. 3. Output of the Pest Identification Module First Phase

mode, the suspected causes, Bird cherry-oat aphid and Green bug aphid are displayed as shown in figure 3. Clicking confirm diagnosis, the secondary observations appear. Choosing the leaf colour to be brown the Bird cherry-oat aphid is taken out of the diagnosis and the Green bug aphid stays with 0.4 certainty as shown in figure 4. The observations that are still being displayed are related to the diagnosed disorder and they are shrinking each time one observation is selected. If they exist the user can reach diagnosis with 1.0 certainty. Applying the same scenarios using the multi-cause diagnosis the two suspected causes are displayed after providing the same observations with these certainties Bird cherry-oat aphid with 0.14 certainty and Green bug aphid with 0.4 certainties as shown in figure 5. As you can see the secondary observations are not shrinking like the single-cause diagnosis because the system tries to diagnose all suspected causes. Each time the user chooses an observation the certainty measure of one or more causes increases based on its relevance to these causes.

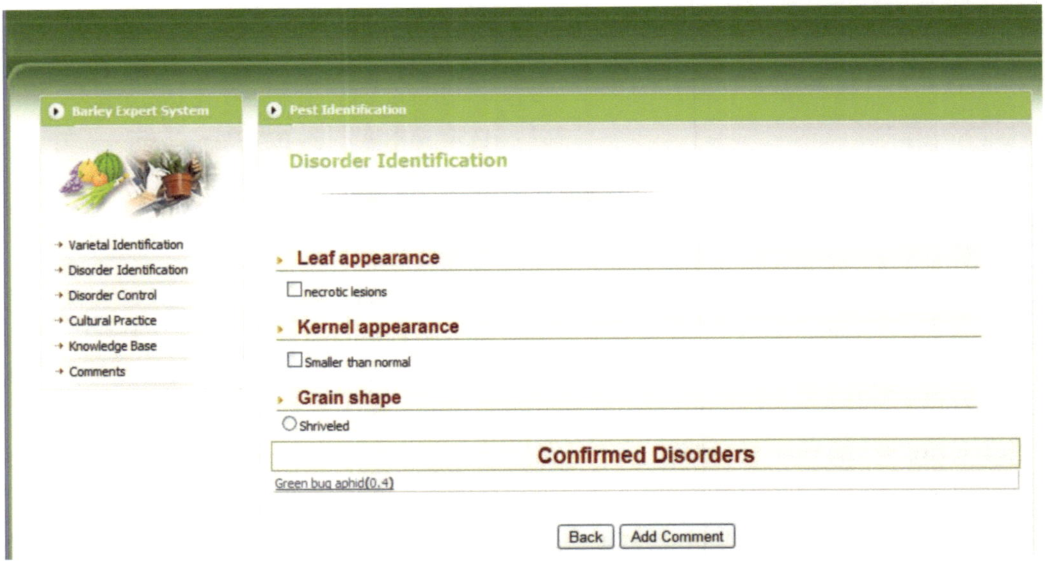

Fig. 4. Output of the Pest Identification Module Second Phase in case of Single-cause Diagnosis

Fig. 5. Output of the Pest Identification Module Second Phase in case of Multi-causes Diagnosis

5.4 Pest control module

The Pest Control module covers the same number of pests covered by the cultural practices module. The difference is that this module is used when a disorder appears and the pest that causes this disorder is diagnosed. For example if leaf rust is diagnosed, the system asks first about the percentage of infected plants, the available pesticide, and then give the recommendation as shown in figure 6.

Fig. 6. Output of the Pest Control Module

6. Conclusion and future work

This paper describes the development of a Web-Based Domain Specific Tool for Building Plant Protection Expert Systems and its usage to build an expert system for Barley protection. The plant protection knowledge has been modelled into four modules: variety selection, cultural practices, pest identification, and pest control. The tasks of the four modules are built-in in the tool. The tool also allows the user to choose the input and outputs of thee system as it has a presentation layer. The main contribution of this work is in building such tool that has the following characteristics: share knowledge acquisition through availing the tool on the Internet, enable human experts to cooperate with knowledge engineer through using the tool, and represent the knowledge in XML which is a standard data language to facilitate knowledge verification and future upgrading. There is still some work to be done to further verify the tool to be more user friendly for human experts and to support more crops with minimum intervention from the tool developer.

7. References

Abdelhamid, Y., Hassan, H., Rafea, A.(1997). An Approach to Automatic KBS Construction From Reusable Domain-specific Components, The 9th International Conference on Software Engineering & knowledge Engineering (SEKE'97).

Abdul-Hadi Z., Asaad S., Bayaa, B. , Dahab, M., Edris, S., El-Azhary,S., El-Bahnasy, K., El-Sayed, A, El-Zemaity, M., Grando, S., Ketata, K., Kumari S., , Malhotra, R., Mosaad, M., Pande, S., Rafea, A. , Ragab, A. , Rao, G., Said, A., Shata, A., Yehyaoui, A.(2006). Rapid Generation of Plant Protection Expert Systems, Computers in Agriculture and Natural Resources, 4th World Congress Conference, Proceedings of the 24-26 July 2006 (Orlando, Florida USA).

Chandrasekaran, B. (1988). Generic taks as building blocks for knowledge-based systems: the diagnostics and routine design examples. Knowledge Engineering Review, 3(3), 183-210.

Clancey, J. (1994). Notes on "Heuristic Classification", Artificial Intelligence, 59, 191- 196.

David, J., Krivi, J., Simmons, R. (1993). , Second Generation Expert Systems, Springer Verlag

El-Korany, A., El-Azhary, E., Yehia, M.(2004). An Approach for Building Generic Diagnosis Model in Agriculture Domain, Fifth International Workshop on Artificial Intelligence in Agriculture(AIA'2004), Cairo, Egypt

Musen, A. (1989). Automated Support for building and extending expert models. Machine Learning, 4(3-4), 347-376

Rafea, A., Hassan, H., Hazman, M. (2003). Automatic Knowledge Acquisition Tool for Irrigation and Fertilization Expert Systems, Expert Systems with Applications- An International Journal Volume 24, Issue 1, January 2003, Pages 49-57

Rothenfluh, E., Gennari, H., Eriksson, H., Puerta, R., Tu, W., Musen, A. (1994). Reusable ontologies, knowledge acquisition tools, and performance systems: PROTOGE-II solutions to Sisyphus-2. In Proc. 8th Banff Knowledge-Based Systems Workshop, 43, 1-30.

Shaalan,K.,Rafea,M.,Rafea,A.(1998). 'KROL: A Knowledge Representation Object Language on Top of Prolog'. Expert Systems with Applications, An International Journal Vol 15 pp 33-46 Elsevier Science Ltd,.

Studer, R., Richard, B., Fensel, D. (1998) Knowledge Engineering: Principles and Methods. Data and Knowledge Engineering , 25(1), , pp. 161-197.

.van Melle, W.J. (1981). System Aids in Constructing Consultation Programs. Ann Arbor MI: UMI Research Press.

Wielingaa, J., Schreiber, Th., Breuker, A. (1992). KADS: A modelling approach to knowledge engineering. Knowledge Acquistion, 4(1)5-53.

12

Expert System for Greenhouse Production Management

Yongguang HU, Jizhang WANG and Pingping LI
Jiangsu University
China

1. Introduction

Greenhouse is a kind of agricultural building structure with glass or plastic roof, where the vegetables or flowers can grow well year round by controlling the inside climatic environment. Fig. 1 shows commercial multispan greenhouses in China. The closed environment of a greenhouse has its own unique requirements, compared with outdoor production. Pests and diseases, and extremes of heat and humidity, have to be controlled, and fertigation is necessary to provide water and nutrients. Significant inputs of heat and light may be required, particularly with winter production of warm-weather vegetables. So greenhouse cost-effectiveness can not be ignored.

Fig. 1. Modern commercial greenhouses

Greenhouses are increasingly important in the food supply of high latitude countries and regions, especially Northern China, because they can allow certain crops to be grown year round such as lettuce and tomato.
Greenhouses protect crops from too much heat or cold, shield plants from dust storms and blizzards, and help to keep out pests or diseases. Light and temperature control allows greenhouses to turn inarable land into arable land. Hydroponics can be used in greenhouses as well to make the most use of the interior space.
Therefore, greenhouse industry is one of the most important parts and symbol of modern agriculture, since it can provide abundant fresh products stably and sustainably. However, greenhouse production process is much more complicated, compared with outdoor production. Precision management is badly needed under such controlled space. Generally, greenhouse system consists of the following elements - surrounding structures, covering, cooling and heating system, shading and light-supplementary system, CO_2 enrichment system, culture facilities, fertigation and automatic control system. Crop cultivation techniques and related equipment are also necessary.
In a word, faced with so huge amount of knowledge and techniques greenhouse engineering and its production management are challengeable, which leads to the emerging of expert system for greenhouse production management.
The application of expert system on greenhouse production management has been emphasized by many researchers, especially on greenhouse cultivation and environment control. A decision analysis and expert system model was applied to the problem of individual nutrient selection for cucumber growth in a controlled environment (Fynn et al., 1994). A computer-aided decision-making expert system for greenhouse cucumber was developed, which included cultivation management, pest and disease diagnosis and prevention (Chen & Li, 2001). VEGES was developed for diagnosis of nutrient deficiency, pest and disease on greenhouse vegetable (Yialouris et al., 1997). The humidity and temperature of a laboratory scale greenhouse are controlled using a rule-based expert system (Türkay, 1994). Artificial neural network was adopted to determine the temperature setpoint for greenhouse tomato by data collection rather than growers' experiences. Compared with conventional expert system it has the advantage of short control time and higher accuracy (Seginer et al., 1996). An expert system based on optimal fuzzy control strategy fulfilled real-time temperature control by on-line adjustment of setpoint (Jacobson et al., 1989). GHMES was developed to carry out the real-time environment control based on crop model and cultivation management (Hu et al., 2006).
The chapter deals with expert system development and application for greenhouse vegetable production management, including general description of greenhouse production system, design on expert system for greenhouse production management, integration of environment control subsystem with the expert system, software fulfilment of the expert system and two application cases in greenhouse vegetable production practice.

2. Design on expert system for greenhouse production management

2.1 System functional structure

According to the analysis of greenhouse and its production process, the expert system is composed of four subsystems (in Fig. 2), which are cultivation techniques, consultation of pest/disease and nutrient deficiency, diagnosis of pest/disease and nutrient deficiency, and environment control decision. Under each subsystem, there are still several subsystems.

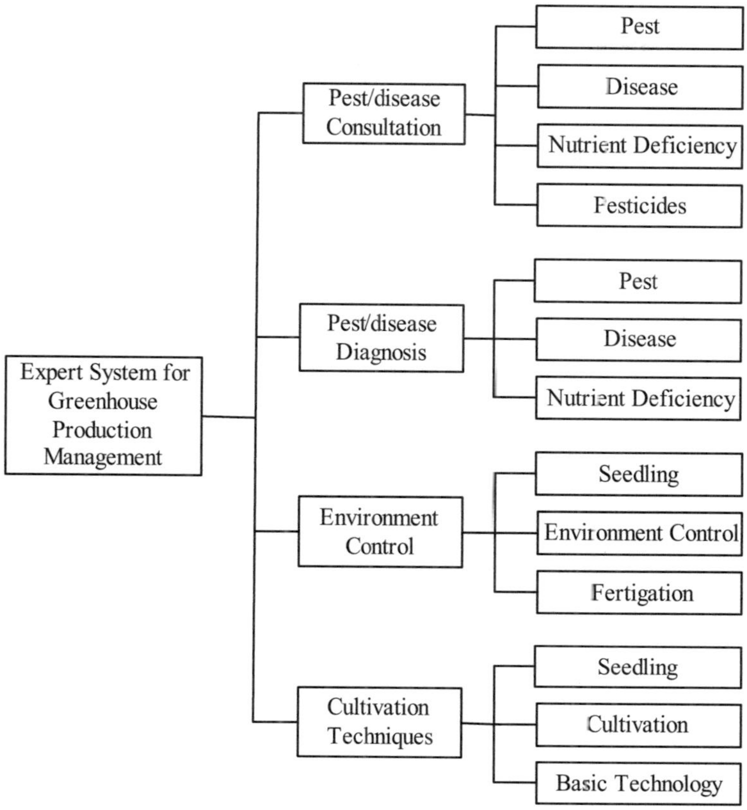

Fig. 2. System structure

2.2 System configuration

Modular design method is adopted to configurate the expert system and every independent module is combined by master module. Main modules of the expert system include inference diagnosis module, database management module, cosultation module, decision on environment control, text browsing module and help module. Correspondingly, system software structure is shown as Fig. 3.

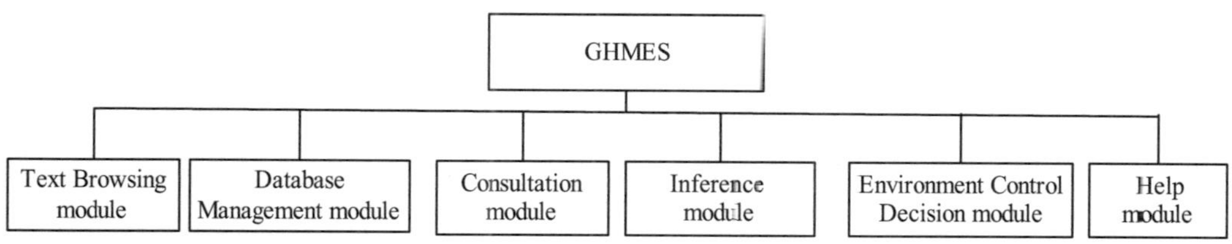

Fig. 3. System software structure

1. Inference and Diagnosis Module

   This is the core part of the expert sytem, which deals with the diagnosis of common pest/disease and nutrient deficiency for greenhouse crops. It can draw a diagnosis conclusion step by step and provide prevention and treantment mothed for user's reference.

2. Database Management Module
   The module is used for creating, editing and modifying knowledge and database. The known data, knowledge and rules of the expert system are also created, edited and modified through the module.
3. Text Browsing Module
   The module describes the botanical and physiological features of several typical greenhouse crops in text. Cultivation techniques and requirements of environment are also involved.
4. Consultation Module
   It includes both pest/disease and nutrient deficiency consultation modules. The module provides users with the type of pest/disease or nutrient deficiency and the expert system goes into the details such as symptom, occurrence regularity, prevention and treatment, and related pictures.
5. Decision of Environment Control Module
   There are two decision modes for greenhouse environment control, suiting for different occasions. One is on-line decision mode and the other is off-line decision mode. Under the on-line mode the expert system is integrated with the environment information collection system, based on which real-time environment control strategy can be worked out to complete the adjustment of greenhouse environment for good growth of crops. Under the off-line mode users input the present environment and crop information by hand and the expert system gives proper decision alternatives for user's reference.

3. Fulfillment of expert system for greenhouse production management

3.1 Database management

Among consultation module, cultivation techniques is called through text mode, and pest/disease, nutrient deficiency and chemicals are based on data dictionary, which result from large amount of searched basic data. For example, intuitive description of disease symptom and its pictures can be given by the system according to user's selection of different diseases.

Moreover, diagnosis module is also based on symptom, but the symptom is represented by particular knowledge. Here production rule knowledge representation based on relational database is adopted, and the knowledge is represented through database tables.

First, E-R model is established, which is an abstraction of real world. E-R model extracts common characteristics and neglects nonessential details, and describes the characteristics accurately using all kinds of concepts. There are three abstractions.

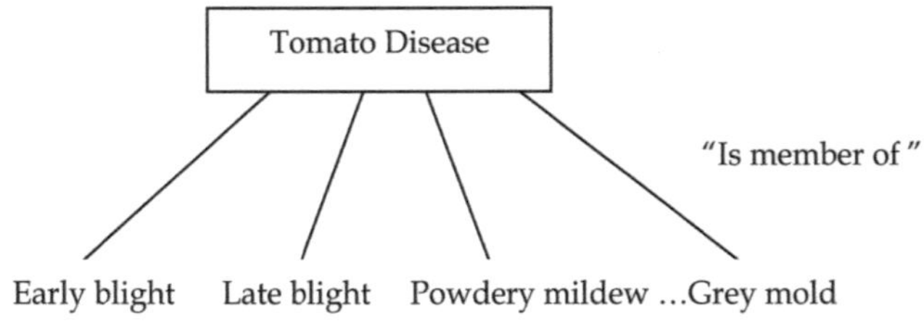

Fig. 4. Classification model

a. Classification defines a certain concept as a type of a group of objects, which have the common features and behaviours. Take tomato as an example, classification model is described in Fig. 4.
b. Aggregation is defined as a component part of a type. An entity is the aggregation of several attributes. In Fig. 5, the relationship between symptom and different parts is an aggregation.
c. Generalization is defined as a certain subset relationship between different types, which includes subtype and supertype. Generalization model is described in Fig. 6.

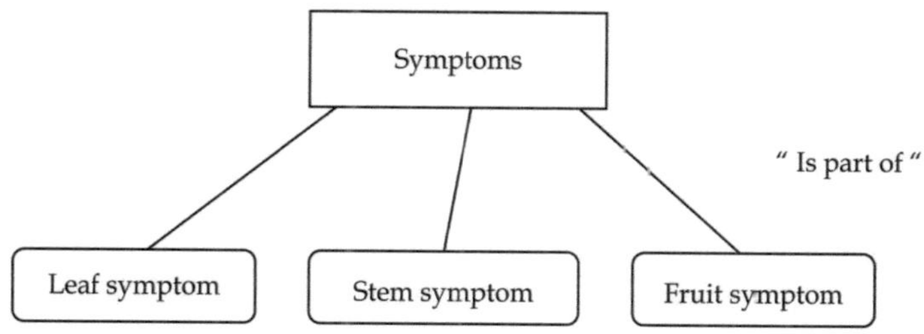

Fig. 5. Aggregation model

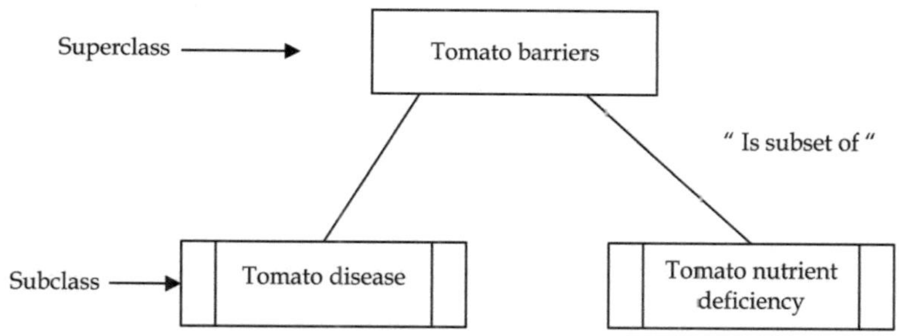

Fig. 6. Generalization model

Therefore, E-R model of the expert system is as follows in Fig. 7.

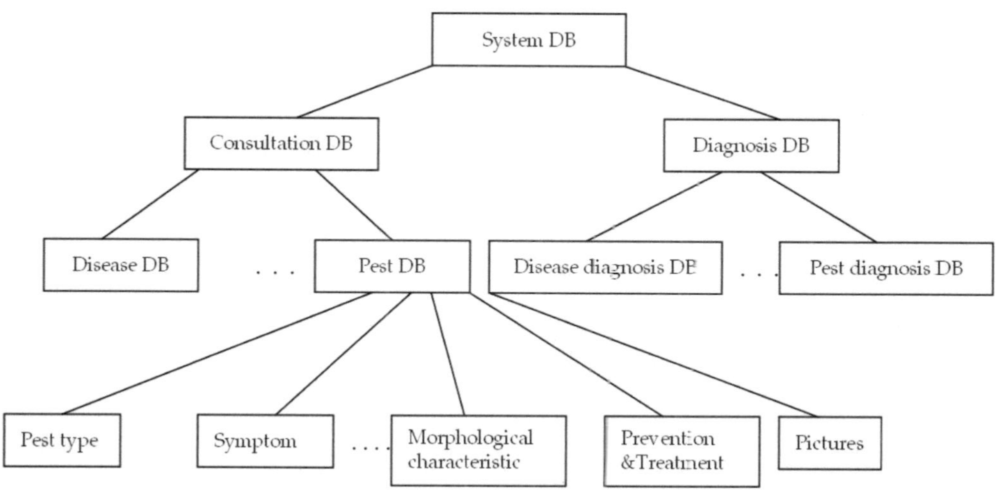

Fig. 7. E-R model

Then, E-R model is transformed into relational model, following the principle: one entity type is transformed into one relational schema, so entity attribute is relation attribute and entity code is relation code. The transformed data model is listed below.

Diseases:

Title	Symptom recognition	Occurrence regularity	Prevention/treatment	Pictures

Pests:

Title	Damage symptom	Morphological feature	Prevention/treatment	Pictures

Finally, the memory size of each data table field is determined, data and knowledge is recorded, and database is built. When using the database, maintenance of adding, deletion and updating is needed.

3.2 Design of knowledge base

3.2.1 Acquisition of knowledge

The source of knowledge is kinds of books, scientific reports and pictures. The reliability of the expert system depends on the quality of knowledge, so accuracy of fact description need to be guaranteed. The knowledge of greenhouse tomato growth barriers is briefly illustrated as follows.

1. Symptom description with natural language

Tomato barrier symptom is described with simple natural language, and a piece of knowledge table is made. For example, as for the case of phosphorus deficiency, symptom and diagnosis is described as follows.

Crop title: Tomato
Symptom: older leaves etiolating with purple brown spots
Older leaves dropping off easily
Short small plant
Thin stem
Olive green leaves
Violet Leaf Venation on the back
Diagnosis: Phosphorus deficiency

Simple language helps to purify and order the knowledge, and forms a description and diagnosis table. Even though there is large number of tomato growth barriers, the most common symptoms and easily-recognized symptoms are listed in Table 1, with which a series of targets (conclusion) can be decided for every barrier. All described symptoms and important facts are linked to the targets, and then proper diagnosis rules are obtained.

2. Rules of knowledge base

Representation of system symptom is based on the form of Object-Attribute-Value (OAV), which is suitable for developing any expert system based on rules. Most of the symptoms have one or several attributes and each attribute has at least one value. All the possible attributes and values of each symptom are collected and prepared.

Knowledge in description/diagnosis table is used to relate disease with its symptom. In the table the columns represent diagnosis and the rows represent symptom. Rules conformed to given column or row units are found out from rules of knowledge base. In addition, if a disease needs to be recognized by several rules, the attribute of the disease will appear in

Disease	Pest	Nutrient deficiency
Grey mold	Whitefly	Potassium
Late blight	Liriomyza sativae blanchard	Nitrogen
Leaf mold	Polyphagotarsonemus latus	Phosphorus
Spot blight	Spodoptera litura	Ferrite
Virus disease	Helicoverpa armigera	Calcium
Cercospora leaf spot		Magnesium
Blossom-end rot		Boron
Bacterial wilt		
Wilt		
Powdery mildew		
Sclerotinia sclerotiorum		

Table 1. Type of tomato diseases, pests and nutrient deficiency

several columns or rows of the table. When coding or decoding the table, rules are sorted out according to the etiopathology or inducement of the disease in Table 2. The rules of Table 2 are described as,

If growth limited with light green/yellow older leaves then Nitrogen deficiency;
If yellow or light yellow young leaves with green texture then Ferrite deficiency.

Symptom	Nutrient deficiency				
	N	N	Fe	Fe	……
Plant:					
Growth limited	X				
Wilting		X			
Color of older leaf:					
Light green	X				
Light yellow		X			
Green-purple					
Color of young leaf:					
Light yellow			X		
Green texture among nervations				X	
…………					

Table 2. Relation between tomato symptom and nutrient deficiency

3.2.2 Knowledge representation method

Knowledge base is essential to expert system and its structure and performance influence the accuracy and efficiency of problem solving. At the same time proper knowledge representation method may enhance the performance of knowledge base.

The knowledge within the expert system is represented and organized by the following types: descriptive knowledge, data knowledge and rule knowledge. Production knowledge representation based on database is used to strengthen the relation among knowledge and to reduce the number of production rules.
Rule base is the knowledge memory of specific field, and its representation is

If < premise > then < conclusion > λ

which means the reliability of conclusion is λ when premise comes into existence. $\lambda=1$ for accurate inference, and λ varies within [0,1] for inaccurate inference. < premise > is the conjunction of facts and assertion.
Semantic model of the rules is expressed as Fig. 8.

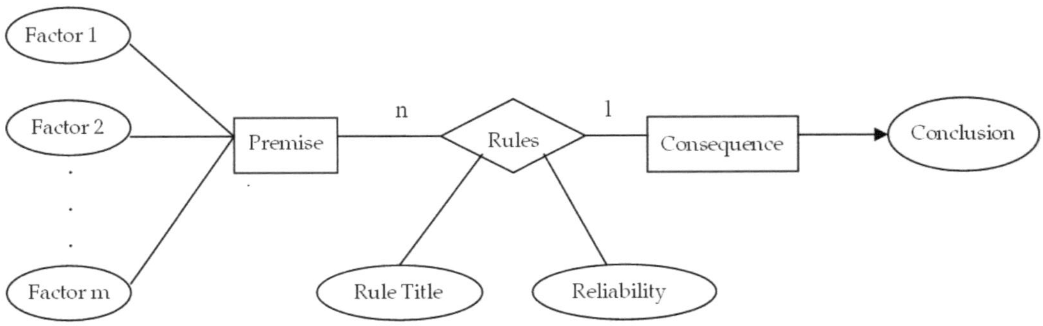

Fig. 8. Semantic model of the rules

Based on above semantic model, relational database and knowledge inference, rules are represented by relational database. Rule premise and conclusion are separated, and put into different database. Rules and related information is stored in rule premise base, and its structure is as follows.

Number of rules	Rule premise	Meet or not?

Rule conclusion and related information is stored in rule conclusion base, and its structure is as follows.

Number of rules	Rule conclusion	Number of premise	Number of auxiliary	contentment

Take a complete production rule as an example,

if < premise 1 >, < premise 2 >, < premise 3 > then < conclusion >

which means number of premise is three and conclusion can be made only when all the three premises meet the requirements.

3.2.3 Establishment of knowledge base

1. Knowledge base of pest/disease diagnosis

Besides rule premise base and rule conclusion base, dictionary base is designed to make knowledge base management easier by storing premise, conclusion and code of the rule base. Its structure is dictionary (fact number, facts, known or not) Knowledge base is essential to expert system and its structure and performance influence the accuracy and efficiency of problem solving. At the same time proper knowledge representation method may enhance the performance of knowledge base. The above three bases are structured through a table in Fig. 9.

2. Knowledge base of environment control decision

① Knowledge base of crop growth

It includes the requirement of growth on temperature, humidity and light intensity during different stages, which is acquired from expert's experiences, experiments and literature.

② Knowledge base of environment control

It covers the basic requirement on inside and outside environment control, priority of control parameter selection, actuator requirement under different climate, diagnosis and control strategy under abnormal situations. For example, roof window must be closed when it rains, or rolling screens must be closed if wind speed is too high.

③ Other auxiliary knowledge base

A. knowledge base of open-close of greenhouse

When the greenhouse actuators are in operation the open-close status of greenhouse is very important. For example, greenhouse must be closed when heating or CO_2 enrichment, or south and north rolling screens must be open and east and west rolling screens must be closed when cooling with sprinkling.

B. knowledge of environmental influence on crop growth

For example, higher temperature is needed to promote the growth of cucumber during the early growth stage, while too low humidity could cause its physiological barrier during the development stage.

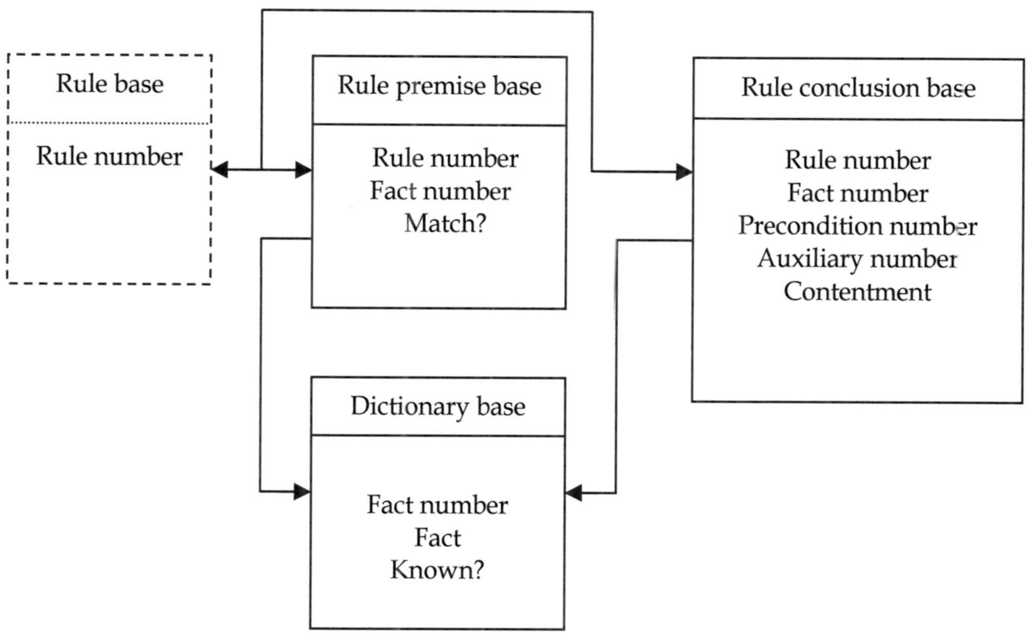

Fig. 9. Table-structured knowledge base

3.2.4 Organization of knowledge base

Knowledge base is organized by database management mechanism of SQL Server 2000, since knowledge is represented through relational database table. This kind of organization has the following advantages.

1. Knowledge base and inference engine are mutually independent, and the internal variation of organizational structure of knowledge base does not affect inference engine.
2. Expansion, maintenance and modification of knowledge are easily done with the help of database.
3. Rule files can be transformed into database files so that the normative and flexibility of knowledge representation are improved.
4. Multimedia knowledge representation is achieved through setting fields of picture, sound and animation in the conclusion base.

3.3 Design of inference engine

Inference engine may control and coordinate the whole expert system for greenhouse production management. The knowledge used for inference is accurate, and inference conclusion is definite.

3.3.1 Diagnosis of pest/disease and nutrient deficiency

Occurrence and development of pest/disease and nutrient deficiency are restricted by many factors, and here cropping system, growth season, temperature and humidity, and time are considered. Diagnosis of pest/disease and nutrient deficiency is based on symptom. The diagnostic flow chart is shown in Fig. 10.

The inference engine is built up with structured query language and forward inference is adopted. According to the given facts, rule premise database is searched to find out the matched record. The matching process is shown in Fig. 11.

For example, when users input information (pupae; oval shape), auxiliary number of rule is not reduced to 0 after inference. The inference conclusion is: greenhouse whitefly and liriomyza sativae blanchard, and detailed information of the two pests is listed. Final decision will be made by watching and judging the further features.

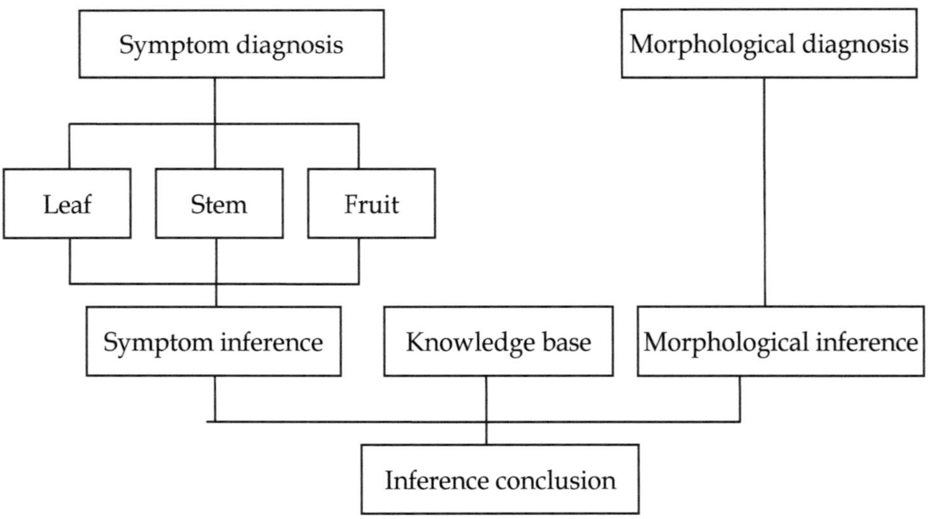

Fig. 10. Flow chart of diagnosis

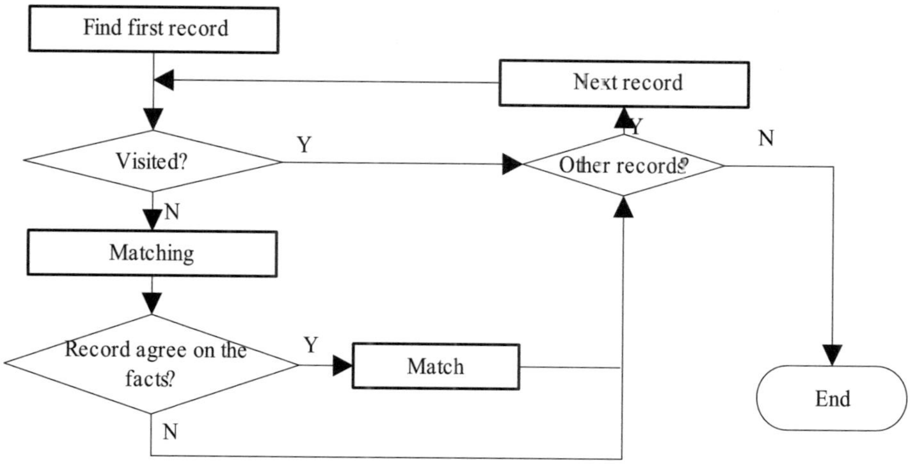

Fig. 11. Flow chart of matching record

3.3.2 Environment control decision based on models

Different combinations of environment control actuators are listed in Table 3 (for summer) and Table 4 (for spring and autumn).

Combination number	Roof window	Rolling screen	Shading	Fan	Wet pad
1	0	0	0	0	0
2	1	0	0	0	0
3	1	1	0	0	0
4	1	1	1	0	0
5	1	1	1	1	0
6	1	1	1	1	1

Table 3. Combinations of environment control actuators for summer

Combination number	Half roof window	Roof window	Rolling screen	Shading	Fan
1	0	0	0	1	0
2	0	0	0	0	0
3	1	0	0	0	0
4	0	1	0	0	0
5	0	1	1	0	0
6	0	1	1	1	0
7	0	1	1	1	1

Table 4. Combinations of environment control actuators for spring and autumn

In Table 3 and Table 4, 1 stands for the status "Open" of the actuators, while 0 stands for the status "Closed" of the actuators.
The inference process is described as Fig. 12. First, users input environment information and the status of actuators manually or automatically through greenhouse environment information collection system. With photosynthetic model and knowledge of crop growth appropriate environment parameters can be figured out. At the same time current environment inside the greenhouse is judged to make sure it conforms to the proper range. Then keep the current status of the actuators. Otherwise, inference of environment control decision must be done in order to output the optimal environment control decision for users' reference.

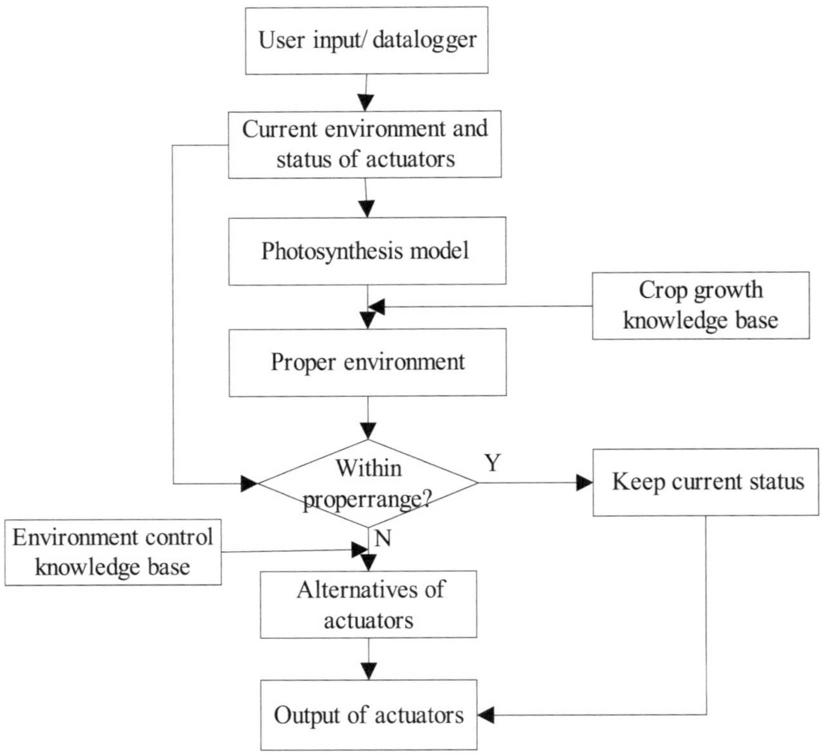

Fig. 12. Inference process of environment control decision based on models

4. Integration of environment information collection with expert system

To integrate obtained models and knowledge, especially current environment and crop information with greenhouse management expert system for vegetables and make better decisions, real-time environment information collection system is indispensable.

4.1 Overall design of environment information collection system

As a sub-system of greenhouse management system, environment information collection system provides expert system with real-time environment information and help to make proper environment control decisions.

4.1.1 Design requirements

The sub-system can collect environment information inside and outside greenhouses independently. All the information is stored in database, and can be used for greenhouse management expert system. The climatic parameters include temperature, relative humidity, light intensity and data of CO_2 concentration wind speed, wind direction and rainfall can also be collected by reserved extensible channels and interfaces for future purpose.

The system needs separate monitoring and unified management

4.1.2 System functions

For greenhouse environment control, single chip microcomputer receives climatic data from kinds of sensors, carries out logical operation and judgement with expert system, and then makes control decisions to adjust greenhouse environment. Meanwhile, it can help growers to analyze history dada and mine good management strategies. The specific functions are listed as follows:

Real-time monitoring greenhouse environment;
Updating the environment information database for expert system;
Information output and display with text, graph table or printout;
Alarming in case of extreme occasions or crop stress.

4.1.3 System configuration

Environment information collection system consists of sensors, data collection module and monitoring software. System configuration is shown in Fig. 13.

Each of the sensors is connected with data collection modules to obtain environment parameters inside and outside greenhouses. All data collection modules communicate with monitoring system (PC) through RS232/485 converter. Monitoring software is developed with configuration software, which is easily customized and interactive.

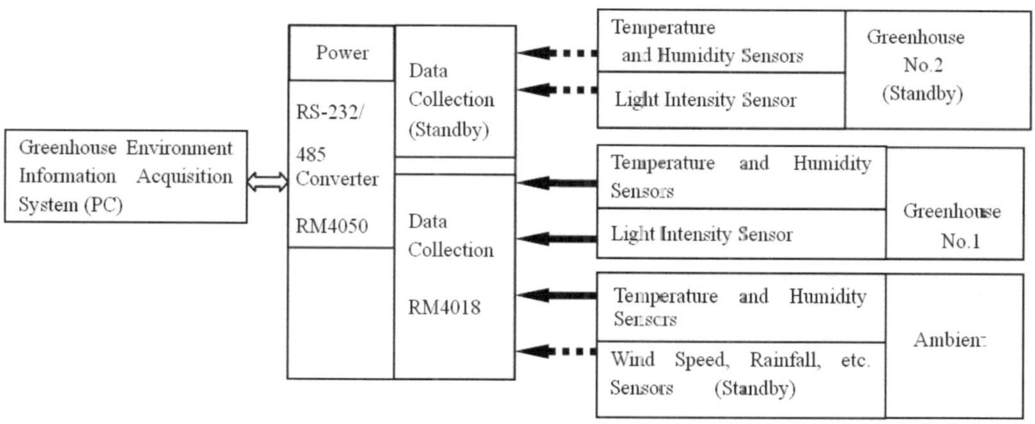

Fig. 13. Configuration of greenhouse environment information collection system

4.2 System hardware design

Selected sensors are used to measure temperature, relative humidity and light intensity. Integrated temperature and humidity sensor LT/W/S and light intensity sensor LT/G

adopt advanced circuit module to transmit signals, and output standard voltage and current, which can be switched by jumping lines. Specification of sensors is shown in Table 5.
8 channels can be linked to data collection module RM4018 and communicate with monitoring computer through the interface of RS485. RM4018 adopts MCU of AT89C2051, 12-bit A/D chip ADS7822 and multiplexer chip MPC508. Photoelectric isolation is used to enhance anti-jamming.

Sensor type	Range	Output	Accuracy
LT/W/S Temperature Humidity	-20~80°C 0~100%	0~20 mA 4~20 mA 0~5 V	±0.5°C ±3%
LT/G	0~100KLux	0~10 V	±3%

Table 5. Specifications of sensors

Module RM4050 adopts the techniques of photoelectric isolation and auto reversion to gain high reliability. System supply voltage and current is DC24V/2A and plastic case is self-made.

4.2 System software design

The software of greenhouse environment information acquisition system is developed on the platform of configuration software PCAuto3.1, which is a kind of special software for data collection and process control. PCAuto3.1 has flexible configuration not programming mode and can provide customers with friendly interface and easy operation.
Configuration software consists of project manager, development system, interface running system, real-time database, I/O driver, network communication program, serial communication program, dialing communication program and web server program.
The software of greenhouse environment information acquisition system includes real-time display, text and graph output, database management and system parameters setting. The main window is shown in Fig. 14.
The database of the software is called by the model base and environment control system, and then control decision can be made based on it.
First, database files of ACCESS is created, entitled data.mdb. Then the database form is correlated with configuration software form by the command of dynamic link library---SQLCreateTable. And one record of environment information is inserted by the command of dynamic link library---SQLInsert.
Finally, expert system directly calls real-time ACCESS database files to be processed for making control decisions.

4.3 System implementation

According to measuring requirement, sensors were put on proper locations and connected with the data collection modules. And the data collection modules were connected with a computer in which monitoring and control software had been installed
The system automatically recorded environment information at a certain interval and was put into expert system by the ACCESS database files. The system ran for 20 days with no software or hardware failures and successfully supported greenhouse management system with proper decision-making.

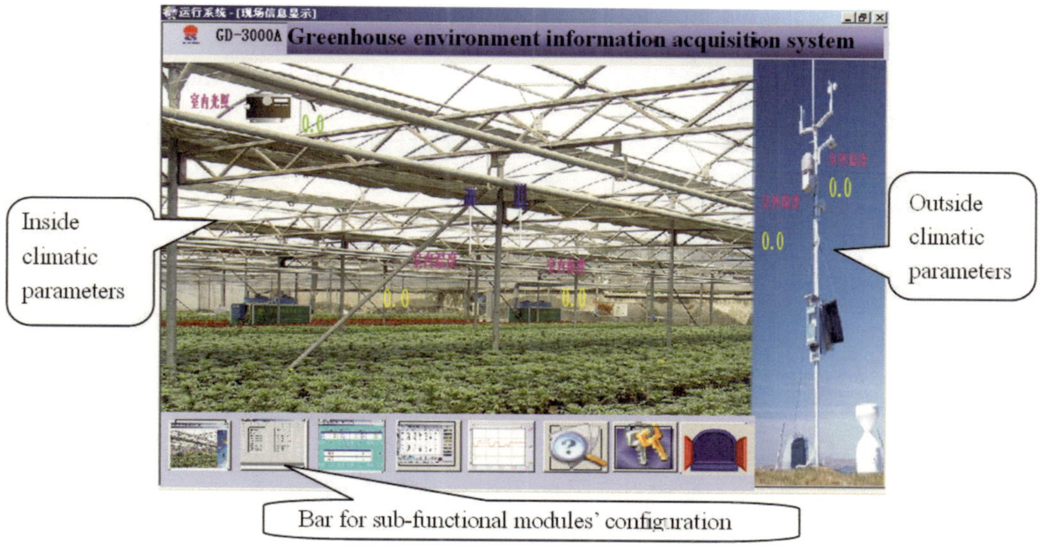

Fig. 14. Main window of the system software

5. Application examples of expert system

The operation of the expert system is simple and easy through menu-driven mode. Given functions include,

1. Consultation of basic cultivation information, dealing with botanical characteristics, requirements of growth environment and cultivation techniques during each growth stage.
2. Consultation of frequent pest/disease and nutrient deficiency symptom in greenhouses and chemicals for prevention and treatment.
3. Diagnosis and recognition of pest/disease and nutrient deficiency.
4. Decision on greenhouse environment control for on/off-line operation mode.

Fig. 15 shows the main interface of the expert system, consisting of title bar, menu bar and shortcut bar. Users can select corresponding functions by clicking them.

Fig. 15. Main interface of the expert system

5.1 Example of disease diagnosis

The general process of diagnosis is briefly described through tomato diseases. Fig. 16 is one of the subforms for diagnosis of tomato diseases. Tomato diseases are diagnosed by their damage symptoms, which have much difference according different growing parts such as leaves, stems and fruits. Users observe the tomato plant on site carefully, and then choose corresponding parts suffering potential diseases in the expert systen. Finally the diseases and their prevetion/treatment motheds are inferred by the expert system.

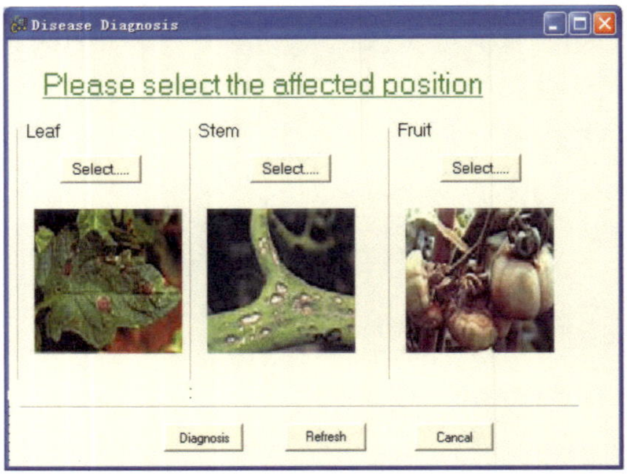

Fig. 16. Interface diagnosis for tomato diseases

Fig. 17, symptom selection dialogue box, will come out when clicking on "Leaf", affected position, in Fig. 16. Then all the disease symptoms related to tomato leaf will appeare in the list box of "selected knowledge or data". After proper selection the knowledge or data will be put into the list box of "selected inference knowledge". Here we choose three pieces of knowledge: "water-stain diseased spots, V-shape extended inwards from leaf edge", "drab or tawny spots" and "with grey mold layer", and save it as a database file.

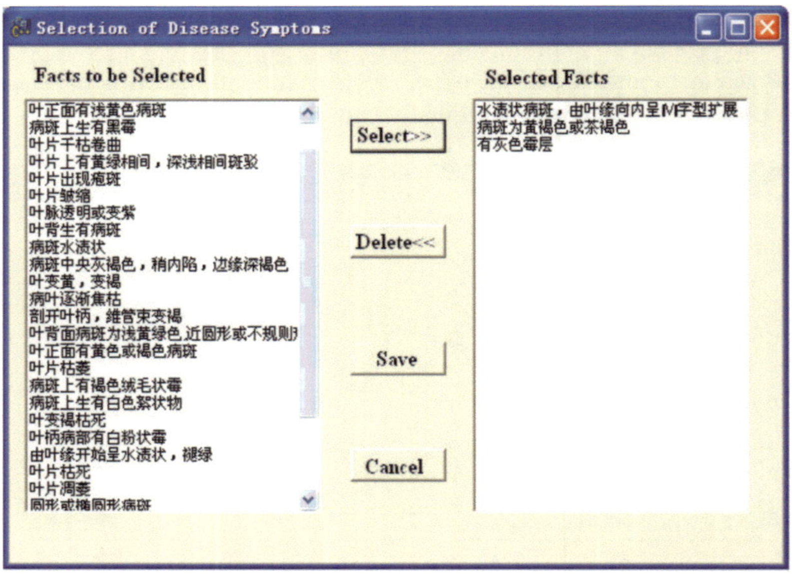

Fig. 17. Dialogue box of leaf symptom selection

For the fruit part, the operation is the same as the leaf part (see Fig. 18). At the same time another database file is created.

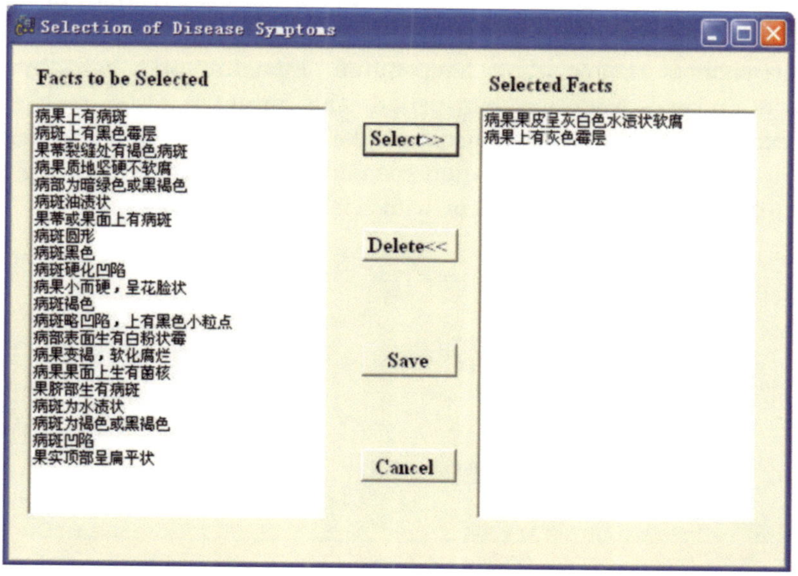

Fig. 18. Dialogue box of fruit symptom selection

After the above two-step selection, click the botton "Inferring" and the conclusion will be made in Fig. 19 by calling the knowledge base of disease diagnosis. The inference result shows that the tomato plant suffers grey mold, whose detailed information is listed in Fig. 19.

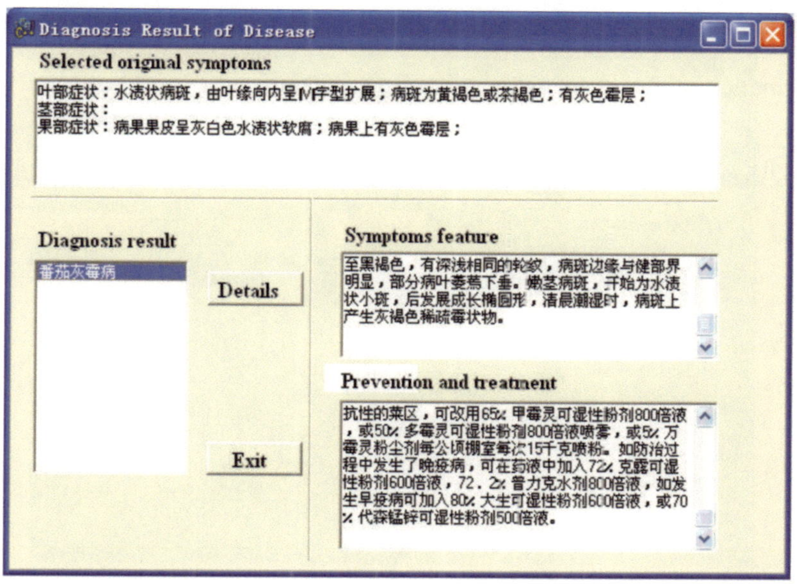

Fig. 19. Diagnosis result of tomato diseases

If only insufficient information is input, several inference conclusions may be obtained for user's reference and selection.

5.2 Example of greenhouse environment control decision

5.2.1 On-line decision

When users choose on-line decision mode the system collects environmental information inside and outside the greenhouse automatically. Fig. 20 shows both inside and outside environment parameters, including temperature, humidity and light intensity. The information is updated every a certain period. The current status of each environment controlling actuator is also shown. According to the specific crops cultivated in greenhouse, optimal environment conditions, irrigation span and recommended actuating alternatives will be decided through the expert system, wihich is shown in Fig. 21.

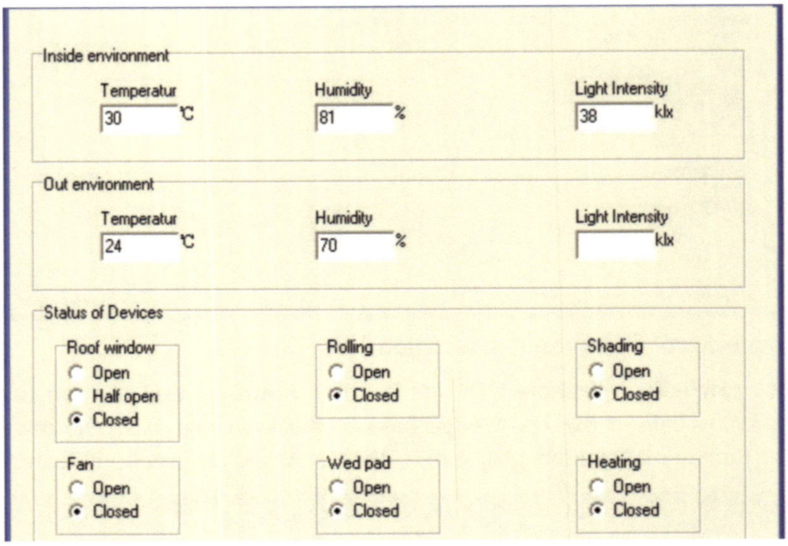

Fig. 20. Information output of greenhouse environment and actuator status

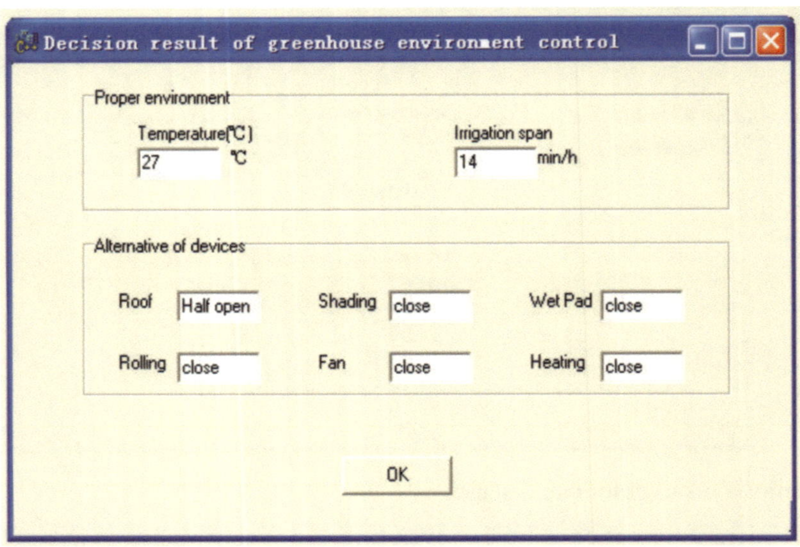

Fig. 21. On-line decision result

5.2.2 Off-line decision

Manual decision is carried out when users input the information of greenhouse environment and actuator status by hand, not through the collection system of environment information. Users may estimate and input light intensity at five levels due to no radiometer available (see Fig. 22). Base on above information off-line decision could be made in Fig. 23.

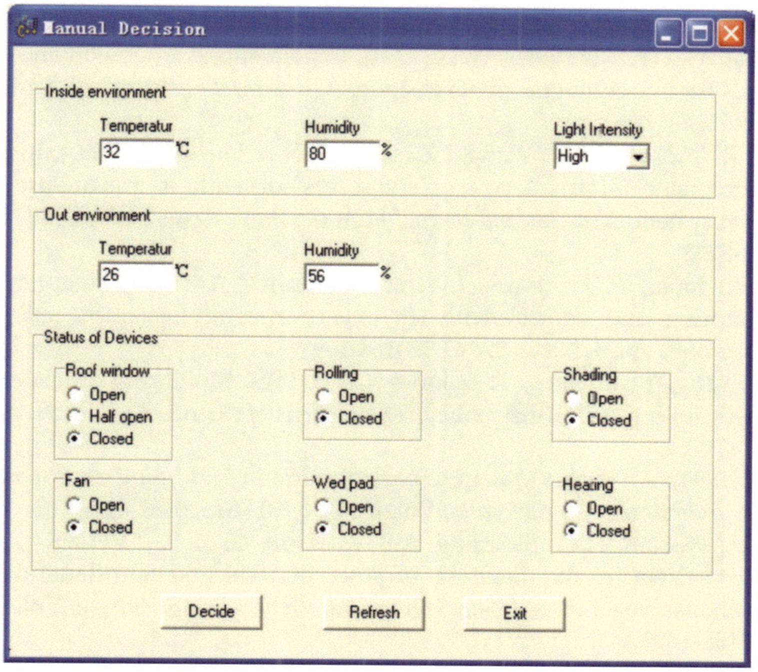

Fig. 22. Manual decision

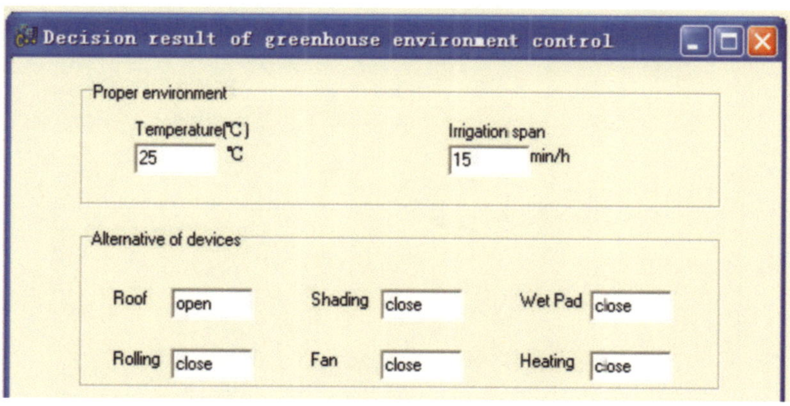

Fig. 23. Off-line decision result

6. Acknowledgements

We sincerely thank Professor Xiliang Zhang and Mr. Zuohua Li for their contributions to the development of greenhouse environment information collection system and pest/disease diagnosis module. The research was also funded by China and Jiangsu Provincial government (Project grant No. 2006BAD11A10, 30771259 and 08KJA21001).

7. References

Chen, Q.Y. & Li, H. (2001). Study on the expert system of cucumber culture management in greenhouse, *Transactions of the CSAE,* Vol. 17, No. 6, 142-146, 1002-6819

Fynn, R.P.; Bauerle, W.L. & Roller, W.L. (1994). Implementing a decision and expert system model for individual nutrient selection, *Agricultural Systems,* Vol. 44, No. 2, 125-142, 0308-521X

Hu, Y.G.; Li, P.P.; Zhang, X.L.; Wang, J.Z.; Chen, L.F. & Liu, W.H. (2007). Integration of an environment information acquisition system with a greenhouse management expert system, *New Zealand Journal of Agricultural Research,* Vol. 50, No. 5, 855-860, 0028-8233

Jacobson, B.K.; Jones, P. H.; Jones, J.W. & Paramore, J.A. (1989). Real-time greenhouse monitoring and control with an expert system, *Computers and Electronics in Agriculture,* Vol. 3, No. 4, 273-285, 0168-1699

Seginer, I.; Hwang, Y.; Boulard, T. & Jones, J.W. (1996). Mimicking an expert greenhouse grower with a neural-net policy, *Transactions of the ASAE,* Vol. 39, No. 1, 299-306, 0001-2351

Türkay, O.S. (1994). An expert system to control humidity and temperature of a laboratory scale greenhouse, *Mechatronics,* Vol. 4, No. 6, 607-615, 0957-4158

Yialouris, C.P.; Passam, H.C.; Sideridis, A.B. & Métin, C. (1997). VEGES—A multilingual expert system for the diagnosis of pests, diseases and nutritional disorders of six greenhouse vegetables, *Computers and Electronics in Agriculture,* Vol. 19, No. 1, 55-67, 0168-1699

13

Developing an Expert System for Predicting Pollutant Dispersion in Natural Streams

Hossien Riahi-Madvar[1] and Seyed Ali Ayyoubzadeh
Department of Water Structures, Tarbiat Modares University of Tehran
Iran

1. Introduction

In recent years, preservation and purgation of rivers is considered by national and international organizations that have responsible of quality control and preservation of water resources. Because of providing public health, it is most important and vital in regions that cities that rivers feed drink waters and large industrial factories located near these rivers (Li et al., 1998; Pourabadei & Kashefipur, 2007; Tayfour & Singh, 2005). So it is clear that estimation and simulation of flow, contaminant and sediment transport in river and water systems have more significance in water resources management. Using precious estimations reduces the risk of contaminant and pollutants on environment in now and future and increases the impact and effectiveness of environmental engineering projects on water recourses quality (Li et al., 1998 ;).

The increasing process of pollution on surface waters necessities the requirement of using mixing and attenuating processes in natural rivers. One of the most important, proper and prosperous methods of river environmental management is using and improving of river self-cleaning ability. Now sinking of several types of agricultural and industrial Remainders into natural rivers to oxidize and elimination of organic materials is a usual management operation in environmental engineering. To control the quality of surface water resources, the sinking of pollutants into natural rivers and open flows should be done under a precious and logical method. This action requires the detailed knowledge and information on pollutant transfer in rivers and the ability of transporting, mixing and self-cleaning of pollutants by river flow (Pourabadei & Kashefipur, 2007 ;).

Contaminants and effluents undergo stages of mixing with flow and dispersed longitudinally, transversely and vertically by advection and dispersion transport processes. Contaminants and effluents due to advective and dispersive processes of river flows, propagates in longitudinal, transversal and vertical directions (Tayfour & Singh, 2005). Ability and power of river and other open channel flows in dispersing additive materials in longitudinal, transverse and vertical directions addressed and described by dispersion coefficients. Three dispersion coefficients K_X, K_Y and K_Z show the dispersion coefficients in longitudinal, transverse and vertical directions respectively (Tayfour & Singh, 2005). Far from the point of injection of pollutants to river where the mixing process is completed over all the cross section, only longitudinal dispersion is dominant and all of the dispersion phenomena are described by K_X

[1] Corresponding author E-mail: Hossien.riahi@gmail.com

coefficient (Chatila, 1997). Rate of longitudinal dispersion is determined by the longitudinal dispersion coefficient and finally the fate of contaminant transport is relevant to the longitudinal mixing and modeling, hazard zoning, monitoring and accurate determination of pollutant conditions in river and natural channels requires the precious estimations for longitudinal dispersion coefficient (Li et al., 1998; Fisher et al., 1979).

2. Important

Accurate estimation of longitudinal dispersion coefficient is required in several applied hydraulic problems such as: river engineering, environmental engineering, intake designs, estuaries problems and risk assessment of injection of hazardous pollutant and contaminants into river flows (Sedighnezhad et al., 2007; Seo & Bake, 2002). Investigation of quality condition of natural rivers by 1-D mathematical models requires the best estimations for longitudinal dispersion coefficient (Fisher et al., 1979). When measurements and real data of mixing processes in river are available, the longitudinal dispersion coefficient is determined simply, but in rivers that the mixing and dispersing data isn't available and these phenomena aren't known, should use alternative methods for estimation of dispersion coefficient values (Kashefipur & Falconer, 2002). In these cases, because of the complexity of mixing phenomena in natural rivers, the best estimations of dispersion coefficients aren't possible and usually these values are determined by several simple regressive equations (Deong et al., 2001). There are several empirical equations for estimation of longitudinal dispersion coefficient in natural rivers that have presented in next sections (Seo & Cheong, 1998). These equations are valid only in their calibrated ranges of flow and geometry conditions and for larger or smaller ranges haven't good results.
The main aim of this chapter is to investigate the method and equations that developed for dispersion coefficient estimation and assessing the accuracy of these methods in comparisons with real data and at least not at end, developing a new and accurate methodology for dispersion coefficient determination. So, In the first step authors have investigated previous studies and in the second step inventionally using adaptive neuro-fuzzy inference system(ANFIS), a new procedure is developed for accurate estimation of longitudinal dispersion coefficients and the results of this new model is compared with previous empirical equations. At follows, firstly we have presented most important equations for longitudinal dispersion coefficient and finally adaptive neuro-fuzzy inference system is described in detail. At the end of the chapter comparison of results of empirical relations with ANFIS model is presented.

3. Materials and methods

In this section, at first theoretical concepts, research background and most important equations that are available for estimations of longitudinal dispersion coefficient are presented and after that adaptive neuro-fuzzy inference system and developing algorithm of this model are presented. Also, the data set that have used in this study and variable ranges of these parameters are presented.

3.1 Theoretical background

The one-dimensional (1D) Fickian-type dispersion equation, which is derived by Taylor (Fisher et al., 1979), has been widely used to obtain reasonable estimates of the rate of longitudinal dispersion. The 1D dispersion equations is

$$\frac{\partial C}{\partial t}+u\frac{\partial C}{\partial x}=K_x\frac{\partial^2 C}{\partial^2 x} \quad (1)$$

Where C: concentration average in section, u: longitudinal average velocity, t: time, x: longitudinal direction in flow stream and K_x: Longitudinal dispersion coefficient. Based on this equation, the fate of pollutant transport in rivers is determined by K_x value. Fisher (Fisher et al., 1979) developed following triple integral term for estimation of it (Tavakollizadeh & Kashefipur, 2007)

$$K_x=-\frac{1}{A}\int_0^B hu'\int_0^y\frac{1}{\varepsilon_t h}\int_0^y hu'dydydy \quad (2)$$

Where K_x: Longitudinal dispersion coefficient, A: cross section area of flow, B: top width of water surface, h: local depth of flow in any transverse point, u′: deviation of depth average flow velocity from cross sectional average velocity, y: transverse location from left bank and ε_t: transverse mixing coefficient. In this equation the unknown term of et is described by several researchers as a transverse turbulent coefficient. It is noticeable that the equation 2 is a basic for several proposed empirical equations of K_X. Fisher et al. (Fisher et al., 1979) used following equation for estimation of ε_t in wide and straight rivers with uniform flow and constant depth in transverse which haven't any transversal dispersions

$$\varepsilon_t=0.15Hu_* \quad (3)$$

Where H: depth average of flow in cross section, u_*: shear velocity and equals to √ (gHSf) and S_f is the longitudinal slope of energy.
Comparisons of real measurements with results of equation 2 shows that in uniform flows average error of this equation is 30% and in non-uniform flows it is reaches to 4 times of real data(FaghforMaghrebi & Givehchi, 2007). It is difficult to use equation 2 in real and applied cases because the geometry of cross section h(y) and transverse velocity profile v(h) aren't available and can't be determined simply and because its impracticalities Fisher et al. (Fisher et al., 1979) using several simple non-dimensional parameters proposed another equation (Tayfour & Singh, 2005)

$$K_x=\frac{I\overline{u'^2}B_1^2}{\varepsilon_t} \quad (4)$$

In this relation B_1: longitudinal scale corresponding with shear resulted from transverse velocity distribution, ε_t: cross sectional average of transverse mixing coefficient and I is non-dimensional integral

$$I=-\int_0^1 h'u''\int_0^{y'}\frac{1}{\varepsilon_t'h'}\int_0^{y'}h'u''dy'dy'dy' \quad (5)$$

Where its non-dimensional parameters are:

$$u''=\frac{u'}{\sqrt{\overline{u'^2}}}h''=\frac{h}{H}y'=\frac{y}{B}\varepsilon_t'=\frac{\varepsilon_t}{\overline{\varepsilon_t}} \quad (6)$$

In this equation √(u'2) is the deviation of velocity and shows size of deviation of average turbulent velocity from cross sectional average velocity (Tayfour & Singh, 2005). Based on the proposed method by fisher and equation 4, researchers have developed several empirical relations which the most important of them are presented in table 1. it is clear that all of these equations determines the longitudinal dispersion coefficient using variables that relates the average conditions of river flow to the longitudinal dispersion processes. These variables are average depth of flow in cross section, average velocity and shear velocity and width of water surface. In this study presented equations in table 1 is compared and the accuracy of them is determined based on real data collected from published data sets. Also input and output parameters of ANFIS model are these variables.

Ref.	*Eq. No.*	*Equation*	*Author(year)*
(Tayfour and Singh, 2005)	*(7)*	$K_x = 5.93Hu_*$	*Elder(1959)*
(Deong et al., 2001)	*(8)*	$K_x = 0.58(\frac{H}{u_*})^2 UB$	*Quien and quifer(1979)*
(Fisher et al., 1979)	*(9)*	$K_x = 0.011\frac{U^2B^2}{Hu_*}$	*Fisher(1976)*
(Seo and Bake, 2002)	*(10)*	$K_x = 0.55\frac{Bu_*}{H^2}$	*Liu and Chen(1980)*
(Seo and Bake, 2002)	*(11)*	$K_x = 0.18(\frac{U}{u_*})^{0.5}(\frac{B}{H})^2 Hu_*$	*Liu(1980)*
(Tavakollizadeh and Kashefipur, 2007)	*(12)*	$K_x = 2.0(\frac{B}{H})^{1.5} Hu_*$	*Awasa and Ottawa(1991)*
(Seo and Cheong, 1998)	*(13)*	$K_x = 5.92(\frac{U}{u_*})^{1.43}(\frac{B}{H})^{0.62} Hu_*$	*Seo and chang(1998)*
(Sedighnezhad et al., 2007)	*(14)*	$K_x = 0.6(\frac{B}{H})^2 Hu_*$	*Kasiez and Rodriguez(1998)*
(FaghforMaghrebi and Givehchi, 2007)	*(15)*	$K_x = 0.2(\frac{B}{H})^{1.3}(\frac{U}{u_*})^{1.2} Hu_*$	*Huang and li(1999)*
(Deong et al., 2001)	*(16)*	$K_x = \frac{0.15}{8\varepsilon_t}(\frac{U}{u_*})^2(\frac{B}{H})^{1.67} Hu_*$ $\varepsilon_t = 0.145 + \frac{1}{3520}(\frac{U}{u_*})(\frac{B}{H})^{1.38}$	*Deong et al.(2001)*
(Kashefipur and Falconer, 2002)	*(17)*	$K_x = 10.612(\frac{U}{u_*})HU$	*Kashefipur and falconer(2002)*
(Tavakollizadeh and Kashefipur, 2007)	*(18)*	$K_x = 7.428 + 1.775(\frac{B}{H})^{0.62}(\frac{U}{u_*})^{1.572} HU$	*Tavakolizadeh(2007)*

Table 1. Empirical equations for estimation of longitudinal dispersion coefficient

Tayfour and Singh (Tayfour & Singh, 2005) based on the ability of artificial neural networks determined longitudinal dispersion coefficient in natural rivers (Tayfour & Singh, 2005). Comparison of results of ANN model with real data shows its superiority than empirical relations of Fisher (Fisher et al., 1979), Kashefipur and Falconer (Kashefipur & Falconer, 2002) and Deong et al. (Deong et al., 2001). Correlation of coefficient of real data with predicted values of ANN model in training stage was 0.7 and root mean square error of 193 (Tayfour & Singh, 2005). Although several studies in environmental engineering used artificial intelligence (ASCE, 2000; Choi & Park, 2001; Chang & Chang, 2006; Maier & Dandy, 1996; Dezfoli, 2003; Rajurkar, 2004; Sadatpour et al., 2005; Karamouz et al., 2004; Lu et al., 2003), only Tayfour and Singh (Tayfour & Singh, 2005) used artificial neural network to estimate longitudinal dispersion coefficient in natural rivers so in this study inventionally a new methodology for estimation of longitudinal dispersion coefficient in rivers is developed and results of this new method is compared with previous empirical relations.

3.2 Fuzzy logic and fuzzy systems

In modern modeling methods, fuzzy systems and fuzzy logics have peculiar places (Zadeh, 1965). The most characteristics of these methods are the ability of implementing human knowledge by tongue labels and fuzzy rules, nonlinearity of these systems and adaptability of these systems (Jang, 1993). A fuzzy system is a logical system based on if-then fuzzy rules and initial point of building and developing a new fuzzy system is the derivation of set of if-then fuzzy rules knowledge of expert person or knowledge of modeling field (Dezfoli, 2003). Having a method or tool to achieve fuzzy rules from Numerical, statistical or tongue information is a suitable and simple method for modeling with fuzzy expert systems (Nayak et al., 2004).

Another, modern modeling method is the artificial neural network and most important ability of these methods is their training ability from train sets (proper input and output pairs). These methods use several training algorithms to extract the relations between input and output parameters (Tashnehlab et al., 2001). Based on the above statements, combining of fuzzy systems, which works based on logical rules, with artificial neural networks, which extract knowledge from numerical information, we can develop models that simultaneously use numerical information and tongue statements to model any phenomenon. This combined method of artificial neural network and fuzzy systems is named adaptive neuro-fuzzy inference system (Jang, 1995; Kisi et al., 2001; Gopakumar & Mujumdar, 2007; Sen & Altunkaynak, 2006).

A fuzzy system is a system based on logical rules of if-then statements. This system images input variable space to output variable space using tongue statements and a fuzzy decision making procedures (Jang, 1995; Dezfoli, 2003). Fuzzy rule sets is a set of logical rules that describes the relations between fuzzy variables and is the most important component of a fuzzy system (Karamouz et al., 2004). Because of the uncertainty of real and field data, a fuzzification transition used to transform deterministic values to fuzzy values and a diffuzification transition is used to transform fuzzy values to deterministic values (Maier & Dandy, 1996; Dezfoli, 2003). Most common types of fuzzy systems is the Sugeno fuzzy system in which fuzzy rules stored in a rule base station. The rules in this system are

$$\text{IF } x_1 \text{ is } A_1 \text{ and } x_2 \text{ is } A_2 \ldots x_n \text{ is } A_n \text{ Then } y=f(x_1,x_2,\ldots,x_n) \tag{19}$$

Where A_i: are the fuzzy sets. In this system the if section of rule is a fuzzy value and the result section of the rule is a real function of the input values and usually is a linear statement such as: $a_1x_1 + a_2x_2 + \ldots + a_nx_n$ (Dezfoli, 2003).

3.3 Fuzzy logic and fuzzy systems

"ANFIS" statement which is the abbreviation of Adaptive neuro-fuzzy inference system is an adaptive fuzzy system which works based on artificial neural networks ability (Jang, 1995). This system is a fuzzy Sugeno by a forwarding network structure. Figure 1 shows a Sugeno fuzzy system with two inputs, one output and two rules and below it, the equivalent ANFIS system is presented (Tashnehlab et al., 2001). This system has two inputs X and Y and one output, where its rule is

$$\begin{array}{l}\text{IF x is } A_1 \text{ and y is } B_1 \text{ Then } f=p_1x + q_1y+r_1 \\ \text{IF x is } A_2 \text{ and y is } B_2 \text{ Then } f=p_2x + q_2y+r_2\end{array} \tag{20}$$

If any layer in this system showed by an O_j(the output of i node in j layer), the ANFIS structure will have five layers (Jang, 1995). Based on the figure 1 the operation of these layers is:

First layer, Input nodes: every node in this layer is a fuzzy set and any output of any node in this layer corresponds to the membership degree of input variable in this fuzzy set. In this layer shape parameters determines the shape of the membership function of the fuzzy set (Zadeh, 1965). Membership functions of fuzzy sets usually showed by bell shape functions such as (Jang, 1993)

$$O_i^1 = \frac{1}{1+\left[(x-c_i)/a_i\right]^{2b_i}} \tag{21}$$

Where X: value of input to i node, and c_i, b_i and a_i are the parameters of membership function of this set. These parameters usually called if (condition) parameters.

Second layer, rule nodes: in this layer every node computes the degree of activation of any rules

$$O_i^2 = w_i = \mu_{Ai}(x) \times \mu_{Bi}(y), i = 1,2 \tag{22}$$

Where $\mu_{Ai}(x)$: membership degree of x in A_i set, $\mu_{Bi}(x)$: is the membership degree of y in B_i set

Third layer, medium nodes: in this layer i node computes the ratio of activity degree of i rule to the sum of activation degrees of all rules

$$O_i^3 = w_i^n = \frac{w_i}{w_1 + w_2}, i = 1,2 \tag{23}$$

In this layer win: normalized membership degree of i rule.

Fourth layer, consequent nodes: in this layer output of any node is calculated

$$O_i^4 = w_i^n f_i = w_i^n.(p_i + q_i + r_i), i = 1,2 \tag{24}$$

In this equation r_i, q_i and p_i are the adaptive parameters of layer and called consequent parameters.

Fifth layer, output nodes: in this layer every node computes the final output value of any node(number of nodes equals to output parameters)

$$O_i^5 = \sum w_i^n f_i = \frac{\sum w_i f_i}{\sum w_i} \tag{25}$$

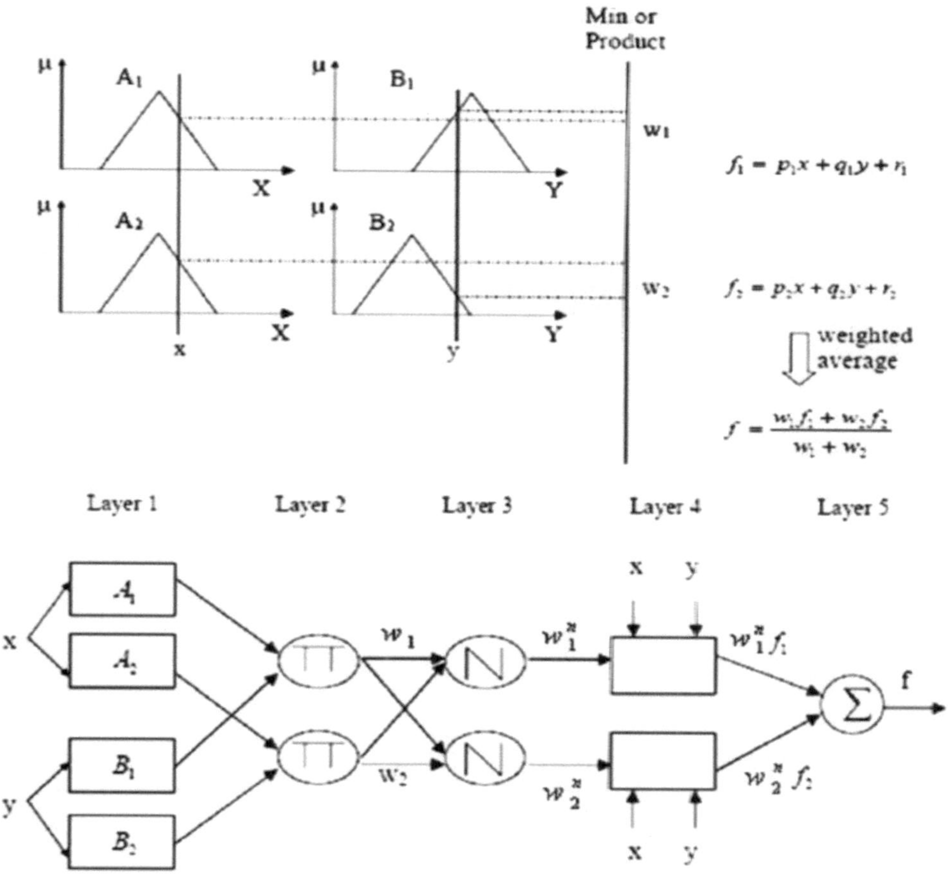

Fig. 1. a Sugeno fuzzy system with triangular membership function and its equivalent neuro-fuzzy system.

In this way a fuzzy system which has the ability of learning can be developed. In this method, main learning algorithm is error back propagation algorithm. In this method, by error descending gradient algorithm, error value is propagated towards the input layers and nodes and model parameters adopted. Based on the figure 1 total output of this system can be written by a linear function of consequent parameters (Zadeh, 1965)

$$\begin{aligned} f &= w_1^n f_1 + w_2^n f_2 \\ &= (w_1^n x)p_1 + (w_1^n y)q_1 + (w_1^n)r_1 \\ &+(w_2^n x)p_2 + (w_2^n y)q_2 + (w_2^n)r_2 \end{aligned} \tag{26}$$

So using least square error method the consequent parameters can be determined. Also combining this method with error back propagation algorithm a hybrid method can bed developed which operates as follows. In this method, in any train epoch, moving forward, the outputs of nodes is calculated normally to forth layer and finally consequent parameters calculated based on the least square error method. In the next step, after calculation of the error, in backward movement, the ratio of error is propagated over if parameters and those values are adapted based on error descent Gradient method (Zadeh, 1965, Sadatpour et al., 2005; Nayak et al., 2004; Gopakumar & Mujumdar, 2007). In this study input parameters of developed model are flow width, flow depth, cross sectional average velocity, shear velocity and output parameter is the longitudinal dispersion coefficient of pollutant.

4. The database

Estimation of longitudinal dispersion coefficient in rivers using equations of table 1 or ANFIS models requires hydraulic and geometry data sets. In this study a wide range of published data in literature is reviewed and finally a data set is prepared. Using this data set the results of empirical equations and ANFIS are compared and assessed. The authors collected such data that have all required parameters in empirical equations. Table 2 shows the range of variation of collected data and its parameters. The data set was collected from several references such as (Li et al., 1998; Pourabadei & Kashefipur, 2007; Tayfour & Singh, 2005; Choi & Park, 2001; Chatila, 1997).

Parameter	*Range*	*Average*
Flow velocity(m/s)	*0.034-2.23*	*0.7116*
Flow depth(m)	*0.22-25.1*	*3.69*
Flow width(m)	*11.89-201*	*137.74*
Shear velocity(m/s)	*0.0024-553*	*0.0956*
$K_x(m^2/s)$	*1.9-2883.5*	*223.1*

Table 2. Range of collected data set

From collected data set (73 series) 70% of them used for training of the ANFIS model and remaining 30% used for testing of the ANFIS model. Train and test sets selected randomly and optimum structure of ANFIS model is determined by default conditions in MATLAB commercial software and trial and error procedure. After developing several models with different structures, the optimum structure of the model is determined. The final optimum structure of the ANFIS model was using grid partitioning procedure for generating of fuzzy rules, Gaussian membership function with 4 input parameter and 3 membership function for any of input parameters with 30 epochs. Detailed description of developing ANFIS models with MATLAB is presented in several published papers (Riahi et al., 2007; Riahi & Ayyoubzadeh, 2007a; Riahi & Ayyoubzadeh, 2007b; Dezfoli, 2003; Sadatpour et al., 2005; Karamouz et al., 2004; Kisi et al., 2001; Nayak et al., 2004; Gopakumar & Mujumdar, 2007).
Tables and figures have to be made in high quality, which is suitable for reproduction and print, taking into account necessary size reduction. Photos have to be in high resolution.

5. Results and discussions

In this section, statistical parameters for accuracy assessing and final results of empirical relations and ANFIS model are presented. At first statistical parameters are described.

5.1 Statistical parameters

The results of empirical relation and ANFIS model assessed using statistical parameters such as: correlation coefficient (R^2), Mean absolute error (MAE), root mean square error (RMSE) and mean square error (MSE). These parameters show an average behavior of error in performance of the models and are global statistics that don't show any information about the error distribution over results. Because of this reasons another two statistical parameters that can assess preciously the performance of models. These parameters, which not only show the performance of model in predictions by an index but also show the distribution of errors over all the results, are: Average Absolute Relative Error (AARE) and Threshold Statistics index (TS) (Maier and Dandy, 2006; FaghforMaghrebi and Givehchi, 2007). The TS_x index for x% of predictions shows the distribution of error in predicted values of any model. This parameter determined for different values of average absolute relative error. The value of TS for x% of predictions determined by

$$TS_x = \frac{Y_x}{n} \cdot 100 \tag{27}$$

Where Y_x: is the number of predicted values (from total number of n) for every value of AARE less than x%. Mathematical equations of these statistical parameters are presented in (Maier & Dandy, 1996; FaghforMaghrebi & Givehchi, 2007; Kisi et al., 2001; Gopakumar & Mujumdar, 2007).

5.2 Results of empirical equations

The results of empirical equations in table 1 are calculated using all of collected data set and results of them are compared with measured data. Table 3 shows the results of empirical equations. Based on the results of table 3, none of these empirical equations have good results and shows considerable errors in comparison with measured data. The best empirical equation is the huang and li (Li et al., 1998;) with R^2=0.48, RMSE=295.7(M2/S), MAE=87439.6(m4/sec2), MAE=132.98(M2/S) and MAAE=68.46%. The values of these statistical indexes show the poor performance of empirical equations for prediction of longitudinal dispersion coefficients.

It is noticeable that based on the results of the table 3 and equations in table 1, poor performance is resulted from equation 8(Li et al., 1998;) that relates K_x directly with square of flow depth. But from physically based of the phenomenon K_x is function of the transverse velocity profile which reduces its effects with increasing of flow depth. Another result is that when flow depth or flow width eliminated from empirical equations, because of elimination of one of the most important parameters the results of these equations reduced considerably in comparison with similar equations. In this case equations of 7, 10, 12 and 14 can be addressed. Also it is clear that the effects of average velocity of flow on K_x are more than the flow width. For example equation 17 without presence of flow width is clearly better than equations without presence of flow velocity such as: 10, 12 and 14.

Figure 2 shows the distribution of error in predicted values by empirical equations. The equations of 7, 8 and 10 with poor performance eliminated from this figure and also bound of maximum error threshold in some equations was greater than 5000% , the upper bound of x-axis was set to 500%. From this figure it is clear that for 50% of predicted values, error is greater than 100% which is very high and equation 15 (the best one) have 300% error for 100% of predicted values, but all of the other equations have 500% errors for 100% of predicted values.

Statistical Parameter					
AARE (%)	*MAE*	*MSE*	*RMSE*	R^2	*Author(year)*
97.18	*217.7*	*204752.5*	*452.5*	*0.12*	*Elder(1959)*
51798.3	*118320.3*	*35870077*	*598974.19*	*0.01*	*Quien and quifer(1979)*
331.5	*833.71*	*3578526.49*	*1891.7*	*0.44*	*Fisher(1976)*
93.12	*218.72*	*207419.03*	*455.43*	*0.10*	*Liu and Chen(1980)*
179.3	*238.39*	*223345.63*	*472.95*	*0.35*	*Liu(1980)*
191.31	*148.87*	*112535.11*	*335.46*	*0.30*	*Awasan and Ottawa(1991)*
637.2	*433.50*	*1044996.01*	*1022.25*	*0.42*	*Seo and chang(1998)*
259.87	*262.61*	*23246.29*	*481.92*	*0.28*	*Kasiez and Rodriguez(1998)*
68.46	*132.98*	*87439.6*	*295.7*	*0.48*	*Huang and li(1999)*
169.2	*352.86*	*708674.88*	*841.83*	*0.38*	*Deon et al.(2001)*
496.83	*330.39*	*826843.83*	*909.31*	*0.35*	*Kashefipur and falconer(2002)*
89.92	*172.17*	*141874.83*	*376.66*	*0.44*	*Tavakolizadeh(2007)*

Table 3. Statistical results of empirical equations in prediction of Kx values

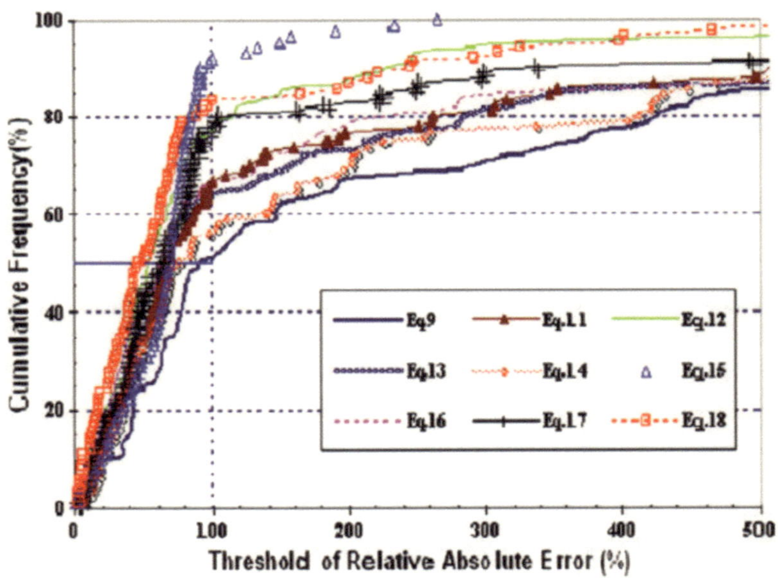

Fig. 2. Distribution of error prediction of empirical equations

5.3 ANFIS model results

Using collected data set, a new model for prediction of longitudinal dispersion coefficient in natural rivers is developed based on the ANFIS method. The results of this new model are presented in figures 3 to 6 in train and testing steps and the statistical results of this model

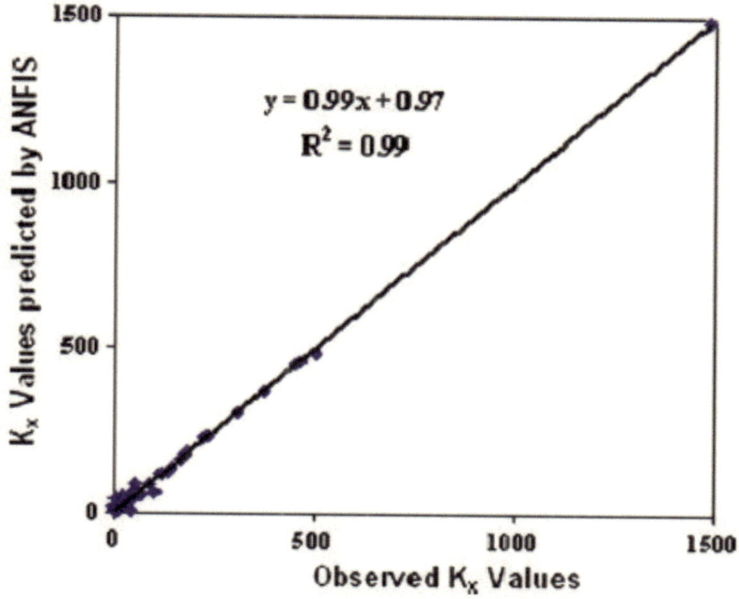

Fig. 3. Comparison between actual and ANFIS model results in training step

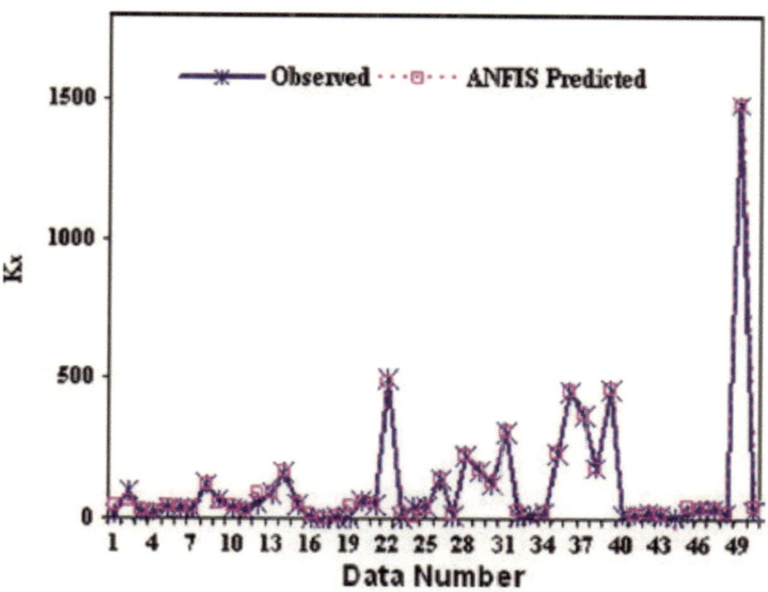

Fig. 4. Performance of ANFIS model results in training step

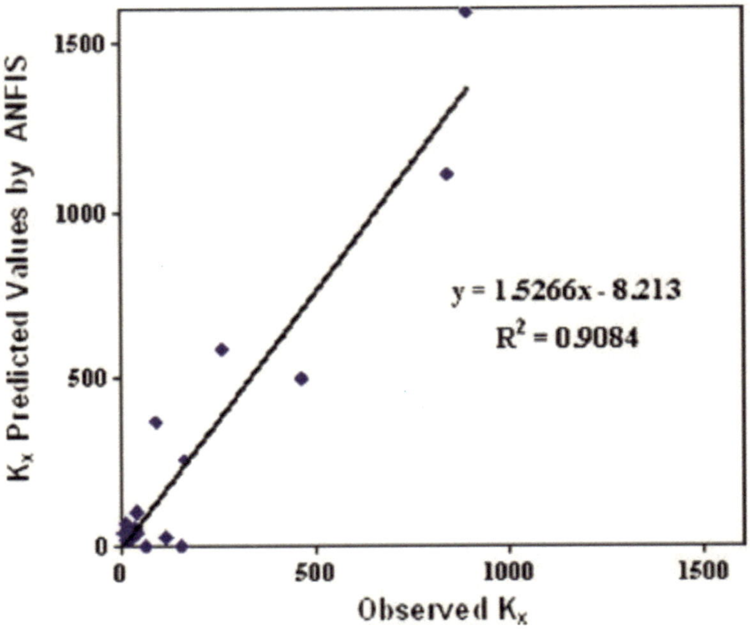

Fig. 5. Comparison between actual and ANFIS model results in Testing step

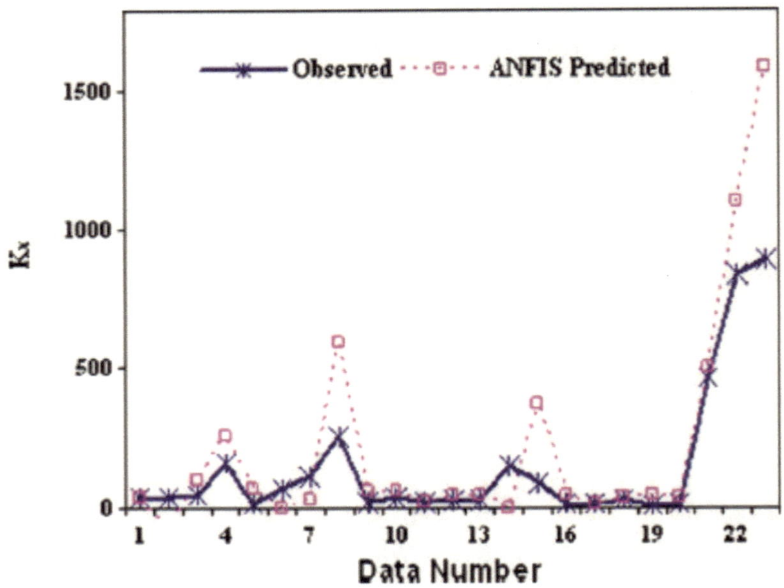

Fig. 6. Performance of ANFIS model results in Testing step

are presented in table 4. The input parameters of this model are: flow width, flow depth, average velocity and shear velocity and output parameter is the longitudinal dispersion coefficient. Figs of 3 to 6 show that the ANFIS model accurately learned the dispersion processes in natural rivers and predicted K_X values accurately. The ANFIS model extracted the dominant phenomena of pollutant transport in natural rivers and simulated its longitudinal dispersions. Comparison of the results of ANFIS model (table 4) with the results of empirical equations (table 3) shows the superiority of the ANFIS model in prediction of K_X values in rivers. Figure 7 compared the error distribution of ANFIS model in train and test steps with the results of best empirical equations in table 3(equation 15 and 18).

Statistical Parameters					*Stage model developing*
AARE (%)	*MAE*	*MSE*	*RMSE*	*R^2*	
63.48	*8.66*	*230.43*	*15.18*	*0.9957*	***Training Stage***
127.68	*104.77*	*35240.14*	*187.8*	*0.9084*	***Testing Stage***

Table 4. Statistical results of ANFIS model in training and testing steps

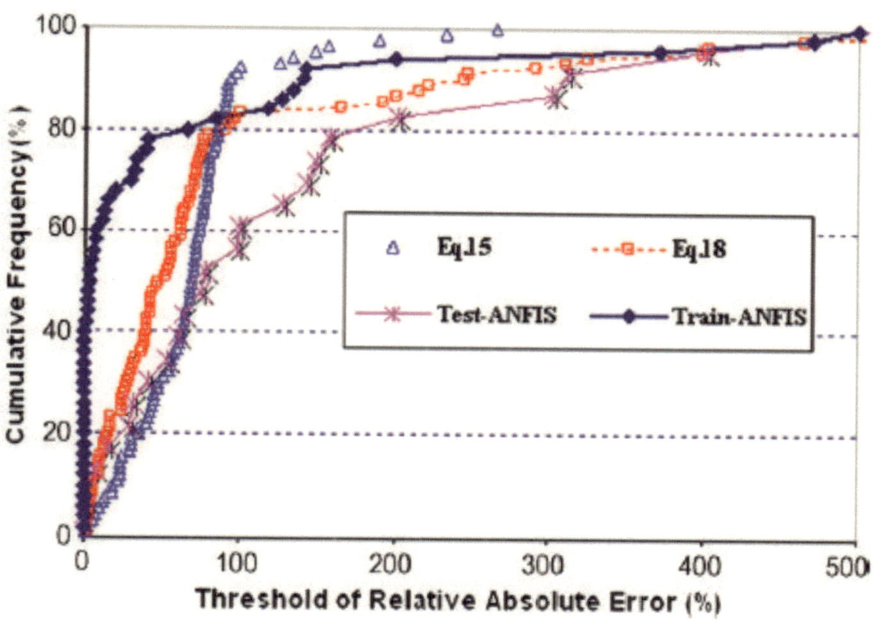

Fig. 7. Error distribution of ANFIS model in train and test steps in comparison with the results of 15 and 18 equations

Base on the results of ANFIS model in figure 7, in 70% of predicted cases the error of ANFIS model in training step is less than 100% and is lesser than from results of the 18 and 15 equations. Also in test step based on the table 4 and figure 7 it is clear that the results of the ANFIS model are better than empirical equations. Good performance of NFIS model in comparison with empirical equations in prediction of K_X values never else of limit number of data series in train and testing steps, wide range of variation of data set parameters and simple and quick developing of ANFIS model, shows the high ability of this model for prediction of K_X values rather than empirical equations without any needs for mathematical equations of the phenomena or numerical solving of them. The results of this study shows that ANFIS model can be used as alternative precious method for prediction of longitudinal dispersion coefficients.

6. Conclusions

In this chapter the authors have investigated the method and available equations for prediction of longitudinal dispersion coefficient in natural rivers and collected a data set to evaluate the performance of these equations. Based on the results, none of these empirical equations have good results and show considerable errors in comparison with measured data. The best empirical equation is the huang and li (Li et al., 1998) with R2=0.48, RMSE=295.7(M2/S), MAE=87439.6(m4/sec2), MAE=132.98(M2/S) and MAAE=68.46%. The values of these statistical indexes show the poor performance of empirical equations for prediction of longitudinal dispersion coefficients. In 50% of predicted values the error of these equations is greater than 100% and is very high and equation 15 (the best one) have 300% error for 100% of predicted values, but all of the other equations have 500% errors. Using collected data set, a new model for prediction of longitudinal dispersion coefficient in natural rivers is developed based on the ANFIS method. The input parameters of this model are: flow width, flow depth, average velocity and shear velocity and output parameter is the longitudinal dispersion coefficient. The results show that the ANFIS model accurately learned the dispersion processes in natural rivers and predicted K_X values accurately. The ANFIS model extracted the dominant phenomena of pollutant transport in natural rivers and simulated its longitudinal dispersions. Comparison of the results of ANFIS model (table 4) with the results of empirical equations (table 3) shows the superiority of the ANFIS model in prediction of K_X values in rivers. Base on the results of ANFIS model, in 70% of predicted cases the error of ANFIS model in training step is less than 100% and is lesser than from results of the 18 and 15 equations. good performance of ANFIS model in comparison with empirical equations in prediction of K_X values never else of limit number of data series in train and testing steps, wide range of variation of data set parameters and simple and quick developing of ANFIS model, shows the high ability of this model for prediction of K_X values rather than empirical equations without any needs for mathematical equations of the phenomena or numerical solving of them. The presented methodology in this chapter is a new approach in estimating dispersion coefficient in streams and can be combined with mathematical models of pollutant transfer or real-time updating of these models.

7. References

ASCE Task Committee, Artificial neural network in hydrology, Journal of Hydrologic Engineering (2000), 5: 124-144.

Bardossy, A. M. Disse, Fuzzy rule-based models for infiltration, Water Resources Research (1993) 29(2): 373-382.

Chang, F.J. Y.T. Chang, Adaptive neuro-fuzzy inference system for prediction of water level in reservoir, Advances in Water Resources(2006) 29:pp. 1-10

Chatila, G. j. Modeling of pollutant transfer in compound open channels, (1997) PhD Dissertation, University of Ottawa, Ontario Canada.

Choi, D.J. H., Park, A hybrid artificial neural network as a software sensor for optimal control of a wastewater treatment process. Water Res(2001), 35: 3959-3967.

Deng, Z.Q. V. P.Singh, L. Bengtsson., Longitudinal dispersion coefficient in single channel streams, journal of hydraulic engineering (2001), ASCE, Vol.128, No. 10, pp.901-916.

Dezfoli, K.A. Principles of Fuzzy theory and its application on water engineering problems, Jihad Press,Tehran, Iran, p227.

FaghforMaghrebi, M. M. Givehchi, using non-dimensional velocity curves for estimation of longitudinal dispersion coefficient, Proceedings of the 7th international symposium river engineering (2007), 16-18 October, Ahwaz, Iran, 87-96.

Fisher, H.B. E. J. List, R. C. Y. Koh, , J. Imberger, N. H. Brooks, Mixing in Inland and Costal Waters, Academic Press(1979),, Inc., San Diego, 104-138.

Gopakumar, R. P. P.Mujumdar. A fuzzy dynamic wave routing model, Hydrological Recesses (2007), 21,pp. 458-467.

Jang, J. S. R. ANFIS: adaptive-network-based fuzzy inference system. IEEE Trans Syst, Man, Cybernet (1993)23(3):pp.665–85.

Jang, J. S. R. N. Gulley, The Fuzzy Logic Toolbox for Use with MATLAB, The Mathworks Inc(1995), Natick, MA.

Karamouz, M. M.Tabehs, A. Nazief,A. Moridi, prediction of pressure in water networks using ANFIS models, Isfahan Journar of water and wastewater(2004), Isfahan, Iran, No.53, pp:3-14.

Kashefipur, S.M. A. Falconer, Longitudinal dispersion coefficients in Natural channels .Cardiff University, Proceedings of the fifth International hydro informatics Conference(2002), pp 95-102, July 1-5.

Kisi, O. Suspended Sediment Estimation Using Neuro-Fuzzy and Neural Network Approaches. J. Hydrological Sciences(2005), 50(4), pp. 683-695.

Kisi, O. M.E. Karahan, Z.Sen, River suspended sediment modeling using a fuzzy logic approach, Hydrological Processes (2006) 20: pp.4351–4362.

L. A. Zadeh, Fuzzy sets, Information Control, (1965) 8(3), 338-353.

Li, Z.H. J. Huang, J. Li, Preliminary study on longitudinal dispersion coefficient for the gorges reservoir, Proceedings of the 7th international symposium environmental hydraulics(1998), 16-18 December, Hong Kong, china.

Lu, W. Z. W. J. Wang, X. K. Wang, Z. B. Xu, A. Y. T. Leung,. Using improved neural network to analyze RSP, NOX and NO2 levels in urban air in Mong Kok, Hong Kong. Environmental Monitoring and Assessment(2003)., 87: 235–254.

Maier, H. R. G. C. Dandy. The use of artificial neural networks for the prediction of water quality parameters. Water Recourses Res(1996), 32(4), 1013-1022.

Nayak, P.C. K.P. Sudheer D.M. Rangan K.S. Ramasastri, A neuro-fuzzy computing technique for modeling hydrological time series, Journal of Hydrology (2004)291, pp.52–66.

Pourabadei, M. S.M. Kashefipour, Investigation of flow parameters on dispersion coefficient of pollutants in canal, Proceedings of the 6th international symposium river engineering(2007), 16-18 October, Ahwaz, Iran, 29-38.

Rajurkar, M.P. U.C.Kothyarib, , U.C. Chaube, Modeling of the daily rainfall-runoff relationship with artificial neural network, Journal of Hydrology(2004), 285: pp. 96–113.

Riahi, H. S.A.Ayyoubzadeh, using neuro-fuzzy in scour hole dimensions, 6th hydraulic conference of Iran(2007), 2-4 September, Shahrekord university, shahrekord, Iran.

Riahi, H. M.Salami, using neuro-fuzzy in drain pipe spacing, 3rd civil engineering conference of Iran(2007), 2-4 September, Tabriz university, Tabriz, Iran.
Riahi, H. S.A.Ayyoubzadeh, Prediction of regime channel treatments using ASNFIS modeling, first national hydraulic and dam engineering(2007), 1-3November, Islamic azad university of Karaj, Karaj, Iran.
Sadatpour, M. M.Afshar, A.Hadad, fuzzy optimized model for river water quality modeling, Isfahan Journar of water and wastewater(2005), Isfahan, Iran, No.64, pp:15-27.
Sedighnezhad, H. H. Salehi, D.Mohein, Comparison of different transport and dispersion of sediments in mard intake by FASTER model, Proceedings of the 7th international symposium river engineering(2007), 16-18 October, Ahwaz, Iran, 45-54.
Sen, Z. A. Altunkaynak,. A comparative fuzzy logic approach to runoff coefficient and runoff estimation, Hydrological Processes (2006) 20:pp. 1993–2009.
Seo, I, W, K.O. Bake, , Estimation of the longitudinal dispersion coefficient using the velocity profile in natural streams, journal of hydraulic engineering, ASCE,(2004), Vol.130, No. 3, pp.227-236.
Seo, I.W. T.S. Cheong, Predicting longitudinal dispersion coefficient in natural Stream, journal of hydraulic engineering, ASCE(1998), Vol. 124, No. 1, PP. 25-32.
Tashnehlab, M. S.Menhaj, Modeling Trip tours using ANFIS modeling, Engineering Journal of Tehran university, (2001) Volume. 31, No. 3. pp:361-370.
Tavakollizadeh, A. S.M. Kashefipur, Effects of dispersion coefficient on quality modeling of surface waters, Proceedings of the 6th international symposium river engineering(2007), 16-18 October, Ahwaz, Iran, 67-78.
Tayfour, G. V.P. Singh, Predicting longitudinal dispersion coefficient in natural streams by artificial neural network, journal of hydraulic engineering(2005), ASCE, Vol.131, No. 11, pp. 991-1000.